ROYAL HISTORIC.

STUDIES IN HI.

New Series

C000262019

PROTESTING ABOUT PAUPERISM

POVERTY, POLITICS AND POOR RELIEF IN LATE-VICTORIAN ENGLAND, 1870–1900

PROTESTING ABOUT PAUPERISM

POVERTY, POLITICS AND POOR RELIEF
IN LATE-VICTORIAN ENGLAND, 1870–1900

Elizabeth T. Hurren

THE ROYAL HISTORICAL SOCIETY
THE BOYDELL PRESS

First published 2007
Paperback edition 2015

A Royal Historical Society publication
Published by The Boydell Press
an imprint of Boydell & Brewer Ltd
PO Box 9, Woodbridge, Suffolk IP12 3DF, UK
and of Boydell & Brewer Inc.
668 Mt Hope Avenue, Rochester, NY 14620–2731, USA
website: www.boydellandbrewer.com

ISBN 978 0 86193 292 4 hardback
ISBN 978 0 86193 329 7 paperback

ISSN 0269–2244

A CIP catalogue record for this book is available
from the British Library

This publication is printed on acid-free paper

THIS BOOK IS DEDICATED WITH LOVE TO

ANGUS, WHO WALKED WITH ME THROUGHOUT,

MATTHEW, FOR HIS CARE, SUPPORT AND NOW FRIENDSHIP,

AND WITH THANKS TO

FIVE 'GENTLE' MEN WHOSE FAITH IN ME HELPED TO
MAKE THIS POSSIBLE

RLA, PWJB, PJRK, SAK AND JWS.

Contents

List of Figures

List of Tables

List of Maps

List of Illustrations

This book was published with the help of a most generous grant from the Scouloudi Foundation, in association with the Institute of Historical Research.

Acknowledgements

This book began as a PhD thesis at the Nene Centre for Research, at University College, Northampton, under the auspices of the University of Leicester. I am grateful to the department of history for sponsoring a PhD bursary to enable the research to be completed.

I have been lucky in my career to receive help and encouragement from academics who exemplify scholarly integrity. In the early stages of the thesis words of encouragement and the interest expressed in this project by Professor Richard Smith and Dr David Thomson were formative experiences. In particular, I hope that this book builds upon David Thomson's thought-provoking work on late-Victorian poverty and welfare. Unquestionably it follows where he led, though any factual errors or interpretations are of course my own.

I owe an enormous intellectual debt to Dr Peter Bartrip and Professor Peter King, my doctoral supervisors. I remember supervisions fondly, especially the good humour at tea-making time. Subsequently, it was a privilege to become one of their colleagues, and after various job moves, still to maintain firm friendships. Without their faith in me this journey would have been much harder. Thank you both for the gentle words of support along the way. I am also grateful to Dr Robert Louis Abrahamson who always makes me think, and for his gentle encouragement to forge ahead.

Over the course of my work on the thesis and subsequently, members of the history department at Oxford Brookes University have been very supportive. In particular, Professor Steven King read a draft of the thesis and gave invaluable feedback at crucial junctures. His help has always been constructive, encouraging and supportive. Likewise, Professor John Stewart extended the hand of friendship, giving assistance on publication plans, and research strategy. Thank you both for red wine and gentle words of enlivening scholarship in a new academic home.

The writing of any book is an editorial journey and I would like to express my sincere thanks to those who have helped me in this regard. Dr Jon Lawrence has been very supportive and personifies what is best about the Royal Historical Society Series and its commitment to mentor younger scholars. Likewise, Christine Linehan, my editor, has been encouraging, reassuring and patient throughout.

I would like to express my thanks to the staff of Northamptonshire Record Office, the British Library Manuscript Department and all those along the research trail who were enthusiastic about this untold story.

Finally, and predictably, much has changed during the writing of this book. In many respects it represents a letting go of the past. Certainly, it has been completed in the spirit of a future that is no longer waiting to take flight.

Elizabeth T. Hurren,
Verio Granta, 2005

xi

Abbreviations

BDODRA   Brixworth District Out Door Relief Association
BL   British Library
Bodl. Lib.   Bodleian Library
COR   Charity Organisation Review
COS   Charity Organisation Society
DMOP   District Medical Officer of the Poor
LGB   Local Government Board
MRDRA   Medical Relief Disqualification Removal Act
NALU   National Agricultural Labourers' Union
NRO   Northampton Record Office
PRO   Public Record Office
TNA   The National Archive

AgHR   *Agricultural History Review*
BJHS   *British Journal of the History of Science*
EcHR   *Economic History Review*
EHR   *English Historical Review*
HJ   *Historical Journal*
JBS   *Journal of British Studies*
JEcH   *Journal of Economic History*
JEEcH   *Journal of European Economic History*
JSHM   *Journal of the Social History of Medicine*
NP&P   *Northamptonshire Past and Present*
P&P   *Past and Present*
SH   *Social History*

Note: Unless otherwise stated, all quotations are cited with original spelling and emphasis.

Introduction

In the late nineteenth century there was a broad consensus in central and local government that publicly funded income support for the needy should be minimised. This book recounts how poverty, politics and poor relief debates clashed when a 'crusade against outdoor relief' dominated English social welfare policy between 1870 and 1900. Traditionally, poor relief in England was paid in the form of small doles to the majority of paupers who lived outside the workhouse.[1] Around 1870, however, a powerful lobby of senior politicians, civil servants, leading economists and influential philanthropists wanted to revive the strict letter of the Poor Law Amendment Act (1834).[2] At first reformers stated that outdoor relief must be withdrawn from the able-bodied, mendicant or work-shy, as the New Poor Law intended.[3] Only indoor relief would be given, inside a workhouse, provided a pauper were truly destitute.[4] Then reformers conceived that a major way to cut local taxes was to try to eradicate outdoor relief altogether. Ideologically this *crusade* was inspired by classical political economy and the self-help rhetoric of the Charity Organisation Society (COS).[5] It fundamentally altered the 'mixed-economy of welfare' and put greater strains on individual 'makeshift' economies, by focusing on arguments against public assistance and in favour of family and individual responsibility.[6] For the first time the aged, disabled, sick and widowed were treated on equal terms with the able-bodied unemployed. The ideological background to, and practical implementation of, that thinking, especially in rural society,[7] is a central feature of this book.

This study analyses the bitter battle over the poor law that was ignited when the labouring poor refused to accept cost-saving measures during the

1   P. Mandler (ed.), *The uses of charity: the poor on relief in the nineteenth-century metropolis*, Philadelphia 1990.
2   G. Himmelfarb, *The demoralisation of society: from Victorian virtues to modern values*, London 1995.
3   H. Southall, 'Poor law statistics and the geography of economic distress', in J. Foreman-Peck (ed.), *New perspectives on the late-Victorian economy: essays in quantitative economic history, 1860–1914*, Cambridge 1991, 180–217.
4   F. Driver, *Power and pauperism: the workhouse system, 1834–1844*, Cambridge 1993.
5   G. R. Boyer, *An economic history of the English poor law, 1750–1850*, Cambridge 1990.
6   M. Katz and C. Sachsse (eds), *The mixed economy of social welfare*, London 1996; P. Thane, 'Old people and their families in the English past', in M. J. Daunton (ed.), *Charity, self interest and welfare in the English past*, London 1996, 113–38.
7   See, for example, a summary of its chief features in rural England in A. Digby, 'The rural poor', in G. E. Mingay, *The Victorian countryside*, London 1981, 591–601; *The poor law in nineteenth-century England and Wales*, London 1982; and *British social policy: from workhouse to workfare*, London 1989. D. Eastwood, *Governing rural England: tradition and transformation in local government, 1780–1840*, Basingstoke–London 1994, provides context.

1

last three decades of the nineteenth century. It explores how ratepayers, alarmed by a growth in agricultural competition from overseas and a series of poor domestic harvests, thought poor law bills were excessive as farming profits plummeted. Thus, they were very receptive to central government's *crusade*. Meanwhile, amongst the labouring poor, there was a general rejection of the idea that only the landed classes should be the beneficiaries of agricultural profits and poor law tax savings. These socio-economic changes and firm opposition of the labouring poor took place in an era of widening democracy.

Rural political life changed fundamentally after the Third Reform Act in 1884.[8] New voters wanted better welfare provision just when central government and poor law unions declared their intention to abolish all outdoor relief. Consequently, a tug of war over the poor law developed. It coincided with changing national political, economic and cultural developments that began to undercut the *crusade* platform in rural life. Later Victorian debates about the limits of personal and public responsibilities in welfare matters provided evidence that pauperism was often involuntary. Labouring demands for the reintroduction of outdoor relief and a greater say in the administration of the poor law did not therefore seem unreasonable. In particular, social scientific investigations by, amongst others, Charles Booth, the New Idealist thinking of academics and the tentative beginnings of socialism started to overturn notions that poverty was caused by individual 'sin' and 'moral' failing. It was the passing of the Local Government Act (1894) that fully democratised the poor law and brought these forces to the fore in rural politics. Paradoxically, the *crusade*, where it was tried and found wanting, was thus a political catalyst for welfare reform. In rural England poverty and local democracy had radicalised the poor law and the 'politics of place' by the close of the nineteenth century.[9]

Since the 1980s many studies have examined the origins and impact of the Poor Law Amendment Act of 1834.[10] Unquestionably this work has

---

[8] P. Lynch, *The Liberal party in rural England, 1885–1910: radicalism and community*, Oxford 2003, 1–7, 22–4, summarises arguments about the impact of these democratic changes.

[9] J. Lawrence, *Speaking for the people: party, language and popular politics in England, 1867–1914*, Cambridge 1998, 1, termed the phrase the 'politics of place'. This book builds upon his notion of the importance of local politics.

[10] See, for example, relevant studies published since the 1990s: A. Brundage, 'The making of the New Poor Law debate: redivivius', *P&P* cxxvii (1990), 183–6; D. Englander and R. O'Day (eds), *Retrieved riches: social investigation in Britain, 1840–1914*, London 1995; P. Thane (ed.), *The foundations of the Welfare State*, London–New York 1996 edn; D. Englander, *Poverty and poor law reform in 19th-century Britain, 1834–1914: from Chadwick to Booth*, New York 1998; L. Hollen-Lees, *The solidarities of strangers: the English poor laws and the people, 1700–1948*, Cambridge 1998; A. J. Kidd, *State, society and the poor in nineteenth-century England*, Oxford 1999; S. A. King, *Poverty and welfare in England, 1700–1850: a regional perspective*, Manchester 2000; A. Brundage, *The English poor laws, 1700–1930*, Basingstoke 2002; and B. Harris, *The origins of the British Welfare State: social welfare in England and Wales, 1800–1945*, Basingstoke 2004.

enhanced historians' understanding of the social welfare debates and practices of the mid-Victorian period. Yet it has also established a broad poor law chronology that marginalises late nineteenth-century welfare policy. A typical modern textbook will discuss various aspects of the administration of the New Poor Law before 1870, and the development of Welfare State legislation after 1900. The intervening three decades, during which the *crusade* was tried and failed, are 'handled uncomfortably or glossed over' by most poor law historians.[11] The *crusade*, as Geoffrey Finlayson and José Harris point out, is seldom the focus of research in its own right.[12] Instead, it tends to be discussed in connection with the expansion of workhouse services,[13] and thus its insignificance is stressed. This mishandling is exacerbated by the fact that the secondary literature on *crusading* is limited[14] when compared with the vast amount written on the mid-Victorian poor law. This trend is mistaken and needs further elucidation by reviewing the paucity of literature that is available.

11 D. Thomson, 'Welfare and the historians', in L. Bonfield, R. M. Smith and K. Wrightson (eds), *The world we have gained: histories of population and social structure*, Cambridge 1986, 225–378 at p. 373. Kidd, *State, society and the poor*, for example, devotes just pp. 45–64 to the later Victorian poor law and only pp. 48–52 to the *crusade*.
12 G. Finlayson, *Citizen, state and social welfare in Britain, 1830–1990*, Oxford 1994; J. Harris, *Private lives, public spheres: a social history of Britain, 1870–1914*, Oxford 1995.
13 See, for example, M.W. Flinn, 'Medical services under the New Poor Law', in D. Fraser, *The New Poor Law in the nineteenth century*, London 1976, 45–66; M. A. Crowther, *The workhouse system, 1834–1929*, London 1981; A. Scull (ed.), *Madhouses, mad-doctors and madmen*, London 1981; J. Pickstone, *Medicine and industrial society: a history of hospital provision in Manchester and its regions, 1752–1946*, Manchester 1985; S. Cherry, *Medical services and the hospitals in Britain, 1860–1939*, Cambridge 1986; F. F. S. Driver, 'The English Bastille: dimensions of the workhouse system, 1834–1884', unpubl. PhD diss. Cambridge 1988; G. Bock and P. Thane (eds), *Maternity and gender politics: women and the rise of the European welfare states, 1880s–1950s*, London–New York 1991; H. Hendrick, *Child welfare: England, 1872–1989*, London 1994; and F. Crompton, *Workhouse children*, Stroud 1997.
14 K. Williams, *From pauperism to poverty*, Manchester 1981; D. Thomson, 'Provision for the elderly in England, 1834–1908', unpubl. PhD diss. Cambridge 1981; 'Workhouse to nursing home: residential care of elderly people in England since 1840', *Ageing and Society* iii (1983), 43–69; '*I am not my father's keeper*: families and the elderly in nineteenth-century England', *Law and History Review* ii (1984), 265–86; 'The decline of social security: falling state support for the elderly since early Victorian times', *Ageing and Society* iv (1984), 451–82; and 'Welfare', 255–378; M. Mackinnon, 'Poor law policy, unemployment and pauperism', *Explorations in Economic History* xxiii (1986), 229–336, and 'English poor law policy and the crusade against outdoor relief', *JEcH* xlvii (1987), 603–25; D. Thomson, 'The welfare of the elderly in the past, a family or community responsibility?', in M. Pelling and R. M. Smith (eds), *Life, death and the elderly: historical perspectives*, Oxford 1991, 194–222, and *World without welfare: New Zealand's colonial experiment*, Auckland 1998.

Context

The history of the nineteenth-century poor law has been dominated by the Whig approach of Sidney and Beatrice Webb,[15] who set out to prove that in the later nineteenth century central government began to move away from the misguided principles of the Poor Law Amendment Act of 1834. They argued that poor law administrators adopted instead a more enlightened set of welfare policies, such as the development and expansion of workhouse medical services, the boarding out of pauper children and so on. This indicated that, by 1900, social policies were more progressive. The problem with this paradigm was that the 'crusade against outdoor relief' did not fit the Webbs' model of social welfare culminating in the early Welfare State. It contradicted notions that social policy outside the workhouse was more advanced by the close of the late-nineteenth century. Rather than analysing the complex nature of the whole poor law experience, the Webbs ignored the fact that most of the labouring poor were claimants of outdoor, not indoor, relief. It was simpler to conclude that the *crusade* was an aberration, a period 'marked by a deliberate attempt to keep all formal collective welfare activity to a minimum, and to maximise individual, family and informal neighbourly assistance when need arose'.[16] As a result the Webbs established a league table of poor law studies, with the decades of the *crusade* relegated to the bottom. This created the mistaken impression that the *crusade* played only a peripheral role in the rise of the early Welfare State. To rediscover the lost *crusading* experience is a primary objective of this book.

Modern scholarship has tended to compound the Webbs' misinterpretations. It is, for instance, noteworthy that in the 1980s interest in the *crusade* seemed to revive. Yet that revisionism was sporadic. Keynote articles by Derek Fraser and Michael Rose, for example, tried to rekindle interest in the neglected *crusade*.[17] However, as the results of detailed empirical research were not provided, the wider academic community was not convinced that the *crusade* merited further reconsideration. Others, such as Robert Humphreys, researched the *crusade* under a COS umbrella,[18] but again this did not encourage poverty historians to follow his lead. Meanwhile, some medical historians were researching the treatment of the sick poor, old age pensions and the workhouse system after 1870. However, this work tended to ring-fence *crusading* topics into specialist research areas, with the result

---

[15] S. Webb and B. Webb, *English poor law history*, London 1927–9.

[16] Thomson, *World without welfare*, 18.

[17] D. Fraser, *The evolution of the British Welfare State*, London 1984 edn; M. E. Rose, 'The crisis of poor relief in England, 1860–1900', in W. Mommsen and W. Mock (eds), *The emergence of the Welfare State in Britain, 1850–1950*, London 1981, 50–70, and *The relief of poverty, 1834–1914*, London–New York 1986 edn.

[18] R. Humphreys, *Sin, organized charity and the poor law in Victorian England*, Basingstoke 1995.

that 'poor law strategy and practice' was 'broken into too many pieces'.[19] Thus, the bigger picture for the later nineteenth-century poor law was lost. It seemed that these trends would be reversed by three key historians, Mary Mackinnon, David Thomson and Karel Williams, who recognised the Webbs' flawed legacy and the need to revisit the *crusade* experience in its entirety. In particular, Williams argued that a missing 'outdoors' perspective meant that welfare historians could not appreciate the extent of the 'brutal dispauperisa-tion' inflicted on those living outside the workhouse in the later Victorian era.[20] Only very rarely could the impoverished afford to live independently at home without basic outdoor relief. Most guardians knew that mutual aid was beyond the meagre means of the poor and that a lack of welfare tended to exacerbate pauperism. In fact it was 'outdoor' paupers, the majority of the labouring poor, who bore the brunt of the *crusade*'s severe socio-economic rationale. Mackinnon, Thomson and Williams believe that the Webbs understated this. Ultimately, this book seeks to build upon the work of these three historians, by exploring the conduct and impact of the *crusade* at a local level.

The case for the later Victorian poor law

Today few welfare textbooks highlight that the late nineteenth century was a pivotal phase in poor law history, thus obscuring the real vibrancy of the period. There are in fact a number of important reasons for studying the *crusade* in its own terms.

It is evident that the Webbs' methodology was flawed. They were poor law historians driven by ideological imperatives and thus they misrepresented the radical nature of the *crusade* campaign.[21] Finlayson notes that studying the Whig theory of poor law history involves embarking on 'a great collective train journey into the future'.[22] *En route* the reader is directed 'to stop at certain "significant" stations – such as 1830 to 1850, 1874 to 1880, 1906 to 1911'. He adds that the chief problem with this approach is that the reader is encouraged to view each phase of poor law history 'in terms of the develop-ment or evolution of the Welfare State', rather than in its historical context. Periods of poor law disjuncture, like the *crusade* decades, are neglected because they do not fit a progressive paradigm. For this reason many welfare textbooks concentrate on local and national welfare policies which seem to indicate

---

19 Williams, *Pauperism*, 94. There is also a large literature on the separate care of children. For two excellent summaries see Hendrick, *Child welfare*, and Crompton, *Workhouse children*.

20 See n. 14 above, and Williams, *Pauperism*, 107.

21 S. Webb and B. Webb, *English poor law policy*, London 1910. Mackinnon, 'English poor law'; Thomson 'Welfare'; and Williams, *Pauperism*, are very critical of the Webbs' Whig-gish approach.

22 Finlayson, *Citizen, state and social welfare*, 2–3.

that poor law provision became more enlightened as the nineteenth century progressed.[23] Yet however progressive local measures were, often those policies were also a reaction against the harshness of radical poor law ideology in the later Victorian period.[24] The extremism of *crusading*, Thomson explains, led to 'working back... to a more normal balance' of social responsibilities and objectives that historians now term the rise of the early Welfare State.[25] Historical understanding of twentieth-century public welfare systems must thus find its foundation in the impact of the *crusade* experiment. In particular, historians need to examine how popular protest against the mechanisms and impact of the *crusade* changed public perceptions of the causes of poverty, creating a more liberal consensus on social policy in central government circles after 1900.[26]

Another important reason for a renewed emphasis on the later Victorian poor law experience is that historians need a firmer understanding of the social and political costs of *crusading*. Empirical research on these matters has been sketchy. Mary Mackinnon suggests that the social cost was too high. During a period of rapid economic change the *crusade* often had a detrimental financial impact upon those living on the margins of late-Victorian society.[27] However, seldom has this important statement been strengthened by primary research. Likewise, in terms of the socio-political consequences of the *crusade* our knowledge remains muted, despite Derek Fraser calling attention to this neglected theme over twenty years ago.[28] John Garrard has explored the political angle in some major northern Victorian industrial towns. He found that as urbanisation accelerated voters became more interested in the local, rather than the national, political scene.[29] Fraser and Garrard remind welfare historians of the need to think more conceptually about the structure and performance of late-Victorian local government, including poor law politics. This book follows up Garrard's suggestion that poor law historians need to engage with some of the questions that political scientists have raised about the nature of local power and how it is under constant negotiation.

---

[23] See, for example, U. R. Q. Henriques, *Before the Welfare State: social administration in early industrial Britain*, London 1979.

[24] Thomson, 'Welfare of the elderly', 212–13.

[25] Ibid. 194.

[26] It should be noted that elsewhere new methods of social investigation helped to change perceptions of poverty, but these did not influence those who controlled the policy of the Brixworth union board of guardians during the *crusade* campaign, c.1873 to 1893.

[27] Mackinnon, 'English poor law', 603–4.

[28] D. Fraser, *The new poor: urban politics in Victorian England: the structure of power in Victorian cities*, Leicester 1978 edn.

[29] J. A. Garrard, *Leaders and politics in nineteenth-century Salford: an historical analysis of urban political power*, Salford 1977; 'The middle classes and nineteenth-century national and local politics', in J. A. Garrard, D. Jary, M. Goldsmith and A. Oldfield (eds), *The middle class in politics*, Farnborough 1977, 35–67; 'Parties, members and voters after 1867: a local study', *HJ* xx (1977), 145–63; *Leadership and power in Victorian industrial towns, 1830–80*, Manchester 1983; and 'Social history, political history and political science: the study of power', *Journal of Social History* iii (1983), 105–23.

A closely related theme is the lack of any detailed understanding of the impact of the coming of poor law democracy in local government. Current texts, on both welfare and political history, often state that there was very limited popular participation in local government politics by working people during the late nineteenth century.[30] Yet the *crusade* and the strong political reaction it engendered challenge such orthodoxy. It is interesting that Pat Ryan, in his exploration of the political impact of the *crusade* in poor law unions in the East End of London, did not find evidence of a strong political reaction, but conceded that his study had 'raised more questions than it resolved'.[31] An unstable migrant population in the East End may explain a lack of interest in local politics. Ryan suggested that more local studies were needed before historians could clarify the impact of the *crusade* on the lives and politics of working people.

Pat Ryan's conclusions have encouraged some poor law historians, like Pat Thane, to undervalue the social and political aspirations of working-class rural voters in the late-Victorian era. The latter claims that 'the scattered evidence from local elections' reveals that 'turnouts were usually low even after the local franchise changes in 1894'.[32] She concludes that 'nowhere did working men flood out to support such reforming candidates, or indeed any others', who supported social welfare issues associated with municipal socialism.[33] Thane acknowledges that 'the variety and implications of interest in municipal socialism in this period deserve more detailed attention', but she does not concede that further research needs to be carried out on poor law politics because she regards the *crusade* campaign as insignificant. She emphasises that only forty-one poor law unions (6.6 per cent) adopted rigorous *crusading* initiatives. However, as Williams points out, it is worth remembering that 16 per cent of the total population in England and Wales lived in areas where a strict *crusading* strategy was maintained for more than twenty years.[34] Moreover, poor law historians still know very little about what made these poor law unions different and why they chose to follow strict *crusading* guidelines.

---

30 Relevant texts include K. O. Morgan, *Rebirth of a nation state: Wales, 1880–1980*, Oxford 1981; K. T. Hoppen, 'The franchise and electoral politics in England and Ireland, 1832–1885', *History* lxx (1985), 202–17; I. G. C. Hutchinson, *A political history of Scotland, 1832–1914: parties, elections and issues*, Edinburgh 1986; P. Hollis, *Ladies elect: women in English local government, 1865–1914*, Oxford 1987; and P. F. Clarke and K. Langford, 'Hodge's politics: the agricultural labourers and the Third Reform Act in Suffolk', in N. Harte and R. Quinault (eds), *Land and society in Britain, 1700–1914: essays in honour of F. M. L. Thompson*, Cambridge 1996, 119–37.

31 P. Ryan, '"Poplarism", 1894–1930', in P. Thane (ed.), *The origins of British social policy*, London 1978, 56–83, and 'Politics and poor relief: East End unions in the late nineteenth and early twentieth centuries', in M. E. Rose (ed.), *The poor and the city: the English poor law in its urban context, 1834–1914*, Leicester 1985, 130–72.

32 P. Thane, 'The working class and state "welfare" in Britain, 1880–1914', *HJ* xxvii (1984), 877–900, repr. (without revision) in D. Gladstone (ed.), *Before Beveridge: welfare before the welfare state*, London 1999, 86–113.

33 Ibid. 892.

34 Williams, *Pauperism*, 104.

It is likely that the policies of these 'model' boards of guardians had a knock-on effect, if only briefly, on many other unions. It is thus possible that the *crusade* campaign produced a strong political reaction, necessitating changes in our understanding of the nature of local government politics and the social welfare aspirations of new voters in this period.

A further reason for a renewed investigation of the *crusade* is that it can elicit new insights into aspects of late-Victorian rural society. In particular, an important aspect of the history of collective working-class rural politics has been neglected. The shibboleths of Swing and agricultural trade unionism have dominated the field of rural political studies for some time.[35] Historians such as John Archer, Alun Howkins, David Morgan and Keith Snell, however, have published more general 'labour' histories of the nineteenth-century countryside[36] to which an analysis of the *crusade* campaign can make a further contribution. The implementation of a deeply impoverishing *crusading* experiment often aroused intense animosity, sometimes producing strong opposition. Although resentment was aroused by a cluster of grievances (poor labour relations, low wages, charity rights, customary parish pensions, etc.), it was usually debates about entitlement to outdoor relief that were the primary force mobilising political activism in some rural communities. Thus, a study of the *crusade* campaign can shed light on the complex nature of political conflict in the countryside.

Finally, local empirical work allows historians to explore in detail the relationship between agricultural trade unionism and the *crusading* experience. In the 1870s trade union agitation against the *crusade* was more extensive

[35] J. P. D. Dunbabin, '"The revolt of the field": the Agricultural Labourers' Movement in the 1870s', *P&P* xxvi (1963), 68–97; A. J. Peacock, *Bread or blood: a study of the agrarian riots in East Anglia in 1816*, London 1965; E. J. Hobsbawm and G. E. Rudé, *Captain swing*, London 1969; J. P. D. Dunbabin, *Rural discontent in nineteenth-century Britain*, London 1974; R. Arnold, 'The "revolt" in the field in Kent, 1872–1879', *P&P* lxiv (1974), 71–95; P. L. R. Horn, *Labouring life in the Victorian countryside*, London 1976; R. Wells, 'The development of the English rural proletariat and social protest, 1700–1850', *Journal of Peasant Studies* vi (1979), 115–39; P. L. R. Horn, *The rural world and social change in the English countryside, 1780–1850*, London 1980; J. P. D. Dunbabin, 'The incidence and organisation of agricultural trades unionism in the 1870s', *AgHR* xvi (1986), 114–41; N. Scotland, 'The National Agricultural Labourers' Union and the demand for the stake in the soil, 1872–1896', in E. F. Biagini (ed.), *Citizenship and community: radicals and collective identities in the British Isles, 1865–1931*, Cambridge 1996, 151–67.
[36] D. H. Morgan, *Harvesters and harvesting, 1840–1900: a study of the rural proletariat*, London 1982; A. Howkins, *Poor labouring men: rural radicalism in Norfolk, 1870–1923*, London 1985; K. Snell, *Annals of the labouring poor: social change in agrarian England, 1660–1990*, Cambridge 1985; J. Archer, 'By a flash and a scare': arson, animal maiming and poaching in East Anglia, 1815–1870, Oxford 1990; A. Howkins, *Reshaping rural England: a social history, 1850–1925*, London 1991; K. Snell, 'Deferential bitterness and the social outlook of the rural proletariat in eighteenth- and nineteenth-century England and Wales', in M. L. Bush (ed.), *Social order and social classes since 1500: studies in social stratification*, London–New York 1992, 158–79; A. Howkins, 'Peasants, servants and labourers: the marginal workforce in British agriculture, 1870–1914', *AgHR* xlii (1994), 49–62.

than general labour histories of the countryside reveal.[37] In some rural areas there was a direct link between the *crusading* campaign and the advent of agricultural trade union combination. Many working people joined local and national agricultural trade unions, such as the National Agricultural Labourers' Union (NALU), not just to increase wages, but also to fight for the reintroduction of outdoor relief. Even though they were not successful until the passing of the Local Government Act (1894), what unfolded was a bitter and prolonged campaign of opposition. By exploring the pivotal role that the 'poor law and the politics of place' could play in labouring communities, this study contributes to labour history by complementing the wealth of work on urban industrial labour relations in the later Victorian period.[38]

The Brixworth union in context

This book focuses on the rural poor law union at Brixworth in Northampton-shire. None of the seven 'strict' model rural unions that supported the *crusade* initiative has yet been the subject of detailed research with the result that historians have little understanding of the impact of the *crusade* in the countryside.[39] Moreover, although studies of 'strict' urban unions like Manchester are available, most research on the *crusade* concentrates on central government policy initiatives, ideology and pauperism statistics.[40] Generally this is the result of an inability to find good local records to explore local performance and achievement. In the case of Brixworth, however, leading participants left a wealth of material recounting the nature of, and reasons for, local support for the *crusade* campaign.

The Brixworth union, moreover, played a leading, and wider, role in the

---

[37] Some agricultural historians have noted the importance of the *crusade* in relation to rural trade union activity. See, for example, A. F. G. Brown, *Meagre harvest: the Essex farm workers' struggle against poverty, 1750–1914*, Chelmsford 1990, 86–87.

[38] For the best relevant summaries see E. H. Hunt, *British labour history, 1815–1914*, Basingstoke 1981; R. Gray, *The aristocracy of labour in 19th-century Britain, 1850–1914*, London 1981; K. D. Brown, *The English labour movement, 1700–1951*, London 1982; C. J. Wrigley (ed.), *A history of British industrial relations, 1875–1914*, i, London–New York 1982; J. Winter (ed.), *The working class in modern British history: essays in honour of Henry Pelling*, Cambridge 1983; J. Benson (ed.), *The working class in England, 1875–1914*, Harlow 1984; E. Roberts, *A woman's place: an oral history of working-class women, 1890–1940*, Oxford 1984, and *Women's work, 1840–1940*, London–New York 1988; H. McLeod, *Religion and the working class in nineteenth-century Britain*, Basingstoke 1984; R. Price, *Labour in British society: an interpretative essay*, London 1986; J. Benson, *The working class in Britain, 1850–1939*, Harlow 1989; and P. Joyce, *Work, society and politics: the culture of the factory in later Victorian England*, Aldershot 1991 edn.

[39] These include Atcham (Salop), Bradfield (Berks), Brixworth (Northants), Faversham, Milton, Tenterden (all Kent) and Wallingford (Berks).

[40] Humphreys, *Sin*, 39–41, discusses the Manchester poor law union. See also Ryan, 'East London', 130–72, and L. J. Feehan, 'The relief of poverty in Liverpool, 1850–1914', unpubl. PhD diss. Liverpool 1988.

crusade campaign and reactions to it. In the late-Victorian period the Local Government Board (LGB) created a league table of the best-performing *crusading* poor law unions in England and Wales. A total of thirty-four urban and seven rural 'model' unions competed annually for a position in the top ten.[41] The Brixworth union was consistently ranked amongst these high achievers. The LGB regarded it as one of its chief *crusading* allies. It featured in the annual reports of central government, in poor law conference proceedings, in national newspapers and in most major journals whenever the *crusade* campaign was discussed.[42] Thus, it was at the centre of national controversy.

Leading members of the Brixworth board of guardians also ensured that this rural union maintained a high profile. In the Brixworth union a powerful cohort of prominent local individuals, including Albert Pell (Conservative MP for south-Leicestershire) and the 5th Earl Spencer (senior Whig peer and leading member of the Liberal party), were key national figures in late-Victorian debates on welfare. These men were successful publicists who used their positions of authority in both houses of parliament and their status on the ruling councils of powerful charitable lobbies, such as the COS, to promote their *crusading* ideology. They organised a formidable 'marketing campaign', creating the impression that they had an unassailable reputation as the poverty experts of their day. They were so successful that they made an important contribution to imperial welfare debates as far afield as New Zealand.[43] David Thomson stresses that the influence and lobbying skills of leading members of the Brixworth union should not be underestimated. It is no coincidence that in most contemporary welfare textbooks this rural 'model' union is cited as emblematic of the *crusade* ideology. Yet its record of poor law administration has never been studied in detail.[44] Although Anthony Brundage did examine the early to mid-Victorian poor law experience in Northamptonshire, his work on the Brixworth union did not extend to the later period.[45] Thus he omitted the wealth of resources that this study brings together.

The presence of so many eminent figures on the Brixworth union board

---

[41] LGB league tables of 'model' unions are cited in C. Booth, *The aged poor in England and Wales: condition*, London 1894, 58–98.

[42] Idem, *Pauperism and the endowment of old age*, London 1892; W. Chance, *The better administration of the poor law*, London 1895; G. Lubbock (ed.), *Some poor relief questions: for and against*, London 1895; P. F. Ashrott, *The English poor law system*, London 1902; T. MacKay, *History of the English poor law*, III: *1834–1898*, London 1904; Webb and Webb, *English poor law* and *English poor law history*.

[43] Thomson, *World without welfare*, 15–18. It must be conceded, however, that between 1865 and 1906 many poor law unions were also importing their welfare ideas from overseas, notably from Germany.

[44] Humphreys, *Sin*, 36–8, cites the Brixworth union but does not check its local administrative record.

[45] Brundage, *English poor laws*, 126, demonstrates that the author has not had an opportunity to revisit his earlier Northamptonshire study to take into account new source material.

of guardians also affords a rare opportunity to explore central–local relations more fully. These men were determined to implement a full-scale *crusading* experiment to prove that their ideology worked in practice and guaranteed savings. In turn, the LGB needed a *crusading* success. It was therefore in the interests of both sides to develop a close working relationship. This book examines that central–local alliance. It ascertains whether relations were ever strained. How, for instance, did committed *crusaders* and central government respond at times of mounting pressure for economic and political change that undermined their campaign? It will be shown that local poor law unions were often very slow to register changing definitions of the causes of poverty and their remedy, and that *crusaders* tended to ignore changes in social policy that did not suit their economic interests. Thus there was often a significant time lapse between more national and liberal social policy trends, and actual changes in the administration of the poor law in the localities. This study uses the poor law as an historical prism to retrace complex central–local dynamics and offers fresh insights into the nature of state intervention by the later nineteenth century. The reader is brought closer to the locus of poor law politics.

A central purpose of this book is to test Pat Thane's view that the coming of local democracy had a very limited impact. It does so by investigating the nature of political activity within the Brixworth union. The study will explore whether political activism developed in a linear fashion, starting with agricultural trade unionism and culminating in working-class representation in the poor law union boardroom. It will also examine whether Liberalism, which dominated Northamptonshire politics, managed to contain and address the aspirations of working people. If it failed to do so then political historians who debate the drift away from Liberalism in the later Victorian and Edwardian era may need to take into account the political ramifications of the *crusade* when they assess the impact of municipal socialism.[46] It would also mean that welfare historians such as Pat Thane would have to revise their view that working-class political activity only emerged as a force in British politics when Labour strengthened its 'chances of attaining local or central power … post 1920'.[47] Essentially, this book evaluates the tense political relationship that developed between *crusaders* and those determined to exploit democracy for welfare ends. Irish poor law historians, such as Bill

---

46 There is a wealth of literature on the subject of whether or not Liberalism declined in the later Victorian period. Useful context is given in A. Sykes, *The rise and fall of British Liberalism, 1776–1988*, Harlow 1997. On Liberal vibrancy see, for example, P. F. Clarke, *Lancashire and new Liberalism*, Cambridge 1971, and *Liberals and social democrats*, Cambridge 1978. Others see Liberalism in early decline: K. Laybourn and J. Reynolds, *Liberalism and the rise of Labour, 1890–1918*, London 1984; G. L. Bernstein, *Liberalism and Liberal politics in Edwardian England*, London 1986; K. Laybourn, *The rise of Labour: the British Labour party, 1890–1979*, London 1988; D. Tanner, *Political change and the Labour party, 1900–1990*, Cambridge 1990; R. McKibbin, *The ideologies of class: social relations in Britain, 1880–1950*, Oxford 1991.

47 Thane, '"Welfare"', 900.

Feingold, have stressed the importance of boards of guardians in rural society, establishing that they were significant arenas of political negotiation in the late nineteenth century.[48] This book will test whether the same was true of some of their English counterparts.

Rethinking the late-Victorian poor law

This study has six broad aims, which will locate the late-Victorian poor law experience.

Initially it will test Williams's view that the *crusade* was a policy of 'brutal dispauperisation by any and every means'. It analyses whether this statement characterises the nature of the local poor law decision-making process. Did the poor living outside the workhouse experience a greater degree of economic hardship when outdoor relief allowances were withdrawn? Was it cruel to ask the poor to resolve the problems of pauperism alone, even if this often exacerbated their poverty? In asking these questions, the study takes issue with the progressive view of the late-Victorian poor law espoused by the Webbs.[49] A second closely related aim is to examine Rose's claim that the *crusade* was a backward-looking initiative. It asks whether the *crusade* reverted to, or radicalised, the strict letter of the New Poor Law. Was the *crusade* much harsher on the poor than previous nineteenth-century poor law practices?[50]

The study then moves on to investigate the impact of the process of local government democratisation. Did gaining the right to vote in poor law elections in 1894 give ordinary working people the means to influence the decision-making process for the first time? Did they grasp the opportunity not simply to oppose the *crusade* but to organise its overthrow? To what extent, therefore, did these new voters support extensive social welfare provision or were they apathetic, failing to capitalise on their new voting rights? Were local politics more accessible and flexible than contemporaries were prepared to admit and conventional modern scholarship appreciates?[51]

It is then important to analyse the complex relationship between central and local poor law authorities. Did the *crusade* give guardians an opportunity to exploit poor law regulations and, if so, to what extent? In what ways did they take advantage of central government initiatives in social policy to promote their ideological viewpoints and cost-cutting measures?

---

[48] S. Clarke and J. S. Donnelly (eds), *Irish peasants and political unrest, 1780–1914*, Manchester 1983; W. L. Feingold, *The revolt of the tenantry: the transformation of local government in Ireland, 1872–1886*, Boston 1984.

[49] Williams, *Pauperism*, 102.

[50] See Rose, 'Crisis of poor relief', 62; Thomson, 'Welfare', 374; and Williams, *Pauperism*, 99. This theme is considered further at pp. 52–6 below, where Williams's views are discussed in more detail.

[51] Thane, '"Welfare"', 892. Howkins, *Poor labouring men*, 178, highlights that rural politics were very complex and more diverse than conventional labour studies often convey.

A further significant issue is the complex question of the changing nature of paternalism during the *crusade* decades. Did the *crusading* ethos, and its practical application, undermine complicated, but meaningful, local perceptions about poor law duties and responsibilities: was there a difference between poor law rhetoric and reality?[52] This study analyses the impact of changes in outdoor relief on the everyday lives of the labouring poor to try to uncover, from the fragments of evidence that have survived, what it felt like to be caught up in various *crusading* initiatives. Finally, it examines the contribution that each social grouping (landowners, farmers, clergy, artisans and labourers) made to local poor law politics. It focuses on what part each played in the implementation, overthrow and aftermath of the *crusade* in the Brixworth union.

This approach allows historians for the first time to focus on the controversy over outdoor relief. It recounts arguments for and against public assistance in a significant location where a version of the *crusade* was tried and found wanting. Structured chronologically into three sections, the book will examine the economic, socio-political and personal dynamics of the New Poor Law as they evolved. In the process it explores the lived experience of the *crusade*. The *crusade* against outdoor relief was a complex jigsaw puzzle; to understand it demands renewed analytical emphasis on the later Victorian poor law. A study of the politics of poor relief, the forces that shaped the *crusading* experience and the impact that those policies had on the poor, is overdue.

---

[52] D. Roberts, *Paternalism in early Victorian England*, London 1979, 2, characterises paternalism in this way.

PART I

THE NATIONAL POOR LAW PICTURE

1

The New Poor Law:
Legal and Theoretical Framework

The origins and immediate impact of the New Poor Law Amendment Act of 1834 have been the subject of considerable historical research in the last thirty years.[1] This review of its statutes and guidelines analyses the framework that should have dictated regional policy. Yet it will also make clear that those legal stipulations were seldom realised. By the 1840s central government preferred to issue so-called interim 'orders', tinkering with the original statute rather than passing new legislation. Naturally, this made poor law administration on the ground complex. It is for this reason that commentators, like Steven King, note that 'what the state *thought* should happen' seldom matched 'what actually *did* happen'.[2]

The principles of the New Poor Law are well-rehearsed in a number of recent textbooks.[3] Essentially, Benthamite utilitarianism, emphasising 'the greatest happiness for the greatest number' in society, framed the new legislation. Bentham stressed individualism and a desire for greater and more efficient central government. Thus, legislation stipulated that local boards of guardians were to be established to achieve administrative uniformity. Guardians were either elected to serve every three years (on the basis of property-owning status), or were non-elected magistrates (*ex-officio*). Each parish was combined into a larger poor law union centred, if possible, upon a market town or city centre. A property tax was levied on residents in each parish to pay for the welfare of their poorer residents.

To achieve minimal taxation guardians were instructed to refuse outdoor relief to able-bodied claimants who applied for parish assistance. Instead, they had to use a workhouse test. This involved a relieving officer assessing each poor law claimant's financial circumstances on behalf of guardians. Goods had to be sold or pawned to make ends meet. Only after all material resources had been liquidated would a pauper be authorised to enter the workhouse. They were given tickets to prove their destitution, dressed in a pauper uniform and became inmates. To ensure that workhouse provision was each pauper's 'less eligible' option, indoor relief care was to be very basic; this had important

---

1   For a list of current work in this field see introduction, n. 10.
2   King, *Poverty and welfare*, 18. Here the emphasis will be on the issue of outdoor relief. A summary of those procedures can be found in Englander, *Poverty and poor law reform*, 13–30.
3   Hollen-Lees, *Solidarities*, provides a comprehensive overview.

economic implications. For instance, only minimal support was to be given to destitute persons during periods of seasonal unemployment, illness or a family crisis.[4] Likewise, those who entered the workhouse and could work had to earn their keep. Men laboured on various work schemes within the workhouse, usually in stone-yards, until their employment circumstances improved. Women were employed to do general menial tasks, such as oakum picking or domestic work. Benthamite reformers believed that a disciplinary work regime would discourage able-bodied claimants from becoming welfare dependants and encourage them to adopt an ethos of self-reliance. The new regulations were also designed to persuade farmers to raise wages, once they realised that customary outdoor relief benefits had been abolished.[5] A key legislative objective was that guardians would treat all poor relief applications made by the able-bodied poor according to the strict letter of the law.[6]

In practice, as numerous regional studies have shown, these principles were not fully implemented because legislation failed to define accurately what the term 'able-bodied' meant. Many guardians exploited this ambiguity in order to retain their traditional discretionary powers.[7] Guardians in urban areas in the north of England, as Michael Rose has shown, struggling with the twin difficulties of high unemployment rates and inadequate workhouse capacity, often ignored outrelief regulations. If they had been implemented they would have caused considerable social unrest.[8] Similarly, in rural districts, many farmer guardians ignored the new directives and used medical outrelief orders to retain labour reserves to meet seasonal farming demands.[9]

In the early years of the New Poor Law central government accepted that in order to get the new procedures underway it would have to defuse local resentment by accepting a measure of non-compliance. This resulted in a high degree of continuity between the Old and New Poor Law.[10] However, once the New Poor Law system was in operation, senior civil servants were instructed to review outrelief procedures; unsurprisingly they found considerable diversity. Central government concluded that it was time to reassert its

[4] M. Blaug, 'The myth of the old poor law and the making of the new', *JEcH* xxiii (1963), 151–84.
[5] Ibid; P. Dunkley, 'Whigs and paupers: the reform of the English poor laws, 1830–34', *JBS* xx (1980), 135.
[6] Fraser, *Evolution*, 23; Englander, *Poverty and poor law reform*, 9–13.
[7] D. Ashforth, 'The urban poor law', in D. Fraser (ed.), *The New Poor Law in the nineteenth century*, London 1976, 128–48, and Digby, *Poor law*, both argue this point. Williams, *Pauperism*, 81–90 is the only historian to have challenged this view.
[8] See introduction, n. 17, for Rose's case studies of northern industrial towns, such as Huddersfield.
[9] A. Digby, 'The labour market and the continuity of social policy after 1834: the case of the eastern counties', *EcHR* 2nd ser. xxviii (1975), 69–83.
[10] Idem, 'The rural poor', 593, and M. E. Rose, 'The allowance system under the New Poor Law', *EcHR* 2nd ser. xxix (1966), 607–20, are just two historians who make this point.

authority by defining what it meant by the term 'able-bodied'. As a result, a decision was taken to issue three new outrelief directives.

In 1842 an Outdoor Labour Test was sent to all poor law unions in England and Wales.[11] This was a pragmatic gesture on the part of central government, which conceded that seasonal work patterns forced large numbers of unemployed able-bodied labourers to apply for parish funding. The new directive gave guardians the option of employing these claimants during the day within the workhouse in return for a small outrelief dole. Most guardians welcomed the directive because poor law unions that were still building their workhouses relied on this type of labour. However, in practice, they tended to subject men, rather than women, to this test.

Consequently another directive was issued two years later with a view to achieving greater compliance. The 1844 Outdoor Relief Prohibitory Order[12] stipulated that outrelief regulations were to be tightened in rural areas. Its primary objective was to ensure that all able-bodied applicants and their dependants had to enter the workhouse or support themselves independently. It was hoped that this would remedy the confusion about poor relief entitlements and bring about more uniform practices. However, this second directive contained a key phrase that undermined its purpose.

One of its subclauses stated that guardians had discretion to award outdoor relief to able-bodied applicants in cases of 'sudden and urgent necessity'. Obviously this wording could be interpreted in a number of ways. It soon became a key administrative loophole. Many rural guardians, as Anne Digby has shown, construed that it gave them the powers to award outdoor relief on medical orders to paupers at times of family crises.[13] Those who had an accident, were disabled at work, fell ill temporarily or could not afford to bury a relative without parish assistance, often received outdoor medical relief. The directive also gave guardians the powers to treat vulnerable poor relief applicants more liberally. Widows with children on low incomes and independent childless widows with no visible means of support could apply for outrelief funding for up to six months after their spouse's death. Guardians had the discretion to relieve the resident family of an absent or removable father and relieving officers often paid rent on behalf of low-income families. In total the Webbs estimated that by 1871 some 371 rural poor law unions were governed by this second order,[14] but it appears to have accentuated, rather than resolved, the problem of diverse practices in the administration of outrelief in rural areas of England and Wales. Rose states that, as a result, most people living in the workhouse were not able-bodied and they only entered at times of family crisis or as a result of severe ill health. Most poor relief claimants received some form of outrelief on a regular basis.[15]

---

11 Rose, 'Allowance system', 618.
12 Englander, *Poverty and poor law reform*, 15, 97, 100.
13 Digby, 'Labour market', 69–83.
14 Webb and Webb, *English poor law policy*, 91.
15 Rose, 'Allowance system', 607–10.

In 1852 a third directive, the Outdoor Relief Regulation Order, was issued.[16] It tried, like its rural predecessor, to clarify eligibility for outdoor relief in urban districts, but failed because it too contained subclauses that gave guardians additional discretion. The new regulations stipulated that poor law unions should have the option of awarding outrelief allowances to all categories of female claimants seeking poor relief. Women, unlike men, were officially no longer subjected to the Labour Test of 1842, even if they were able-bodied. Central government conceded that guardians were justified in not institutionalising female claimants unless it was absolutely necessary on the grounds of ill health. Similarly, the directive gave guardians an opportunity to treat able-bodied male applicants more leniently. As well as transferring able-bodied men under the Labour Test directive of 1842 to a parish work scheme, guardians now had the right to add payments in kind (usually bread, meat, etc.) to their meagre outrelief doles. Central government only made one proviso: that not less than 50 per cent of each claimant's total outrelief allowance should be given in a non-monetary form.[17] This created a new official scale of outrelief in kind with a minimum threshold but, crucially, no upper limit. These three directives encouraged many guardians, who believed that the 'line of demarcation between poverty and destitution was often imperceptible', to act even more pragmatically.[18] The directives officially governed outrelief provision in England and Wales until July 1896, when the LGB passed another Outdoor Relief Order. However, for the twenty years between 1873 and 1893 a set of outrelief recommendations, known as the Longley Strategy, dominated government thinking on welfare provision. This symbolised what has become labelled in so much poor law historiography as 'the *crusade* against outrelief'.

The origins of the *crusade* were rooted in a major recession during the 1860s. In 1863–4 outrelief provision came under a renewed attack following a series of trade slumps, and industrial crises in Lancashire and London, which caused national poor relief expenditure to rise by about 20 per cent.[19] Many guardians, who feared that higher levels of unemployment and a lack of outrelief provision might result in social unrest, ignored regulations concerning able-bodied males, and expenditure rose as a result. For a time that threat appeared to be very real, particularly in London when, during trade slumps in the years 1855, 1860–1 and 1866–7, food riots broke out in the East End.[20] However, the Poor Law Board, replaced by the LGB in 1871, did not recognise that trade problems and a 16 per cent rise in London's population in the decade 1861 to 1871 were responsible for the rise in poor law expenditure. Instead they blamed recalcitrant boards of guardians who gave liberal outrelief to

---

[16] Digby, *Poor law*, 21.

[17] Kidd, *State, society and the poor*, 32–3.

[18] Digby, 'The rural poor', 593.

[19] Rose, 'Crisis of poor relief', 57, calculates that during 1862 poor relief applications in the Lancashire cotton districts increased by 'some 300%'.

[20] Englander, *Poverty and poor law reform*, 20.

unemployed claimants. Thus, a decision was taken to promote the efficacy of the workhouse test by initiating three policy changes.[21]

The first of these was spearheaded by senior civil servants at the Poor Law Board, who negotiated with large organised charitable bodies in London, most notably the COS (founded 1869), to try to prevent indiscriminate almsgiving.[22] Senior civil servants aimed to create welfare partnerships with private charitable organisations to try to eradicate liberal outrelief expenditure and random acts of charity. This objective was outlined in a new central government outrelief circular known as the Goschen Minute of 1869, named after a future president of the LGB, who drew it up. Goschen proposed that each board of guardians in London should form an administrative partnership with members of the COS. Senior civil servants were given the power to co-opt any COS member onto boards of guardians for this purpose. Each poor law union would then act as a sort of pauper 'clearing house'. Relieving officers were instructed to report outrelief claimants to boards of guardians fortnightly. But each case came before a full board meeting only after it had been investigated thoroughly by a local poor law official, generally a guardian, and/or a COS representative.

If an outrelief application merited assistance, guardians were encouraged to withhold poor relief and instead to refer the case on to their local COS branch via their co-opted COS member. COS authorities would then re-interview each case and compile a home case study report before making a recommendation for temporary charitable relief for a fixed period of around four weeks. If the claimant's circumstances did not improve after one month they were referred back to their poor law union and had to accept indoor relief. In London, central government co-opted many leading COS members onto boards of guardians. The profile of COS membership has been likened to a 'new urban squirearchy' of middle-class professionals who strongly emphasised 'leadership and deference'.[23] They envisaged that their role was to separate the 'respectable poor' from the undeserving. This would ensure that genuine claimants would be supported and the work-shy would be disciplined in workhouses.[24]

Meanwhile, junior civil servants saw the need for a second policy change to resolve the growing rating crises in urban England. This problem began following the passing of the Poor Law Removal Act of 1846 and the Irremovability Act of 1861, when residency qualifications for parish relief were reduced from five to three years respectively. Obviously this increased rates in districts where pauper numbers swelled as the rural unemployed migrated

---

[21] Humphreys, *Sin*, 20–1.

[22] Kidd, *State, society and the poor*, 45–8.

[23] Englander, *Poverty and poor law reform*, 21–2.

[24] See chapter 2 below for a detailed examination of *crusaders'* rhetoric and that of their critics.

in search of work.[25] Prior to 1865 each individual parish paid for the costs of its own poorer residents from local rates levied amongst residents to spread the cost of poor law expenditure. On the one hand this meant that major landowners in closed villages often encouraged paupers to migrate. On the other hand large ratepayers tried to avoid paying high local taxes by asking tenants to leave rented premises over the rate assessment period (usually in the spring): empty premises had a lower rateable value so that larger ratepayers thus avoided paying their share of poor law bills. Poor law coffers, therefore, never had enough tax income to pay for adequate workhouse expansion to meet increasing demand. This in turn necessitated larger outdoor relief bills. Central government was therefore determined to reform the parochial rating system and the way that poor law rates were levied. Smaller householders, who contributed a disproportionate amount of their income to the poor rate, welcomed the Parochial Assessment Bill of 1862 and the Union Chargeability Act of 1865. The first of these stopped wealthier landowners from interfering with rating procedures, while the second revised rateable assessments by making 'property rather than poverty, ... the basis of parish contributions to the common expenses of the union'.[26] Regardless of who was living in a property or the number of paupers in a parish, a fixed rateable value was levied according to the size of the premises. This latter measure was very significant because it led to the *crusade* against outrelief.

The Union Chargeability Act stipulated that parish rates had to be pooled into a union-wide fund.[27] Creating a larger revenue base made all parishes responsible for every pauper within a poor law union. It also provided more income to fund loans for improvements in workhouse facilities, notably medical dispensaries. London's problems were resolved by passing a Common Metropolitan Poor Act in 1867 under which rates were pooled into a Common Poor Law Fund to pay for the construction and maintenance of workhouse property in the capital. This finally brought eleven metropolitan districts under the New Poor Law.[28] Civil servants hoped that the 1865 and 1867 bills would stop parishes acting like a number of 'quarrelling member states' both in the provinces and the capital, and that expanded workhouse capacity would prevent high levels of outrelief.[29] In reality, wealthier ratepayers scrutinised outrelief expenditure because they resented having to pay for their neighbour's pauperism. Central government could not have predicted this outcome but it was not unwelcome. It was a catalyst that led to the *crusade* against outrelief in many unions even before central government's campaign of retrenchment got underway officially.

The third policy change was that in 1871 the Poor Law Board merged

[25] M. E. Rose, 'Settlement, removal and the New Poor Law', in Fraser, *New Poor Law*, 25–44 at pp. 26–38.

[26] Englander, *Poverty and poor law reform*, 21.

[27] Rose, 'Crisis of poor relief', 50–70, discusses 1865 revenue changes.

[28] Englander, *Poverty and poor law reform*, 21.

[29] Rose, 'Crisis of poor relief', 59.

with the newly created LGB to form a new ministry of state, controlling most aspects of local government administration.[30] The LGB was more powerful than its predecessor because it ranked amongst the most senior government departments and its president had a seat in Cabinet. From its inception a decision was taken to try to raise the LGB's profile by again reviewing all outrelief procedures. Alarm was expressed immediately when senior civil servants calculated that only about 16 per cent of paupers were being relieved within workhouses, despite the revenue changes that had been brought in after 1865 to improve indoor relief capacity.[31] The secretary of the LGB, Henry Fleming, re-examined outrelief procedures personally and concluded that a new set of guidelines should be issued to every poor law union in England and Wales outlining revised outrelief procedures. This was to have a domino effect on administrative practices on a regional and local basis.

The Fleming Circular of December 1871 stated that 'neither locality, trade, seasons, weather, population' trends or a 10 per cent retail price growth during the 1860s had been the cause of higher levels of outrelief funding.[32] Recalcitrant boards of guardians in London and the provinces were held responsible for the spiralling cost of relief. Fleming's report presented the issue of outrelief in moral terms. Guardians had failed in their duty to protect the interests of local ratepayers because their lax administrative methods accentuated levels of pauperism. The review recommended the propriety of the workhouse test, stating that it was a safeguard that addressed the social evil of poverty. However, its chief objective was to introduce a system of greater financial accountability. Fleming stressed the need to introduce cost-saving initiatives. Under the new directive guardians were authorised to grant outrelief only in very exceptional circumstances, and for a maximum period of three months.[33] This had an immediate impact on the 'makeshift' economies of poor relief claimants. For example, some females whom guardians chose to relieve under the 1844 and 1852 Orders now had their outrelief funding withdrawn. These included single able-bodied females with or without illegitimate children, as well as women deserted by their spouses. All mothers with young children were now expected to accept indoor relief. They were encouraged to hand over the care of their children to workhouse personnel who would arrange to board them out and educate them, giving women the freedom to seek employment. Similarly, older unemployable men were judged to be burdens on the community and their outrelief funding was withdrawn. All outrelief cases had to be inspected on a regular basis, by means of a home visit from either relieving officers or a District Medical Officer for the Poor (DMOP), although only the former now had the authority to grant outrelief. Able-

---

30 See C. Bellamy, *Administering central–local relations: the Local Government Board in its fiscal and cultural context*, Manchester 1988, for the most comprehensive account of the LGB's record of administration.
31 Humphreys, *Sin*, 21–8.
32 Ibid. 24.
33 Ibid. 24–5, analyses the Fleming Report.

bodied cases were reviewed weekly and medical cases not less than once a quarter. This was the beginning of what contemporaries dubbed the *crusade*.

In 1873 the LGB commissioned another report on outrelief procedures. It investigated whether Fleming's directive was being implemented uniformly. This review was undertaken by one of the most eminent senior inspectors at the LGB, Henry Longley.[34] He found that there was still a high degree of local autonomy and so a third anti-outrelief initiative, the Longley Report, was issued. It reiterated the themes of the Goschen Minute of 1869 and the Fleming Circular of 1871, but also proposed more radical deterrents. Longley believed that the recommendations of Goschen and Fleming were appropriate, but failed to increase compliance because they did not state explicitly that all types of outrelief funding should be abolished. Longley asserted that only by stating that outrelief funding was illegal would expenditure on poor relief be reduced. Guardians might disagree in principle with a ban, but abolition would expose those who refused to co-operate and central government could then concentrate on eradicating non-compliance. Once offending poor law unions had been identified, pressure would be brought to bear on them to conform. Longley believed this was the only way to eradicate local autonomy and cut expenditure on poor relief nationally. These strategies and the nature of their deployment arose out of a complex array of political, theoretical and experiential forces in nineteenth-century England.

Changing ideas on welfare provision in the nineteenth century

By 1870 Henry Longley, the LGB, major charity organisations and politicians were buffeted by a series of distinctive theoretical and practical agendas that reshaped poor law policy debates. First, numerous economic theories informed politicians and the public about welfare entitlements. Second, welfare ideas from elsewhere, notably Scotland and Ireland, were influential. Third, changing political discourse, whether re-styled 'New Liberalism' or 'popular Toryism', may have informed poor law change. The *crusade* stood at the confluence of these trends.

Economic theory

Unquestionably classical economic theorists, like Adam Smith, John Locke, Thomas Malthus and David Richardo were *crusade* heroes.[35] With their emphasis on free market economics, wealth creation and the need to give individuals in society freedom of economic opportunity,[36] they inspired Jeremy Bentham to formulate the notion of *laissez-faire* government. Bentham's utili-

---

[34] Williams, *Pauperism*, 96–107, provides the most comprehensive analysis of the Longley Strategy.

[35] Fraser, *Evolution*, 99–125.

[36] G. Himmelfarb, *The idea of poverty: England in the early industrial age*, London 1984, 133–46.

tarian welfare vision underpinned the New Poor Law. He championed *laissez-faire* government, administrative uniformity and limited welfare provision for the destitute.[37] Some collectivist action, he argued, was needed to improve the health, welfare and economic viability of the nation. The sick, infirm, disabled and so on did not have the same level of labour to offer as the able-bodied. However, economic needs in a society must be harmonised to create 'the greatest happiness of the greatest number'. Only under exceptional economic conditions, therefore, should central government adopt interventionist welfare policies. Instead, throughout the mid-Victorian period there was a vibrant self-help literature exemplified by Samuel Smiles's *Self-help: with illustrations of conduct and perseverance* (1859) and *Character, thrift and duty* (1871). Values such as individual hard work, determination, independence, self-discipline and self-improvement were emphasised.[38] This meant that the poor were expected to practise mutual aid before seeking welfare help. Consequently, the English poor relief system was complex and structured by a 'mixed economy of welfare' in most areas. Often the poor relied on 'makeshift economies' to make ends meet. Moreover, at the macro-level, the politics of poor relief were complicated because a 'help from within' attitude could not compensate the poor in dire need.[39] Where could the labouring poor turn to instead? Some social theorists, notably Herbert Spencer, seemed to offer an answer, thereby influencing *crusaders*.

Herbert Spencer's *The proper sphere of government* (1843) and *Social statics* [sic] (1851) stated that all classical economists should be arch-opponents of the state. He championed Malthus and anticipated Darwin's work, arguing that in nature the 'survival of the fittest' had evolved for rational economic reasons. The resources of any species were limited. Non-achievers should not be allowed to destroy the 'natural' economic order. When the state stepped in to help the weak, it often confused 'sympathy with justice'.[40] Spencer was not a heartless free market capitalist, but like many Victorians he emphasised that the charity sector should share the welfare burden with government.[41] Later the COS would follow his lead (a theme elaborated in chapter 2).

Many committed *crusaders*, therefore, insisted on regulated but limited charitable provision. The poor needed a new form of 'moral education' to help themselves. Charities should kick-start material improvement; but thereafter it was up to the pauper to act independently. As for the non-productive poor, they should be categorised and identified as of lower economic status and less biological worth. Those who bred too much must be rejected for draining too many welfare resources. Eugenics and biology thus underpinned many late-Victorian discourses on poverty. Essentially, science gave *crusaders*

---

37 Humphreys, *Sin*, 150.
38 Hunt, *British labour history*, 111.
39 See n. 9 above.
40 Humpreys, *Sin*, 51.
41 M. J. D. Roberts, *Making English morals: voluntary association and moral reform in England, 1787–1886*, Cambridge 2004, 143–5.

a new commerce of knowledge about human nature, which they exploited for economic reasons. However, as Gareth Stedman Jones notes, critics soon recognised that ideas on, and theories of, poverty had produced social typologies that lumped the genuine poor together into a 'casual labour' mass, giving rise to a degenerative discourse about their 'grime dirt and disease'.[42] In particular, a group of Oxbridge academics, dubbed the Idealists, challenged the Spencerian notion that altruism could replace state action.

The New Idealists were a group of predominately academic thinkers. By the late-Victorian period, they were concerned about welfare ideology and social problems. They asked why so much charity was necessary, if self-help was such a great success. It was obvious that the poor had not disappeared and it was surely dangerous to ignore them? Idealists like Thomas Hill Green (Oxford), together with Henry Sidgwick and Alfred Marshall[43] (both at Cambridge) started to lecture on these socio-economic challenges. Essentially, they tried to reconcile a free market ethos with the idea of a positive view of the state, necessitating intervention in social policy.

Alfred Marshall argued in *The economic of industry* (1879) that personal economic progress had four facets.[44] First, an individual had the chance either to 'improve' on the gifts of nature or to 'waste them'. Second, they could choose either to exploit or neglect their physical strength and energy in hard work or laziness. Third, individual mental ability and self-knowledge might help to change economic circumstances. Finally, a person's 'moral' character, notably their attitude to work, was very relevant to their economic success or failure. Harnessing a person's positive attributes, Marshall argued, would have knock-on economic benefits.[45] Likewise, Green insisted that everyone in society needed an equal chance to create wealth allowing each to 'contribute to the social good'. The poor were part of society and needed to be helped not rejected, as *crusaders* insisted. The New Idealists, therefore, reformulated Adam Smith's political economic vision. Some individuals had more freedom than others. The poor often suffered economic constraints that required state help. D. G. Ritchie, summarised the Idealist viewpoint:

> The history of progress is the record of the gradual diminution of waste. The lower the stage, the greater is the waste involved in the attainment of any end. In the lower organisms, nature is reckless in her expenditure of life. ... When we come to human beings in society, the State is the chief instrument by which waste is prevented. ... By freeing the individual from

---

[42] G. Stedman Jones, *Outcast London: a study of the relationship between classes in Victorian society*, Oxford 1971, 1–16.

[43] See also A. Marshall, 'How far do remediable causes influence prejudicially a) continuity of employment, b) the rate of wages?', in *Industrial conference*, London 1885, 173–4.

[44] Ibid.

[45] G. Jones, *Social Darwinism and English thought: the interaction between biological and social theory*, Brighton 1980, 6.

the necessity of perpetual struggle for the mere conditions of life, it [the State] can set free individuality.[46]

Essentially New Idealists tried to 'detach liberalism from a purely negative view of the state's function'.[47] If the poor were better educated, fed, housed and given improved medical care, most could become a national asset, instead of a welfare drain. However, the New Idealists failed to reconcile demands for more social welfare provision with the need to uphold the state's economic interests and maintain minimal taxation. Most New Idealists (like those classical political economists who preceded them) were creative theorists but lacked pragmatism.[48] They created 'ambiguity', allowing more room for competing ideas 'as to what was actually needed to bring improvement in the condition of the poor'.[49] This exposed their *naïveté* and limited the political appeal of New Idealism. Instead, *crusaders* turned to welfare ideas developing on the peripheries of Britain. In particular, there were inspired by Irish and Scottish cost-saving measures.

Irish and Scottish welfare ideas
Since the 1960s the English system of poor relief has dominated welfare historiography.[50] Only recently, have a number of groundbreaking studies challenged this trend and begun to highlight the importance of influences from other countries on English policy.[51] (Parts II and III will recount how Earl Spencer, a leading guardian in the Brixworth union, imported Celtic welfare ideals.)[52] Irish poor law historians, like Virginia Crossman, show that throughout the eighteenth and nineteenth centuries poverty in Ireland was the focus of extensive debate.[53] It was difficult to ignore the fact that pauperism was pernicious. By 1833, therefore, a Royal Commission on the Condition of the Poorer Classes in Ireland convened, taking three years to report its findings. The final report concluded that an Irish poor law system

---

46 D. G. Ritchie, 'Mr. Spencer's individualism and his conception of society', *Contemporary Review* (Nov. 1886), 50.
47 Jones, *Social Darwinism*, 60.
48 S. Pedersen and P. Mandler (eds), *After the Victorians: private conscience and public duty in modern Britain: essays in memory of John Clive*, London 1994, 1–31.
49 Humphreys, *Sin*, 14.
50 Finlayson, *State, society and the poor*; Fraser, *Evolution*.
51 A national Welfare Peripheries Research Group was formed in July 2004 at the Department of History, Oxford Brookes University. It consists of a consortium of historians researching on Ireland, Scotland, Wales and England who are working towards a national project on welfare states.
52 See pp. 28–30 below.
53 See, for example, D. Dickson, 'In search of the old Irish poor law', in R. Mitchinson and P. Roebuck (eds), *Economy and society in Scotland and Ireland, 1500–1939*, Edinburgh 1988, 149–59, and V. Crossman, 'Welfare and nationality: the poor laws in nineteenth-century Ireland', in S. A King and J. W Stewart (eds), *Welfare peripheries*, Oxford 2005, 26–52.

must not mirror the English New Poor Law.[54] There was little point in forcing the Irish poor into workhouses that lacked the capacity to house them. The Irish were encouraged to recognise the difference between 'living in poverty' and 'destitution'. George Nicholls, an English poor law commissioner, was sent to emphasise this new categorisation. He would later use that experience to champion an English *crusade*; his stance and original attitude in Ireland is therefore instructive.[55]

Nicholls insisted that absentee Irish landlords must bear the costs of poor relief. He recognised, however, that if the principle of outdoor relief were extended to Ireland, ratepayers would be overwhelmed. Instead, he stated that only the destitute would be relieved in workhouses; others had to learn self-help. This set a poor law benchmark that *crusaders* revived in England after 1870. Crossman shows that by the end of 1842 Ireland had been divided up into 130 unions with workhouses planned, being built or almost complete in most areas. Yet although the system was operational sooner than its English counterpart, it was also in a fundamental funding crisis from its inception. The 'Great Famine' meant that the Irish poor law system almost collapsed because of unprecedented levels of destitution.[56] Quite simply, as Christine Kinealy shows, workhouses could not cope with either the influx of claimants or the scale of disease, death and starvation.[57] Mary Daly estimates that workhouse numbers more than doubled, from 417,000 in 1847 to 932,000 by 1849.[58]

None the less, after the famine poor relief levels stabilised to an average of 35, 000 annual claimants by 1859. Thereafter, attitudes, debates and poor law issues were very similar to those in England. How much relief was needed, who should pay, could poor relief levels be reduced? In 1861 a Select Committee on Poor Relief in Ireland reviewed the system and concluded that there was considerable regional diversity, as there was in the English system. Moreover, the issue of outdoor relief still divided commissioners, guardians, ratepayers and social commentators. The arrival in Ireland of a new lord lieutenant, the 5th Earl Spencer, in 1868 brought these issues to a head.[59]

When Spencer arrived in Ireland he ascertained that endemic poverty, the religious question and an iniquitous landlord system were three of the most pressing social questions. For most of his time in office he was preoccupied with the Irish poor law. Since he later became a keen *crusader*, his time in Ireland demonstrates how debates on the welfare periphery could interchange

---

54 *Third report from the commissioners for the inquiring into the condition of the poorer classes in Ireland*, PP 1836 xxxxiii.

55 Sir George Nicholls, *A history of the Irish poor law*, London 1856.

56 See, for example, M. E. Daly, *The famine in Ireland*, Dublin 1986, for an excellent summary of the vast famine historiography.

57 C. Kinealy, 'The poor law during the great famine: an administration in crisis', in E. M. Crawford (ed.), *Famine: the Irish experience, 900–1900*, Edinburgh 1989, 160–85.

58 Ibid.

59 C. Spencer, *The Spencer family*, London 1999, 255–88.

with Westminster. Spencer called on the expertise of Sir Alfred Power, chief commissioner on the Select Committee on Poor Relief in Ireland (1861). Power was a Whig who believed that the state's duty was to be disinterested and practise non-interference for the sake of the economy. Spencer commissioned Power to re-examine the current state of the poor law in Ireland: the report was later published as A *paper on outdoor relief in Ireland prepared at Earl Spencer's request* (1875). In it Power extolled virtues akin to, and, at the same time, anticipating, later *crusade* rhetoric. He declared that outdoor relief had a 'very demoralising tendency', exacerbating rather than resolving poverty. It destroyed self-reliance and few paupers learned to help themselves. Although the famine had been unprecedented, some fifteen years later poverty was endemic because poor law boards were too generous. The report convinced Spencer that the Irish were idle, profligate and lazy. By the time he returned to Ireland for his second tenure (1885–6) during the Home Rule crisis, his attitudes had hardened even more.[60] Interestingly, Spencer relied on the expertise of his former private secretary in Ireland, Courtenany Boyle, to keep him abreast of English poor law practices. By 1874 Boyle was LGB poor law inspector for East Anglia, placing him at the heart of the *crusade* in England to abolish outdoor relief. Together, an influential senior member of the Liberal government and a leading English poor law civil servant disseminated Irish welfare ideas in the English system during the formative years of the *crusade*. Boyle often debated poor law theory and practice with Spencer. A letter in 1885 summarises Boyle's advice to him on what to read and which relevant welfare ideas were in circulation:

> I am glad you are still looking into what is said by the Great Theorists. ... I will in a day or two make a suggestion as to certain books which Mr F could collect for you when you get back to Althorp. But be careful about abandoning the bone of sound practical judgement for the recipe of wide philosophical reading, you have dealt successfully with very complicated and difficult problems which men crammed with [J.S.] Mill, Adam Smith ... would have theorised about ... but without arriving at such practical conclusions. Jeremy Bentham glances at it in his Principles of Legislation. The development of Local Government is a question of recent growth. What strikes me as remarkable is the extraordinary demand for State interference ... Politicians are forever inquiring that the state should step in to do this and the other, while they clamour for individual freedom.[61]

Boyle advised Spencer to ignore Westminster edicts or political economic theories unless he believed that they 'were sound'. Poor law democratisation worried both men. In Ireland the poor law had become a vehicle for wider

---

[60] C. Boyle to John Poyntz Spencer, 5th Earl Spencer, 28 Nov. 1873, BL, MSS Althorp, K387.
[61] Boyle to Spencer, 25 Aug. 1885, ibid.

nationalist grievances.[62] Boards of guardians were infiltrated and then taken over by the Land League. This was a lesson Spencer noted and would monitor carefully on his return to England. Meanwhile his poor law studies only reaffirmed a *crusading* outlook he had formulated in Ireland. He was also aware of influential Scottish welfare debates.

Traditionally many nineteenth-century contemporaries viewed the Scottish poor law system in a harsh light because the Poor Law Amendment Act (Scotland) of 1845 seemed ungenerous.[63] Scottish reformers believed that statutory poor relief and a poor rate levied from local property taxes would exacerbate rather than resolve pauperism.[64] Poor law critics conceived that whereas the 'respectable' Scottish poor might sometimes *need* poor relief; the indolent and work-shy *wanted* regular assistance, an important distinction. The Scottish poor law system did not provide unemployment relief. Entitlement, therefore, was very difficult to establish and the poor had first to appeal to local parochial boards in each parish and then, if that failed, to a Central Board of Supervision. Poor relief applicants had to prove their 'respectability', residency rights for five years or more in a parish and to confirm that they had not begged to make ends meet. The system was complicated by the fact that Scottish ratepayers were not compelled by law to pay for their poor-rates: they were a voluntary not statutory duty. In time, English *crusaders* were very influenced by these long-established Scottish poor law perspectives, and their originators, notably Thomas Chalmers.

Chalmers was arguably the most influential figure in Scotland and beyond.[65] His importance for English *crusaders* was three-fold. First, he believed that poor law administrators should be appointed for life, adopting business attitudes.[66] Second, he upheld the principle of voluntary taxation. This ensured that poor relief was based on a gift relationship between giver and receiver, encouraging more self-reliance and lowering expectations. Third, Chalmers agreed with Malthus that rapid population expansion by the profligate poor was the root cause of pauperism. It must be stopped both for the sake of ratepayers and national economic growth. His emphasis on voluntarism, therefore, exemplified common nineteenth-century welfare ideas both north and south of the border with England. These Scottish reformers set out to influence their English counterparts – a crucial point neglected in standard poor law historiography with an Anglo-American bias. By all means give charity,

---

62 Feingold, *Revolt of the tenantry*; V. Crossman, 'With the experience of 1846 and 1847 before them: the politics of emergency relief, 1879–84', in P. Gray (ed.), *Victoria's Ireland? Irishness and Britishness, 1837–1901*, Dublin 2004, 167–81.

63 See, for example, R. Mitchinson, *The old poor law in Scotland: the experience of poverty, 1574–1845*, Edinburgh 2000.

64 R. A. Cage, The *Scottish poor law system, 1745–1845*, Edinburgh 1981; J. Smyth, '"Seems decent": respectability and poor relief in Glasgow, c. 1861–1911', in A. Gestrich, S. A. King and L. Raphael (eds), *Being poor in modern Europe*, Oxford 2004, 1–27.

65 S. J. Brown, *Thomas Chalmers and the godly commonweal in Scotland*, Oxford 1982.

66 Cage, *Scottish poor law system*, 90–109.

Chalmers argued, but do so in secret. Target the needy, establish their gratitude and thereby improve their 'moral' character, all to be English *crusader*
attitudes.[67] Scotland, like Ireland, therefore, was a breeding ground for
crusading attitudes.[68]

While debates about classical political economy form the backdrop to this
study of the *crusade*, as it was executed at a local level, it is less clear how wider
political debates centring on Liberal and Conservative social policy impacted
on local poor law administration in practical terms. At Westminster, the
Liberal and Conservative parties dominated but neither had a cohesive social
welfare agenda in the late-Victorian era. Regardless of their political leanings, rarely were politicians prepared to compromise free market principles or
increase taxes to fund welfare reform. The majority also felt threatened by 'the
emergence of the Labour party – with its strong commitment to the construction of rational democracy'.[69] Increasingly this meant that in social policy
terms the relationship between any political party and the expanding electorate was 'highly ambiguous' before 1914.[70]Against this complex backdrop
'it is essential to recapture what politicians *thought* they were arguing about'
when they spoke of the need for welfare reform in late-Victorian society.[71]
How did a very 'loose-textured political vocabulary' translate into poor law
reality? To what extent did political discourse, both Liberal and Conservative, reshape ideas about late nineteenth-century welfare provision?

Liberalism

There is no easy or definitive way to define nineteenth-century Liberalism.
It is a complex issue. Modern political historians 'have long disagreed over
the extent to which it is possible to provide a single, coherent definition of
Liberal party beliefs, especially for the unsettled period between Gladstone's
first government and the development of New Liberal ideas in the Edwardian
era'.[72] Traditional histories of Liberalism suggest that there were four political

[67] A. S. Cheyne (ed.), *The practical and the pious: essays on Thomas Chalmers*, Edinburgh
1985. Chalmers set up a renowned voluntary poor relief experiment in St Johns parish,
Glasgow. Although lauded by *crusaders*, it was actually a failure.
[68] See, for example, D. Roberts, *Modern Scottish Catholicism*, Glasgow 1979; O. Checkland, *Philanthropy in Victorian Scotland: social welfare and the voluntary principle*, Edinburgh
1980; I. Levitt, *Poverty and welfare in Scotland, 1890–1948*, Edinburgh 1988; and J. J.
Smyth, *Labour in Glasgow, 1896–1936: socialism, suffrage, sectarianism*, East Linton 2000.
[69] Lawrence, *Speaking for the people*, 61.
[70] Ibid. 164.
[71] S. Collini, *Liberalism and sociology: L. T. Hobhouse and political argument in England
c. 1880–1914*, Cambridge 1979, 14–15.
[72] Lynch, *Liberal party*, 8.

strands in the party in the Victorian period:[73] Whig, Gladstonianism,[74] Radicalism[75] and New Liberalism[76] respectively. Yet, to suggest that these had a teleological development or were ring-fenced into separate political ideologies would be mistaken.[77] British Liberalism, like Conservativism, covered a spectrum of politicians motivated by a complex mixture of ideology, pragmatism and opportunism.[78] Moreover, a single Liberal MP could espouse any of the four political strands, depending on the issues involved. The average Liberal MP tended to take a 'broader approach to their political ideology' than traditional histories have tended to convey.[79] It can hence be difficult to make sense of the political backdrop to changes in poor law policy at a local level without some exploration of the core social welfare values of Liberalism and ideological shifts after 1870.

In general terms nineteenth-century Liberalism has been characterised by an emphasis on 'individualism'. It personified 'a belief in maximising the individual citizen's freedom from restraint and a corresponding commitment to restricting the role of the state'.[80] It espoused the notion of 'an enabling state' that provided law, order and defence but thereafter left (indeed required) its citizens to get on with their working lives. Thus, historically, it has been identified 'with protest against religious and political authority' and often with a determination to challenge any power and privilege derived from land.[81] The New Poor Law exemplified these ideals. Legislation freed those in poverty to achieve their economic potential by forcing employers to raise wages when outdoor poor relief allowances were withdrawn from localities. The *quid pro quo* was that each pauper had 'a right and duty to make the best of their oppor-

[73] See, for example, M. Bentley, *Politics without democracy, Great Britain, 1815–1914*, London 1984, 204; J. Vincent, *The formation of the Liberal party, 1857–1868*, Cambridge 1966; *How Victorians voted*, Cambridge 1967; and *The governing passion: cabinet government and party politics, 1885–6*, Brighton 1974; P. Weiler, *The new Liberalism: Liberal theory in Great Britain, 1889–1914*, London–New York 1982, 53; and J. P. Parry, 'High and low politics in modern Britain: review article', *HJ* xxix (1986), 753–70.

[74] B. Hamilton, 'Gladstone's theological politics', in M. Bentley and J. Stevenson (eds), *High and low politics in modern Britain*, Oxford 1983, 28–57.

[75] For the Radical alliance see D. Nicholls, *The lost prime minister: a life of Sir Charles Dilke*, Oxford 1985.

[76] See M. Freeden, *The new Liberalism: an ideology of social reform*, Oxford 1978, and 'The New Liberalism and its aftermath', in R. Bellamy (ed.), *Victorian Liberalism: nineteenth-century political thought and practice*, Oxford 1990, 175–93. Both argue from the perspective of a political theorist.

[77] Lawrence, *Speaking for the people*, 1.

[78] This point is made forcibly by G. R. Searle, *The Liberal party: triumph and disintegration, 1886–1929*, Basingstoke 1992; D. Powell, 'The Liberal ministries and Labour, 1892–1895', *History* lxiii (1993), 408–26; E. F. Biagini (ed.), *Citizenship and community: Liberals, radicals and collective identities in the British Isles, 1865–1931*, Cambridge 1996; and S. J. Lee, *British political history, 1815–1914*, London 1996 edn.

[79] Bernstein, *Liberalism and Liberal politics*, 3.

[80] Collini, *Liberalism and sociology*, 1.

[81] Ibid.

tunity'.[82] This meant that those who failed to work and were unwilling to try mutual-aid were to suffer 'the penalty of being treated as a pauper'. Liberals regarded 'idleness as a social pest, to be stamped out like crime'. This political vision gave the party a broad appeal especially in Nonconformist and radical circles. Above all, Liberalism saw itself as the party of *'peace, retrenchment and reform'*.[83] It liked to think that it was governed by 'moderation, reason and restraint' and resolved social problems in terms of 'rational discourse, compromise and consent'.[84] Aspects of these positive attributes were seen to have contributed to electoral success in 1868, 1885 and again in 1892.

Yet, 'action and priorities in politics', rather than rhetoric, matter in the long run.[85] And it is undeniable that this positive spin on Liberalism paints too rosy a picture because 'there was a constant dragging of feet' over social welfare reform, which came to dominate both 'high' and 'low' politics. A vast amount has been written on debates about the failings of Liberal social policy and whether these contributed to the demise of the party in the later Victorian and early Edwardian eras.[86] None the less, most political historians concur that social welfare was a major issue for Liberals. On the surface the party appeared to be successful at election time but when it came to developments in social welfare it often looked clumsy. The problem was that in terms of social reform the party rank and file was 'complex' and therefore ideologically 'far from static' throughout the late-Victorian period.[87] This meant that party managers struggled to retain unity, satisfy their more traditional membership and attract new voters. Often these goals were incompatible in social policy terms, particularly for Gladstone who was at the party's helm during most of the late-Victorian era.

In 1868, when Gladstone's first term of office began, his political vision was akin to that of his Liberal forefathers. Any Liberal reform, he explained, must seek to liberate the individual but 'without damaging the fabric of society'.[88] Yet during this period, a very slow but basic ideological transition within Liberalism started. Essentially the 'profound belief in individual liberty and a government who had a responsibility to free up that potential' found expression in social welfare debates, and was to have important implications for the party's future cohesiveness and ideological direction.[89] Such views tended to be espoused by the Radical wing of the party, a heterogeneous set of political alliances. None the less, most Radicals (regardless of their political diversity)

---

82 Ibid. 139.
83 E. F. Biagini, *Liberty, retrenchment and reform: popular Liberalism in the age of Gladstone, 1860–1900*, Cambridge 1992.
84 Bernstein, *Liberalism and Liberal politics*, 198.
85 McKibbin, *Ideologies of class*, 93.
86 See introduction, n. 46.
87 S. Collini, *Public moralists: political thought and intellectual life in Britain, 1850–1930*, Oxford 1991, 181.
88 Bentley, *Politics without democracy*, 204.
89 Bernstein, *Liberalism and Liberal politics*, 48.

began to 'emphasise that state intervention was *sometimes* necessary to secure the freedom of the individual to realise their potential'.[90] Gladstone's political strength was exemplified by his ability to contain this ideological shift by stating that politics had a moral, not socially exclusive, purpose. Education and sanitary measures, for instance, improved the nation's fabric. Although Radicals were unconvinced by this political spin, Gladstone remained obstinate about the need for social reform and over the next two decades this single issue often divided the party, being especially of concern to those on the left who became very despondent about the party's future electoral appeal. That said, it is important to clarify what mainstream Liberals 'meant went they spoke of the need for *social reform*'.[91] Often, this entailed more, not less, emphasis on 'the need to reform social behaviour', rather than the structure of society. Moreover, if social reform meant larger tax bills or altered the rate-paying *status quo* in local government, then moderate Liberals were often very sceptical about its desirability. Gladstone appealed to their conservatism and for a time contained Radical calls for poor law reform. However, he was also aware that 'Radical inclusion within the Liberal coalition was always partial and conditional' and that the *status quo* was shaky by the 1880s.[92]

During the 1880s two major issues confronted Liberalism, the extension of the parliamentary franchise and the rise of more liberal elements of Radicalism. Historians disagree on the nature and impact of these factors on Liberal identity and policy. In particular, opinion is split on how to interpret the publication of Joseph Chamberlain's 'Unauthorised Programme' of 1885. It has been seen as designed to attract new working-class voters to the party, as launched for reasons of personal aggrandisement, or as a combination of both.[93] At the same time, commentators debate the significance of developments in Liberal social policy against the backdrop of well-known late nineteenth-century extensions to the franchise.[94] There is no doubt that the prospect of full democracy filled many Liberals with deep anxiety in the last three decades of the nineteenth century. Most party members feared losing their propertied privileges: low taxes, small poor relief bills and dominance in local government. To many, there seemed to be an inevitable drift to the left of British politics, which Liberalism could either ignore or try to redress. Moreover, party doctrine about the harmony of class interests within the Liberal fold, that capital and labour were not opposed since both were fighting the same 'Tory enemy', seemed empty rhetoric against the backdrop of the impersonal

---

90 Ibid.

91 Lawrence, *Speaking for the people*, 219.

92 Ibid. 172.

93 These are outlined in D. A. Hamer (ed.), *The radical programme: Joseph Chamberlain and others*, Brighton 1971, pp. xxxiv–xxxv, xi.

94 See, for example, H. Pelling, *Popular politics and society in late-Victorian Britain*, London 1979; H. V. Emy, *Liberals, radicals and social politics, 1892–1914*, Cambridge 1973; and D. A. Hamer, *Liberal politics in the age of Gladstone and Rosebery: a study in leadership and policy*, Oxford 1972.

forces of the market, which often had tragic personal consequences for the labouring poor.[95] This had been the theme of Chamberlain's 'Unauthorised Programme' and explains why it ignited such controversy about the future direction of Radical Liberalism and social policy debates. It pointed out that the lives of the greater part of the population, in cities and the countryside, were always precarious, relying on meagre 'makeshift' economies and a main breadwinner in each family. Life-cycle crises (childbirth, sickness and death) or major recessions in manufacturing and agriculture during the 1880s often exacerbated poverty. Liberalism had to respond to the challenge of social policy. But at the same time few could reconcile that thinking with the party's free market principles. Perhaps a radical ideological shift might also exacerbate disunity?[96] That situation was complicated in the spring of 1886 by the Irish question, which has been seen as either the occasion or the major cause of the splitting into Liberals and Liberal Unionists. In social policy terms the period from 1885 to 1895 was a critical decade for the Liberal party.

A number of vital political issues dominated. Would the Home Rule *débâcle* of the spring of 1886 strengthen or weaken the party? It might provide a greater sense of unity at Westminster. Alternatively, there was a real danger that it would expose the factionalism of the Liberal rump under Gladstone's control, a clear electoral liability.[97] Closely related was whether the Third Reform Act marked the beginning of the end for British Liberalism?[98] Liberals had every expectation of making gains in the countryside where extending the new householder franchise had been a popular move. At the same time deepening rural recession meant that this was not guaranteed. And gains seemed to be masking electoral problems in urban and borough constituencies. Liberals were experiencing a political backlash in towns and cities. Worried party election agents reported being squeezed out of some suburban and industrial areas where economic problems dominated elections. Attrition on two fronts complicated so-called 'class politics' and made it much harder to envisage social welfare solutions. Another important issue was whether the Liberal party was incapable of, or unwilling to, revamp its predominately middle-class caucus organisation to attract working-class

---

95 See, for example, K. Laybourn and D. James (eds), *'The rising sun of Liberalism': the Independent Labour Party in the textile district of the West Riding of Yorkshire between 1890–1914*, Bradford 1991.

96 The question of Liberal unity/disunity is contentious. See Bernstein, *Liberalism and Liberal politics*, 3, 8–10, for a summary of debates.

97 There are two schools of thought on this subject. Vincent, *The governing passion*, 54–5, argues that Home Rule was an issue that Gladstone did not intend to win. It was a rallying cry to divert attention from Radicalism. Others view the decision as more complex, a genuine desire to resolve Irish problems and a wish to preserve a Gladstonian legacy. See, for example, M. Cowling, *Religion and public doctrine in England*, Cambridge 1981; J. P. Parry, *Democracy and religion: Gladstone and the Liberal party, 1867–1875*, Cambridge 1986; and M. Bentley, *The climax of Liberal politics: British Liberalism in theory and practice, 1868–1914*, London 1987.

98 See, for example, Hamer, *Liberal politics*.

voters and representatives?[99] Perhaps, the party failed to 'socialise' its new electorate and thereby 'tame' popular politics?[100] Finally, was 'New Liberalism' a popular move that revived or undermined the party's fortunes in the 1890s? At what stage, if ever, did the party make the transition from 'New Liberal' ideology to 'New Liberal' political practice?[101]

Yet, although these issues predominated in 'high' political circles at Westminster, because of the general neglect of the late-Victorian poor law and its local political backdrop, it is difficult to assess how much impact they had on the everyday administration of the poor law. This book will show that working people were not convinced that the Liberal party would endorse social reform or extend measures to the poor law. Liberalism, therefore, often seemed irrelevant in the context of working people's daily 'material life and popular politics'. Consequently, the 'poor law and the politics of place' became the focus of the lives of the labouring poor in most areas. This was very apparent where a *crusade* was tried and found wanting. During the *crusading* decades new voters focused on their immediate poor law 'social and economic circumstances' and these tended to shape 'Labour politics on the ground'.[102] 'High' and 'low' politics, therefore, drifted further apart in the late nineteenth century and it was the poor law that seemed to drive a political wedge between the centre and local government. Increasingly, poor law elections, once democracy rolled out to them, became the conduit for all sorts of socio-economic grievances. In poor law terms this complicated the 'story of democratisation in Victorian and Edwardian Britain'. This book, therefore, builds upon the most recent trends in political history by emphasising the importance of micro-political studies and their wider historical lessons in terms of social policy.[103] For, although in the 1880s social reform was in the air, it was not yet central to partisan politics. However, by the 1890s it had taken centre stage in poor law elections, especially where the *crusade* was blamed for exacerbating the impoverishment of so many of the labouring poor. The defeat of the *crusade* at local poor law elections in the 1890s, therefore, may be a crucial missing jigsaw piece in the vital transition between the politics of the 1880s and the intense focus on social reform at successive general elections in the Edwardian era. For this reason, poor relief questions often crossed 'class' boundaries; the social welfare aspirations of most new voters were first expressed during poor law elections; and those political struggles complicated the story of 'class' politics after the Third Reform Act.[104] This is not to suggest that the Liberal party did not recognise the threat of social democracy in the

---

[99] Pelling, *Popular politics*, sees a failure of caucus politics as the basis of 'decline'.

[100] Lawrence, *Speaking for the people*, 178, now stresses the '*incompleteness* of party control' at a local level.

[101] Tanner, *Political change*, 420–2, 424, 427, 431–2, 437, stresses that what really mattered was 'politics on the ground.'

[102] Lawrence, *Speaking for the people*, 1; Tanner, *Political change*, 420–2.

[103] Lynch, *Liberal party*, 5, 8.

[104] The notion of the 'rise of class politics' is refuted by Tanner, *Political change*; P. Joyce,

1890s. It did and so it is important to clarify the extent to which 'New Liberalism' was a vote winner or an electoral liability by the 1890s.

It is very difficult precisely to date the start of 'New Liberal' thinking, but 1889 seems to have been a watershed year.[105] The publication of *Fabian essays on socialism* (1889), the successful London dockers' strike and Charles Booth's poverty studies, all seemed to demand a new political response.[106] Theorists like T. H. Green, L. T. Hobhouse and J. A. Hobhouse tried to reformulate Liberal theory to take account of the need for wider social welfare provision. Essentially, these New Idealists tried to 'integrate new terms such as reform, intervention and community' into Liberal tradition.[107] These notions, however, tended to appeal to specific interest groups in the party, predominately Radicals, some moderates and MPs who had previously been businessmen. Supporters therefore wanted practical welfare solutions but, as in the past, they were also wary of reform that challenged the *status quo*.[108] Estimates vary, but Henry James calculated that about '150 MPs' espoused aspects of 'New Liberal' thinking by 1890; though few would have described themselves as 'New Liberal' politicians.[109] And this was the chief problem with 'New Liberalism'. It gained some, but by no means extensive, ideological ground in terms of 'high' politics. At the same time its impact was minimal in terms of 'low' poor law politics. Thus, the inroads that 'New Liberalism' made on the party in terms of social welfare provision have been questioned.

Some welfare historians, notably Humphreys, maintain that 'New Liberalism' changed the terms of social welfare debates in the party by showing that the New Poor Law was unfair to the vast majority of the labouring poor whose poverty was involuntary.[110] Other political historians are very sceptical about the impact of 'New Liberalism' prior to 1900.[111] In particular Keith Laybourn and David James have argued that the appeal of 'New Liberalism' was often 'limited to the rarefied atmosphere of high politics'.[112] Meanwhile, in the localities, 'New Liberalism' was viewed as just empty rhetoric and political window-dressing. McKibbin and Lawrence point out that seldom did either the Newcastle Programme (1891) (which helped the party get re-elected in 1892 but also in many respects just rehashed the promises of the 'Unauthorised Programme') or central party propaganda espouse practical 'New Liberal'

Visions of the people: industrial England and the question of class, 1848–1914, Cambridge 1991; and Lawrence, *Speaking for the people*, introduction.

105 Clarke, *Lancashire*, 3–7.

106 Weiler, *New Liberalism*, 46.

107 Ibid. 35–40.

108 Freeden, 'New Liberalism', 176.

109 For James's estimates see J. Chamberlain, diary entry for 5 Dec. 1890, in G. L. Garvin and J. Amery, *The life of Joseph Chamberlain*, London 1932–69, ii. 409.

110 Humphreys, *Sin*, 1–4.

111 Tanner, *Political change*; Bernstein, *Liberalism and Liberal politics*; McKibbin, *Ideologies of class*.

112 Laybourn and James, 'The rising sun'.

measures.[113] Yet, some commentators, like Peter Clarke, insist that whatever the national context 'New Liberal' ideas could under specific electoral conditions, notably in Lancashire, permeate down to a local level because party activists were successful at rallying support at the grass roots.[114] Elsewhere few have found evidence to support Clarke's Lancashire findings. Indeed, Collini asserts that it is important 'not to overstate how much "New Liberal" theory challenged' local issues that mattered to electorates like reform of the Poor Law.[115] 'New Liberal' theorists still believed that there was a 'deserving' and 'undeserving' class in society. Liberalism in social policy terms, therefore, often looked irrelevant in a fast-changing industrial or agricultural world in the midst of late-Victorian recession. Moreover, whilst these complex debates about the success or failure of 'New Liberalism' are important and ongoing, it is undeniable that Liberalism contained a wide variety of (national and local) competing, contradictory and occasionally mutually exclusive political and social welfare ideologies, as well as individual politician's career aspirations and strategies. 'The remarkable thing' is not the failure or demise of Liberalism but that such 'anachronistic' and, in the end, rather limited practical ideas about social policy, 'should have lasted so long' in the late-Victorian period.[116]

While there were other major issues that divided and troubled the party, a failure to resolve social welfare debates was a key weakness arising out of its creeds and the tensions between its national and local political imperatives. During Gladstone' first (1868–74) and second ministries (1885–6) more radical elements in the party understood that social welfare reform was an important political hot potato in an era of widening democracy. The 'Unauthorised Programme', the 'Newcastle Programme' and 'New Liberal' thinking tried to offer political solutions to widen the party's appeal. But progress was very limited. For this reason, the nadir of Liberalism's electoral fortunes probably 'came in 1895'.[117] Increasingly, in social policy terms Liberalism had lost its potency. In the context of the poor law, the Liberal party experienced a political backlash because of its lack of imagination, empathy and political inaction over social welfare reform. Seldom did 'New Liberal' theory gain purchase amongst voters in *crusading* unions before 1900. Not until after 1906 did the Liberal party try to revive its fortunes by developing 'centralised and programmatic party politics' concerned with 'state-directed social reform that would head off emerging class politics and create a genuine rational (and hence Liberal) democracy'.[118] These manifesto commitments were future political challenges, in the Edwardian era, and outside the time scale of this discussion. Nevertheless, this stormy Liberal political sea did impact at the

113 McKibbin, *Ideologies of class*, 90; Lawrence, *Speaking for the people*, 217.
114 Clarke, *Lancashire*, 3–7.
115 Collini, *Liberalism and sociology*, 139.
116 McKibbin, *Ideologies of class*, 90.
117 Lawrence, *Speaking for the people*, 220.
118 Ibid. 225

local level. Ordinary voters used the political vehicle of poor law democracy to materially improve their lives when Liberal politicians failed them on social welfare reform. Although a standard 'New Liberal' defence was that they stood for 'a fuller appreciation and realisation of individual liberty contained in the provision of equal opportunities for self-development',[119] that meant little to the average voter if it seldom translated into poor law reality. As a result, the politics of everyday life were murky in later Victorian England. Perhaps Conservative opportunism could succeed where Liberal social policy failed?

Conservatism

In the 1830s the Conservative party emerged as a 'defensive reaction of rank, property and privilege'.[120] Although Conservative ascendancy has been attributed to the political watershed of the Great Reform Bill (1832), in reality it made slow progress in Victorian England. Moreover, a 'Conservative' label was adopted by some landowning patricians and ignored by others who remained Whigs. Conservatism, like its Liberal counterpart, was therefore often fractured. Gradually contemporaries 'witnessed a change of style and presentation rather than of fundamental purpose' on the political right.[121] Thus, Conservatism came to represent 'constitutional monarchy and aristocratic parliamentarianism'; it was 'self-consciously traditionalist with its main focus on Parliament and government'. Most Conservatives believed in the God-given 'natural order' of the state. Communities, 'like the family, and the nation gave meaning and significance to the individual' in the Conservative world-view.[122] British Conservatism saw itself as the guardian of political equilibrium, a role that suited its predominately agricultural membership prior to 1880. Yet Conservative politicians were often just as capricious as Liberals, sharing many of the same concerns about the need for economic stability, the threat of the coming of democracy and the rise of the left in British politics. There were no easy Conservative social policy solutions to these dilemmas.[123] In poor law terms, the Conservative party represented the dominance of a magistracy, a property-owning elite, often to the detriment of the vast majority of the labouring poor. Thus Conservatives might have expected to fare worse at the polls in an era of widening democracy. Yet, their appeal seemed to expand as Liberalism's shrank. This has been attributed to the concept of 'popular Toryism' based on patriotism (empire, Church and monarchy) and its promise to protect the 'pleasures of the people' (drink,

---

119 Collini, *Liberalism and sociology*, 31.
120 B. Coleman, *Conservatism and the Conservative party in nineteenth-century Britain*, London 1988, 1.
121 Ibid. 89.
122 M. Pearce and G. Stewart, *British political history, 1867–1995: democracy and decline*, London 1996, 67–107, quotation at p. 69.
123 Ibid.

football, half-day holiday on Saturday afternoon and suchlike).[124] Despite internal social policy debates and disputes, therefore, Conservatives made steady electoral headway. It is important to emphasis, however, that this triumph was seldom linear, often patchy in the regions and at times appeared to falter in the critical period between 1875 and 1895.

At first, the Conservatives, led by Benjamin Disraeli (1868–81), 'did not represent a single style of Conservatism'.[125] The party stood for an amalgam of principles and one of its chief electoral problems was that in many respects it did not look that different from traditional Liberalism. Conservative doctrine emphasised the sanctity of property rights, freedom of contract and low public expenditure. It took a 'negative approach to taxation and social policy', which it believed would be more popular than an interventionist one. The average Conservative voter espoused traditional causes: 'defending the Church establishment, religious education, private property, the Empire, the monarchy and the union with Ireland against the depredations of radicalism'.[126] The enduring popularity of late-Victorian Conservatism, therefore, seems a contradiction in an era of widening democracy. How did the party reconcile the demands of labour and at the same time retreat from popular aspirations for more social welfare provision?

Skilfully, in 1872, Disraeli promised to redress 'the health of the nation' since it 'was the most important question for a statesman'.[127] His form of Conservatism was soon dubbed 'one-nation' and his followers were quick to play up his social reform credentials. For a time this proved to be a clever political ruse. However, in power, Conservatives enacted limited and unimaginative measures for social reform.[128] In the end Disraeli's tenure was judged unadventurous: 'pragmatism tempered by prejudice'. In *Punch* Dizzy was described as a political 'conjuror', a 'juggler' and a 'tightrope walker'. Any claims to social policy creativity and imagination were dubious.[129] Disraeli was a master of political spin. His reforming image was just political 'window-dressing'. Essentially he 'stuck very close to the mood and requirements of his party'.[130] Disraeli's success derived from his ability to make 'existing Conservative support count for more' at election time by manipulating the franchise.

---

124 M. Pugh, *The making of modern British politics, 1867–1945*, Oxford 2002 edn, 42–59.
125 Coleman, *Conservatism*, 145.
126 Pugh, *Modern British politics*, 51.
127 P. Adleman, *Gladstone, Disraeli and later Victorian politics*, London 1970; R. Blake, *The Conservative party: Peel to Churchill*, London 1985 edn; M. Pugh, *The Tories and the people*, Oxford 1985.
128 P. Smith, *Disraelian Conservatism and social reform*, London–Toronto 1967; P. R. Ghosh, 'Style and substance in Disraelian social reform c. 1860–80', in P. J. Waller (ed.), *Politics and social change in modern Britain*, Brighton 1987, 59–90.
129 Pearce and Stewart, *British political history*, 76–82. Measures included the Criminal Law Amendment Act (1871), the Factory Act (1872), the Workmen's Act (1875), the Conspiracy and Protection of Property Act (1875), the Public Health Act (1875) and the River Pollution Act (1876).
130 Coleman, *Conservatism*, 159.

Yet this also meant that the Conservative party after Disraeli's death in 1881 seemed to face a very uncertain electoral future.[131] However, most Conservatives, unlike many Liberal theorists, were political realists. The former perceived that it was essential not to remain a mixture of endeavour and nonendeavour in order to achieve party consensus by the Home Rule crisis.[132]

In 1886 Lord Salisbury led the party to a second late-Victorian election victory. At first, Salisbury's government still seemed to resemble Disraeli's.[133] For example, Salisbury had a deep-seated contempt for democracy. He described proposals to extend the revamped parliamentary franchise to the poor law as 'like the cat being given the cream'. Thus he was very wary of substantive constitutional changes that might challenge the landed interest and erode the party's traditional support base. However, like Disraeli, he paid careful attention to social policy, local government and poor law debates. Salisbury recognised that the Home Rule *débâcle* gave Conservatism a unique opportunity to align with Liberal Unionism provided he support a legislative programme that appealed to the electorate and yet preserved the underlying *status quo*. This meant that whilst 'he did not shrink from a little judicious assistance to the poor', as 'a general rule' he 'prescribed self-help'.[134] Salisbury predominantly attracted middle-class voters 'who had not quit Liberalism in order to pay higher taxes or suffer more legal constraint under the Conservatives'.[135] In any case Conservatives were 'caught in the dilemma of financing social policies under a free enterprise system'.[136] Future electoral success depended on a tricky political balancing act. They had to achieve momentum in social policy but yet disguise the fact that Conservative social policy, whilst creative, was not extensive. This meant that, 'for late-Victorian Conservatives the key to their appeal lay in capitalising upon the unchanging and unifying issues like empire and the foreigner, while leaving the radicals to suffer the consequences of dashed expectations and disturbing innovation'.[137] Something from Conservatism, it was argued, was better than mere rhetoric from powerless Radicals within the Liberal coalition.

It is, however, noteworthy that Salisbury was adaptive rather than inflexible.[138] He recognised the need to espouse 'a long established theme of popular Toryism', with its commitment 'to pass legislation that would be of direct benefit to working men'.[139] A good example is the issue of housing reform (to

---

131 Pugh, *Modern British politics*, 42.
132 Coleman, *Conservatism*, 149.
133 P. Marsh, *The discipline of popular government: Lord Salisbury's domestic statecraft, 1881–1902*, Brighton 1978; Coleman, *Conservatism*.
134 Pugh, *Modern British politics*, 59–60.
135 Ibid. 61.
136 Ibid. 63.
137 Ibid. 64.
138 Marsh, *Lord Salisbury*; D. Steel, *Lord Salisbury: a political biography*, London 2000.
139 R. McKenzie and A. Silver, *Angels in marble: working-class Conservatives in urban England*, London 1968; Smith, *Disraelian Conservatism*; R. Shannon, *The age of Disraeli, 1868–1881: the rise of Tory democracy*, London 1992; Lawrence, *Speaking for the people*, 106,

deal with overcrowding and poor sanitation) that seemed a logical and popu-
list proposal in the 1880s.[140] Salisbury recognised that it was an ambiguous
and fluid political issue, which could enable the Conservative party to grasp
the centre ground from Liberals, given their paralysis on such issues at the
time. It could also be dropped at need without causing any serious political
damage. His strategy, therefore, was to make political capital out of proposals
for modest social reform by concentrating on major issues, not details of
policy. Liberals did the reverse, focusing so much on the details of reform
that little overall progress was made in terms of actual policy-making. And
often when they did get around to formulating policy measures, they seemed
clumsy and irrelevant. By 1895 this contributed to the Conservative's election victory and left Liberalism floundering. Whilst Liberals argued about the
need to adopt temperance policies like giving local government the powers
to ban the consumption of alcohol, Conservatives defended a working man's
right to enjoy his drink at the pub. The Conservative party did not preach to
its voters about the need to reform their morals. It was courteous and paternalistic in its belief that there was a social order. Neither the aristocrat nor
the artisan should interfere with each other's private lives. Conservatism,
therefore, was pragmatic, recognising that Liberalism's 'moral' reforming zeal
was an electoral liability. Instead, local Conservative organisations, like the
Primrose League, concentrated on the appeal of regular, free and attractive
local entertainment, such as bands, teas, garden parties and summer fetes.
These did much for the Conservatives' image as the party of the 'pleasures of
the people'. By contrast, Liberal organisations in many regions often floun-
dered, beset by arguments about drinking habits and social exclusivity at
earnest political meetings timed around elections only. Liberalism's mistake
in the area of social reform was its continued emphasis on 'the personal habits
of individuals, rather than the social and economic circumstances of their
lives', thus offending new voters.[141] Paradoxically, Conservatives seemed to
be the party committed to the logic of democracy, notably passing the Local
Government Act (1888) which set up county councils. They were also seen
to champion social welfare measures that materially improved voters' lives,
like old age pensions, even though in many respects such warm promises later
became for them political albatrosses. Meanwhile, many Conservatives felt
very uncertain about the meaning of 'mass democracy'. However, the broad
appeal of 'popular Toryism', in cities, towns and the countryside, meant they
did not experience the same political malaise as Liberalism at local polls by
1895. They did feel threatened by the rise of Labour, the spectre of a Liberal-
Progressive pact and the shift to the left in British politics. Tories also recognised that the political landscape of Britain was changing rapidly and that

and 'Class and gender in the making of urban Toryism, 1880–1914', EHR 3rd ser. cxvii
(1993), 629–52.
[140] A. Wohl, The eternal slum: housing and social policy in Victorian London, Belfast 1977.
[141] Lawrence, Speaking for the people, 108.

without doubt social welfare debates were an intrinsic part of a complex 'political game' for everyone. But these were future challenges, well into the Edwardian era.

High politics and low poor law politics

While political economy, social theory and welfare ideas in Ireland and Scotland, together with social policy initiatives by the Liberal and Conservative parties shaped the late-Victorian poor law world, their influence should not be overstated. National debates had to be mediated at a local level. Although the *crusade* against outdoor relief was a national campaign, it was given form by local initiative. This meant that those in local government enforced welfare policy in either a positive or negative way according to their economic interests. When 'high' politics did not reflect poor law realities, the local simply ignored the centre. Thus local politicians kept abreast of, and sometimes ignored, policy initiatives at Westminster. As a result there was often a strong disconnection between national debates and the practicalities of everyday political life. Proposals for the implementation of social reform were, therefore, seldom uniform. In reality, national politicians could not dictate poor law political style at the local level. Of course, successive Liberal and Conservative governments stressed their social welfare credentials. Frequently, however, their political economy was ignored. Party election agents reported that local social welfare issues, like reform of the poor law, were vote winners. Frequently, unpopular manifesto commitments were given short shrift. Thus, the coming of democracy complicated the game of 'class politics' and it was the poor law that became the focus of new voters' welfare aspirations before 1895.

In most places the poor law was the administrative vehicle of local government. Yet, political histories often ignore its importance and significant political struggles. By contrast, contemporaries monitored poor law political change closely. Few denied that where the *crusade* was implemented it was despised. Most recognised that it would have significant local political ramifications. The social and economic terms under which the poor law had been offered were offensive to new voters. It was no longer acceptable to say that sometime in the future incremental reform might be more generous. The poor law, therefore, was subject to numerous local socio-economic and political pressures by the later Victorian period.

Linear historical models outlining major shifts in social welfare cannot do justice to the complexities of local poor law change in the late-Victorian era. Social policy was translated in myriad forms and often depended on how committed guardians were, or were not, to the *crusading* ethos in practical terms. Again this reinforces the fact that there was both a working-down and a working-up of social reform in the context of the poor law, between centre and local, as well as *vice-versa*. The realities, both of economic life and the political economy of poor relief, meant that new voters were often very sceptical about warm political promises at Westminster. They also understood that political divisions over social reform within both Liberal and Conservative parties did not map neatly onto poor law political allegiances in the localities. Guardians of the poor were often capricious. They might favour social reform during the reading of a new bill at Westminster and at the same time worry about its economic cost and hence unpopularity amongst ratepayers at home. They might espouse poor law largesse to get elected and act conservatively when in power, fearful of damaging the economic and social order. They might also form a coalition to support a pauper whom they felt obliged to fund and then reject a similar but unknown case. Poor law politics, therefore, represent an exemplar of the tensions between national and local politics, especially during an era of widening democracy. In many respects poor law elections anticipated how social reform became central to partisan politics in the Edwardian era.

In the late-Victorian period there were large rural constituencies that played an important role in national and local political life. Yet their importance has been neglected in favour of urban political studies. This is regrettable since the rural labouring poor lobbied in poor law elections for the sort of social reform that was pivotal to the partisan politics of the Edwardian era. A study of the *crusading* experience shows that the rural labouring poor were eager to participate fully in debates about the political economy of the poor law, especially individuals who had crossed the threshold between relative to absolute poverty. Likewise, ratepayers resisted changes in the poor law, determined to limit their liabilities in this respect against the backdrop of a deepening rural recession. Thus the rolling out of poor law democracy increased the political awareness of everyone in rural society. On the one hand those in power felt threatened by the numerically stronger lower classes. On the other hand the labouring poor had the political means and will to fight for permanent change in the poor law. The poor law, therefore, was an important political vehicle in rural England; and yet its broader significance remains misunderstood and undervalued. The coming of poor law democracy altered the terms of political debates, on both a local and national stage, about the need for more generous social reform. Democracy was a catalyst. In poor law elections new social welfare ideas first found expression. It was poor law politicians who experienced first hand the genesis of this new political reality. They learned that social reform was very important to an expanding electorate. National politicians did not necessarily have to confront equivalent electoral pressure or wide-ranging social policy demands until the Edwardian era. Those gifted with political acumen, however, recognised that change in the poor law was a precursor of the future direction of British welfare policy. Throughout, therefore, this book rethinks the broader significance of the poor law and its place in national and local political life. Meanwhile, it is important to turn to the national statistics of the *crusade* campaign in order to understand more fully not just its ideological and political backdrop but also its execution and impact in practical terms.

The *crusade*: a statistical overview

The Longley Strategy, or the '*crusade* campaign', was a 'brilliant short-run success' in statistical terms.[142] Karel Williams estimates that between 1871 and 1876 the total number nationally of paupers on outrelief fell by around 33 per cent (*see* figs 1 and 2), thereby reducing the percentage of the total population claiming outrelief from 3.8 per cent to 2.4 per cent, with expenditure decreasing by some £276,000.[143] Outdoor pauper numbers fell steeply from an average of 791,000 in the 1860s to just 567,000 in 1876. Thereafter numbers stabilised to an average of 542,000 claimants between 1877 and 1892, although regional patterns were often quite diverse. For example, in many of the rural areas that experienced an agricultural crisis in the late 1870s, outrelief was reintroduced to alleviate widespread impoverishment. Nevertheless, between 1871 and 1893 outdoor pauper numbers fell by 338,000 (40 per cent), despite a rising population.[144] Williams calculates that this reduction was achieved on a broad front, with 39 per cent fewer women and children, and 33 per cent fewer non-able bodied paupers, claiming outrelief by 1893. He estimates that 'in 1871, 3.8 per cent of the population drew outrelief and by 1893, only 1.7% of the population drew outrelief'.[145] However, as David Thomson points out, Karel Williams does not take account of the changing age profile of the population. The significant point about the reduction in outrelief is that despite the fact that the proportion of elderly persons in the total population in England and Wales was increasing, the number receiving 'some form of public assistance' in 1890 'was less than half of what it had been in 1870'.[146] This attack on provision for the elderly had never been tried before on such a scale and this is what made the *crusade* so different.[147]

Those who opposed central government's experiment in retrenchment feared that the numbers receiving indoor relief would rise proportionally to the reduction in outdoor relief, thus increasing rates. Initially these fears were unfounded as numbers in receipt of indoor relief fell between 1871 and

---

142 Williams, *Pauperism*, 102. Economic historians often disagree about the pauperism statistics produced by central government. Overall, however, the pattern of reduction in outdoor relief quoted here is that accepted in the works cited in the introduction.
143 Ibid. 104.
144 Williams, *Pauperism*, 102–4, 107, and Englander, *Poverty and poor law reform*, 23, broadly accept these figures, although Humphreys, *Sin*, 28 calculates that the cost of outdoor relief nationally fell by 28.6% between 1871 and 1876.
145 Williams, *Pauperism*, 107.
146 Thomson, 'Welfare and the historians', 374.
147 On this aspect of the *crusade* see, for example, Thane, 'Old people and their families', 113–38.

Figure 1
Mean number of paupers in receipt of outdoor relief in England and Wales, c. 1860–1900

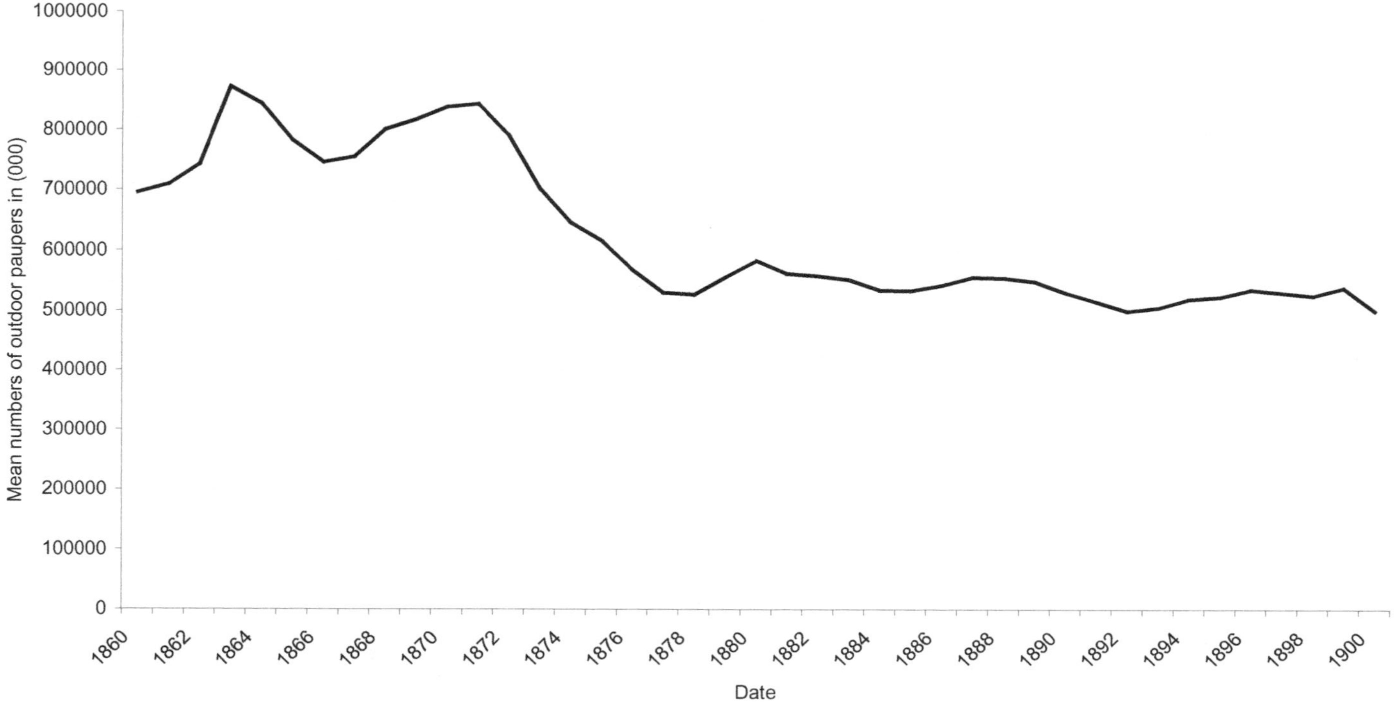

Source (figs 1–5): Williams, *Pauperism*, 97–104, and appendices.

Figure 2

Rates of outdoor paupers per 1,000 of estimated total population in England and Wales, c. 1860–1900

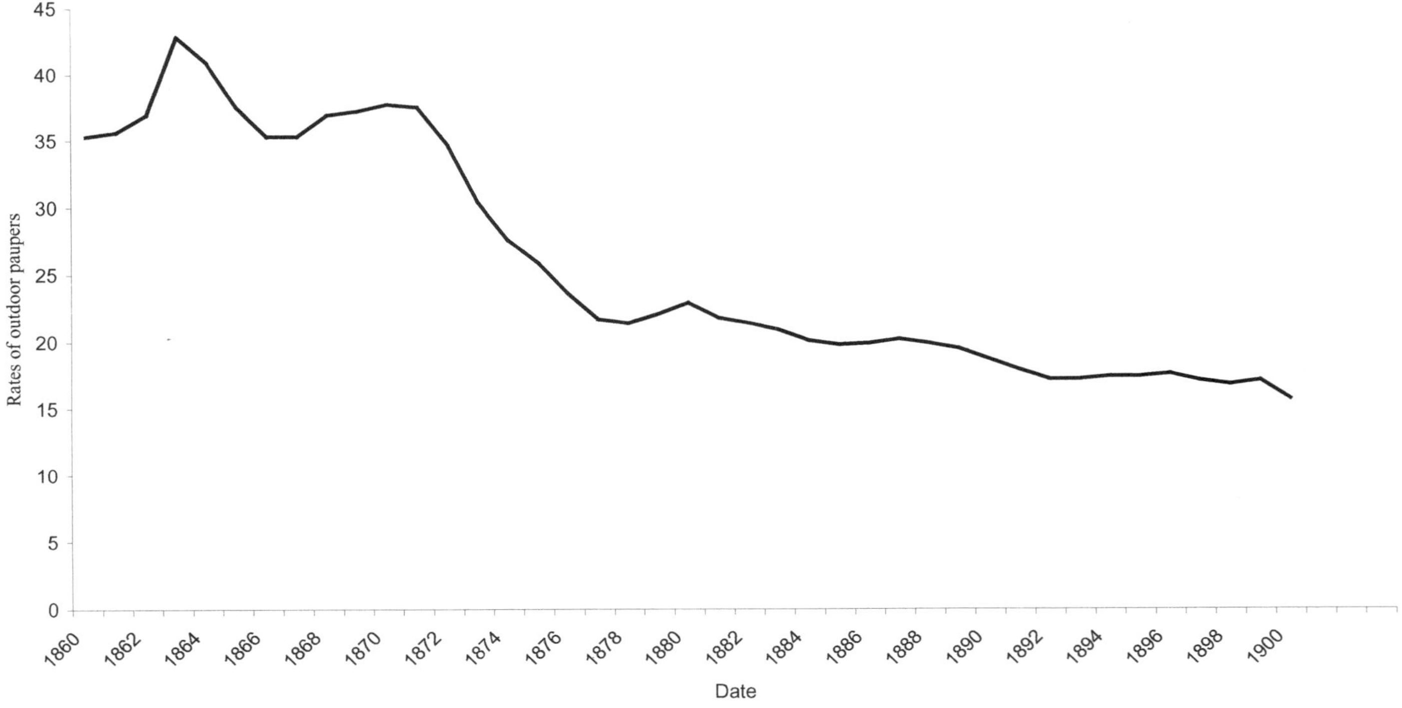

Figure 3

Mean number of paupers in receipt of indoor relief in England and Wales, c. 1860–1900

1876 by about 11 per cent, or 15,000 (*see* fig. 3).[148] Mary Mackinnon points out that improvements in living standards and the fact that real incomes rose after 1870 probably contributed to this trend.[149] It is evident, however, that after 1876 guardians began to send in returns to central government recording higher numbers of indoor relief claimants. Official records show that indoor relief levels increased by 44,000 (35 per cent) between 1876 and 1893 (*see* fig. 3), which meant that even when general population growth has been factored in, rates of indoor relief per head continued to rise slightly (*see* fig. 4).[150] Comparing the cost of outdoor to indoor relief, it is evident that the latter did increase the rates in real terms.[151] In total, outrelief expenditure fell by £903,000 (25 per cent) between 1871 and 1876, and then by a further £390,000 by 1893. Yet, as critics feared, although the total cost of expenditure on poor relief decreased by £551,000 (7 per cent) between 1871 and 1876, overall it increased by £1,331,000 (17 per cent) in the period between 1871 and 1893 (*see* fig. 5). Karel Williams points out that total expenditure 'increased substantially' because the 'direct and indirect costs of building and running' larger workhouses were substantial. Moreover ' "in-maintenance", maintenance of lunatics and loan charges', 'together increased by 62% or £1,577,000' between 1871 and 1893.[152] At the same time expenditure per head of population fell only slightly, from 6s. 11½ d. to 6s. 6¼ d., between 1871 and 1893.[153] If the *crusade*'s underlying aim was to save money, then it was not an unqualified success.

It is conventional to point out that thirty-four urban and seven rural unions, each registering less than 30 per cent of paupers on outdoor relief, were the engine of the new policy.[154] In numerical terms this appears to be a small proportion of the total number of unions, around 6.6 per cent, forty-one out of a total of 622. However, 'the group of forty-one achieved a 57% reduction in outdoor numbers against a national reduction of 35%' in the period between 1871 and 1876 and then a '68% reduction ... against a national 37% reduction' between 1871 and 1893.[155] Overall, these unions contained '16 per cent of the total population in England and Wales and they accounted for a 28 per cent national reduction in outdoor numbers' between 1871 and 1893. Consequently, these 'model' unions were influential. But the crucial point is that the national *crusade* would have not got underway without the initial support of a significant proportion of other poor law unions, which later relaxed regulations: themes to be explored later. Meanwhile, the reason why the forty-one were different is that they were more determined to retain their

---

148 Williams, *Pauperism*, 102.
149 Mackinnon, 'Poor law policy', 229–336 at p. 299.
150 Williams, *Pauperism*, table 3.1 at p. 102.
151 Ibid. 103.
152 Ibid.108.
153 Ibid. appendix, section C, table 4.6 at p. 170.
154 For figures on 'model' unions see Booth, *Aged poor*, 58–98.
155 Williams, *Pauperism*, 106–7.

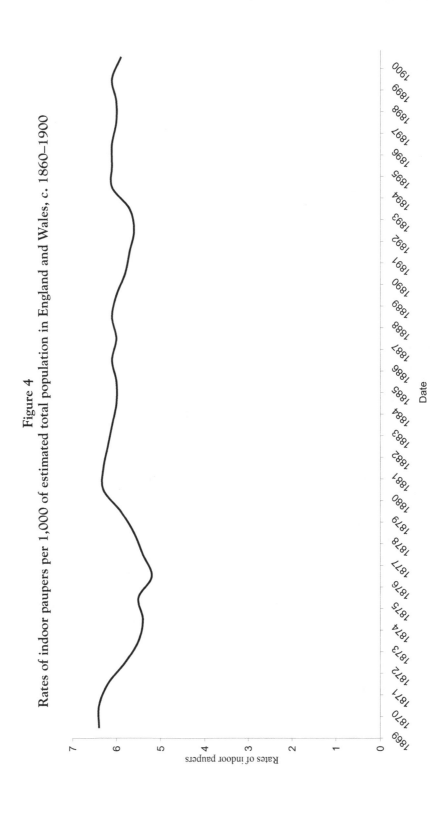

Figure 4
Rates of indoor paupers per 1,000 of estimated total population in England and Wales, c. 1860–1900

Figure 5

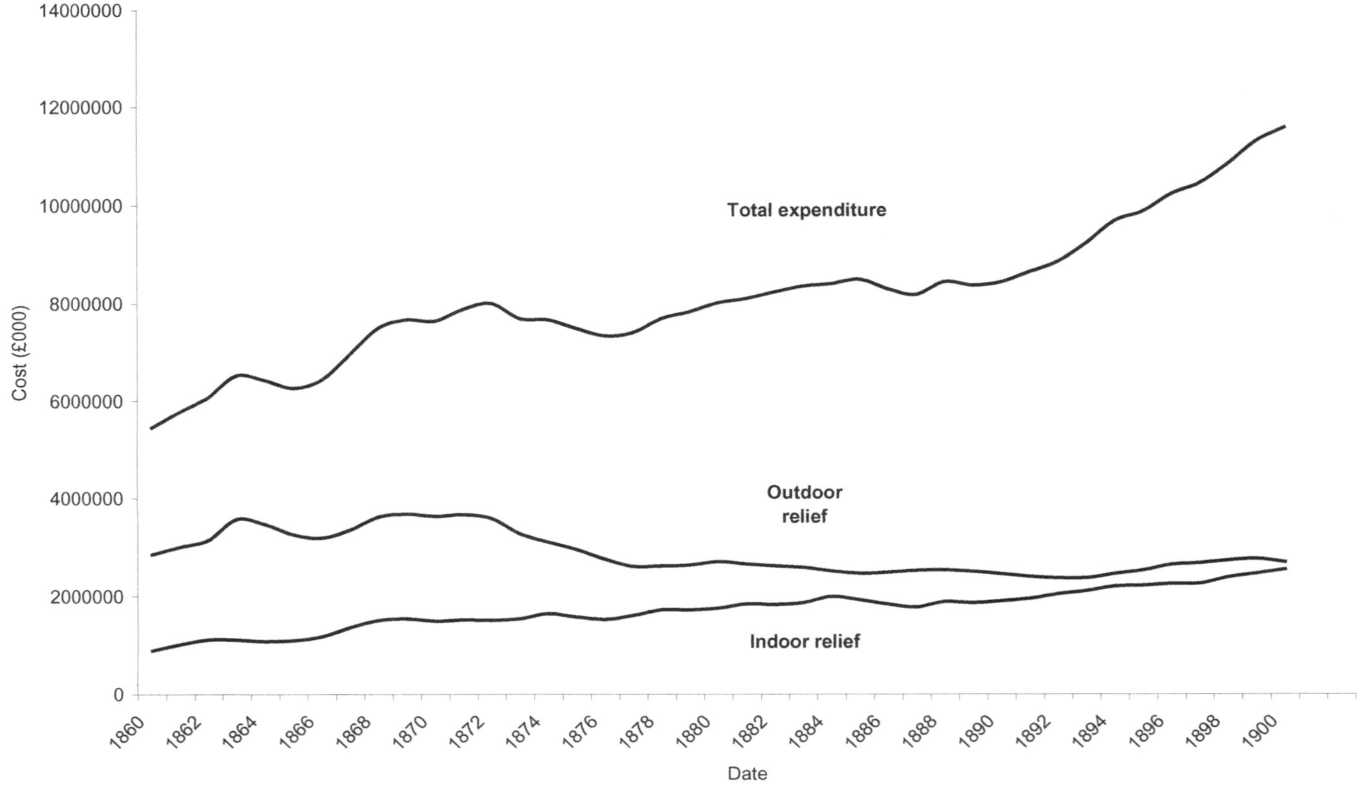

Amount spent on indoor and outdoor relief compared to the total cost of poor relief in England and Wales (including cost of lunatic paupers, loan charges, salaries and workhouse maintenance), c. 1860–1900

policies for ideological and economic reasons.[156] The ruthlessness with which they pursued policies of deterrence, especially those seven rural unions that maintained the *crusade* during the late-Victorian agricultural crisis, should not be under-estimated.[157] Curiously, little is known about this key aspect of poor law reality.

The ending of the *crusade* campaign is conventionally fixed at 1893, the year when property qualifications for suffrage in poor law elections were reduced to just £5 *per annum*.[158] This was followed by the Local Government Act (1894) which, by abolishing property qualifications, introduced the principle of one-person-one vote (men and women) in rural poor law elections for the first time. Magistrates' *ex-officio* status was repealed and women were officially allowed to stand for office. Finally, each poor law union became a democratically elected urban or district rural council. At the same time central government issued a new outdoor relief circular in July 1896, which stated that the LGB accepted that guardians were justified in granting outrelief to 'deserving' pauper claimants. There was now widespread recognition that most workhouses had become care homes for the elderly.[159] At the close of the nineteenth century welfare debates centred on the need for social measures 'to raise living standards', in order to 'promote industrial and social efficiency essential to the maintenance of British imperial power'.[160]

Debates and disputes: statistics and their meaning

Only one welfare historian in the last twenty years has focused upon the *crusade*. Karel Williams argues that the way that historians view the *crusade* decades hinges on their perception of central government's intention regarding outrelief funding after 1834. Welfare historians, such as David Ashforth, Anne Digby and Michael Rose, state that central government legislated in 1834 to try to eradicate all types of outrelief funding, particularly able-bodied female and male provision.[161] They assert that the Outdoor Labour Test of 1842, the Outdoor Relief Prohibitory Order of 1844 and the Outdoor Regulation Order of 1852 were genuine attempts by central government to reassert its authority. However, since those directives were so badly drafted, guardians could retain

---

[156] In March 1886 Joseph Chamberlain, president of the LGB, issued a new circular on outdoor relief which noted that guardians were authorised to provide schemes of work for 'steady and respectable' labourers. This initiative coincided with changing attitudes in society about the nature of poverty, as exemplified in Charles Booth's social investigations. It is difficult to assess its reception in rural unions as there are too few case studies to allow comparisons. Stedman Jones, *Outcast London*, provides an overview of unemployment riots in London in 1880s, as does Englander in *Poverty and poor law reform*, 27–8.

[157] Pauperism calculations are problematical and should be used carefully.

[158] Williams, *Pauperism*, 103.

[159] Thomson, 'Workhouse to nursing home', 47.

[160] Englander, *Poverty and poor law reform*, 73.

[161] See introduction.

a high degree of autonomy. Consequently, the New Poor Law did not succeed in its original objectives with regard to outrelief until the introduction of a *crusade* against outrelief. Thus, the New Poor Law, concludes Rose, was the creation of the late-1860s, not the 1830s.[162] The *crusade* experiment was an extension of the original ethos of 1834, a backward-looking policy initiative.

Karel Williams criticises such notions. He believes that too many poor law historians embarked on research in the 1970s without first questioning the Webbs' premise that outrelief directives were imprecise in the mid-Victorian era.[163] Welfare historians set out to uncover patterns of resistance to central government policy, but their conclusions were often misleading because the language of outrelief directives was misread. Williams, by contrast, believes that the outrelief directives between 1834 and 1870 were not 'colander-like', but designed only to eradicate the funding of outdoor relief for males.[164] Those guardians that continued to support other pauper categories on outrelief orders were following central government's guidelines, not opposing them. The *crusade* initiative was not therefore a reiteration of the ethos of 1834, but a new, far more radical, strategy to abolish outrelief. Williams agrees with Rose that welfare retrenchment evolved against the background of industrial crisis, rating changes and the expansion of workhouse capacity, but feels that he underestimates the extremist nature of the *crusade* ethos.[165]

Williams adopted a rather unusual methodology to support his viewpoint. He examined the context of the discourse of outrelief directives in the mid-Victorian period to prove that his fellow poor law historians misunderstand the intentions of central government.[166] His close reading of the 1834 strategy concludes that from the outset legislators intended 'to differentiate the kind of relief given to one class and another' because provision was made for the 'remedial' treatment of female able-bodied and other non able-bodied pauper claimants.[167] He found that the original poor law commissioners 'simply assumed that the workhouses of a reformed poor law would contain *some* old and sick persons', but not all and this was why guardians retained the right to award outrelief in cases of 'sudden and urgent necessity'. He then compared the language of the outrelief directives of the mid-Victorian period with the Goschen, Fleming and Longley recommendations. He found that these did not reiterate the 1834 ethos, as Rose claims, but were far more radical.

Williams believes that the Longley Strategy exemplifies the *crusade* ideology and that its profound social cost has been overlooked. It contained several elements of policy that brought about significant changes in central

---

[162] Rose, 'Crisis of poor relief', 50–70.
[163] Williams, *Pauperism*, 91–6.
[164] Humphreys, *Sin*, 17, and Kidd, *State, society and the poor*, 31–2, echo this claim.
[165] See Williams, *Pauperism*, 59–90, for his views on the funding of the able-bodied between 1834 and 1870.
[166] Williams's theoretical credentials are outlined ibid. 3–4.
[167] Ibid. 56–8 summarises Williams's reading of the strategy of 1834.

government policy and local poor law administration.[168] He explains that after 1834 guardians were given responsibility for deciding poor relief cases in poor law unions by developing 'a knowledge of the poor', in order to assess their eligibility for outrelief funding. Often they referred cases to poor law officials, such as doctors, to guide them in best practice. The Longley Strategy represented a momentous shift in policy because it reversed previous administrative guidelines by emphasising 'knowledge by the poor' of their poor law predicament. They now had to prove to guardians that they were entitled to outrelief.[169] Paupers were to be educated to adopt self-help by means of a series of new recommendations published in the form of a *crusade* charter placed in every workhouse waiting room. Williams stresses that this authorised guardians to ignore the fate of paupers struck off outrelief registers, since it was assumed that they had been educated not to become welfare dependants and no further enquiry was needed to establish the social cost of the *crusade* policy. Central government only asked guardians to report the outcome of certain medical cases who refused to enter the workhouse for treatment. For example, guardians were responsible for ensuring that a pauper on medical outrelief suffering from a communicable disease that might infect the wider community entered the workhouse isolation wards. One of the more radical recommendations of the Longley Strategy was that it encouraged guardians to recover all poor relief costs, by prosecuting the adult children of elderly or sick paupers to force them to contribute to their destitute relative's maintenance.[170] The Longley Report thus contained a more proactive policy of deterrence than the ethos of 1834.

Williams explains that Longley set out to create a New Poor Law climate by fostering a 'crudely repressive' competitive atmosphere amongst poor law unions in London and the regions.[171] Poor law conferences were established to share best practice and were a forum for central government to promote its *crusade* policies. Annual performance league tables were published praising those that adopted the Longley Strategy and damning those who refused to comply. Astutely the Longley directive was not published as a legally binding order, as had been the mid-Victorian outrelief directives. Instead it was issued as a set of recommendations in order to defuse popular resentment at far-reaching changes. Unfortunately, this gave extremist guardians greater autonomy because they were not restricted by official orders. Longley stressed the need to educate the poor, but those determined to cut costs ruthlessly ignored that ethos, and the new strategy 'turned into another kind of event', with many guardians pursuing 'brutal dispauperisation by any and every means'.[172]

Recently Karel Williams has been criticised by welfare historians, such as

168 Ibid. 96–102.
169 Ibid. 99.
170 Ibid.
171 Ibid. 102.
172 Ibid.

David Englander, who, while not doubting the important contribution that he has made, have questioned three aspects of his work.[173] First, Williams produced such a wealth of statistical information to support his claim that male able-bodied outrelief provision was almost eradicated by 1850, that the reader is often confounded by his empiricism. He also adopted a very unusual methodological approach for an historian in his detailed analysis of language. Consequently, no one has checked his calculations or interrogated his theoretical perspective. 'The profession', as Englander observes, 'has in general praised the statistical resource which has been created but ignored the conclusion derived from it.'[174] Englander notes that Williams's work has yet to be scrutinised by a suitably qualified historian and this is to be regretted since he raises some challenging lines of enquiry. Second, Williams takes a contradictory approach to poor law research. On the one hand, he downplays the value of local studies because he is very critical of those historians who study poor law unions to uncover patterns of resistance to central government policy in the mid-Victorian era. On the other hand, he asserts that the *crusade* decades must be studied in context. Williams, like Mackinnon, believes this can only be done by reference to central government indicators, but these are often a rather crude way to gauge the impact of regional poor law change.[175]

Third, Williams checks his analysis of legislative language against central government pauperism returns to ascertain policy trends. The problem with this is that whilst it recognises that language should be contextualised, it neglects to do the same with centrally collected statistics. Pauper returns, like a poor law discourse, need to be understood in the context in which they were produced. Local poor law statistics could be manipulated in various ways, a factor that criminal historians, such as Howard Taylor, emphasise.[176] Digby criticises Williams for accepting pauperism returns at face value.[177]

By the 1990s Williams had become the set text on the *crusade*. Indeed over the past twenty years countless poor law textbooks have rehashed his findings without checking their statistical credentials.[178] Furthermore, Williams's emphasis on national pauperism statistics has been a disincentive to local studies of the *crusading* experience. Subsequent research has been scattered and cannot counter-balance Williams's lack of regional and local primary research.[179] Williams has also been allowed to judge the *crusade*.[180] Few poor law historians seem to have misgivings about this precedent. Most do not

---

173 Englander, *Poverty and poor law reform*, 85–6.
174 Ibid. 86.
175 Mackinnon, 'Poor law policy', 229–336, and 'English poor law', 603–25.
176 H. Taylor, 'Rationing crime: the political economy of criminal statistics since the 1850s', *EHR* 3rd ser. xi (1998), 569–90.
177 Digby, *Poor law*, 23, and R. N. Thompson, 'The working of the poor law amendment act in Cumbria, 1836–1871', *Northern History* xv (1979), 128, also make this point.
178 See, for example, Hollen-Lees, *Solidarities*, and Kidd, *State, society and the poor*.
179 King, *Poverty and welfare*, represents the new trend of studying 'regional states of welfare'.
180 For an interpretation of Williams see Brundage, *English poor laws*, 110–17.

comment on the fact that a post-modern statistician might have missed an infinite number of ambiguities that could have arisen when guardians tried to interpret complex statutes and guidelines on outdoor relief. In fact it is only by close analysis of the internal workings of the poor law system, and an unravelling of its complexities, that historians can start to uncover its anomalies and distinctive regional, inter-regional and local variations in the late-nineteenth century. When central–local relations are considered from the perspective of the 'poor law and the politics of place', it is clear that pauperism statistics were much more fluid than Williams appreciates. At best, destitution figures are impressionistic. There is a more potent and subtle poor law story to be told for the *crusade* decades. The *crusading* experiment drove those in deepest poverty to enter a system in which they were shuffled about to save costs. After 1870 the poor relief system was confining, demeaning and, above all, prohibitive. It deterred those most in need. Paupers got lost in a plethora of central government returns. They literally fell off the pauperism scales and disappeared from poor law view. Historians can relocate them, research their parlous lives and start to retell their neglected *crusading* histories.

The case of Margaret Price

The nineteenth-century poor law world was very murky, awash with welfare ideas both backward- and forward-looking. Paupers had to navigate their way around a system rife with contradictions. But how did it feel to be on the receiving end of so much theorising and political intransigence? The best way to illustrate this is to let a pauper tell her own poor law story.

In September 1874, at the start of the *crusade*, a civil servant in the poor law department of the LGB pasted into his incoming correspondence ledger a lengthy letter:

> I am a dwarf and that has caused me to be a pauper these last few years and daughter of that unfortunate family that was knocked about Norton I have had the sum of half a crown a week and now they taken that of[f] me and I am nearly 27 years of age and I am not able to get my bread. ... I am with my parents and we are in lodgings 6 of us and little room and no door to it and my Mother says with tears in her eyes that we are quite indecent and the parish to pay 4 shillings a week and Mother one shilling a week. ... Always paid our rent and my parents are got on in years My Father 67 and Mother upwards of 60 and Mother says she has reared 7 children out of 11 and never troubled the parish in the whole of the time for she was a great slave and chaired [charred] at respectable houses and more is the pity My father is not everybody's workman for he is not very handy and does not always like work but it is true he had got a bad alement [ailment] that he is not always able for work but when there used to be thrashing with thrushells he could manage that but now there is not much of it he is glad to catch a days work here and there where he can and he cannot get work for every day in the week and we have one child that is 8 years old that we keeps

without troubling the parish and we have only 1 shilling a week and now they have taken that of[f] us and we have only the sum of 1 and 6 pence to keep me as a dwarf and to [add] more [to our troubles] this last week they say we asked them for shoes because we were so bad off and not fit to go to school and Mother is so fond of sending us to school that she would send us to school barefoot if the governess would have us... If we should have a house to ourselves if it was but a cattle shed... it is impossible for me to live on 1 and 6 pence a week but our useage that we had last winter would melt the heart of a stone and if it had not been for a good Union doctor we should not of[f] wanted shelter now and likewise no fault to find of the relieving officer but we are 6 in a little bit of a room Mother often says we are no better than pigs in a litter Mother brought me up to read and write as you can plainly see [181]

This narrative gives us a window on the apparently well-known competing ideas about the legitimacy of welfare provision in the English regions. It is significant for three key reasons. First, it marks the start of the *crusade*. This letter shows how the sudden withdrawal of outdoor relief could impact on a vulnerable section of society, such as the disabled. Second, investigating the letter's background reveals that the pauper, Margaret Price, wrote this long explanation herself. This is a precious testimony, even if its author might have been manipulative and was ultimately unsuccessful. Third, the letter received no reply. It was filed and annotated 'Is the story authentic? What do current poor law guidelines say? Why are they not in the workhouse? Are they destitute or on its margins? The case is a difficult one. No reply. File.'[182]

The lack of a reply and her underlying problems with the poor law could reflect the fact that Margaret Price had to navigate a set of fixed poor law rules, suggestive orders and myriad local interpretations that were intertwined with wider ideological debates. In fact, it seems noteworthy that the letter draws on nearly all the classical political economic strands.

On close reading it is apparent that Margaret Price recognises that she must begin her poor law claim by categorising her pauperism – she is disabled. This emphasises that her plight is involuntary. Moreover, her use of the language of 'deserving' is not coincidental. Her strategy appears to be to key into a poor law discourse. Thus Margaret also stresses her self-help and mutual-aid credentials, notwithstanding her narrow family and kinship network. She stresses that her family has tried to remain semi-independent despite problems such as a lack of work, young children to feed and ageing parents. Her determination to work, the fact of a basic education and shame at having to share sleeping arrangements, are detailed to stress the family's 'respectability'. In case her letter is assessed on biological grounds, she emphasises her work record despite her disability and that the family has reared their children

---

[181] Margaret Price to LGB, 30 Sept. 1874, TNA, PRO, MH 25/225, LGB memo no. 62953.
[182] Ibid.

without recourse to poor relief. But as well as reflecting nineteenth-century welfare discourses, this letter also looks forward.

Margaret Price seems to suspect that the tenor of the New Poor Law is changing on the eve of the *crusade*. Maybe this is why her letter is lengthy: one reading is that its case-study style mirrors COS inquiry methods. Furthermore, she not only displays an understanding of her predicament but also seems to know that she must be proactive in conveying it in her letter. Margaret must have had at least a broad sense of the new *crusading* rules. Longley stated that the poor should understand their predicament and prove their poor law worth. Perhaps Margaret read a *crusade* charter on the workhouse waiting room wall, or on a local church door. Maybe the relieving officer advised her that only lengthy and persistent claims would be funded from now on. Whatever the letter's background, and her underlying motivations, one outcome is certain: Margaret recognises that *crusaders* may want to know more, inquire further and will try to deny her claim to outdoor relief. She could not navigate all of their rhetoric because its entire substance would have been unfamiliar still. Thus, she tried to establish a lengthy dialogue, perhaps hoping that a similar reply would give her a sense of the best tactical approach. The fact that her letter went unanswered must have spoken volumes to her about her worsening plight. Evidently guardians of the poor were adopting and refining classical political economic terminology to suit their *crusading* design.

This is only one potential reading of the letter. To understand its historical context properly and the stormy sea changes in the poor law that it seems to be trying to navigate, chapter 2 focuses upon the *crusaders'* rhetoric. What had Margaret Price come up against? Why was she being ignored? Who, if anyone, would take responsibility for her plight? Delving deeper into *crusaders'* rhetoric makes it possible to understand Margaret Price's predicament. It is worth emphasising that wherever there was doubt, *crusaders* maintained their convictions. In a fast-changing world their outlook was obdurate. Margaret Price seems to have caused no one in authority a sleepless night, or a moral qualm. She was simply filed and forgotten.

2

Retrenchment Rhetoric:
Crusaders and their Critics

In 1870 Britain seemed confident of her imperial might and economic pre-eminence in the world order.[1] On the international stage her economy was amongst the richest. In global terms she produced around one third of all manufactured goods. Likewise, British businesses were responsible for about one third of Europe's commercial transactions. This meant that Britain had an unrivalled export record in terms of her gross national production (GNP), standing at around 43 per cent *per annum*.[2] The possession of a large empire meant that surplus goods could be sold on colonial markets, notably in India. As a result, Victorian economists estimated that gross national income rose from £523.3m. in 1851 to £668m. in 1861, and again to £916.6m. by 1871.[3] In major manufacturing cities like Manchester, the nation's wealth was being produced. But this rosy picture should not be taken at face value. There were significant structural problems in the later Victorian economy. Credit booms, for example, in 1852–7, 1861–6 and 1869–73, fuelled economic expansion. But that trend was dependent on heavy borrowing. So long as prices were buoyant, economic growth was assured. Yet, sales were by no means robust since recession was common. Moreover, a growing urban population threatened to absorb a greater proportion of the nation's surplus wealth in larger poor relief bills, for instance, leading to increasing tax demands which in turn undermined profitability. Against the backdrop of growing overseas competition in industrial and agricultural products, central government, charity giving organisations, poor law reformers and ratepayers perceived that something must be done to limit poor law expenditure. They argued that Britain seemed rife with economic anxieties and extremes despite her celebrated imperial might.[4] It seemed that everyone might be threatened by a 'deceleration in national prosperity growth' in the English regions.[5]

It was also obvious to many contemporaries that wealth was unevenly distributed in Victorian society, and that this created deep-seated social tensions. Few could deny that recessions were unavoidable when the national economy was subject to the vagaries of a changing and complex international

1   Eric. J. Hobsbawm, *The age of empire, 1875–1914*, London 1987.
2   R. Floud, *The people and the British economy, 1830–1914*, Oxford 1997.
3   G. Best, *Mid-Victorian Britain, 1851–75*, London 1990 edn, 19–23; Pearce and Stewart, *British political history*, 1–27.
4   D. Cannadine, *The decline and fall of the British aristocracy*, London 1992.
5   Humphreys, *Sin*, 2.

trading situation. This was the theme of new social commentators, like Henry George in *Poverty and progress* (1881). Urban ratepayers complained that the bulk of rural society, about 30 per cent of the total population of England and Wales, migrated to towns between 1881 and 1901 in search of work following a major agricultural recession.[6] Perhaps, pondered Henry George, punitive taxes on land were needed to resolve a poor relief crisis in towns and cities. George asserted that welfare provision was needed when workhouse capacity was filled. Often paupers experienced involuntary poverty. He noted that from as early as 1870 civil servants started to debate whether the rate base had the capacity, or should be expected, to continue to foot the bill for extensive poor relief. Alarm was expressed that total government spending on state intervention in the 1860s was already £65–70m. *per annum*, around 8 per cent of GNP.[7] In the same decade ratepayers' bills across Britain had risen by a phenomenal 16 per cent to pay for poor relief. Economic growth seemed threatened by guardians' liberal attitudes, resulting in tense central–local relations. Against this backdrop *crusaders* climbed onto a political platform to express their view that a new science of poverty was needed. That thinking led to a campaign to eradicate outdoor relief, spearheaded by the COS. This chapter examines the ideology of, and criticisms made about, the COS, including the critique of its position by opposition groups, during the *crusading* decades.

The Charity Organisation Society

On 29 April 1869 'The Society for Organising Charitable Relief and Repressing Mendicity', soon dubbed the COS, was established.[8] The COS was in the vanguard of anti-welfare action, with many leading *crusaders* among its rank and file. Members believed that indiscriminate welfare provision undermined individual self-help and exacerbated pauperism by encouraging the work-shy, idle and profligate to claim welfare instead of seeking alternative assistance

6   Lynch, *Liberal party*, 129.
7   Pearce and Stewart, *British political history*, 17.
8   See C. L. Mowat, *The Charity Organisation Society, 1869–1913: its ideas and work*, London 1963; J. Harris, *Unemployment and politics: a study of English social policy, 1886–1914*, Oxford 1972; P. L. J. H. Gosden, *Self-help*, London 1973; Henriques, *Before the welfare state*; J. Fido, 'The Charity Organisation Society and social casework in London, 1869–1900', in A. P. Donajgrodski (ed.), *Social control in nineteenth-century Britain*, London 1977, 207–30; F. K. Prochaska, *Women and philanthropy in nineteenth-century England*, Oxford 1980; A. W. Vincent, 'The poor law reports of 1909 and the Charity Organisation Society', *Victorian Studies* xxvii (1983–4), 343–65; Stedman Jones, *Outcast London*; A. J. Kidd, 'Charity organisation and the unemployed in Manchester, c. 1870–1914', *SH* ix (1984), 45–66; P. Johnson, *Saving and spending: the working class economy in Britain, 1870–1939*, Oxford 1985; B. Dennis and S. Skilton, *Reform and intellectual debate in Victorian England*, London 1987; L. Hollen-Lees, *Poverty and pauperism in nineteenth-century London*, London 1988; and Humphreys, *Sin*.

elsewhere. Too many charities, it was claimed, were bamboozled and duped by the 'undeserving' poor. As a result, attempts to encourage Victorian ideals, like thrift, hard work, self-reliance and sobriety, were undermined by generosity. COS ideology, therefore, was an amalgamation of classical political economic theories and Irish and Scottish welfare ideas.[9] Sampling articles in the *Charity Organisation Review* (COR), the COS organ, reveals its common core aims and ideology.

The Revd L. R. Phelps, chairman of the Oxford COS and a national spokesman, recalled in several articles in the COR why he was an ardent *crusader*. Although the following quotations are lengthy, they are worth citing in full because they exemplify COS ideology. They also provide an important template for understanding the depths of commitment and strength of feeling expressed for the *crusading* cause in the Brixworth union. Often poor law practice duplicated COS rhetoric because committed *crusaders* never wavered during a prolonged and bitter political battle. Thus, Phelps wrote:

> In Oxford an immense deal of charity was dispensed year by year. There were endowed Charities administered by the Charity Trustees, and others connected with parishes. There were alms distributed by ministers of religion. There was a large incalculable amount of money, of necessaries and comforts given away by private individuals. If only these were given to the right individuals, they were amply sufficient to provide for all the cases, which had hitherto been the despair of the thoughtful guardian. But to secure this, namely that charity should reach its proper object and be suited to them, some permanent organisation was required to guarantee full knowledge of an applicant's needs, no less than continuity and adequacy. So [we] called in the Charity Organisation Society, and from that day to this relief of the poor has been effected by the co-operation of that Society with the Board of Guardians.[10]

He went on to explain that

> When a case comes before the Board, which would be considered suitable for out-door relief, relief is given for a fortnight, and the case referred to the Charity Organisation Society for their consideration. At the end of the fortnight the Society report to the Board. If the Society undertakes it, the case is left to them. ... A voluntary society can bring to bear on a case a far greater number of forms of help than a Board of Guardians can command. It can give much of sympathy and encouragement, which it secures by interesting some member of the Society in the case, who reports constantly to the Committee, and notes its varying needs.[11]

9   See, for example, pp. 27–31 above, where these intellectual strands are discussed.
10   Revd L. R. Phelps, *The administration of the poor law in Oxford: a letter to the principal of Brasenose*, Oxford 1900, 1–6, Oxfordshire County Record Office, pamphlet 362.5.
11   Ibid.

Phelps claimed that the case-work system functioned 'excellently' and that the number of claims for outdoor relief dwindled once the society became established on a regional basis.[12] The same sentiments, often repeated verbatim, would be evident in the Brixworth union.

The COS was supported by many leading figures in central government. George Goschen, for example, was a keen supporter.[13] As vice-president of the COS he envisaged a long-overdue rationalisation of the poor law. Goschen believed that 'scientific investigation, by means of categorisation and co-ordination' of welfare agencies could reproduce a 'composite relief system' with a 'core of moral activities' creating more uniform administrative practices. Thus, the drunk, the idle and the profligate should be rejected on moral grounds because they drained resources and hoodwinked charities and guardians. Instead the COS concentrated on destitution. Too much poor relief undermined character-forming experiences, limiting the development of a spirit of independence, 'dignity, self-esteem and self-respect' in paupers.

This rhetoric shaped government directives on outdoor relief in the early 1870s. In particular, COS ideals were embedded in the Fleming Directive (1871). The *First Local Government Report* (1871–2) outlined Fleming's new rules on outdoor relief. Amongst the eleven new recommendations, civil servants stated that no outdoor relief was to be granted to any able-bodied applicant, male or female – even if he or she had children. If a husband deserted his wife, she would not be granted outdoor relief until a period of twelve months had elapsed. The same rule applied to able-bodied widows with children. The financial situation of each pauper had to be investigated. Account would be taken of 'their respective families, with the ages and number of children employed, amount of wages of the several members of the family at work, cause of destitution', and so on. If they had previously claimed regular outdoor relief, guardians should treat their claim unfavourably because generosity had been unsuccessful. Anyone granted outdoor relief would only receive assistance for a maximum of three months. Men taken into labour yards to work on a temporary basis would only be relieved on a week-by-week basis. Thus guardians could monitor the local employment situation and assess the merit of public works.[14]

Relieving officers now had to visit claimants every fortnight. Medical relief would only be authorised on receipt of a report from a DMOP. In larger unions Fleming recommended that 'inspectors of out-relief' should be appointed to check on the work of relieving officers. Central government hoped that these new guidelines would encourage guardian compliance. The subsequent Longley Strategy extended their vision on retrenchment and integrated COS rhetoric. Longley stated that the poor must be categorised

[12] Humphreys, *Sin*, 171.
[13] Ibid. 21.
[14] Henry Fleming Secretary, 'Report no. 20 outdoor relief circular from the Local Government Board to the poor law inspectors', *First report of the Local Government Board, 1871–2*, PP, 63–8.

in line with COS thinking. However, Social Darwinism could easily slip into decision-making on this issue too.[15] COS literature explained that guardians were following the maxim of 'natural selection' when they categorised paupers into 'deserving and undeserving' classes. Poor relief should not be given to a pauper residuum. Those who displayed incurable hereditary characteristics, like laziness, idleness or drunkenness should be ignored. Likewise, ratepayers must disregard the demands of illegitimate children and their profligate mothers. Essentially, regular but resolute enquiry into pauper claims ensured that poor law administration 'did as little harm as possible' to the evolutionary potential or otherwise of society.[16] Thus Longley reiterated that welfare agencies must 'administer relief so as to offer the minimum discouragement to the formation by the poor of provident and independent habits'. Guardians must be educators, encouraging independence. So the rules, regulations and recommendations of the Goschen Minute, Fleming Directive and Longley Strategy were combined into a single poster that reported minimal outdoor relief entitlements. This was posted in workhouse waiting rooms, on church doors and in public houses, usually anywhere the labouring poor might congregate. In this way central government publicised that the poor lacked entitlement and should seek help elsewhere, or enter the workhouse. The passing of the Union Chargeability Act (1865) made this system viable by creating the workhouse capacity to absorb outdoor claimants coming indoors. However, reformers knew that indoor relief was more expensive than outdoor relief. Thus, the so-called rules and regulations were severe and amounted to deterrence. To illustrate this point Karl Williams focuses on Longley's statement with respect to the 'disabled' class, the aged and infirm:

> No outrelief should be given to applicants of the disabled class (being capable of removal to the workhouse):
> (a) where their home is such that they cannot be properly cared for there.
> (b) where they are of bad character.
> (c) where it appears that they have relatives able or liable to contribute to their maintenance, who refrain from doing so.
> (d) where they have made no provision for their future wants, having been previously in receipt of wages as to allow them to do so.[17]

Here the *crusaders'* mindset is self-evident. Clearly it often overlapped with COS thinking. Notions such as 'bad character' are emotive and very subjective. Who judged whether an aged pauper was being 'properly cared for' was very controversial. It involved prying into family circumstances and inferred that poor relief was an unequal gift relationship. The emphasis on children paying for their parents' care reiterated the expectation of self-help. Perhaps, the most offensive notion is that poverty was a condition of 'wants', not

---

15 Jones, *Social Darwinism*.
16 Williams, *Pauperism*, 96–107.
17 Ibid. 98.

needs. It was questionable whether any unskilled worker, poorly paid agricultural labourer, or casual labourer had the means to save for old age. Likewise, widows were treated very harshly. Most had to put their children into the workhouse and go to work to obtain even a meagre outdoor allowance. This was very hard on women who had been in a ratepaying class and had slipped from relative to absolute poverty because of the death of their spouse. Longley, when criticised, retorted that the intention of the *crusade* was to be 'gradualist'. In reality, as Williams points out, 'there was not much difference between these conditional rules' and the 'direct prohibition' of outdoor relief.[18] The poor knew that the writing was quite literally on the poor law wall: their needs were irrelevant.

The Longley Strategy marked the golden years of COS influence. This said, Robert Humphreys and George Behlmer disagree about COS poor law success at a local level. Humphreys believes that the COS had a disorganised and poorly run infrastructure in the regions.[19] There was, therefore, considerable difference between COS rhetoric and reality. Behlmer insists that it is vital not to dismiss COS members' poor law record.[20] He suggests that COS guardians could be flexible and adaptive. For these reasons they often shaped local government debates about welfare provision in the early 1870s, even though they fell short of a *crusade* ideal. The vast in-letter files of the LGB around 1873/4 are instructive. They reveal that correspondents sometimes wrote to support the *crusade*, and at other times complained about COS rhetoric being adopted wholesale as government policy. Critics, however, tended to write in more frequently.

Critics of the COS

Joseph Turnell, former relieving officer and leading member of the Sheffield board of guardians, published a pamphlet on the subject of outdoor relief in 1873.[21] It caused a sensation in poor law circles. Turnell criticised the LGB for adopting COS methods. He claimed in a follow-up letter that

> Hundreds of thousands of our aged poor and infirm are in the most miserable condition; that the small allowance which we make to them is not sufficient to sustain nature, and that the horses, nay the very dogs of our

18 Ibid.
19 Humphreys, *Sin*, 7.
20 See, for example, G. K. Behlmer, *Friends of the family: the English home and its guardians, 1850–1940*, Stanford 1998, and G. K. Behlmer and F. M. Leventhal (eds), *Singular continuities: tradition, nostalgia and society in modern Britain*, Stanford 2000.
21 Joseph Turnell, *Pamphlet suggestions for the amendment of the administration of the poor law by which double relief could be given to the aged and infirm, materially increase that given to the widow and orphan, and a great reduction of the rates to the ratepayer*, Sheffield 1873.

aristocracy are better stabled, kennelled, and fed than our deserving poor are housed, clothed and fed. [22]

Turnell insisted that during his twenty-year stint as a relieving officer he learned that co-ordinating charity in order to cut back on outdoor relief resulted in 'gross mismanagement'. Experience taught him that poverty and pauperism were two sides of the same coin. Historically, ratepayers experienced a series of poor relief peaks and troughs. In his opinion the COS and the *crusade* had swung too far, 'to an extremity of cruelty, which is painful to contemplate'. Why, he asked, was the COS allowed to hijack poor law debates and policy-making in the capital? The long experience, considerable knowledge of the poor and pragmatic financial skills of the guardians was being devalued. He warned that the *crusade* was 'disreputable' and would result in significant welfare 'inequality'. Above all, he was very angry that Mr [Andrew] Doyle, LGB inspector for the north of England, had criticised the work of northern guardians. In the appendix to the *First local government report* (1872–3), Doyle claimed that pauperism was unchecked and as high as 10.8 per cent of the total population in many manufacturing districts. Turnell called this calculation a fiction.

A wave of similar petitions and letters of protest from northern and midland unions reiterated Turnell's criticisms. Most resented the directive that guardians must revive and retrieve old charities to fund poor relief. Mr [George] Searle, a leading spokesman for northern guardians, asserted that it was inappropriate for 'boards of guardians to enquire into the monies left by the sacred of past ages for their sole use and benefit, with a view to getting them back again'.[23] Other northern guardians queried why, if central government wanted administrative uniformity, they did not set 'a national rate' and implement 'a national chargeability' system? In that way everyone everywhere would be responsible for the funding of each other's poor. A larger common fund would lessen the burden on individual ratepayers. If a 'national rate' was set at 'three shillings in the £', then, as one leading spokesman for midlands unions calculated, it 'would enable us to double the relief given to the aged and infirm poor'. A majority of guardians, in around 66 per cent of poor law unions, felt that COS retrenchment was 'an insult to God'. It contravened the sentiment and spirit of the poor law since Elizabethan times. Newspapers soon resounded with similar criticisms.[24]

When the LGB was established civil servants in the poor law department were allocated areas of the country to monitor. A series of maps was compiled

---

22 J. Turnell, Sheffield union, 14 Jan. 1874, MH 25/24, LGB misc. correspondence between civil servants and poor law officials, misc. file, 1874.

23 Mr Searle to LGB, dated '1874', MH 25/25, ibid.

24 MH 25/25, misc. file, 1874, records incoming letters. Corresponding replies and private civil servant discussion can be cross-referenced to outgoing misc. file, 1874, MH 19/85.

for each union.[25] Relieving officers, parish-by-parish, were instructed to record levels of pauperism. Each parish was coloured red, blue or black, according to the number of paupers in receipt of outdoor relief. Those in the 'red' were identified as places where guardians needed to target their energies in order to reduce pauper numbers outside the workhouse. At the same time civil servants were aware that this was a crude instrument. Consequently, relevant regional and national newspapers were read on a regular basis to monitor public opinion. Noteworthy articles were pasted union-by-union into LGB files, and were used to compile a regional picture of pauperism across England. They give a flavour of the sorts of welfare ideas that were in circulation and the criticisms being made of current government policies on welfare. The fact that civil servants took the time to monitor newspaper editorials indicates the importance of the articles selected for retention. In January 1874, for instance, a typical newspaper article, originally featured in the *Midlands Free Press* and later picked up by both the *Daily News* and *The Times*, was stuck into an LGB miscellaneous file:

Prison diet per week	Pauper diet per week
8lb bread	5lb bread
16oz meat	10oz meat
2lb 8oz potatoes	16oz potatoes
16oz pudding	24oz pudding
7 pints of gruel	24oz Irish stew
3 pints soup	2 pints soup
7 pints cocoa	Paupers have to eat Australian meat of poorer quality

Conclusion: If God treats man for sin as man treats man for poverty, woe unto the Sons of Adam![26]

Civil servants assessed that the unwitting testimony and bitter tone of this piece reflected the range of criticisms being made about COS thinking on the poor law and its practical implications. Their notes in the margin suggest that COS rhetoric had made in-roads into the popular imagination in three ways. First, the article criticised a COS mindset that equated criminality with poverty. The public's perception seemed to be that the COS wanted to punish the idle poor for pauperism. Civil servants did not disagree with this thinking but they did note the article's bitter tone; 'perhaps it set a dangerous precedent for the future'? Second, the article suggested that the workhouse was already the lowest common denominator for most poor relief claimants, worse than prison. The editorial line assumed that this aspect of COS thinking was very familiar to readers. Again the bitter tone suggested that far from abusing the

---

[25] It seems that these maps were destroyed during the Second World War. They are often referred to in LGB files during the early *crusade*.
[26] The *Midlands Free Press* covered Derbys., Leics., Northants and Notts. See also *Paupers and Prisoners*, 20 Jan. 1874, MH 25/25, LGB newspaper and article misc. files, 1874.

rates, most workhouse residents were in dire need; civil servants speculated 'whether future poor law tax savings might be difficult to impose'? Third, the journalist assumed that contemporary readers would understand that a poor quality workhouse diet reflected the complex nature of a shifting pauper population. For instance, meat was second-rate, fit for a pauper residuum, and Irish stew was a staple of the workhouse menu. A migrant pauper population, often not assimilated into society, appeared to be a growing social problem. Unskilled, usually Irish, workers were frequently caught up in a casual labour market swelling workhouse lists; again civil servants speculated whether 'they could be ignored and at what social cost?' Yet, according to COS thinking, these paupers were work-shy and should be underfed in the workhouse. Civil servants noted that the journalist questioned the economic sense of that argument. Surely the malnourished would only return for more, and more costly, poor relief later; and what about the Bible's edict to 'love your neighbour as yourself'? An internal LGB memorandum discussion concluded in a confidential summary that poverty was a 'complex problem' and 'often defied COS rhetoric'. On this occasion the LGB did not come to the defence of the COS. Nevertheless the COS publicity machine kept putting out the same message: the poor could help themselves.

In April 1895 W. G. Chance (honorary secretary of the central Poor Law Conference, a Farnham union guardian and COS keynote member) recalled his convictions in the COR. His comments confirm that *crusading* attitudes often hardened in the face of mounting criticism over the course of the late nineteenth century:

> They want to bring everything down to one dead level – to mend the house by undermining its foundations – is quite consistent in advocating out-relief. The more miserable, discontented and demoralised the people become the better he is pleased, because it helps towards the establishment of his Utopia, where there are no rich and no poor – where indeed individual responsibility is annihilated, and everyone is made to fit. ... He dislikes the name of charity, which he calls the patronage of the poor by the rich. His whole creed is dependence on the State, and he well appreciates the fact that outdoor relief, which if generally extended will leave charity no field to work in, leads to that dependence. ... They may be misled by spurious promises for a time, but they will soon be undeceived, and then I shall be sorry for those who have been misled.[27]

According to Chance the poor law should be 'regenerative'. It must not interfere with the labour market because poor law supplements reduced wages in real terms. Why would an employer pay higher wages if his fellow ratepayers were prepared to supplement pauper incomes? Generous poor relief only undermined 'individual thrift and independence in the nation'. Surely, there was a difference between being '*legally* destitute' and '*morally* destitute'?

---

[27] William G. Chance, 'State administration of relief', COR (Apr. 1896), 138–45.

The former was someone who was friendless and had nothing. If he or she did not enter the workhouse, the alternative was starvation and death. The latter had financial options. Outdoor relief was therefore a 'demoralising substitute' when a 'combination of help' could see a pauper through a crisis. Poor law inspectors and civil servants tended to agree with these sentiments. Mr J. S Davy, a leading LGB inspector, was typical:

> It is very easy to make things pleasant all round by the grant of public money; pleasant to the applicant, pleasant to the Guardians themselves, who in granting the relief feel the joy of benevolence, which though it is vicarious, is none the less genuine after its kind. The hard task is that of the Board who administer relief as conscientious trustees of the public money; who insist that their officers shall give the fullest information with regard to each case; who form a painstaking judgement as to the amount and the kind of relief which is necessary; and who, finally, in coming to their decision, hold the immediate interest of the individual subordinate to the general well-being of the class from which the applicant comes.[28]

Repeatedly this attitude is echoed in LGB files, reflecting the outlook of the COS and of *crusading* guardians. Thus, a leading *crusader* wrote in the COR in March 1887 that:

> in helping a poor man nothing on earth should be done to degrade him. It was no use to take the rose of a watering-pot and sprinkle tickets and shillings and sixpencees and threepenny-bits among the people. Mere almsgiving in driblets did no good. It kept up a sort of irritation – a little feverishness – morbid hunger and thirst which degraded instead of assisting men.[29]

In the same issue HRH the duke of Albany, chairman of the council of the COS, declared in a lengthy annual speech to members that sometimes mendacity work was disagreeable. 'For it so happens', he stated, 'that the ways in which we can do the most for the poor seem to them at first sight irksome and unkind.' In the past too many charity-giving organisations, around 640 in the early nineteenth century and an additional 144 in the 1850s, did much harm. 'If we really want to improve the condition of the poor', he advised, 'we must compel them to send their children to school; we must keep down outdoor relief; we must check indiscriminate almsgiving.' He recognised that 'in doing these things we are in danger of appearing to the poor rather as pedagogues than as parents — as though we were always enforcing unpleasant truths'.[30] But was the COS so obdurate and unfeeling? Did their ideology shift during the later decades of the nineteenth century?

Robert Humphreys points out that 'COS and LGB traditionalists scarcely wavered from the individualistic principles that brought them together in

[28] Ibid. 144.
[29] Editorial, 'Annual meeting report', COR (Mar. 1887), 107–20.
[30] Ibid. 119.

1869' at the time of the Goschen Minute.[31] This alliance was forged and remained fixed 'in spite of trends towards an interventionist state having gained wider public acceptance by 1890'. That was a fatal error. In an era of widening democracy, few accepted that they had to be categorised, housed in a workhouse and stigmatised in order to receive poor relief. In the meantime, however, COS exponents concentrated on the 'moral health' of the nation, ignoring significant socio-economic and political changes that coincided with changes in the definition of poverty in the 1880s. This meant that their influence waned, although the timing of that sea-change has been hotly debated.

COS influence probably peaked sometime between 1877 and 1885.[32] In these years industrial and agricultural recessions were severe throughout England.[33] In many respects the financial problems that poor law reformers had flagged up in the 1860s had came to fruition by the 1880s.[34] A rural exodus over-stretched resources in towns and cities. Public health, housing and the poor law struggled to meet the demands of a growing population seeking work. Against this backdrop, older notions that poverty derived from 'sin' and a 'moral' failing seemed outdated. Around 1885, therefore, COS rhetoric appeared implacable and irrelevant. A vibrant journal literature reflected this fundamental shift. Publications like the *Contemporary Review*, the *Fortnightly Review* and the *Nineteenth Century* publicised the changing ideas about the poor law and welfare that were in circulation. It is not possible here to retrace the dynamics of those vibrant debates everywhere. Yet, sampling several influential articles is instructive.

The Times, for example, described economic conditions at the start of the 1880s in dire terms. A leading editorial noted that 'trade, which for several years past has been struggling with falling prices, has reached a point approaching stagnation'. Likewise, agriculture was in crisis due to 'the complete failure of the harvest'. Throughout Britain, especially in 'Sheffield ... the Potteries ... and in Lancashire', work was in short supply. The article concluded that 'if the upper and middle classes suffer, why not the lower?'[35] *Punch* agreed. It was very critical of the COS and its *crusading* ethos. For example, on 27 March 1886 it published a wry poem reflecting on bitter debates about self-help and charity. How could the poor survive when basic outdoor relief was withheld?

> Sikes on Self-Help (For the 'Unemployed')
> A person wot is unemployed,
> Accetin' of relief,
> Is hindependence 'as destroyed;
> Which therefore I turned thief.

---

[31] Humphreys, *Sin*, 159.
[32] Williams, *Pauperism*, 103, notes this watershed. He also stresses that after 1893 the coming of democracy was significant.
[33] Hunt, *British labour history*.
[34] E. P. Hennock, 'Poverty and social theory in England: the experience of the eighteen-eighties', *SH* i (1976), 68–91.
[35] *Times*, 30 Jan. 1880.

No charity to 'elp distress,
Says swells, but wot's to blame;
Demoralizin', more or less,
Receivers of the same.

Blow charity, assistance blow,
And blowed employment be!
So long as I can plunderin' go,
You don't demoralize me!

Self-elp it is the means and plan
I choose to pursue;
So, consequently, all I can,
I 'elps myself unto.[36]

Oliver Twist's enemy Bill Sykes had taken COS rhetoric at face value. Self-help and thieving go hand-in-hand. This, hinted Punch's editorial line, is what happens under an excessive *crusade*: a life of crime has more appeal than living with the certainty of absolute poverty. Sykes's work ethic peverts Samuel Smiles's *Self-help* manual. Aligning criminality with a life of pauperism in this way also echoes early criticisms of the *crusade*. Critics often pointed out that better prison diets exposed the appalling nature of their pauper equivalent. By 1895 even a more conservative journal like the *Quarterly Review* suggested that driving paupers into a life of crime was questionable.[37] 'We may', it commented, 'pay too high a price for the independence of the poor; we may inflict too great a hardship if we hurry too fast the withdrawal of... facilities for relief.' It was undeniable, it maintained in its editorial, that 'pauperism was a social evil, and society should be ready, if necessary, to pay highly' to 'reduce its dimensions'. Clearly, the influence of harsher sentiments towards the poor and their relief was starting to wane.

The key point about traditionalists' wavering, is that it gave COS critics an opportunity to challenge ingrained *crusader* attitudes. Thus, in July 1885, the *Fortnightly Review* (a more liberal journal), queried the arrogance of the COS. Why, it asked, 'after centuries of trial and failures it had been reserved' for the COS 'to stumble upon a remedy' of charity organisation?[38] COS conceit convinced the short-sighted that *crusaders* were 'destined to allay all the miseries and remove all the burdens that oppress society', giving them a name 'amongst the foremost social reformers of modern times'. Too often, the journal argued, *crusaders* surveyed 'the world from the serene altitudes of the political economist; it is necessary to tell them that there is a considerable number of human beings already suffering below'. How could it be denied 'that their need of relief is pressing and immediate?' The editor maintained that the COS mind-set was outdated: they 'would abolish all charity at all

---

[36] *Punch*, 27 Mar. 1886. See also COR (Apr. 1886), 141, for the official COS response.

[37] Editorial, 'The abuse of statistics', *Quarterly Review* cccxxix (July–Oct. 1894), 466.

[38] Lord Stanley of Alderley, 'Two days in the Brixworth union', *Fortnightly Review* (July 1885), 42–55.

hazard and at once'. Outdoor relief was '<u>not</u> an unmitigated evil', as the COS claimed, nor was it 'worse than mendicancy or starvation'. The COS would have everyone believe, continued the editor, that it was 'better to starve any number of poor people than violate one jot of the ... theories on political economy'. The article concluded that the COS and the *crusade* could be summed up in the disreputable refrain 'perish the poor for poor law profit'.

Did the views expressed in such journals reflect wider public opinion? It is clear that increasingly journalists regarded the *crusade* as the welfare issue of its day; it raised fundamental questions about who was responsible for poverty, the individual or the state? Unsurprisingly, the issue also took centre stage in political circles. However, it is noteworthy that wider public opinion was also informed by a complex array of powerful older literature, as well as by ground-breaking humanitarian writers and social scientific studies that challenged COS thinking. Collectively they seemed to cut to the heart of the *crusaders'* socio-economic reasoning.

In the mid-Victorian period novelists like Charles Dickens, Mrs Gaskell and Charles Kingsley highlighted the dire economic predicament of the poor. Few who read *Hard Times* or *Oliver Twist* could deny that pauperism was often the downside of industrialisation. Likewise, Henry Mayhew's *London labour and the London poor* (1851) suggested that there were structural poverty crises in the poorer districts of the capital. Although COS rhetoric was a reaction against this older literature, Dickens and his contemporaries were read avidly and entered the popular imagination. So much so that literary depictions of penury may have helped to prepare the ground for changing ideas on poverty in the 1880s when everyone seemed to have been affected by recession.[39] The landowner, farmer, shopkeeper, businessman, skilled artisan and unskilled labourer knew that their financial losses resulted from broader economic trends and not individual failing. How could the poor be blamed for their sad plight when everyone was in the same situation? Thus, by the 1880s, the *Illustrated London News* captured a receptive audience with its 'recent revelations as to the misery of the abject poor that have profoundly touched the heart of the nation'.[40] It ran a campaign that focused on a growing awareness of endemic poverty. A new wave of humanitarians soon followed, often recapitulating early Victorian ideas about the causes of poverty.

It is difficult to capture the complexity and variety of discourse on poverty in the 1880s. A range of opinion was expressed by leading charities, politicians, social groups, radicals, social imperialists, social science investigators and humanitarians. Of these, Andrew Mearns's *The bitter cry of outcast London* (1883) seemed shocking.[41] Mearns was a Congregationalist minister, who decided to publish a small pamphlet critiquing social conditions. He

---

39 Fraser, *Evolution*, 132–3.
40 Quoted by A. S. Wohl in the introduction to A. Mearns, *Bitter cry of outcast London*, London 1970, 9.
41 Fraser, *Evolution*, 132–3.

did so from the perspective of a 'traditional moralist'. His language was 'emotive and emotional'. He stated that there was a quantifiable environmental link between endemic pauperism and poor housing, which caused the moral degradation of the poor, not the other way around. Likewise, the Revd William Preston, who assisted Mearns, repeated Macaulay's dictum that 'if people are forced to live in hog-sties they eventually behave like hogs'. Both Mearns and Preston highlighted London's numerous and poverty-ridden slums; evidently the poor were not responsible for their plight. Mearns asked how could London, the largest and wealthiest city in western Europe, harbour unchecked such widespread poverty?

Mearns's emphasis on housing needs led W. T. Stead, editor of the *Pall Mall Gazette*, to run a campaign in 1885 exposing the appalling housing conditions in London and the regions. Stead estimated that 'one-third of the agricultural houses of Britain are required to be rebuilt', around 700, 000 dwellings. Likewise in major cities, like Birmingham, property speculators exacerbated pauperism. In the late 1840s dwellings were built 'for as little as £60 a-piece: the capital cost was kept down by making the supporting walls only 4½ inches thick, putting in joists measuring 5½ by 1½ inches, and fixing them 17 inches apart'.[42] Short-term investment for large profits caused misery amongst the most vulnerable in urban society. Inadequate housing subsided or fell down by the 1880s. The COS, Stead pointed out, still maintained that the way to resolve poor housing and overcrowding was to force 'everyone, everywhere into the workhouse'. In his opinion this was a ludicrous solution. Such debates coincided with social scientific studies, which tried to take debates on the causes of poverty forward and tended to isolate the COS.

In the 1880s 'there was an increased realisation that environment, social and physical, played' a critical role in the fortunes of the poor, so much so that few could control their economic destiny. Yet 'at the same time nobody had any clear notion of how extensive poverty was'.[43] Two groundbreaking studies were decisive. Charles Booth's *The life and labour of the people of London* (1889–1903), and Joseph Rowntree's survey of poverty in York in *Poverty: a study of town life* (1901), estimated that around 30 per cent of the nation lived in pauperism not of their own making. These two unsentimental rationalists tried to observe poverty to understand its statistical basis. They noted that casual earnings, old age and, especially in York, low wages, exacerbated pauperism. They stressed that these problems were beyond the scope of charity organisation when they involved one third of the population. State intervention was needed. Thus, alongside the growing public awareness of poverty, a diversity of social and cultural forces had begun to erode *crusade* thinking by the turn of the century.

One example, among the many critiques in circulation, was the Fabian Society tract *Why are the many poor?* (1884). Its themes were typical of many

---

42 Best, *Mid-Victorian Britain*, 39.
43 Fraser, *Evolution*, 135.

writings on the root causes of poverty in the decade 1885–95. It began 'we live in a competitive society with Capital in the hands of individuals – what are the results. A few are very rich, some well off, the MAJORITY IN POVERTY, and a vast number in misery'. Capital, it argued, dominated society. Therefore 'if Capital be socialised, Labour will benefit by it fully, but while capital is left in the hands of the few, Poverty must be the lot of the many'. Thus:

> Whilst the capitalist often retires with a fortune on which he, his children, and his children's children live without useful industry. Here is one out of many instances. The son of an owner of ironworks is now in the House of Lords; he has a fine town house; his children are brought up in ease and luxury. But where are the children of those whose work made the fortune? They toil from morning to night for a bare living, as did their fathers before them.[44]

The significant point about these attitudes is that they reflected wider debates about the causes of and remedy for poverty, which often took place against the backdrop of a confluence of social, economic, cultural and political demands for changes in the poor law. Slowly at first, but gradually gaining momentum in the course of the 1880s, those arguments appeared to threaten COS dominance. It needed to react quickly. Instead, and fatally, it was obdurate.

Ignoring socio-economic change: the intransigence of the COS

During the 1880s the COS rank and file reacted in a very conservative way to the groundswell of newspaper criticism, social commentary and social scientific investigation that challenged its ideology. Members were determined to maintain their view that the issue of poverty, as opposed to pauperism, was the business of the COS. This made them appear out-dated. The Edwardian historian G. H. Gretton wrote that

> In the year 1888 it seemed that many currents of restlessness – the restlessness not only of the working people and the people on the 'starvation line', but of educated and thoughtful people also in regard to the responsibilities of citizenship – were producing a genuine effect. ... But some were resistant.[45]

The COR often reflected the stubborn resistance of the *crusaders*. In March 1887, for example, members were still debating the 1860s issue of legitimate charity:

> May I add one word upon the charitable world? That is a most fearful phrase. Who invented it? What is the meaning of it? What is the use of the 'chari-

---

44 Anon, 'Why are the many poor?' (Fabian Society, tract i, 1884).
45 G. H. Gretton, *A modern history of the English people*, I: *1880–1898*, London 1913, 223.

table world'? It seems to me that its functions are to relieve without pains and individual responsibility. How does it appear before the public? What is the charitable world doing? It is constantly appealing to the Government. It is doing it now. It is appealing to Government to emigrate people, to pass Acts for open spaces, to weaken the poor Law, and do a vast number of things, which, when worth the doing, the people would probably do for themselves without any charitable world to suggest it to them.[46]

Likewise, in September 1889, the COR was still sticking to its strict New Poor Law principles:

That out-relief is insufficient, that it is frequently bestowed on unworthy persons, and that finally, it should rarely, if ever, be given at all, is the unanimous conclusion of those who have worked longest and kept their heads coolest amongst the London poor.[47]

At successive annual meetings of the Church Congress in the 1880s COS members clung to the same message, that charity exacerbated pauperism:

The City of London, with an endowed income of over £100,000 a year in parochial charities, a decreasing population of only 76,000, and a forest of churches, is conspicuous for its pauperism. As its wealth increases, so does this blot and sore, till the ludicrous is reached. ... About 70 persons in a thousand residents are in receipt of parish relief in this Babylon reeking with wealth.[48]

Some of their suggestions were positively offensive to those who fell from relative to absolute poverty in the 1880s. At the North Midland district poor law conference held in Leicester on 13 December 1886, COS delegates insisted that poor people wasted their resources. Mr Mossop, Leicester COS member and guardian for Holbeach union, stated that

something might be done to save the great waste involved by each family doing its own cooking – by co-operation the cooking might be done far better and at much less cost. Food should be cooked by steam, and probably the system adopted in the German Army, would be found most economical (they regularly cooked by steam).[49]

---

[46] Editorial, 'Annual meeting', COR (Mar. 1887), 108.
[47] Editorial, 'Poor relief: out-relief ii', COR (Sept. 1889), 359.
[48] D. J. Vaughan (ed.), *Report of the church congress held at Leicester September 28–Oct. 1, 1880*, London 1881.
[49] Editorial, 'Annual poor law conference for the north midland district held at the board room Leicester in Pockington's Walk, on Mon. 13 Dec., 1886', *Poor law conference reports*, London 1886, 407–26.

A fellow speaker, the Revd. J. Bird from the Barrow-on-Soar union, concluded that the poor ignored 'many' remedies for pauperism. He observed that amongst the many proposed at central conference that year were suggestions about 'Australian beef, German cookery, cricket clubs (exercise), less rent (by negotiation), and the discouragement of early marriages'. Yet, these solutions were also petty. They emphasised that *crusaders* were either incapable, or unwilling to see the bigger picture of poverty in the later Victorian era.

From this snapshot of core COS values and of the thinking behind them, one lesson stands out. In an era of economic complexity and uncertainty, the COS was often resolute and intractable. Even though in most corners of late-Victorian society, strong criticism was being made of its ideology and *modus operandi*, the COS stuck to its principles. *Crusaders* stressed self-help, mutual aid and independence, principles which could not be implemented in an era of recurring recessions in industry and agriculture. Their philosophy could only work if the poor could find alternative forms of employment. It is debatable whether this was practicable. Moreover, while the COS 'demanded abject deference'[50] from applicants for poor relief, in an era of widening democracy most new voters thought that welfare entitlements should accompany full citizenship rights. In ignoring poor law realities the COS made a fatal mistake. That said, there was some tinkering around the edges of COS convictions, notably a commitment by figures such as Octavia Hill to lobby for better housing for the poor. Nevertheless most COS members maintained a myopic vision of welfare provision, 'belief in the overriding dominance of individual character', which 'remained' their 'strong distinguishing feature'.[51] Generally the average COS acolyte did not waver in the face of considerable pressure to reintroduce outdoor relief. Nor did he or she feel the need to react to the weight of evidence that showed pauperism to be the downside of much industrial or rural capitalism. This was why a pauper like Margaret Price got nowhere with her claim to poor relief around 1874. In an uncertain world, the narrow COS perspective was built around ignorance of what a 'world-without-welfare' meant for the vast majority of the labouring poor.

Crusaders lacked the ideological vision to respond to a changing material world in which a cross-section of society recognised that the margin between relative and absolute poverty was often slim. Once increasing numbers of respectable ratepayers, like bankrupt small businessmen, tenant farmers and artisans, came into the ambit of the poor law in the 1880s, the hold of the COS on the popular imagination started to slip. They were exposed as sincere, and sincerely wrong. Meanwhile, the labouring poor would pay a high social cost for a *crusading* experiment that set out to prove that poor law ideology could remedy pauperism and reduce taxation. To fully appreciate that bigger poor law picture it is necessary to examine how *crusading* was organised and run

50 Humphreys, *Sin*, 173.
51 Ibid. 4, 144–5.

on a local basis. A close analysis of *crusading* activities reveals what happened where and with what result.

Part II takes up this agenda with a case study of the Brixworth union. Here, protesting about pauperism reached fever pitch when poverty, politics and poor relief policies clashed in late-Victorian England.

PART II

THE LOCAL POOR LAW LANDSCAPE

3

The Northamptonshire Poor Law Experience, 1834–1900

'This county of wooded hills – many with the steeple of an ancient church thrusting up between the trees – of villages, churches and country houses built of stone of many colours from the dark brown ironstone to golden yellow limestone, is less regarded than it should be.'[1]

Early commentators dubbed Northamptonshire the 'middle-kingdom' of England.[2] Cartographers observed that it was a very inland area, with a distinctive shape. It has been described as 'rather like a diving seal, its head lunging into the fringe of the Cotswolds in the South West, its tail trailing the Fens in the North East and one flipper thrust into Buckinghamshire'.[3] It is bordered by nine counties.[4]

In the past, travellers stressed that Northamptonshire's location made it of prime strategic importance for agricultural and industrial trade. Its significant communication and transportation links included Roman roads like Watling Street, the Great North Road and the main stretch of the Grand Union canal. Today it remains at a conjunction of major travel routes. The M1 motorway crosses Northamptonshire's 642,393 acres, just seventy miles from London; likewise the A1/M and A14 transect the county. Thus, it is still very much at the centre of everyday Midlands' life.

Northamptonshire has always been famous for two staples of its local economy, its world-famous shoe-making industry and agricultural prosperity. A New Domesday survey, *The return of the owners of land in England and Wales* (1873) called it the county of *'squires, spires and mires'*. It reported that '57% of the land in Northamptonshire was owned by 102 landlords with landed estates of a thousand acres or more and just under half of this was in the hands of 16 persons owning estates of between 5,000 and 20,000 acres'.[5] Bill Rubenstein observes that this made the county exceptional. He notes that 'the degree of landowning concentration was phenomenal', with sixteen major

1 J. Smith, *Northamptonshire: a Shell guide*, London 1968, introduction.
2 J. Bridges, *The history and antiquities of Northamptonshire*, London 1791; G. T. Baker, *The history and antiquities of the county of Northamptonshire*, Northampton 1823–30, 1836–41.
3 Geographical layout is detailed in the introduction to J. Morton, *Natural history of Northamptonshire*, London 1712, and also in J. M. Steane, *The Northamptonshire landscape*, London 1974.
4 These include Leics. and Rutland (to the north); Bucks and Oxon. (in the south); Warwicks. (to the west) and Cambs., Hunts. and Beds. (in the east).
5 *The return of the owners of land in England and Wales*, London 1873 (NRO).

Map 1. Northamptonshire: a Midlands county in the nineteenth century.

landowners owning an estimated 65–74.9 per cent of the land in county in 1873.[6] Yet, the nature of that landed society was never static – the gentry came and went over the centuries.[7] In the nineteenth century, however, influential landowners were a consistent feature of Northamptonshire life.[8] Despite political divisions and inter-family rivalries, landowners shared a vision. They had endured because land equalled power in both economic and political terms. The established Church underpinned that ethos, happy to thrive on generous landed patronage. Local consensus (involving landowners, clergy and farmers) about the value of agricultural prestige meant that the *status quo* was seldom questioned. Landed society in the county was confident, having consolidated its political authority since the sixteenth century. This did not abate until the coming of democracy created county councils (1888) and parish councils (1894), later abolishing property qualifications in poor law elections (1895) and thus handing political power to ordinary people for the first time.

It is important to consider Northamptonshire life in broad socio-economic terms before the *crusade* against outdoor relief got underway. It is very odd, given its strategic location and the continuing presence of major landowners, that there is no substantial history of the county. Since, moreover, the agricultural interest in the county often dominated central government, its neglect is something of an anachronism. This discussion hence uses primary research to probe how the poor law fitted into a dense pattern of influential landownership. The poor law landscape across Northamptonshire was undeniably complex. None the less, a landowning elite staffed boards of guardians, thereby maintaining their predominant Tory or Whig supremacy. Most were determined to remain at the political apex of poor law life at all costs and with minimal interference from central government. Thus the New Poor Law was administered in accordance with their economic interests. As a result, there was much continuity between Old and New Poor Law practices. This meant that the 'mixed economy of welfare' was always skewed in favour of those in power and the labouring poor had to 'makeshift' their meagre economies accordingly.[9] In Northamptonshire this basic socio-economic fact of local life shaped how parish politics and Westminster interacted in poor law matters.

---

6   W. D. Rubenstein (ed.), *Wealth and the wealthy in the modern world*, London 1980, introduction; *Men of property: the very wealthy in Britain since the industrial revolution*, London 1981; and *Elites and the wealthy in modern British history: essays in social and economic history*, London 1987; Cannadine, *Decline and fall*, 88–138.
7   This point is made forcibly in J. V. Beckett, *The aristocracy in England, 1660–1914*, Cambridge 1986, and L. Stone and J. C. Fawtier Stone, *An open elite? England, 1540–1880*, London 1984.
8   R. L. Greenall, *A history of Northamptonshire and the soke of Peterborough*, Chichester–London 1979.
9   See, for example, S. A. King and A. Tomkins (eds), *The poor in England, 1700–1850: an economy of makeshifts*, Manchester 2003.

Getting started: the New Poor Law in Northamptonshire

On the eve of the New Poor Law in 1834 Northamptonshire had a prosperous economy; however, wealth, and therefore power, tended to be concentrated in the hands of those with a rather conservative outlook.[10] Central government consequently judged that the reception of the New Poor Law in Northamptonshire was probably going to be contentious.[11] Parishes were predominantly rural, so the early poor law commissioners put in charge of combining them into poor law unions expected to run into a hedge of local interests. Initially, central government focused on Northamptonshire as a priority case: if it could get the New Poor Law procedures up and running in an area with such a high number of resident gentry then it would be a very good public relations exercise.

An assistant poor law commissioner, Richard Earle, was assigned to Northamptonshire and initially seems to have had a great deal of success (*see* table 1).[12] His early reports stress that he won the confidence of Northamptonshire's landowners, who were prepared to co-operate in the combining of 345 parishes into twelve poor law unions across the county.[13] On closer reading, however, it is apparent that such co-operation was the result of Earle's considerable bureaucratic flexibility.

Earle's returns to central government belie the fact that he had to agree to combine estate villages into small poor law units. For instance, eight of the duke of Grafton's estate villages were combined into the Pottersbury union, which had a total population of only 5,934. To appease Lord Grafton, and thereby reinforce his dominance, Pottesbury union was also not centred in a market town, contravening legislation.

It was common for major landholders to apply this type of pressure.[14] For example, at Brackley union the Cartwright family of Aynho Park dominated proceedings, while Sir Charles Knightley of Fawlsey Hall held influence over Daventry union. In each case the market town principle was compromised if it did not suit the interests of a landed proprietor. Worst affected was Hardingstone union, on the outskirts of Northampton town. Local magnates refused to lose parishes to Northampton union. Instead, Edward Bouverie (a Whig squire) and the marquess of Northampton (based at Castle Ashby) applied political pressure to ensure that their local status was consolidated at Hardingstone. As a result, Northampton poor law union was a 'long straggling agglomeration of parishes', in which landed magnates had little interest

---

[10] Greenall, *Northamptonshire*, 79–82.

[11] A. Brundage, 'The landed interest and the New Poor Law: a reappraisal of the revolution in government', *EHR* lxxxvii (1972), 27–48.

[12] *Report of his majesty's commissioners for inquiring into the administration and practical operation of the poor laws*, PP 1834 xxvii–xxix.

[13] Brundage, 'The New Poor Law', 34–5

[14] Ibid. 31.

Table 1
Poor law unions and their population levels
in Northamptonshire, 1835–6

Poor law union	Ex-officio guardians	Elected guardians	Parishes	Population
Pottersbury	4	18	11	5,954
Towcester	6	31	23	12,142
Brackley	11	33	33	13,351
Brixworth	3	38	33	13,571
Hardingstone	4	22	20	8,019
Wellingborough	5	36	26	18,383
Northampton	2	31	17	21,761
Kettering	6	33	30	15,502
Daventry	7	34	28	19,137
Thrapston	2	30	25	11,105
Oundle	4	40	32	12,120
Peterborough	8	45	40	20,934

Source: Brundage, 'The New Poor Law', 43.

Note that the listing of poor law unions reflects source material.

or judged irrelevant to their wider political concerns.[15] It was therefore one of the few poor law boardrooms in the county where middle-class professionals, tradesmen and a shopkeeping elite had some influence. This would have important, and unanticipated, political implications in the 1890s with the coming of poor law democracy, when new political leaders in Northampton town helped to rally opposition to demand poor relief, pension and welfare changes.

Meanwhile, some unions were combined around market towns, notably at Towcester, Peterborough and Oundle. But this added to, rather than detracted from, the power of families living in the hinterlands of those county towns. Thus, the Fermors of Easton Neston continued to dominate poor law matters around Towcester; 'Lords Cardigan, Westmorland, Montagu and Winchelsea' crowded Oundle union's boardroom, making it a Tory enclave; and Earl Fitzwilliam (Milton Park) and the marquess of Exeter (Burghley House) applied considerable political pressure in the Peterborough union to maintain Whig influence.[16] Throughout Northamptonshire the poor law redrew and reinforced social cohesion. Little wonder that central government reported that 'whenever the bonds which united landlords and tenants have been, from past causes, loosened, the association of the two classes at the several

15 Ibid. 38–9.
16 Ibid. 34–7.

boards of guardians throughout the country will tend to re-establish that connection, which, for the advantage of both, should ever subsist between them'.[17] The New Poor Law in Northamptonshire was thus characterised by continuities.

Three features of the Northamptonshire poor law experience provide ample proof of such continuities. At first property qualifications were introduced in guardian elections, under clause 40 of the New Poor Law. Antony Brundage explains how it operated in rural Northamptonshire:

> Landowners could cast one vote for the first £50 of annual land value, and a further vote for each £25, up to a maximum of six. Furthermore, owners were allowed to vote by proxy. The new ratepayer franchise was one vote for land valued up to £200, two votes for land between £200 and £400, and three votes for land valued over £400. Thus power in the parish was transferred to the large proprietors and tenants and away from small farmers and tradesmen who often controlled the democratically elected parish vestry. An individual could vote both as owner and ratepayer, and thus it was entirely possible for a large resident proprietor to cast nine votes.[18]

The dominance of the propertied class at election time was intensified by Justice of the Peace *ex-officio* status. Consequently landowners and their tenant farmers controlled the local social and political scene. Eleven out of thirty-three Brackley union guardian seats, for instance, were allocated to magistrates. This evidence contrasts with the findings of Byung Khun Song and David Eastwood for Oxfordshire, where the magistracy had been influential but thereafter its authority declined.[19] Put simply, in Northamptonshire there were just too many 'squires and spires' on the ground for there to have been immediate and substantial changes in the poor law. The landed influence may have been eroded as the nineteenth century progressed, but in the Midlands agricultural heartland that decline would be very slow, preserved by numerical strength.[20]

Also underlying poor law continuity in Northamptonshire was the uneven distribution of guardian seats. Small villages often elected a disproportionate number of guardians. Hanging Houghton had just thirteen residents and two guardians: it elected the same number of guardians as Moulton village with 1,319 inhabitants.[21] Large landowners also pressurised the assistant poor law

---

[17] *Report into the administration of the poor laws*, 410.

[18] Brundage, 'The New Poor Law', 29–30. See also, for example, the following older but none the less still excellent books: V. D. Lipman, *Local government areas, 1834–1945*, London 1949; B. Keith-Lucas, *The English local government franchise: a short history*, London 1952, and *English local government in the nineteenth and twentieth centuries*, London 1977; K. B. Smellie, *A history of local government*, 4th edn, London 1968; and J. Redlich and F. W. Hirst, *The history of local government in England*, 2nd edn, London 1970.

[19] B. K. Song, 'Continuity and change in English rural society: the formation of poor law unions in Oxfordshire', *EHR* lxiv (1999), 314–38; Eastwood, *Governing rural England*.

[20] Cannadine, *Decline and fall*, introduction.

[21] Brundage, 'New Poor Law', 42.

commissioner into letting let them manipulate safe guardian seats. They alone had the power to sign guardian nomination papers at election time in their estate villages. In this way they could move into power a land agent, clergyman or tenant farmer who would act in the interests of the absentee landowner. Such gerrymandering remained a prime grievance until the Local Government Act of 1894 redistributed seats per head of population.

A final aspect of continuity was that even when landowners took little interest in poor law matters, their more enthusiastic lieutenants (land agents, clergy, tenant farmers) were often elected on a regular basis. Local poor law politics gave ambitious men a forum to promote their interests, whether economic and political, or provided a means of social climbing. Absent landlords were thus free to enjoy their traditional sporting pastimes, hunting and fishing or socialising during the season in London, secure in the knowledge that their representatives were managing their poor law interests.[22] Northamptonshire poor law records are filled with examples of this type of political bargaining between landlord and tenant, as the specific practicalities of the Brixworth union will show.

Meanwhile, other equally important socio-economic changes that impacted upon poor law matters were taking place: enclosure and the commercialisation of agriculture; industrialisation (both proto-industrialisation and the growth of concentrated manufacturing) and urbanisation; and population growth which increased mobility and stretched resources (notably, housing, sanitation, employment opportunities) in certain localities. Each of these factors influenced the development of poor law decision-making in the region.

Ron Greenall observes that Northamptonshire in 1750 was 'predominately [an] open-field county, only a quarter or so of its parishes being enclosed – a century later open-field cultivation had virtually all gone'.[23] The heyday of local enclosure was between 1760 and 1792. Greenall points out that 'so much of Northamptonshire was enclosed ... the county might serve as a textbook example'. Certainly Jeanette Neeson has shown in her study of enclosure patterns that the process was very extensive and resulted in the poor losing significant common rights across Northamptonshire.[24] Greenall concurs pointing out that 'enclosure satisfied all the people that mattered in rural society – the large landowner, the parson and the farmer'. Yet there has been some dispute about the value of the loss of common rights across the county too. Leigh Shaw Taylor's recent work on the duke of Buccleuch's Boughton estate at Weekly parish near Kettering has queried the material value of common rights, while more widely Peter King has shown the significance to poor people of gleaning, firewood gathering and grazing on common land in south-east England. King emphasises that shrinking customary rights were

22 Howkins, *Reshaping rural England*.
23 Greenall, *Northamptonshire*, 83.
24 J. Neeson, *Commoners, common right, enclosure and social change, 1700–1820*, Cambridge 1993.

seen as a loss.[25] Perception, rather than reality, therefore, probably shaped poor people's reaction to enclosure: debates about common rights never receded. Moreover, despite apparent social stability elsewhere in the county, in the Brixworth union protests about enclosure and the loss of common rights did break out. At West Haddon, for example, there was an enclosure riot in 1764, followed by several 'Swing' incidents in the 1830s. Such protests about socio-economic injustices set an important precedent for future demands for poor law reform. Meanwhile, what mattered to labourers was that enclosure generated economic hardship. It also concentrated local power. Over time that power base acted as a political bulwark, limiting the labouring poor's ability to voice socio-economic and political grievances. Moreover, the New Poor Law reaffirmed the landed *status quo* by denying the poor traditional access to the magistracy appeal process under the Old Poor Law. It is a striking feature of Northamptonshire society that this did not result in widespread social unrest, unlike nearby East Anglian counties such as Norfolk. The predominance of the shoemaking industry explains the relative stability of social relations.

The proto-industrialisation of rural society has been the subject of considerable study in England and Europe.[26] In Northamptonshire shoemaking infiltrated local cottage economies; its importance helps to explain how labourers lacking common rights were able to take advantage of different earning opportunities in the wake of enclosure. The industry developed in stages across Northamptonshire. What began as a cottage industry evolved, with mechanisation, into a factory-based economy. Thus at first Northamptonshire's mixed-farming region supplied cattle skins to the tanning industry, which were sold on to shoe artisans. The advent of war often brought economic prosperity. Contracts for army boots supported a growing trade. Small-scale manufacturers, however, did not rely on military contracts. They diversified, supplying stockings, leather goods, saddles and such-like cheaply to London purchasers. As a result, the industry underwent a slow expansion between 1777 and 1817. Generally shoes were carried on the Grand Union canal (opened in 1815), or later on the railway to expanding markets. Villagers began to rely on shoe work. Miss Doreen Norton Walker, the niece of a small-scale shoe manufacturer, explains in her oral history how this worked in Walgrave, a village close to Kettering:

---

[25] See, for example, J. Humphries, 'Enclosures, common rights and women: the proletarianisation of families in the late eighteenth and early nineteenth centuries', *JEcH* i (1990), 117–42; N. Reed, 'Gnawing it out: a new look at economic relations in nineteenth-century rural England', *Rural History* i (1990), 83–94; and T. Hitchcock, P. King and P. Sharpe (eds), *Chronicling poverty: the voices and strategies of the English poor, 1640–1840*, Basingstoke 1997, notably introduction and ch. vii for Peter King's ground-breaking work on gleaning. L. Shaw-Taylor, 'Labourers, cows, common rights and parliamentary enclosure: the evidence of contemporary comment c. 1760–1810', *P&P* v (2001), 95–127, and 'Parliamentary enclosure and the emergence of an English proletariat', *JEcH* iii (2001), 640–62, challenges current orthodoxy.

[26] There has been a vast literature on this topic, summarised in the bibliography to S. A. King and J. G. Timmins, *Making sense of the industrial revolution*, Manchester 2001.

Stephen Norton Walker owned a small business at Walgrave. His work was mainly army boot contracts. The Crimean, Franco-Prussian and African Boer wars boosted his trade. Shoe and boot patterns as well as leather was collected from the train at Lamport halt, about seven miles from Northampton. The skins and lasts were delivered to each cottage in the surrounding villages in a basket. Monday was the dropping off day, Friday the collection day. Labourers often supplemented their field incomes in the winter with a little shoe work.[27]

It was this type of cottage-based industry that sustained many local economies, even though 51 per cent of the county's population still worked the land. By 1831 it is estimated that one labourer in three did some shoe work.[28] However when mechanisation became more common around 1859, shoe-making techniques and working patterns changed. For instance, the riveting of the upper soles of men's heavy boots had to be done in town on specialised machinery. Agricultural workers were drawn from the land into rural industries and then town factories, in search of more regular work. Women did rural lace-making and straw-plaiting to supplement incomes, but this work was hard, monotonous and caused eye-strain. Gradually, women too drifted into shoe work in town. Some employers in traditional industries responded by relocating to towns. Thus, Northampton, Towcester and Wellingborough became important lace- and shoe-making centres, and, as the nineteenth century progressed, work opportunities in the towns diversified, making urban life an appealing prospect.

The pace of urbanisation in Northamptonshire was similar to that of its Midlands neighbours. The population of the town of Northampton, for example, grew considerably, while that of the county as a whole rose by 61 per cent between 1800 and 1851, from 132,000 to 212,000. Then between 1861 and 1900 it grew by a further 93 per cent, from 212,000 to 336,000 (see fig. 6).[29] Similar figures were recorded in other shoe-manufacturing centres: Kettering, Rushden and Wellingborough grew substantially. In 1801 Kettering had a population of 3,198; by 1901 it this had risen to over 30,000. Workers moved in response to enclosure, the loss of common rights and the decline of an older, less competitive, weaving industry (out-priced by northern manufacturing techniques). Thus Ron Greenall estimates that, again at Kettering, there were forty-five shoe manufacturers, turning out between 50,000 and 60,000 boots per week by 1890. Yet the socio-economic transition from traditional industries to shoe-manufacturing was seldom smooth. The plight of the poor across Northamptonshire was acute between 1794 and 1834; for example, in the 1820s, at the former weaving centres of Kettering and Long Buckby, residents were 'half-starved ... and their sufferings would last for

---

27 Miss Doreen Norton Walker (1999), Brixworth union project, oral history.
28 Greenall, *Northamptonshire*, 103–7.
29 *Northampton town census returns for Northamptonshire, 1841–1901* (NRO).

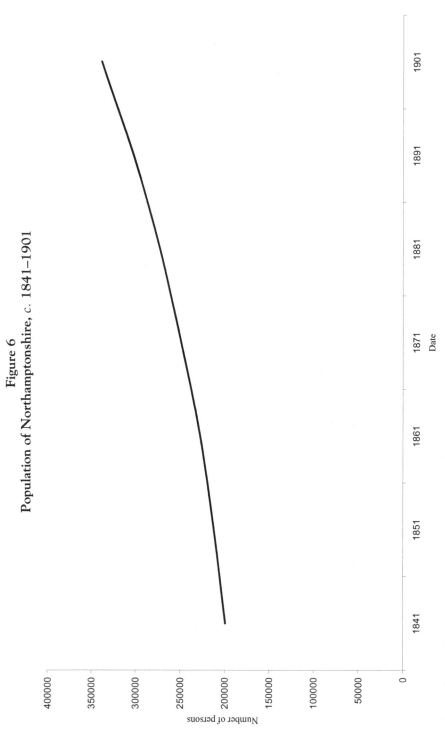

Figure 6
Population of Northamptonshire, c. 1841–1901

Number of persons

Date

400000
350000
300000
250000
200000
150000
100000
50000
0

1841   1851   1861   1871   1881   1891   1901

Source: Brixworth union, census returns, 1841–1901, NRO

nearly two generations'.[30] Employment options were patchy. As late as the 1890s poor people in villages often depended on small-scale shoe work at home in order to survive without recourse to poor relief.

Urbanisation, however, was not a boon for everyone. Often it caused endemic social problems. Greater mobility motivated migrants but it also stretched housing stocks, resulting in inadequate sanitary standards. Likewise insufficient medical services were strained. Thus, death, disease and destitution were common experiences in growing towns.[31] Of course, these social problems were not new. Fire, plague and epidemics had all been overcome in the past. Yet, it was the rate of population pressure and the degree of socio-economic change that threatened to overwhelm local resources. Ratepayers became very concerned about the impact of this level of socio-economic change on the poor law. Could the rates cope with so many claimants? Who would house the poor flooding into towns? These questions were repeated in local weekly newspapers such as the *Northampton Mercury* (Liberal) and *Northampton Herald* (Conservative). By contrast, the *Northampton Guardian* supported the radical view that 'something has to be, nay must be done, for the poor'.[32] Journalists reported that there were considerable discrepancies in wage rates across the county and that these influenced poor law decision-making.

Economic historians, such as Jane Humphries and Peter Lindert, remind us that the calculation of real earnings is complex.[33] Variables such as life-cycle, gender, physical fitness, ill-health, as well as access to a range of work opportunities, all have to be taken into account. In addition, the 'actual achievements' of working people, as Amartya Sen observes, and their 'capability to function' as independent earners need to be quantified.[34] 'Significant wage diversities' can distort realities and result in an 'empirical mess' if handled uncritically. Nevertheless, any welfare history needs at least a broad sense of the complexities of relative versus absolute poverty. In Northamptonshire, although there is very little empirical work, it is possible to estimate some general, though complex, income levels.

Average wage levels for shoe-making in Northamptonshire varied considerably. For example, manufacturers with numerous factories often paid according to skills, output and contract demands. If the army needed boots because of a shortage, extra wages were paid to increase productivity rates.

---

30 Greenall, *Northamptonshire*, 103–7.

31 A. Hardy, *The epidemic streets: infectious disease and the rise of preventative medicine, 1856–1900*, Oxford 1993, provides an excellent appraisal of the medical challenges and dilemmas arising from urbanisation, and the various solutions proposed.

32 The *Northampton Guardian* ran a campaign on this issue throughout 1873–4.

33 See, for example, S. Horrell and J. Humphries, 'Old questions, new data, and alternative perspectives: families' living standards in the industrial revolution', *JEcH* lii (1992), 849–80, and P. Lindert, 'Unequal living standards', in R. Floud and D. McCloskey (eds), *The economic history of Britain since 1700, I: 1700–1800*, Cambridge 1994 edn, 357–86.

34 A. Sen, *Inequality re-examined*, Oxford 1992, 109–10, 116, 135, 150.

That said an average shoe worker in the Midlands could expect to earn more per week than his/her agricultural counterpart.[35] This meant that whilst a rural labourer earned around 13s. per week by the 1890s, the equivalent take-home pay for shoe hands was 17s. If a labourer were a skilled shoe hand, he or she might earn almost 20s. in a good week. Of course few were skilled. It took time to train and become factory efficient. Nevertheless, a worker in a shoe factory was usually better off than a field labourer. Factory conditions also improved considerably over the course of the nineteenth century. Although noisy and cramped, buildings were warm.[36] By contrast, damp fieldwork caused severe rheumatism. Most common day labourers were forced to retire by the age of fifty. Yet few abandoned agricultural work altogether. This was because they lacked the transferable skills to get regular shoe work following mechanisation. Life, for those lagging behind on the land, was hard.

Pamela Horn's research on labourers' earnings in Northamptonshire shows that rural wages were around 9s. per week in the 1850s, rising to 11s. in the 1860s, and on average 13s. by the 1890s.[37] However, these income levels should not be taken at face value. It is noteworthy (see chapter 5) that the agricultural sector experienced an unprecedented recession in the 1880s. Wage levels were seldom static. Even where there was a measure of stability of employment fewer labourers shared in shrinking profit margins. Consequently, it is worth reiterating that whilst there was a consistent drift from the land into towns, that process took time and many families managed their finances by engaging in both urban and rural work. It is this complex wage pattern that is so difficult to quantify.

Welfare historians could, of course, try to characterise income levels by comparing wage rates to the density of population. This might indicate the relative prosperity of the labouring community across the county. Ian Levitt estimates that the density of paupers as a percentage of the total population of Northamptonshire was between 7.5 per cent and 8.49 per cent in 1837. This compares with between 5.5 per cent and 6.49 per cent around 1869 and between 2.5 per cent and 3.49 per cent by 1909.[38] However, like average wage levels, these statistics, which were centrally collected, must not be accepted uncritically. Poor law performance judged exclusively from pauperism returns often skews reality. Unquestionably local elites disguised both the causes and the levels of pauperism from poor law district auditors.

The implications of these general socio-economic findings are that on the eve of the *crusading* experiment Northamptonshire was relatively pros-

[35] A. Fox, *A history of the National Boot and Shoe Operatives, 1874–1957*, London 1958.

[36] F. T. Markland, 'Boot and shoe industry buildings: an examination of the large 19th-century factory buildings in Northamptonshire', unpubl. MSc. diss. Oxford Brookes 1998.

[37] P. L. R. Horn, 'Nineteenth-century Naseby farm workers', *NP&P* iii (1968/1970), 167–73, and *Rural world*.

[38] I. Levitt 'Poor law and pauperism', in J. Langton and R. J. Morris (eds), *An atlas of industrialising Britain, 1780–1914*, London 1986, 160–3.

perous. Agriculture dominated local life, but industrialisation was reshaping the landscape in the way that enclosure had a century earlier. The county had no major city, but in common with nearby agricultural districts, major towns like Northampton, Kettering and Wellingborough were growing fast in population terms. Rapid urbanisation brought endemic social problems and increased mobility. The coming of the railway, wider newspaper circulation and proximity to London, meant that national issues started to influence local life. Nevertheless, Northamptonshire was also a deeply conservative county, led by a landowning elite that protected its economic interests. Against this backdrop the New Poor Law was supported by a coalition of aristocrats, gentry, clergy and tenant-farming magistrates. They viewed the new legislation as an opportunity to reconfigure their power, thereby ensuring that it continued. The future looked set to replicate the past, especially in the specific socio-economic and political landscape of the Brixworth union.

The Brixworth poor law union

The Brixworth union was at the centre of a Northamptonshire poor law world. In 1835 the assistant poor law commissioner for the area completed the delicate task of negotiating its boundaries. The 3rd Earl Spencer scrutinised the New Poor Law arrangements: he intended to influence how the those boundaries were drawn. As a leading member of the Whig government and lord lieutenant of the county he pressurised the relevant central government authorities to allocate his Althorp estate villages to a rural poor law union that he could control. Consequently, the Brixworth union was an odd geographical shape, stretching from the edge of Northampton, northwards to the outskirts of Market Harborough, and west towards Daventry (see map 2). It was not based upon a market town; instead a workhouse was built in 1835–6 in Brixworth parish itself, the logical centre of the district.

The population of the Brixworth union in 1834–5 was 13,571, covering thirty-three parishes, each of which elected a guardian of the poor.[39] The assistant poor law commissioner allocated guardian seats under section 38 of the New Poor Law Amendment Act. Although the legislation stipulated that at least one seat ought to be assigned to each parish, it made no special provision for more populous districts. Clearly this could skew the distribution of seats per head of population. In this case it resulted in major landowners having proportionately greater power on the Brixworth union board of guardians. Antony Brundage estimates that 'the twenty least populous parishes' in the Brixworth union 'provided twenty elected guardians', which gave them 'a majority of the elective part of the board', although they only represented

---

39 *Kelly's directory*, Northampton 1894, summarises the Brixworth union's features between 1834 and 1894. The number of parishes was later increased to thirty-six under boundary changes.

Map 2. Mid-Northamptonshire showing the location of Brixworth and the surrounding villages of the Brixworth union in the nineteenth century.

around '24% of the total population' of the district.[40] This was one of a series of poor law discrepancies that would spark much political tension amongst ordinary working people. Farmers, in particular, would learn to their political cost that ignoring such grievances was a key error. For whereas in 1871 Brixworth was a farmers' parliament, by 1895 it would be a labouring democracy. How, therefore, did farming interests dominate the poor law scene for so long in economic terms?

Although, in the Brixworth union, farming interests controlled the administration of the poor law, giving farmer guardians considerable economic and political power, this was by no means guaranteed: agriculture in the county experienced four distinct periods of change in the course of the nineteenth century. Greenall dates these as the era that culminated in the ending of the Napoleonic Wars in 1815: the period of the corn laws, 1815–46; the high-farming experience of 1846–74; and the agricultural crisis and its aftermath, 1874–1914.[41] Whilst agricultural historians dispute the timings of each shift and their impact on different communities, these were the general farming trends that influenced the local economy. The Brixworth union was a mixed-farming district due to the richness of its soil. Major cereal crops, such as wheat, were grown. The area was also a large-scale producer of wool and meat, with animal skins sold on to the local shoemaking industry. Accurate statistics on farming were not collected until 1866, when it was recorded that Northamptonshire had a total of 271,000 acres of arable land and 252,000 acres under grass for pasture.[42] Although there is no equivalent data available for the Brixworth union, farming in the area appears to have reflected county trends.

There were, in the nineteenth century, five major landowners resident in the Brixworth union who dominated agricultural life: Earl Spencer (Althorp, 17,030 acres), Lord Overstone (Overstone, 15,045 acres), Sir James Langham (Cottesbrooke, 9,118 acres), Viscount Clifden (Holdenby, 4,774 acres) and Sir Charles. Isham (Lamport, 3,112 acres) (*see* map 1). Collectively these men controlled 49,079 acres out of a total acreage of 60,376 in the Brixworth union area (*see* table 2). Moreover, three of the largest estates were brought together under the management of the Spencer family's land agent, for when the 5th Earl Spencer succeeded in 1857 he agreed to merge control of his estate with that of his brother-in-law Viscount Clifden (who lived abroad)[43] and Lord Overstone (a family friend, political ally and London banker). The Spencers' land agent was instructed to co-ordinate farming practices to

---

40 Brundage, 'The New Poor Law', 42.
41 Greenall, *Northamptonshire*, 89.
42 *Royal Commission on the Employment of Children, Young Persons and Women in Agriculture, 1st report* 1867, PP xvii, evidence of F. H. Norman, inspector for Northamptonshire, at pp. 110–21.
43 Spencer, *Spencer family*, 260, explains that Viscount Clifden was married to Lilah Seymour, eldest sister of the 5th Earl Spencer's wife, Charlotte Francis Frederica Seymour.

Table 2
Parishes of the Brixworth union, Northamptonshire, 1871

Parish	Area in acres	Inhabited houses
Cold Ashby	1,940	101
Naseby	3,690	148
Thornby	1,212	54
Guilsborough &		140
Hollowell	3,080	61
Cottesbrooke	2,780	48
Great Creaton	790	112
Spratton &		201
Little Creaton	2,810	13
Ravensthorpe	1,330	104
Coton	860	20
Teeton	681	22
Holdenby	1,855	34
East Haddon	2,572	155
Brington &		188
Althorp	3,761	16
Harlestone	2,530	136
Church Brampton	1,100	34
Chapel Brampton	1,330	43
Pitsford	2,700	136
Boughton	1,850	87
Moulton	1,680	394
Moulton Park	450	2
Overstone	1,940	47
Holcot	1,670	96
Brixworth	3,410	246
Scaldwell	1,060	92
Lamport &		29
Hanging Houghton	1,440	26
Haselbech	1,648	34
Maidwell	1,650	51
Draughton	1,477	37
Faxton &		18
Mawsley	2,120	2
Old	1,650	99
Walgrave	2,040	154
Harrington	1,270	45
Totals	**60,376**	**3,225**

Source: Brixworth union poor law records, census returns, 1841–1900.

Note that parishes do not equate with guardian seats, and that that the listing of poor law unions reflects source material.

maximise profits. In 1866 the agent informed central government that he was in the rare position of having *de facto* control over the whole district. He managed about 1,000 tenants and set the tone in farming practices for the whole of the Brixworth union.[44]

The Spencers' land agent was John Noble Beasley, a renowned agriculturalist. In 1838 he helped his employer found the English Agricultural Society (later the Royal Agricultural Society of England) and began to transform farming in the Brixworth union.[45] Beasley promoted new scientific farming techniques by writing handbooks on drainage, crop rotation and fertilisation methods, stressing the importance of larger capital investment in farm improvements.[46] He was fond of quoting this maxim when farmers asked him about best work practice:

> A little less indulgence in the bed,
> A little more arrangement in the head,
> A little more devotion in the mind,
> Would quite prevent your being so behind.[47]

Beasley's influence, with his employer's support, persuaded many tenant farmers in the Brixworth union to initiate major farm improvements and building works in the mid-Victorian period. These were usually financed by large loans through the new farming bank in the area, the Northampton Union Bank Ltd.[48] Capital outlay was offset against improved crop yields and buoyant meat or wool prices at market to repay loan interest. Steadily farming became a larger-scale business. By the later Victorian period the development of high-farming caused significant changes in local wage conditions. The records of Spencer's land agent show that tenant farmers employed a diverse rural workforce. In common with nearby East Anglian counties, like Norfolk, workers were paid on a sliding wage scale, with skilled workers paid more than their unskilled counterparts.[49] However, in this area of mixed-farming, arable and animal husbandry skills were respected equally. The team man who drove the horses to plough or harvest crops was usually paid at the same

44 *Royal Commission on the Employment of Women*, evidence of J. Beasley, q.19 at pp. 430–1.
45 N. Goddard, *Harvests of change: the Royal Agricultural Society of England, 1938–1988*, Warwick 1988.
46 J. Beasley, *A lecture delivered to the members of the Faringdon Agricultural Club on the duties and privileges of the landowners, occupiers and cultivators of the soil*, London 1860, 1–48; R. Greenall, 'Three nineteenth-century agriculturists', *NP&P* vii (1988/9), 457–9. Beasley worked for the Spencer family from the 1840s until his death in 1874 when he was succeeded by his son Joseph Noble Beasley (1874–85) and then by John Morley (1885–1910).
47 Beasley, *Duties and privileges*, 37.
48 The archive of the Northampton Union Bank Ltd has recently been opened to scholars by its successor the National Westminster Bank plc at their headquarters in Cornhill, London.
49 Howkins, *Poor labouring men*, 26.

Table 3
Wage levels in Brington parishes in the Brixworth union, Northamptonshire, 1870–1

Occupation	Weekly wage levels	Charitable or outrelief supplements
Skilled labourers		
Grazier/stockman	20s.	No
Under gamekeeper	17s.	No
Stableman	15s.	2 weeks bread/meat/shoes
Waggoner/carter	14s.	2 weeks bread/meat/shoes
Shepherd	14s.	2 weeks bread/meat/shoes
Groom	12s.	No
Skilled artisans		
Mason	20s.	No
Carpenter	16s.	No
Blacksmith	16s.	No
Brickmaker	15s.	Gift of shoes per annum.
Sawyer (woodsman)	15s.	No
Fence carpenter	13s. 6d.	1 week meat
Unskilled labour		
Labourers	12s.	2 weeks bread/meat/shoes + outrelief 2s. 6d. per week

Source: J. Beasley, 'The number of the poor and working class people in Brington parish taken in December, 1871', NRO, MSS Spencer, misc. vol., 7f 5.

rate as the stockman who looked after cattle. Shepherds, carters and yardmen were generally better paid than common labourers (*see* table 3).

Further analysis of comparable land agents' records would be needed in order to assess how representative the wage structure outlined in table 3 was, but it provides insights into pay scales on the largest landed estate in the area. A leading guardian was later to describe the occupational profile of the district on the eve of the *Crusade* in 1870 as follows:

> The union in which I acted as a guardian might be termed a rural one in 1870. I do not remember a factory at that time in it; each village, except the smallest, had a shoemaker or cobbler, a hedge carpenter, a baker, a publican, a tailor, possibly a butcher, and many skilled labourers, clever thatchers, hedge-cutters, and drainers, of whom it might be said that most took a pride in their work ... but ... if you paraded all the inhabitants – peers, parsons, squires, yeomen, farmers, gentleman at large, and the residue, big and little – one out of every twelve in the assemblage was a pauper.[50]

[50] A. Pell, *The reminiscences of Albert Pell sometime MP for south-Leicestershire*, ed.

For this reason gifts of bread, meat and shoes on the Althorp estate were important supplements to income, even for better paid skilled workers.[51] In general farm 'labourers' did most of the daily agricultural tasks, but this generic term encompassed a very diverse range of workers.[52] Little is known about their rates of pay, but sampling the records of Spencer's land agent reveals that most were annual, common and day labourers paid according to their skill and local wage agreements with individual tenant farmers. The Royal Commission on Women, Young Persons and Children Employed in Agriculture (1867) recorded that on average male labourers earned 12s. per week and so were the lowest paid agricultural workers, but many worked for as little as 9s. in years of bad harvest. Spencer's land agent recorded that increasingly labourers were paid at piecework rates, which varied considerably according to seasonal requirements and the nature of the task.[53] He further noted that relations between employer and employee became somewhat tense and antagonistic because of the growth of this wage pattern. This was one reason why labourers on the Althorp estate received more income supplements. The unpredictability of seasonal wage rates, loss of work on rainy days and disagreements about productivity rates, strained labour relations. As Keith Snell suggests, 'rural antagonism' in the East Anglian Victorian countryside was 'predominantly landlord/farmer/clergyman versus labourer' over issues, such as 'unemployment, farm machinery, enclosure, … the game laws, low wages, tied cottage insecurity, the operation of the poor law' and the control of charities.[54]

Research on the nature of class antagonism in rural Northamptonshire is patchy. Eric Hobsbawm and George Rudé found that there was a total of only nineteen 'Swing' incidents in the county prior to the New Poor Law, compared to 208 in Hampshire, 88 in Norfolk and 40 in Suffolk.[55] Although Northamptonshire figures are low, five of the major 'Swing' incidents (26%) occurred within the Brixworth union. Why rural antagonism was more marked in this part of Northamptonshire is unclear. Ron Greenall suggests that the Brixworth union had a definite Nonconformist character: Baptists and Congregationalists had a strong presence throughout the nineteenth century.[56] In addition, 'Old Dissent and even older strains of Puritanism' surviving from the Cromwellian era had deep roots in the area, which may have been linked to a strong radical tradition. Recent work by Bridget Lewis on the allotment movement in the 1830s reveals that some landowners, like Sir

---

T. McKay, London 1908, 163. This book was an autobiography but McKay agreed to edit and write the introduction as a favour to Pell for his COS work.

51 These were usually given at Christmas.

52 Howkins, 'Peasants, servants and labourers', 49–62, makes this point about the diversity of labourers' work.

53 *Royal Commission on the Employment of Women*, Beasley q. 19, at pp. 429–31.

54 Snell, 'Deferential bitterness', 160.

55 Hobsbawm and Rudé, *Captain swing*, appendix 1 at pp. 148–9.

56 Greenall, *Northamptonshire*, 78.

James Langham of Cottesbrooke, feared the growth of this type of radicalism and responded by promoting allotment schemes to diffuse social tensions.[57] That reaction to social unrest seems to have set a precedent to which farmers reverted whenever relations were more strained. Thus, sampling Spencer's land agent's labour books reveals that when relationships between farmers and labourers started to deteriorate as a result of changes in the poor law and in farming practices, a series of income supplements were restored to try to temper welfare grievances.[58]

The coming of the New Poor Law unquestionably represented a harsh change in official poor law practices. In particular, guardians now administered outdoor relief as a gift, when it had previously been seen as a parish birthright.[59] The New Poor Law altered social relations to such an extent that by the 1850s the farming community was concerned that endemic social tensions might undermine their long-term economic interests.[60] In the Brixworth union, therefore, almshouses for widows, regular medical outdoor relief doles for the sick poor and charitable provision (gifts of clothing, food, fuel and shoes to the poor) were revived.[61] By the 1860s larger landowners, like Spencer, often paid long-serving estate workers small loyalty pensions in old age, usually the equivalent of average outdoor relief doles of 2s. 6d. per week.[62] Guardians also paid funeral costs on behalf of poorer residents who wanted to bury their loved ones in a customary manner. A medical order claim covered both the cost of a new woollen shroud to lay out a body for inspection during the brief period of mourning and the purchase of the basic wooden coffin, usually made by a local carpenter. Although the range and variety of these benefits was diverse and hence it is difficult to generalise about their effects on different parishes, they do seem to have mitigated the worst aspects of the New Poor Law and profit-driven farming. It is important to note that these benefits did not replace outdoor relief. Instead, the poor regarded charity and outdoor relief as essential income supplements. Moreover, poor law records also indicate that these poverty safety nets altered the subtle balance of socio-economic relations in several significant ways.

---

[57] I am indebted to Bridget Lewis for sharing with me her research on allotments from her thesis 'Charitable provision in Northamptonshire, 1785–1870', unpubl. PhD diss. Leicester 2002, ch. vii. This can be cross-referenced to 'Petition of tenants, Cottesbrooke to Sir James Langham, 6th Dec. 1830', MSS Langham, NRO, L(C) 1163.

[58] See, for example, misc. vol. 7cl, Althorp farm labour books, 1842–57; misc. vol. 7c2, Brampton farm book, 1844–53; misc. vol. 7b3, Althorp Park daily journal of labourers' work, 1859–76, MSS Spencer.

[59] Snell, *Annals of the labouring poor*, 227, argues that the loss of parish birthright created a 'heritage of distrust' in nineteenth-century rural life.

[60] Howkins, *Reshaping rural England*, 74, comments that this was a common reaction in many rural areas during the high-farming era.

[61] H. Nethercote to Spencer, 31 Oct. 1869, MSS Althorp, K383, discusses the importance of medical outdoor relief customary payments in the Brixworth union by the 1860s.

[62] J. Beasley to Spencer, 1871–2, MSS Spencer, Sox 571, outlines these conventions. See, for example, letters of 14, 15 Feb. 1871, and 7 May 1872.

The problem with reviving older customary notions of social responsibility was that farmers in the area were trying to achieve two incompatible goals. On the one hand, they rejuvenated customary expectations to ensure greater social stability and thus protect profitability. On the other hand, they stressed that paternalistic gestures were gifts that could be withdrawn if profits plummeted, which undermined their first aim. Over time this raised the expectations of poorer residents with regard to 'entitlements', which later proved difficult to eradicate. Temporary poor law leniency, therefore, often inflamed, rather than resolved, deep-seated social tensions. Any future farming developments that undermined precarious 'makeshift' economies, whether this involved withdrawing charity, lower wages or harsher poor law attitudes, were resented. The complexities of unstable economic relations are difficult to tease out in the 1860s. Nevertheless they existed and shaped a delicate 'mixed economy of welfare' in the Brixworth union prior to the outdoor relief controversy.

John Archer comments that revived notions of paternalism had only a partial success in the high-farming era, otherwise agricultural trade unionism would not have emerged with such force in the early 1870s in rural England.[63] A major flash point was the perennial problem of underemployment which was a motivating factor behind union combination. A leading gentleman farmer in the Brixworth union, Albert Pell, described employment difficulties in the high-farming period:

> I was soon settled in the Midlands, taking a farm dreadfully out of order, foul, wet and exhausted. A steam plough was just designed at Reading, so I squared up the fields into parallelograms ready for its use. … I took a twenty-one years' lease of the land, 300 acres, and at once proceeded to make bricks and drain pipes. The clay was excellent, labour was cheap and good of its kind, and the new farm premises were soon up. When winter came, I began to put the pipes in the ground. Any number of men were at my disposal, though the parish and those immediately adjacent were 'close' parishes, and the men had to walk in some cases three or four miles to their work. Sometimes I had as many as thirty applicants for work in one day.[64]

Pell stated that life was precarious for poorer families who lacked a major breadwinner in regular employment; most lived in cramped cottages, lacking basic sanitation. These families were often ill because poor diet and infected water supplies made them vulnerable to diseases such as typhoid.

Pell gave evidence to the Royal Commission on Agriculture in 1867, outlining the budget of an average family that relied on regular outdoor relief (see table 4).[65] It showed that even though guardians awarded a regular medical outdoor relief allowance to 'Mr. G.', who earned little because of long-term

63 Archer, 'By a flash and a scare', 256.
64 Pell, Reminiscences, 163.
65 Royal Commission on the Employment of Women, 2nd report, PP 1878, evidence of A. Pell, q. 12 at p. 426.

Table 4
Budget of average labouring family in receipt of medical outdoor relief, 1867

Weekly income		£	s	d
Mr G.	aged 55	ill and earned nothing		
Mrs G.	aged 44	0	2	6
Elizabeth	aged 23	lived and worked in town		
Henry	aged 18	lived and worked in town		
Daniel	aged 15	0	8	0
Sarah	aged 13	worked in service		
Kate	aged 10	earned nothing		
John	aged 7	earned nothing		
Annie	aged 5	earned nothing		
Weekly income total		0	10	6
Additional annual earnings				
Mrs G., gleaning (17 stone of flour)		0	50	0
Daniel, harvest wages		0	32	0
Daniel, harvest beer wages		0	10	0
John, bird scaring wages		0	20	0
Donations				
Milk		0	10	0
Firewood		0	5	0
Subscription to clothing club		0	10	0
Average weekly value of annual earnings & donations		0	2	8
Average earnings per week		0	13	2
Expenditure				
Rent, food, food, clothing, linen, club subscriptions		1	6	2
Weekly budget deficit before poor relief		0	13	0
Weekly medical outrelief allowance for Mr G.				
Money		0	4	0
Five loaves (6lbs)		0	4	3 ½
Weekly budget deficit		0	4	8 ½
Annual budget deficit (weekly x 52)		12	4	10

Source: Royal Commission on the Employment of Women, 1st and 2nd reports, Pell, qq. 12–13b, 20–2, pp. 426–7, 431–4.

illness, the family could not make ends meet. Donations of milk, firewood and clothing were important for subsistence. Children were often sent away into service to earn money and to save food costs. Yet, Sarah, aged thirteen, was still an economic burden because the family was liable for her clothing. The older children lived and worked in town, but do not seem to have been able to afford to send money home regularly. It is evident that the right to glean was a vital income supplement, providing seventeen stone of flour to feed the family over the winter period. This family had no opportunity to save their harvest monies to pay their rent over the winter period. Compulsory admission into the workhouse would have been inevitable without outdoor relief.

In the 1870s Pell became a committed *crusader*. His evidence therefore provides an intriguing perspective on the nature of life for 'respectable' poorer residents, whom he later came to regard as 'undeserving'. This family was living just above the local poverty line by pooling their meagre resources and applying for whatever income supplements were available. Although the question of typicality needs to be taken into account here (no record of equivalent skilled labourer or artisan income levels was recorded), it is evident that changeable employment factors could seriously disrupt a family's income.

Generally agricultural wages were stable in spring and summer provided workers stayed healthy and inclement weather did not disrupt work. However, working '6 to 6 in autumn and from 7 until dark in winter' six days a week took its toll on many common labourers, like Mr G.[66] By the 1860s few could compete with fitter younger workers when labour was more plentiful. Consequently, population levels in the Brixworth union started to decline in this period, from a high of 15,065 in 1861 to 13,866 by 1871, a reduction of 8.6 per cent.[67] This should have improved employment prospects for older labourers, but farmers, who were still continuing to focus on productivity rates, remained less willing to offer regular work. Thus the traditional problems of seasonal work and reduced wages in old age were exacerbated by underemployment.

Reflecting on the Northamptonshire poor law experience

It is apparent that the socio-economic landscape was complex in the Brixworth union when high-farming was at its peak in the 1860s. Moreover, landowners and tenant farmers dominated the board of guardians by virtue of their economic hegemony, holding on average two-thirds of the seats. The New Poor Law franchise protected their interests, by discriminating against small farmers, traders and artisans. Despite its harmonious appearance, social

---

66 Ibid. 112, notes these difficulties.
67 Brixworth union, census returns, 1841–1901, NRO

relations in the area were tense because labour relations were antagonistic. Piecework and seasonal labour requirements forced many inhabitants to rely on regular outdoor relief. Some artisans, like shoemakers and agricultural workers, began to migrate to local manufacturing towns in search of better-paid work and more stable incomes to feed their families. For the disadvantaged in rural society, who could not afford to migrate, or chose to remain, outdoor relief in cash and kind was a necessity if they wanted to avoid the workhouse. From their perspective the prosperity produced by high farming was an 'illusion' that gave way to 'the pragmatic experience of pauperism', particularly as they aged.[68]

The use of case studies provides an avenue into complex issues such as central–local relations, the changing nature of paternalism and the impact of socio-economic change at a local poor law level. By exploring the changing nature of poor relief administration this book can begin to reconstruct how it felt to be in control of, or subject to, *crusading* initiatives. The Brixworth union was moderate in poor law terms for much of the mid-Victorian period. Why it then became a test-bed for committed *crusaders*, therefore, needs further explanation. Certainly problems of underemployment meant that many working people relied on poor relief supplements on a regular basis. Some ratepayers were less inclined to fund the needy when harvest years were poor. Equally, however, many guardians recognised the economic highs and lows of local life and were resigned to higher tax bills. It is rather startling that those same guardians later became *crusaders*, ignoring the evidence of their own eyes that periodically rural society was rife with pauperism: after 1870 the advantaged turned their backs on the disadvantaged in a move with far-reaching implications. As the next chapter shows, that socio-economic context set the stage for a bitter poor law fight over the next twenty-five years.

[68] Archer, '*By a flash and a scare*', 124.

4

Setting the Poor Law Stage to Stigmatise Paupers

The previous chapter outlined how the New Poor Law created a high degree of administrative continuity throughout Northamptonshire. The large number of major landowners in the county meant that both economic and political power was remarkably stable. Indeed, contemporary accounts suggest that the New Poor Law settled down into a regular administrative pattern. This was notable in the Brixworth union. After 1865, however, the economic and political climate of the area started to change. There was a general attack on medical outdoor relief which, though unsuccessful, changed the sentiment and tone of poor law administration. Moreover, it convinced three leading guardians to become ardent *crusaders* for economic and political reasons. At the same time a series of poor harvests undermined farming profits around 1865 so that increasing financial pressure convinced a majority of farmer guardians to work together drastically to reduce outdoor relief. Most were very angry about a new threat of trade union combination at a time of low harvest yields, and were determined to use the poor law to make a pre-emptive strike against them. They adopted a *crusading* attitude to save money and to reassert their authority over the labouring poor. This finding is significant because it reveals how local conditions could drive national poor law change, anticipating central government's new *crusading* campaign. The complex relationship between unionisation and the *crusading* controversy is seldom discussed in welfare textbooks, although agricultural historians such as Arthur Brown, Pamela Horn and Alun Howkins have noted its influence.[1] Case-study analysis presents an important opportunity to examine a well-documented account of the political battle over outdoor relief from its earliest stages. By revisiting the experience of being poor and the importance of outdoor relief in local life, it is possible to start to unravel the impact of the *crusade* from its inception.

Being poor and outdoor relief

In 1866 a Royal Commission inspector for Northamptonshire visiting the Brixworth union examined employment conditions for women and children. He reported that irregular, and low wages and underemployment were the chief

---

1 See, for example, introduction, nn. 36–8.

problems for poorer residents.[2] The economies of labourers' families varied according to individual skills and ages. However, for almost all of them there were two vulnerable points in the life-cycle: young adults struggled financially as soon as they started a family; and physical decline in old age made it harder to work long and arduous hours in the field.[3] Poorer families also had very basic diets. Though rich in carbohydrates they often lacked proteins. Diseases of the 'bones, glands, eyes and skin [were] common' because of vitamin deficiencies.[4] Damp fieldwork exacerbated common medical conditions, such as asthma, bronchitis and painful rheumatic conditions. Two eminent doctors who ran the Northampton and Peterborough infirmaries noted that 'there is no question that the poor (especially women) are insufficiently fed and many of the diseases, which they are subject to, might be avoided if they had better food'.[5] The doctors commented that many women gave their food allowances to their children. For these reasons the provision of outdoor medical relief, in the form of food, medicines or help with rent, was a basic necessity in the area. Moreover, poorer families often lived in rather rudimentary and overcrowded cottages, lacking proper sanitation. Most tried to rent an average allotment of six poles (about one quarter of an acre), where they grew vegetables and potatoes (and the more fortunate kept a pig). A key expense was that rents in those parishes not controlled by a single landowner tended to be very high. Property speculators rented overcrowded tenements at exorbitant rents of around £4–5 *per annum* compared to £2–3 on landed estate villages.[6] A related financial difficulty was that most local work was allocated to estate workers and this meant that outside day labourers sometimes had to walk three or four miles to labour in the fields. If they were late for work the lost time was deducted from their weekly wages, or they earned less piece money. Spencer's land agent's records reveal that as working people aged, impoverishment was a real threat outside the workhouse. However, most people were determined to avoid indoor relief at almost any cost. In the 1890s Sidney Ward, a labourer who became a spokesman for working people, explained why the elderly feared the workhouse:

> Suppose say now, Sir, I have the privileges of liberty, a man who has lived in a cottage for years he has got a little home; it is a little castle to him, and they say when he has lived there over fifty years he and his wife have to break up their home and go into the house. He has to sell his furniture bit by bit before they go in, because if they have anything they will not give him a paper. He has to part with all, and then when he goes in he has

---

[2] *Royal Commission on the Employment of Women* (1867), Norman, pp. 110–21.

[3] See, for example, A. Digby, *Making a medical living: doctors and patients in the English market place for medicine, 1720–1911*, Cambridge 1994, and A. Hardy, *Health and medicine in Britain since 1860*, London 2001.

[4] *Royal Commission on the Employment of Women* (1867), evidence of Dr(s) W. Paley and T. Walker, qq. 14–15 at pp. 427–8.

[5] Ibid. 428.

[6] Ibid. evidence of Mrs G., q. 162 at pp. 456–7.

to part with his clothing too... He was a man who... used to go about the fields all his lifetime ... being confined there after having his liberty is very hard.[7]

The loss of liberty, having to sell possessions accumulated over fifty years, and being made to wear a pauper uniform were to be avoided if at all possible. Charitable provision (bread, fuel, clothing, meat and milk) and medical outdoor relief were therefore prized by the labouring poor in the area.

Traditional intermediaries in rural society, such as land agents and clergymen, usually distributed these benefits. A typical request from Spencer's land agent in the early 1870s gives a flavour of what life was like for older labourers:

> John Manning. He is 78 years of age has worked all his life for Lord Spencer and is predominantly a good honest man. He is now left quite alone in the world and has nothing but his parish allowance and is literally starving. An addition to his income of 2 or even one shilling would be a great boon ... Thomas Worley ... he has been a useful and valuable man. Whatever, however, he had saved is now gone. He suffers painfully from heart disease and has been unable to work but little for some time, indeed he cannot walk to work.[8]

Worley worked as a mason and then a common day labourer on Spencer's Althorp estate throughout his working life. He was a conscientious man who saved hard and contributed to a sick club so he could remain independent in old age. Unfortunately his progressive heart disease incurred a 'doctor's bill of £40', his entire life savings. When he tried to claim sickness benefit from the Great Brington Friendly Society he discovered that it was bankrupt. In the 1860s guardians started to cut back on medical outdoor relief expenditure and friendly societies were inundated with sickness claims. This was one of the chief problems with the rhetoric of self-help: it only worked if friendly societies were solvent. The land agent explained that Worley tried to work even in the depths of winter because he was determined to avoid the shame of admission to the workhouse, but this only exacerbated his ill health. Spencer agreed to give Manning and Worley small customary pensions of 2s. 6d. per week, the equivalent of their meagre outdoor relief doles. However, these were only temporary allowances because he had already asked his land agent to review all estate pensions, with a view to cutting expenditure radically:

> I wish some plan would be discussed for some superannuation fund for all whom I employ. I Would act as a Banker and pay a percentage to the Fund. It would not be difficult to draw a scheme out. Provision would be made for

---

7 *Report of the Royal Commission on Poor Relief in the case of Destitution by Incapacity for Work from Old Age, Final report*, London 1895, evidence of S. Ward, qq. 15761–4.
8 Beasley to Boyle, 30 Apr. 1872, MSS Spencer, Sox 571.

them to withdraw money. It would then be made that no parish pension would be thereafter granted.[9]

In the early 1870s there were two reasons why Spencer took this stance. He was very concerned about the Union Chargeability Act of 1865 because it altered the way that rates were levied across the district. Previously each parish was responsible for the care of all those paupers who had settlement rights.[10] In richer parishes, where a landowner might award generous charitable benefits to vulnerable members of the community, rateable expenditure on outdoor relief was low when compared to large parishes where fewer income supplements were provided. However, after 1865, every pauper in Brixworth union became the responsibility of all its parishes. Rates were pooled into one coffer, administered by the whole board of guardians.[11] In time this would lead to an overall reduction in the numbers on outdoor relief. Prior to 1865 Spencer calculated that it was in his interest to keep rates low by providing alternative sources of outdoor relief funding, such as estate pensions and charitable provision. After 1865 this was no longer a financially viable option because his charitable commitments were passing cost-saving benefits onto ratepayers throughout the Brixworth union. Thus he began to re-examine the customary system of estate pensions on his land.

A second reason for Spencer making cuts was that landowners and farmers in the area experienced a series of poorer harvests after 1865, which reduced yields. There is evidence that 'the actual level of harvest earnings' fell across East Anglia in the late 1860s, alarming farmers who had become rather complacent about 'the relative prosperity' of the high-farming period.[12] Albert Pell commented that 1867–8 was a season of very poor yields.[13] Landowners and their tenant-farmer guardians were anxious to keep rateable bills low at a time of falling profits. Consequently, most began to scrutinise expenditure on medical outdoor relief, which had risen steadily in the mid-Victorian period to nearly £6,000 per annum. When yields were poor, it was no longer advantageous, nor did it make sense, to use medical relief to retain surplus labour in the area during periods of underemployment. This signalled the beginning of the end as far as paternalistic gestures in the Brixworth union were concerned. By the 1890s they would be almost eradicated. It also marked the tentative beginnings of crusading activity.

The first significant indication that the tone and sentiment of poor law administration was shifting in the Brixworth union occurred in December

---

9 Spencer to Beasley, 15 Feb. 1871, ibid.
10 Englander, Poverty and poor law reform, 3, 12–15, 18, 44, explains that settlement rights up to 1865 were complex and usually acquired on the basis of having been born in a parish or through the paternal line. They were stipulated on a settlement certificate that had to be verified by parish overseers.
11 Rose, 'Crisis of poor relief', 50–70, is one of the few welfare historians to emphasise the significance of the Union Chargeability Act of 1865.
12 Howkins, Poor labouring men, 62.
13 Pell, Reminiscences, 233.

1866 when Albert Pell raised the controversial issue of funding medical outdoor relief.[14] He proposed that guardians should cut expenditure on medical outdoor relief and replace benefits with sickness clubs and a workhouse dispensary. The schemes would be designed along the lines of similar ventures that Pell had seen in operation in the Staffordshire potteries.[15] By April 1867 he had persuaded enough farmers to support a motion to review all medical outdoor relief procedures in the area,[16] and a committee was set up to re-examine all cases, whether applying for or already in receipt of medical outdoor relief. Expenditure patterns in the period 1846–66 were examined to ascertain 'whether the feeling of the poor is as independent as it was, or whether they are abandoning their own resources for Medical Relief out of the rates'.[17] The review took more than two years to complete. It reported in the autumn of 1869 that expenditure on medical outdoor relief was excessive and recommended that it should be abolished. At this juncture most of the farmers would not support such far-reaching recommendations, but they agreed to limit medical extras and to reduce both payments in kind and cash allowances on medical orders.[18] The threat this action posed to poorer families strained social relations in the area. It is significant that a clergy guardian who opposed the changes recalled that cuts in medical provision motivated unionisation in the area. In 1875 he reminded Spencer privately that 'I have good reason to know that the most violent agitators of the Labourers' Union derived their main influence in this Parish [Scaldwell] from the apprehension of extreme measures on the part of Guardians in the 1860s.'[19] However, this does not explain why union combination specifically developed in the district in the spring of 1872.

The guardians did not mount a full-scale attack against medical outdoor relief in 1869. Pell had failed to win the argument that lower medical bills would decrease tax bills in the long term. Crucially, however, by early 1871 attitudes amongst farmer guardians were hardening. Pell explained that in the intervening period there had been more years of low yields: 'the drought in 1870 was excessive. ... It had been remarkable in 1868, but this year was hotter and drier. ... The grass did not furnish sufficient food for livestock, and we had to lop trees for fodder'.[20] Whereas arable losses in the 1860s had been offset against buoyant wool or meat sales, by 1870–1 more expensive feeding costs reduced profits from stock. Therefore, around the same time that the Fleming Report (December 1871) was issued, recommending severe cuts in expenditure on outdoor relief, farmers in the Brixworth union were already considering taking similar local action to cut the costs of poor

14 Brixworth union guardian minute books, 2 Dec. 1866, NRO, P/L 2/14.
15 A. Pell to Spencer, 2 Dec. 1866, MSS Althorp, K372.
16 Pell to Spencer, 30 Apr. 1867, ibid.
17 Ibid.
18 Nethercote to Spencer, 31 Oct. 1869, ibid. K383.
19 J. Roberts to Spencer, 20 Mar. 1875, ibid. K157.
20 Pell, Reminiscences, 233.

relief. This exposed the true nature of social relations. It demonstrated in a visible manner that long-held notions of communal responsibility were a sham. Instead farming profit margins took precedence. However, although farmers were more amenable to a *crusading* ethos than they had been earlier, it was three COS zealots on the board of guardians who convinced them that harsher actions were justified. Essentially, they lectured to a willing audience on the merits of cutbacks in the poor law.

Three *crusading* zealots

Three guardians of the poor, all of them leading proponents of the COS ethos, championed the *crusading* cause in the Brixworth union. Of these, Albert Pell was primarily responsible for driving forward a *crusade* against outdoor relief. In 1868 he was Conservative MP for south Leicestershire and recently appointed *ex-officio* guardian of the poor for Haselbech parish. Pell's standing in the district was also derived from his extensive land holdings. He leased 685 acres of farmland on the Northamptonshire-Leicestershire border from Sir Charles Isham (his wife's cousin), and he owned the freehold of Wilburton Manor in Cambridgeshire jointly with his two brothers. In addition, his father had left him substantial property in St George-in-the-East in London.[21] When the COS was established in 1869 Pell became one of its leading members.[22] He believed that poverty was the moral fault of each individual and lax outdoor administration encouraged work-shy individuals to become welfare dependants. The COS historian Thomas MacKay described Pell's poor law convictions: 'As I have already said, upon all Poor Law matters he was a Whig of the highest economic orthodoxy, going rather beyond the famous Poor Law Commission Report of 1834, in his aversion to outdoor relief, and scotching all proposals for Old Age Pensions.'[23]

This type of self-help ideology originally 'forged the New Poor ... and located the prime responsibility for poverty upon those deemed able to help themselves'.[24] After 1870 the newly formed COS worked in close co-operation with central government to promote *crusading* initiatives in the capital and the regions. The COS was convinced that outdoor relief was a dangerous social evil and organised a formidable campaign to promote this viewpoint. Members, like Pell, were encouraged to publish articles on the subject, to raise the issue in the House of Commons and to seek office on any national body set up to debate welfare provision. Thus Pell served as chairman of the

---

21 I am indebted to David Hughes Bt, who shared with me the Pell archive still in his family's possession at Wilburton Manor, Cambridgeshire. Pell's wife was Elizabeth Barbara Pell, *née* Halford, daughter of Sir Henry Halford of Wistow Hall, Leicestershire. His father, Sir Albert Julian Pell, had been a judge in the court review of bankruptcy in London.

22 For COS historiography see chapter 2, n. 8 above.

23 McKay in Pell, *Reminiscences*, p. xiv.

24 Kidd, *State, society and the poor*, 60–3.

central committee of poor law conferences from their inception in 1869 until his retirement in the later 1890s.[25] He was an obvious choice because he was a prominent national figure with good local connections.

Pell first became interested in debates on outdoor relief when he met Mr Stevens of the Bradfield union at Westminster. Stevens had been one of the original assistant poor law commissioners, and was later a leading light in Berkshire political life and in the House of Commons. He advised Pell that many guardians did not follow outdoor relief guidelines and that this was contributing to the spiralling cost of poor relief. Pell asked him to recommend some reading on the subject. Stevens suggested a study of 'Walker, (The Original), Dr.Chalmers, Arthur Young and above all the Reports of the great Poor Law Commissioners in the 1830s'.[26] This reading list reiterates how welfare ideas on the periphery, notably in Scotland, shaped the world view of the *crusaders*. Pell's research convinced him that a *crusade* against outdoor relief was necessary:

> The administration of the Poor Laws is a matter of police, not sentiment, and should be applied unswervingly in obedience to fixed principles, and not become the haphazard display of sentiment and a counterfeit charity.... [otherwise] the incentives of industry are weakened; the fear of the consequences such as cold, hunger and distress, is diminished or vanishes; and a distinct and pernicious inducement offered to the practice of deceit and fraud, and the total abandonment of conscientious, honest effort for self-maintenance unfolds.[27]

Pell published numerous articles outlining his convictions. He was fond of repeating Arthur Young's remark that, 'in England the more money is expended, even well, and humanely, the more poor are created, and that the degree of indigence and misery is exactly in proportion to the assistance given them by rates'.[28] He was convinced that outdoor relief created a culture of welfare dependency and that guardians therefore had a duty to teach the poor that outdoor allowances were not a customary right.

Pell decided to become a committed *crusader* in the two poor law unions in which he served as a guardian. In St George-in-the-East in London he had the support of a number of national COS leaders, such as George Crowder, but in the Brixworth union he lacked supporters. Consequently he focused attention initially on the high cost of medical outdoor relief. Pell needed to

---

25 Digby, 'Rural poor', 591–602, explains that the poor law conference movement began in 1868 in the west Midlands. A central conference was established in 1869 and then this led to district conferences in all other regions by 1877.

26 Pell, *Reminiscences*, 236–7.

27 A. Pell, 'Out-relief: a paper read at a poor law conference as chairman of the central committee held at the Crewe Arms Hotel on Tuesday October 14th 1890', in *Tracts, 1843–1893*, London 1900, 1–16 (BL, ref. 8277 d. e. 29).

28 Idem, 'Arthur Young: agriculturalist, author and statesman', *Journal of the Farmers' Club* iv (1882), 62.

convince a number of leading guardians in the district that his opinions on retrenchment were correct. He decided to approach the largest landowner in the district, the 5th Earl Spencer.

Spencer was a leading Whig grandee, a close political ally of W. E. Gladstone (then prime minister) and lord lieutenant of the county. He was therefore a figure of considerable national and local political influence.[29] Pell first became acquainted with Spencer when they served together on a number of charitable bodies in the early 1860s. Spencer was kept informed by his land agent of Pell's failed attempts to abolish medical outdoor relief in 1866–9. Thereafter, both Spencer and Pell discovered that, although their political allegiances differed (Pell was a staunch Conservative, Spencer was an ardent Liberal), they agreed on poor law matters. Spencer always believed in the strict application of a workhouse test, but like most Whig grandees he preferred to delegate the tedious business of managing poor relief to his fellow guardian clients, clergy and tenant farmers.[30] However, during his first tenure as lord lieutenant of Ireland, he had begun to take a closer interest in the management of poor relief because one of his duties was to oversee a review of outdoor relief there.[31] As a leading member of a government hostile to outdoor relief, he needed to be seen to be promoting *crusading* initiatives, which were initiated by the LGB.[32] Pell envisaged Spencer exploiting his position as honorary chairman of the Brixworth union to raise the profile of a *crusading* campaign. He also saw that the Brixworth union could become a test case for the success of *crusading* (he never envisaged failure). The desire to preserve poor law power, enhance personal political prestige and a pragmatic determination to reduce the costs of pauperism, motivated men like Spencer and Pell to unite.

It is difficult to establish Spencer's motivations and the timing of his conversion to the *crusading* cause for he was a notoriously secretive man who guarded his privacy jealously. All his correspondents were asked to comply with a confidentiality agreement before he would discuss even the most mundane matters on paper. According to two Irish poor law historians

> Spencer's public personality cast him as an extremely able man who lacked a public face. In the circumstances his failure to find a biographer was not particularly remarkable. He hid the private side of his character so successfully even his colleagues were led to wonder whether it existed. No one ever got to know Spencer well.[33]

[29] Pell to Spencer, 2, 21 Jan., 19 Feb. 1861, MSS Althorp, K372.
[30] J. P. D. Gordon (ed.), *The red earl: the papers of the 5th Earl Spencer, 1835–1910*, i, Northampton 1981, 1–20, outlines Spencer's COS ethos.
[31] Power, *A paper on out-door relief*, summarises the Irish review.
[32] Sykes, *Rise and fall*, 75–87, outlines the first Liberal government's poor relief retrenchment priorities.
[33] A. B. Cooke and J. R. Vincent, 'Lord Spencer on the Phoenix Park murders', *Irish Historical Studies* xviii (1973), 585.

Edmund Gosse, librarian of the House of Lords in 1904, met Spencer and recorded that he was 'very intimidating ... although I admire him intensely ... he is certainly the most alarming figure I have yet encountered here'.[34] Spencer personified the sort of Whig who was still attached to the Liberal party in 1870, in that he supported primogeniture, religious freedom and retrenchment. It is true that he has never attracted a biographer, but despite his best efforts to hide his private self he left a remarkable record of his convictions in his intimate family correspondence and in letters to his inner circle of fellow aristocrats. He was also frank in his dealings with his trusted land agents. In public Spencer often appeared reticent but this was because he was intensely shy. Few knew that his brusque manner was a mask, hiding repeated bouts of ill health (due to severe eczema and a bad lung condition), rather than malice. Yet it must be conceded that he was also a formidable opponent when roused. He has recently been described as a 'man of spotless character in public life', but given 'his hands-on style of management' such generalisations need to be balanced with a careful appraisal of his role in local government, especially during the *crusading* decades.[35] Certainly Pell recognised in Spencer a man with considerable influence on poor law matters (both at the centre and the periphery). However, both men also needed to win the support of a local guardian, one who attended poor law board meetings regularly, for Pell and Spencer were often absent at Westminster and in Ireland respectively. That guardian needed to be a conscientious administrator and skilled bureaucrat. He had to be capable of outwitting opponents who tried to ignore poor law technicalities. Pell found his ideal candidate in his local rector, the Revd William Bury.

William Bury, rector and guardian of the poor for the parish of Haselbech, was not a natural ally for Pell. In the early 1860s he had believed in the generous provision of outdoor relief. He had a reputation for being sympathetic to the plight of the labouring poor. Bury was a pragmatist, like many guardians. However, Pell was determined to convert him to his cause. He persuaded Bury to visit every pauper on Haselbech's relieving officer's lists and apply the workhouse test. Pell hoped that this would teach Bury that the labouring poor were abusing the poor law system. Bury found that many pauper families had some savings or relatives who could support them. However, he argued that it was a clergyman's 'duty to protect these unfortunates, and that any confidences' about other sources of funding 'should not be betrayed' to the relieving officer.[36] Consequently, Pell took him on a tour of the homes of elderly paupers in the neighbourhood and showed him the appalling conditions in which they were living. The substandard housing, poor sanitation and depths of endemic poverty convinced Bury that outdoor relief only accentuated pauperism. They visited one bed-ridden female pauper

34 Gosse diary, entry for 14 Mar. 1904, House of Lords Library, London, MSS Gosse, L32.
35 Spencer, *Spencer family*, 263, 280.
36 Pell, *Reminiscences*, 238–9.

who lived 'in a miserable hut of only one room, the wall of which was made of cobble or red earth', where she slept in a recess that had been cut out of the wall.[37] She was a lace-maker, 'half- blind' from doing intricate and under-paid piece-work living in her poorly lit cottage. Pell argued that as 'the pay, supplemented by the Poor Law dole, was starvation pay' she should be forced to enter the workhouse. He informed Bury that a clergyman ought to use his position to 'guide and govern' his parishioners. As a result of these enquiries, Bury became a COS convert and a zealous *crusader*. He defended his conver-sion on the basis that although

> a reform so radical ... cannot have been effected without a certain amount of suffering often endured in silence, escaping the notice of the most careful investigation and difficult to estimate as it is to prevent. Yet, at the same time it should be remembered that such consequences, however, much to be deplored, are really due not to the reform itself, but to the neglect in former years which rendered such reform necessary.[38]

It is somewhat ironic that Bury took this viewpoint. After all, prior to 1870 abuses of outdoor relief were the result of his lax administration. But for ideo-logical reasons he was now prepared to overlook his previous poor law record and sympathy for the impoverished. Bury, like Pell, published numerous papers outlining the reasons for his conversion. He argued that 'exceptional cases of hardship, can, ought to be, and are met by individual charity', which was a much more discriminating way of relieving the poor.[39] This prevented guardians acting impulsively because 'kindness to an individual ... often means cruelty to a class'. Charity was not a legal, civil or customary right. Its judicious management encouraged thrift and independence. Instead of giving generous outdoor relief allowances, which would be 'injurious', charity could be 'safely and widely exercised'. Bury was convinced that charity, not outdoor funding, was the only appropriate safety net for the poverty-stricken in society. He explained that 'the *desire* to do good is easy enough, but to *do* good was the hardest thing' because it meant taking unpopular decisions.

By 1871 Spencer, Pell and Bury had decided to try to implement a *crusading* experiment in the Brixworth union. Pell and Bury were primarily motivated by ideology, whereas Spencer believed in a COS ethos because it was politically expedient and would cut his expenditure. At first, Pell faced overwhelming opposition amongst farmer guardians, but Spencer's influence and the growth of agricultural trade unionism in the district during 1871 persuaded many of his opponents to change allegiance. Farmers exploited Pell's *crusading* ambi-tions to make a pre-emptive strike against union combination.

---

[37] Ibid. 240–1.

[38] W. Bury, 'Report on outdoor pauperism in the Brixworth Union', in *Third annual report of the Local Government Board*, London 1873, appendix b, pp. 19–125.

[39] Idem, 'Charity and the poor law', *Poor law conference report*, London 1876, 44, and 'Poor law progress and reform', *Poor law conference report*, London 1889, 319.

Crusading and agricultural trade unionism

The timing and growth of agricultural trade unionism in south-eastern England varied considerably.[40] Pamela Horn's studies of Midlands counties suggest that in Northamptonshire it began around the early summer of 1872.[41] She found that by 1874 a number of small trade union branches in the Brixworth union were allied to the Market Harborough regional office of Joseph Arch's NALU. For example, local newspapers reported that 220 labourers met to advance union combination at the annual commemoration of the Battle of Naseby. [42] However, the recently catalogued Spencer archive reveals that agricultural trade unionism in the Brixworth union began a little earlier than Horn suggests, around March/April 1872. This confirms John Dunbabin's findings that there was some early union combination in 1871 (and more in 1872) in many corn-growing areas of south-eastern England.[43] Labourers were aggrieved at their low wage levels (around 12s. per week) when farmers were still making substantial profits. They wanted an equitable share of the profits of their labour, a 'stake in the soil', at a time when they believed that farmers could afford to pay them higher wages.[44] The advent of union combination, although highly localised at first, made a significant impact in the Brixworth union because farmers believed it undermined the traditional social order by challenging their authority.

In late March 1872 a fellow Liberal squire and *ex-officio* guardian, H. O. Nethercote, wrote to Spencer in Ireland that union combination was underway. He observed that 'the weather is winterly to a degree and the contemplated Labourers' strikes will probably be deferred to a more *convenient season* ... how the farmers are to meet increasing wages and decreasing prices I do not see'.[45] In early April Spencer's land agent reported that the outdoor relief controversy had convinced an increasing number of labourers to establish union branches: 'The Labourers are giving much trouble and forming Unions. Our own people have hitherto behaved well but I fear will get contaminated.'[46] These comments reveal that social relations in the district were very strained by the spring of 1872. Moreover, Beasley (the land agent) noted that the labourers' main complaint was that farmers expected them to put aside their differences during the harvest in the interests of profitability, but in the autumn they refused to listen to their legitimate wage demands.[47] Furthermore, traditional poor relief claimants believed that guardians were

---

40 For agricultural trade unionism see, for example, introduction, n. 36,
41 Horn, 'Nineteenth-century Naseby', 167–73, and 'Northamptonshire agricultural labourers', 371–7.
42 Idem, 'Nineteenth century Naseby', 167–8.
43 Dunbabin, '"The revolt of the field"', 68–97.
44 Ibid. 68.
45 Nethercote to Spencer, 29 Mar. 1872, MSS Althorp, K383.
46 Beasley to Spencer, 8 Apr. 1872, MSS Spencer, Sox 571.
47 Beasley to Spencer, 1 Apr. 1873, ibid.

using union combination as an excuse to act in a harsh manner. Their actions anticipated the second stage of central government's *crusading* campaign, as outlined in the Fleming Report.

Guardians defended their position by arguing that labour rates were set by market conditions and for this reason many tenant farmers had introduced piece-work wages, which paid each worker for their productivity. Beasley was one of the few guardians who understood why poorer families resented the insecurity of this unpredictable seasonal wage pattern.[48] In private he had considerable sympathy for their precarious financial situation.[49] Local newspapers also sided with the labourers' cause. 'Facts', an editorial in the *Northampton Radical* warned, 'make short work of bombastic rhetoric, about happy and contented labourers.'[50]

One of the first local unions to be formed on the Althorp estate was the 'Brington, Harlestone, Brampton and Whilton' branch, comprising 'over 200 members' in early 1872. There is no evidence that this branch was affiliated at this stage to the NALU in Warwickshire. However, a hand-written copy of a farm labourers' catechism penned by the chairman of the North Essex NALU has survived amongst Spencer papers dating from the spring of 1872.[51] It suggests that the NALU probably sent recruitment officers into the Brixworth union at that time and found a ready audience. Spencer's land agent kept a copy of the NALU's recruitment material and monitored the growing tensions between farmers and labourers. In a letter of early April 1872, Beasley informed Spencer that although a meeting had been convened between the two sides in late March to discuss wage differences, it had not been a resounding success. Though estate labourers had been persuaded not to strike *en masse* immediately, Beasley anticipated further tensions during the summer when, from the labourers' viewpoint, it would be more effective to strike during harvest. He commented that

> Your Lordships Tenants have all hired a sufficient number of men to get the Harvest and plenty more are to be had. They are giving higher wages and there have been some strikes but could not discover if the difficulty had been greater in this neighbourhood than elsewhere. I quite believe that if Farmers and labourers are left to make their own arrangements, the difficulty will soon subside. The labourers will get higher wages, which the farmers are able and willing to pay. If however busy bodies and men who want to make political capital out of anything, will unite here much mischief will be done.[52]

---

[48] Beasley to Boyle, 7 May 1872, ibid.

[49] Ibid.

[50] *Northampton Radical*, 11 Nov. 1874.

[51] 'The farm labourers' catechism – prepared for special use of those agricultural labourers who are not in a union by the chairman of the North Essex district of the National Agricultural Labourers' Union, price one penny' (undated but found in Beasley's land agent files for the Spring of 1872), MSS Spencer, Sox 393.

[52] Beasley to Spencer, 8 Apr. 1872, ibid. Sox 571.

This quotation reveals three important points. First, that one of the problems labourers faced, even during harvest, was underemployment, which decreased wage levels. Some farmers were increasing wages during harvest and then using piece-work rates to make pay cuts in the autumn, which was deeply resented. Second, even though farmers were concerned about lower profit margins, most conceded privately that higher wage demands were justified and they could afford to pay them. Third, farmers feared the growth of the NALU in the area and were determined to oppose union combination. They would not tolerate an intermediary in the district. Farmers were convinced that unionisation was encouraging labourers to make excessive demands and, if they increased wages under union pressure, they would be setting a dangerous precedent.

The Brington union did not strike in the summer of 1872. Instead its leaders tried to negotiate a wage increase. When one was temporarily introduced during harvest and then withdrawn they petitioned Spencer directly during March 1873.[53] They asked him for 'an advance of wages of 2/- [s.] per week, owing to the price of bread and all other commodities'. Farmers in the area had offered a permanent 'extra 1/- [s.] per week' but this the labourers rejected because they wanted 'a fair days pay, for a fair days work'. They explained that if they could not earn a living wage of 16s. per week they would not be able to raise their families 'respectfully': it would be impossible to remain outside the workhouse without wage increases to replace medical outdoor relief and charitable supplements. If guardians withdrew further provision of outdoor relief, then farmers would have to introduce a commensurate rise in wages, otherwise more labouring families would be impoverished. The petitioners explained that labourers could 'leave their employ to seek work at a better market' in town but that would have meant giving up their homes in tied estate cottages too, which families could not afford to do. Many young men were willing to migrate elsewhere, but married labourers with young families and older labourers were reluctant to relocate.

The Brington union was established by eight Althorp estate workers who lived in tied cottages. They risked losing their homes and their jobs. Spencer's land agent's records reveal that the union's committee members earned an average wage of 12s. per week .[54] The highest paid was a blacksmith, John Manning, aged forty-one, who earned 16s. per week. However, as well as having a wife and one daughter to support, the fact that he was an artisan/ tradesman on the Althorp estate meant that he was paid at piece-work rates, and so his wages fluctuated considerably. One of the lowest paid men was an elderly labourer, John Anderson, aged seventy-four, who earned just 10s. per week. He lived with his middle-aged son (a common day labourer on the

53 'Brington, Harlestone, Brampton and Whilton National Agricultural Labourer's Union branch petition to the 5th Earl Spencer', 27 Mar. 1873, ibid. Sox 393; Horn, 'Nineteenth-century Naseby', 167.
54 J. Beasley, 'The number of the poor and working class people in Brington parish taken in December, 1871', ibid. 7f 5, misc. vol.

Althorp estate), his daughter-in-law and their five children all aged under nine. A labourer who lived in Pitsford village in the early 1870s recalled that 12s. per week was the average wage in most villages in the Brixworth union, a reduction from the wage levels of the 1860s, and that most labouring families could barely make ends meet.[55] It seems likely that many agricultural workers in the Brixworth union who hoped to avoid compulsory admission to the workhouse felt that they had no option but to combine into trade unions. For this reason the Brington members officially joined the NALU in 1874 to try to increase their bargaining power.

The Brington petitioners asked Spencer for the use of a schoolroom on his estate for their union activities. Spencer reacted angrily, telling his land agent to 'reply to the memorialists that I am unable to alter my position, decision as to the school room'. He felt that 'it would be inconvenient to have the school room used for meetings of various grouches'.[56] Spencer, like his tenant farmers, believed that unionisation would upset the traditional social order and might have far-reaching repercussions. He therefore stressed the apolitical nature of his decision, hoping that this would dispel any class tensions, but his tenant farmers took the opposite view. Spencer's land agent revealed that the farmers supported a full-scale *crusading* campaign in order to penalise labourers for union combination:

> The Labourers have no doubt a right to form Unions, but they are doing an immense amount of mischief, and causing great disorganisation. The Farmers in several parishes have met and resolved not to increase wages at the dictation of any union. I regret this... I think it is best for employers to be passive... The farmers would be willing to meet the Labourers upon the question, but they will not meet the Union agents. It is intolerable that they should dictate terms... and that all men, skilled and unskilled, old and young, able or partly disabled, should have the same wages, is a condition to which I am sure the Farmers will never submit... One of the effects of the Unions is that many of the members have left off going to Church, and that the Poor Law Guardians have become very stringent, I think too stringent in administration of relief ... the farmers have left off subscribing to clothing and Sick Clubs, to Coal Clubs, etc. All this is creating bad feeling.[57]

Farmers retaliated against the growth of the NALU in the Brixworth union in three ways. First, they refused to negotiate with union agents which meant that wage grievances were not resolved quickly, thus accentuating local tensions. This was a common reaction for 'there was an element of double think in the

[55] T. G. Tucker, 'Memories of Pitsford one hundred years ago', NP&P i (1978), 51.
[56] 'Spencer's reply to the Brington petition', 3 Apr. 1873, MSS Spencer, Sox 393. His reply was written across the top of the petition in a characteristic memo to his private secretary on how to deal with correspondence.
[57] Beasley to Spencer, 1 Apr. 1873, ibid. Sox 571.

farmers' response to unionism'.[58] They would negotiate with labourers but not intermediaries, stressing that the latter were outside agitators. Farmers believed that they were entitled to act defensively because they, not union agents, were the labourers' true friends. Unsurprisingly, the labourers took the opposite view. Secondly, customary charitable payments, which were indispensable to labouring families, were being withheld to penalise union members and their labouring supporters. In fact 'it was common to threaten to abandon paternalism for a rigid adherence to the dictates of economics'.[59] Most farmers in the Brixworth union decided to take very harsh retaliatory action, regardless of the social cost. Thirdly, farmers changed allegiance on the poor law board and supported *crusading* initiatives. Although this was a short-sighted response, they were determined to take pre-emptive action against union combination. Attacking charity and outdoor relief was a blow from the perspective of the poor, exacerbating already very bitter social tensions.

Regional studies, notably those by Arthur Brown and Pamela Horn, have shown that many farmer guardians reacted thus. Similar discrimination in poor relief was so rife in Oxfordshire, for example, that boards of guardians in the area passed a motion at their annual conference in 1873 deploring this type of retaliatory behaviour.[60] In Essex boards of guardians acted like farmer guardians in the Brixworth union, refusing all outdoor relief applications until the NALU left the area and local branches were disbanded. One NALU Essex leader explained that retaliatory poor law action was an effective weapon: 'There lingers in their minds the cursed fear that they might be punished if they join.'[61] However, it was a very dangerous strategy. On the one hand it enabled farmer guardians to reassert their authority over the labouring community, but on the other hand it accentuated the pace of unionisation. Spencer's land agent noted that attendance at Church of England services had fallen sharply, as absence was one way of registering protest against the traditional sources of authority in the area. He also observed that labourers refused to compromise their demands when farmers acted harshly. It was probably unrealistic to demand one wage rate for every type of labourer regardless of their productivity, but the problem with the farmers' stubborn attitude was that it made labourers' intransigence seem reasonable. Increasing numbers of wage disputes and the controversy over outdoor relief created tense social divisions throughout 1872–3, but the Brixworth union farmers would not relent. In Ravensthorpe parish, on the Holdenby estate owned by Spencer's brother-in-law, farmers even 'met and bound themselves in a £50 penalty not

58 Dunbabin, '"The revolt of the field"', 87.
59 Ibid. 81.
60 Horn, 'Northamptonshire agricultural labourers', 199 n. 3, quotes reports in the *Labourers' Union Chronicle* of 8 January 1873 on discrimination at Oxford. See also, for example, *Royal Leamington Chronicle*, 13 June 1874, which cites similar cases. J. Dunlop, *The farm labourer*, London 1913, 154, recounts discrimination in Warwickshire, and Brown, *Meagre harvests*, 86–7, details similar cases in Essex.
61 Brown, *Meagre harvests*, 86.

to employ any Union man'.[62] This drove even more labourers into local trade unions.

In the Brixworth union the growth of unionisation was both a problem and an opportunity for guardians who wanted to adopt various *crusading* initiatives. Farmers feared that unionism threatened their oligarchy and so their action was extreme. Yet though Spencer worried about increasing farmer–labourer social tensions, Pell was delighted by this turn of events: he had won the support of disgruntled tenant farmers who held the largest block vote on the board of guardians, around two-thirds of the available seats.[63] Pell could now forge ahead with a local *crusade* by inflaming the farmers' worst anxieties over the NALU. In the future, it would be very difficult to reintroduce outdoor relief once he had instigated cost-saving reforms. Pell thus had an opportunity to consolidate his position and he acted decisively.

On 2 January 1873 Pell gave notice at a Brixworth union board meeting that he intended 'to ask for a Committee of the Guardians to consider the mode of administration of Outdoor relief in this and other Unions'.[64] He expanded his enquiries across the whole district. A committee was set up consisting of Pell (as chairman), Bury and three farmers. They visited every pauper on the relieving officers' outdoor relief schedule, and promptly struck off 240 cases.[65] Central government was delighted, for by 1872 outdoor claimants in the Brixworth union had risen to an unprecedented 1,062 out of a total population of just under 14,000, at a cost of £5,899.[66] A poor law inspector was despatched to the district. He drew up a map of the union, coloured according to the scales of pauperism in each parish. Another senior inspector, Courtney Boyle, told Spencer personally that outdoor relief levels were highest in his Althorp estate parishes, which had been marked in 'black' and 'red'. Boyle told Spencer that 'Brington is the highest of all, an inevitable result of where there is charity … the less the poor depend on relief the more valuable they are to the nation; Ergo: do all one can to diminish out relief'.[67]

The report of Pell's committee, published in early 1874, confirmed the LGB's findings. The average ratio of outdoor to indoor paupers in England and Wales was 5:1 at a cost of 6s. 11d. per head. In the Brixworth union that ratio was much higher, 17:1 at a cost of 12s. 1½d. per head. Pell claimed that in 'no other union is the disproportion so great'.[68] His committee recommended

---

[62] *Northampton Guardian*, 25 Nov. 1876, reports that Arch recalled in a speech to labourers at Ravensthorpe how farmers had made a £50 pact in 1872/3.

[63] Unfortunately voting patterns were not recorded in the guardians' minute books, so it is impossible to analyse political allegiances accurately in this period.

[64] Brixworth union guardians' minute books, entry for 20 Jan. 1873, P/L 2/14.

[65] Bury, 'Outdoor pauperism', 125

[66] 'Outdoor relief committee report of the Brixworth union', Northampton 1874, [Spencer's copy], MSS Spencer, Sox 393. Its claims are verified in Pell, *Reminiscences*, 357.

[67] These maps have not survived in government records. Boyle corresponded regularly with Spencer regarding poor law matters and the problems of inspection. See, for example, Boyle to Spencer 1 May, 20 June, 2 July, 21 Aug., 28 Nov. 1873, MSS Althorp, K398.

[68] Pell, *Reminiscences*, 291.

that the guardians adopt the Longley Strategy. Reform should not just limit but should work towards abolishing outdoor relief altogether. The guardians published a *crusading* charter, which was placed in the Brixworth union workhouse boardroom and on local church doors. The guidelines were harsh. Even the 'deserving' poor were to be deterred from applying for outdoor relief. If the elderly, infirm, disabled and widowed wanted to avoid the workhouse they had to resort to their kinship and friendship networks. Moreover, general medical outdoor relief was cancelled. Medical extras were only granted to very sick workhouse inmates or members of sick clubs. In practice, most paupers gave up applying for medical aid. As a result, the Brixworth union's expenditure on 'fevers and epidemics' rose in 1873–4.[69] Ironically, paupers were now sick for longer periods and were often admitted to the workhouse infirmary, thus increasing indoor poor relief bills, for it cost more to keep a pauper indoors than out. In practical terms, as Karel Williams explains, the new regulations were a form of 'brutal dispauperisation'.[70] Guardians purged outdoor lists with ruthless enthusiasm, whatever the social cost. They were determined to ignore the 'world-without-welfare' outside the workhouse.[71] Yet, at the same time, some guardians were uneasy about the reforms. Within a short period of time criticisms began to be made and greater moderation advocated.

Many guardians felt uneasy about cancelling further outdoor relief allowances. NALU membership had begun to level off and farmers realised that union combination was not as great a threat as they had first feared. They also calculated that abolishing outdoor relief was damaging the local economy because it forced the able-bodied labouring poor to migrate, creating labour shortages during harvest. The chaplain of the Brixworth union workhouse, the Revd J. L. Roberts, became a spokesman for guardians who wanted to revert to a more moderate policy of outdoor relief. In a letter to Spencer in March 1875, outlining his fellow guardians concerns, he stated that whilst a majority of guardians were in favour of the 'application of the House test in proved cases of improvidence or of notorious bad conduct', most did not believe that 'the aged or Infirm Labourer, & of his widow [*sic*]' should be treated like able-bodied applicants. He argued that the poor law made provision for elderly paupers because legislators recognised that few could save enough from their wages for their old age:

at least for the closing generation, there has been an implied contract upon which the agricultural labourer has given his life's work ... And, at the end of their days for the employer, who has received his consideration to the full, to withhold from the poor man his equivalent, appears to me a most oppressive, if not actually dishonest course. In addition to this, the Workhouse is not <u>and cannot be made</u>, a substitute home for the declining years

69 *Second annual report of the Local Government Board*, xxix, London 1872–3, evidence of Bury, appendix 32, c.748, at p. 74.
70 Williams, *Pauperism*, 107.
71 See, for example, phrasing taken from Thomson, *World without welfare*.

of the Labourers and their widows, who have a right to be considered, and in many cases are, to the full as respectable as the classes above them ... The widow of the respectable cottager should not be compelled to eat, live, sleep and die in the same room of society, <u>unreformed</u>.[72]

Roberts stated that although he met 'some of the roughest specimens' of the agricultural labouring class in the course of his poor law duties, he also encountered 'men and women whose honesty of principle and frugality of life and deep piety of character' filled him with 'admiration'. He insisted that 'the more intelligent guardians know perfectly well' that most could not avoid the workhouse. Many farmer guardians had started to recognise that the sudden withdrawal of outdoor relief had created a 'bitterness among the suffering class which may change them into dangerous classes'. One effect of the farmers' parsimonious actions was that it encouraged 'the most violent agitator's of the labourer's union ... from the apprehension of extreme measures on the part of the Guardians'.[73] No record of Spencer's reply has survived but guardian minute books indicate that a number of farmer guardians were expressing similar concerns.[74] They may have been influenced by the bad publicity that they were receiving in local newspapers. One letter gives a flavour of the criticism:

> Sir – I was glad to see the account of the Brixworth Board of Guardians in your paper on Saturday last and feel quite certain the ratepayers of the Union cannot wish the poor to be oppressed in the way they are now. The letter contained several cases of oppression, but from what one hears and knows, it is not a tenth of a tithe of hard cases. Every one must regret to see one class set against another but what the guardians are now doing so most effects [sic]. Why could their alterations not be made in the same way as other Unions? ... One thing is quite certain ratepayers should be very careful whom they entrust to administer the rates; some Guardians know how to deal with the poor justly and firmly; whilst others don't care how the poor suffer so long as they can save their pockets ... I remain – PAUPER on 1s. 6d. and LOAF.[75]

The *Northampton Mercury*, which carried this letter, had a strong Liberal bias and so such criticisms were not unexpected. Moreover, the peculiar brand of radicalism in this part of Northamptonshire (Old Dissent, Puritanism, Chartism and Bradlaughism) gave voice to resentment about Pell's *crusade* from its inception.[76] For example, an editorial in the same issue of the *Mercury* noted that 'Guardians are going Pell-mell for economy' and expressed the

---

[72] Roberts to Spencer, 20 Mar. 1875, MSS Althorp, K157.
[73] Ibid.
[74] Brixworth union guardians' minute books, P/L 2/15. The issue was raised throughout 1875.
[75] *Northampton Mercury*, 10 May 1873.
[76] Greenall, *Northamptonshire*, 78. J. Howarth, 'The liberal revival in Northamptonshire;

hope that moderates would win the day in the Brixworth union. However, the timing of this criticism coincided with a workhouse scandal which seems to have persuaded moderate guardians to close ranks behind Pell.

Two workhouse deaths

In December 1874 local newspapers reported that two elderly paupers, Thomas Hanson and Thomas Cooper, had died in the Brixworth union workhouse in suspicious circumstances.[77] An editorial explained that it was difficult to ascertain the facts of the cases because guardians were acting furtively, but it was reported that the two men had died as a result of medical neglect. This created a furore in the district because the men had been forced to accept indoor relief after being struck off the outdoor registers in 1873. Although only the bare facts of the deaths were recorded in guardian minute books, central government demanded a full report, which although never published, has survived, and confirms the truth of local rumours.[78]

The facts of the case are that in the winter of 1874 Hanson, aged sixty, and Cooper, aged seventy-eight, were admitted to the workhouse. On 1 December, a Sunday evening, the two men fell ill and the master of the workhouse asked the Brixworth union surgeon, a Dr Harpur, to make a visit. The doctor examined both men that evening and injected each of them with '8 minimums [milligrams] of morphine'. At 7 a.m. on Monday morning a workhouse nurse checked both patients and reported that they were 'fast asleep'. The master asked her to continue checking them at two-hourly intervals. At 9 o'clock she reported that the patients were 'thought queer'. Immediately, the master sent for the doctor. However, it was not until around 10 o'clock that he tried, and failed, to revive the patients with cold water. The doctor did not return to the workhouse until 5.30 p.m. on Monday evening, after completing his rounds. He found that one patient had died at 5 p.m. and the other had sunk into a deep coma, dying at 7 o'clock that evening.

At the inquest into the deaths held on 4 December, the coroner cross-examined the union doctor.[79] As local newspapers were denied full access to the proceedings, only central government files detail the cross-examination. The coroner asked the doctor why he did not attend promptly upon the patients. Harpur explained that he called at the union workhouse at 2 o'clock

---

a case-study in late nineteenth-century elections', *HJ* xii (1969), 78–118, discusses local strands of Liberalism.

[77] The case was given widespread coverage and reported verbatim throughout December 1874 in the *Northampton Herald*, *Northampton Mercury* and *Northampton Guardian* (Conservative, Liberal and radical Liberal newspapers respectively).

[78] Letter from 'RJP' to LGB marked 'private', 'Dec. 1874', Brixworth union correspondence book, 1865–98, MH 12/8700. See also memos ibid. discussing the facts of the case 'dated 4 Dec. 1874' and decision 'to let guardians resolve the matter themselves'.

[79] Ibid.

on Monday afternoon, but no one answered the bell, so he completed his rounds and returned in the evening. This rather feeble excuse did not persuade the coroner. The autopsies had shown that both the deceased had been suffering from kidney disease, a common complaint in elderly, worn-out labourers, and one that current medical opinion held was aggravated by morphine. Moreover the doctor had injected the patients with '8 minimums', instead of the prescribed maximum of '6 minimums' of the drug. The coroner concluded that the doctor's misdiagnosis and overdose of morphine had killed the paupers. Harpur denied knowing that Cooper and Hanson suffered from kidney disease and argued that he 'thought 8 minimums would revive better'. He refused to accept medical culpability.

Even though local newspapers could only report a fraction of the proceedings, what little they did discover caused an outcry. A leading editorial in the *Northampton Mercury* noted that it seemed to have been prearranged by leading magistrates in the Brixworth union that the vice-chairman of the board of guardians, a large farmer who supported Pell, should chair the inquest jury. The newspaper alleged that he instructed his fellow jurors to record a verdict of 'death from natural causes' in the face of the evidence to the contrary. Editorials in all the local newspapers were unanimous in their condemnation of this action: they did not divide along traditional Radical/ Liberal/Conservative lines. They agreed that, at the very least, the chairman of the Brixworth union should have reprimanded the doctor for his medical neglect in a public statement.[80] Newspaper reporters also complained about the guardians' silence on the matter, commenting that the exclusion of journalists from the coroner's court seemed to indicate foul play. Central government and the guardians alone knew the full facts of the cases, but these were not recorded fully in local official records to ensure confidentiality and because the findings were so sensitive. However, correspondence from a relative of a local clergy guardian, placed in central government files alongside the rather mundane official report on the matter, reveals what really happened:

> My brother-in-law (who tells me the Enquiry made the case blacker than ever) has sent you the resolution which he and Lord Spencer and Mr Pell... proposed. The Doctor's Friends back him well; though there can be no earthly doubt that the Paupers were killed by the Opium (& in my opinion) might have been saved had proper attempts to save them been made. My reason for believing they would have been saved under the treatment is: that they lived for 20 hrs after the morphine was given. The Master on finding ... they would not wake up put some cold water on their faces and sent for the Doctor and this was the sum of the treatment. I have no doubt the 12 [guardians who supported the doctor on the jury] take an econom-

---

[80] See, for example, *Northampton Herald*, *Northampton Mercury* and *Northampton Guardian*, throughout December 1874.

ical view ... of the matter- holding that Paupers are relieved of their woes and the rates relieved the Paupers ... and [they] join classes/chums.[81]

This letter gives a rare insight into the social cost of changes in the system of medical outdoor relief and the true attitudes of Pell and his supporters. It suggests that Pell's party covered up the scandal and supported the *crusading* initiatives for purely economic reasons. Reduced medical care options outside the workhouse were not balanced by an expansion of indoor medical services.[82] Dr Harpur was evidently responsible for the paupers' deaths. This was the view of two of his medical colleagues who, in a letter to the LGB, accused him of misdiagnosing the two deceased men and neglecting them for business reasons.[83] Harpur himself admitted that having gone to the workhouse about 2 o'clock, and receiving no reply at the door, he went on to a neighbouring village to make a lengthy house call. In his defence he held that the note sent by the workhouse master did not alert him to the seriousness of the problem and that even if he had attended immediately, the men were beyond help. He was censured by the LGB who felt that his conduct was 'unsatisfactory'. The medical regime within the workhouse also failed the paupers. A poorly paid nurse and a busy workhouse master tried to revive the patients, but failed.

The evidence indicates that charges of negligence against the doctor were not pursued for two reasons. First, Pell needed to retain the support of poor law medical officers in the area to implement his experiment in retrenchment. He, and those of his supporters who sat on the jury, appear to have arranged before the inquest to exonerate the doctor. Second, moderate farmers seem to have judged that to protect their standing in the community, they should close ranks, putting on a united front in public despite their reservations. However critical they were in private, it was imperative that they did not criticise the *crusading* regime or acknowledge culpability.

It is very difficult to assess the impact of these two deaths on the psyche of the elderly labouring poor: no record of individual reactions has survived. Local newspapers, however, reported that the deaths and subsequent inquest heightened labourers' fear of the workhouse. This was expressed in the language of biblical Nonconformity in an editorial in the *Northampton Guardian*, which warned guardians in the Brixworth union that

> He that oppresseth the Poor reproacheth his Maker, but he that honoureth him hath mercy on the Poor (Proverbs Chp. 14 v. 31). ... Rob not the poor because he is poor, neither oppress the afflicted in the gate, for the Lord will plead their cause and spoil the soul of those that spoiled them (Proverbs Chp. 22 v. 23).[84]

---

81 Memos concerning medical deaths in the Brixworth workhouse, 4 Dec. 1874, MH 12/8700.
82 This contradicts Webb and Webb, *English poor law history*.
83 Mortimer and Wilson to LGB, 4 Dec. 1874, MH 12/8700.
84 *Northampton Guardian*, 12 Dec. 1874.

This was a sensitive case and it seems unlikely that guardians would have closed ranks had they not feared its local impact. It was visible proof of the power of the retrenchment party and the powerlessness of the labouring poor. Uncharacteristically, neither Pell, nor Spencer, nor Bury ever made a public statement about the scandal and private correspondence on the matter between them has not survived. Bury supported Pell in public, but confined his comments to statements about the success of *crusading* on the national scene, probably to deflect attention from the local situation. Significantly, he did not chair the inquest jury. Instead, he left the vice-chairman of the Brixworth union to prearrange matters, which suggests that privately he may have been critical. It also seems from his later actions that Bury hoped to stand as chairman of the board of guardians at the next election. Thus he may have been distancing himself from the controversy in order to enhance his chances.

Although few sources have survived that comment on these controversial deaths, letters did flood into the LGB from guardians, ratepayers and paupers complaining about the high social cost of the new *crusading* measures.[85] Most were ignored. Other poor law unions also began to complain about the radical policies of the Brixworth union board of guardians. Critics were offended by LGB promotion of the Brixworth union in successive annual reports. Why was central government supporting such dehumanising policies? Was deterring genuine welfare claimants who feared the workhouse not morally questionable? Why was the Brixworth union allowed to set policy standards for urban areas when it was an agricultural district? One fierce critic was the Sheffield union. It sent a petition to the LGB complaining that 'by publishing the resolutions of the Brixworth union board of guardians not to give outdoor relief' civil servants were 'giving encouragement to resolutions, which are contrary to the spirit of the law'. In the words of their relieving officer:

> Hundreds of thousands of our aged and inform poor are in the most miserable condition; that the small [out-relief] allowance, which we make them is not sufficient to sustain nature, and that the horses, nay the very dogs of our aristocracy, are better stabled, kennelled and fed than our deserving poor are housed, clothed and fed.[86]

Sheffield guardians felt that the high social cost of the *crusade* in the Brixworth union was 'painful to contemplate', especially in the light of recent rumours about the two workhouse fatalities. An internal LGB review concluded that all complaints did 'not ... merit the special attention of the Board' and a standard reply was sent outlining that civil servants were not authorised to intervene in specific outdoor relief cases. It was not in the government's

---

[85] Letters 7 Mar. 1871, 13 May, 2 June 1873, MH 12/8699; Brixworth union guardians' minute books, 31 Dec. 1874, P/L 2/15.

[86] Searle, chairman of the Sheffield union to LGB, 14 Jan. 1874, and Joseph Turnell, pamphlet on outdoor relief sent to LGB, 1874, MH 25/25.

interest to criticise the Brixworth union in public. Instead, it needed to be seen to support a loyal and 'model' poor law union for publicity reasons, even if that meant ignoring poor law realities.[87]

Because of the attitude of central government authorities and the way that Brixworth union guardians closed ranks after the paupers' deaths, Pell now had a unique opportunity to consolidate his poor law power. He knew that some of his supporters were wavering but by moving quickly he could introduce a number of administrative changes that would make a later reversal of policies very difficult. Quickly, he created subcommittees for finance and outdoor relief which would deal with all matters of expenditure. Staffed by committed *crusaders*, they dealt with all applications for outdoor relief. This ensured that such cases were never debated by the full board. Some farmer guardians argued that medical procedures should be reviewed after the workhouse deaths. Pell pre-empted this proposal too. He asked Spencer to establish sick and burial clubs to compel the poor to save for illness and funeral expenses. Although he enhanced the role of the medical dispensary at the workhouse, there was no increase in expenditure on indoor relief to fund the changes. Instead, Pell created more bureaucracy for the master and nurses who did not have the time or the resources to introduce substantial procedural changes. As a result, the standards of workhouse medical care declined. But this was cost effective because the wary poor made even fewer claims for medical assistance. Finally, Pell persuaded the acting chairman of the board of guardians, the Revd Robert Isham (a moderate), to resign. Isham had been ill for some time and Pell argued that now was the moment to appoint a successor. Bury was rewarded for his loyalty to Pell by being elected to the chairmanship.[88] This meant that although Pell had come to office in the early 1870s, he did not achieve dominance over the poor law at Brixworth until 1874 when the farmers give him the mandate to take full control. For the next twenty years, the *crusading* party had *carte blanche* on the board of guardians to the detriment of the poor.

Crusading underway

It is apparent that residents within the Brixworth union 'inhabited a world structured by their relationship to economic and social power'.[89] Agricultural historians, notably Eric Collins, suggest that the agricultural labour market

---

87 J. W. Stewart and S. A. King, 'Death in Llantrisant: Henry Williams and the New Poor Law in Wales', *Rural History* i (2004), 69–87. They argue (p. 83) that the failure of the New Poor Law was to make medical care 'an administrative' rather than a 'people-centred process'. This comment is valid for the Brixworth union.

88 Pell to Spencer, 10 Apr. 1874, discusses the chairmanship; D. Morton to Spencer, 15 Aug. 1874, discusses the chairman's ill health, MSS Althorp, K154.

89 S. Banks, 'Open and closed parishes in nineteenth-century England', unpubl. PhD. diss. Reading 1982, 426, quoted in Howkins, *Reshaping rural England*, 28.

began to deteriorate critically in rural England after 1860, 'the chief problem being no longer to absorb a labour surplus but to obtain sufficient labour for key summer operations'.[90] Yet evidence here indicates that despite migration and falling farming profits, the labour market was by no means flooded. Underemployment was a key problem even during better harvest years, as Spencer's land agent reports reveal, so that that the poor needed a series of customary rights to make ends meet. Farmers revived notions of communal responsibility only in pursuit of increased profits in the high-farming period. That factor altered the triangular matrix of socio-economic relations in this locality, between landowners, farmers and labourers. Whereas in the past customary expectations governed everyday income levels framing wage relations, charitable provision and poor relief expenditure, by the mid-1860s that situation had changed.[91] Furthermore, although medical outdoor relief was very useful to the arable farmer as a device to maintain his labour supply, it was also expensive. Consequently, outdoor relief was the focus of consistent guardian frugality and strong reaction by labourers.[92] The Union Chargeability Act (1865), passed at a time of poor harvests, meant that the parsimonious attitudes of farmer guardians hardened. From their perspective the *crusade* was timely. It seemed to offer a way out of local socio-economic problems. There is evidence of this in the winter of 1871, during a peak underemployment season, when agricultural trade unionism started to be discussed in many rural areas. It was very unfortunate that agricultural workers asked for wage increases at the end of an era of prosperity because their demands seemed unreasonable in a hostile economic climate.[93] This convinced farmer guardians that their position as leaders of rural society was under threat and they took pre-emptive action, withdrawing outdoor relief to penalise paupers for union combination. Consequently, guardians in the Brixworth union anticipated both the Fleming Report and the Longley Strategy, mirroring what was happening in nearby Essex and Oxfordshire.

Crusading was an incremental experience, often locally driven.[94] Guardians were influenced by higher rates, poorer harvests, union combination and cost-saving recommendations from central government. In addition, the role of individual COS supporters, like Pell, Spencer and Bury, cannot be discounted. They provided the leadership and drive to push forward changes in the administration of the poor law. Their ethos was simple and there-

---

[90] E. J. T. Collins, 'Harvest technology and labour supply in Britain, 1780–1870', unpubl. PhD diss. Nottingham 1979, 89, quoted in Howkins, *Reshaping rural England*, 96.
[91] For Peter King's notion of a triangular matrix of social relations see Hitchcock, King and Sharpe, *Chronicling Poverty*, introduction.
[92] Dunbabin, '"The revolt in the field"', 68–96.
[93] Ibid.
[94] There is no mention of the impact of changes in medical outdoor relief on union combination in the standard set texts on the *crusading* decades. However, Digby, *The poor law*, and *British social policy*, both stress the importance of medical outdoor relief in rural society for both farmers and labourers.

fore appealed to those farmers who wanted immediate solutions to urgent economic problems. The poor were work-shy and undeserving, and should be more independent. Taking away outdoor relief was, therefore, a moral duty. So *crusaders* treated paupers as a statistical calculation, hidden in bureaucratic jargon. This, however, contrasted with the reactions of the labourerers for the vulnerable were concerned about deepening impoverishment. Moreover, the growth of agricultural trade unionism and the two pauper deaths in the work-house were very important formative events in the *crusading* process in the Brixworth union. The pauper deaths, though unintended, were themselves one of a number of measures which would later motivate the labouring poor to unite and overthrow the *crusaders* once the poor law was democratised. Union combination, therefore, marked the tentative beginnings of a political journey for working people in the Brixworth union.

Setting these events into the national poor law picture reaffirms Mary Mackinnon's suggestion that welfare historians have 'underplayed the social impact of the 1870s *crusade* against outdoor relief'.[95] In the coming years *crusading* guardians would use 'any and every means' to attack outdoor relief.[96] This involved a wide spectrum of *crusading* techniques often disguised under the generic and unsuitable term, 'the crusade against outdoor relief'. Essentially, in rural localities, many traditional poor relief claimants were not simply bargaining for a 'stake in the soil', but for their very existence outside the workhouse in the 1870s. In time the advent of democracy in local government would empower them to claim back their 'right' to parish funding, a right that central government and local guardians had tried to remove. Meanwhile, attempts by the guardians to create a 'world-without-welfare' would simply strengthen the determination of the labouring poor to protest about their pauperism.

[95] Mackinnon, 'Poor law policy', 299–336, and 'English poor law policy', 603–25; Humphreys, *Sin*, 21.
[96] Williams, *Pauperism*, 102.

5

A World-Without-Welfare? Penalising the Poor with Welfare-to-Work Schemes

By 1873 the Brixworth union guardians had set the stage for a prolonged battle over outdoor relief. They had been influenced by a national trend to reduce rates. At the same time trade union combination seemed to threaten their economic dominance and so they exploited the *crusading* campaign to suit their interests. Reducing medical outdoor relief and closing ranks to cover up the deaths of two workhouse paupers, were indications of their unified power. Yet, neither their subsequent *crusading* activities nor the ways in which those policies exacerbated pauperism have been studied in depth. This chapter, therefore, is primarily interested in rediscovering the impact of a major rural recession upon those who administered the poor law, those who tried to claim outdoor relief and those who were rejected by the *crusading* process in the Brixworth union. It begins by considering four new and very controversial *crusading* strategies that were implemented in order to cut poor law costs severely, and then goes on to explain how, in the face of mounting criticism, leading *crusaders* hid the high social cost of their actions from central government. Instead, guardians informed the assistant poor law commissioner that poor law reform had not been harsh because they had set up welfare-to-work schemes to provide alternative forms of employment. Local sources are used to discover whether these measures were enlightened or financially viable. If they were inadequate, did they persuade the majority of the paupers to migrate so that the Brixworth union exported its poor law problems elsewhere? It is important to engage with how the poor law was perceived; specifically to consider the ways in which cost-cutting measures were experienced by those seeking to maintain power and those subject to harsh retrenchment measures during a period of economic crisis. Central government statistics belie the reality of performance and achievement in the localities at this critical time. It is noteworthy that it was in this period that the Brixworth union guardians, and those elsewhere, often exploited poor law recommendations. The implication of this for poor law historiography is that *crusading* against outdoor relief was an economic and political tool, emerging at different times, in different places and for different reasons. This produced a complicated scattering of *crusading* responses. By examining what happened in the Brixworth union it is possible to reconstruct for the first time what measures were tried and when. Primary evidence will show that the LGB's *crusade* initiated on a local basis is of broader significance to poor law historiography. In fact, retracing its local impact will enable future researchers to test whether a *crusading* template developed that was tried in most locations.

Guardians and their four major *crusading* activities

In 1872 fifty-three guardians sat on the Brixworth union board.[1] Ten were Justices of the Peace, appointed *ex-officio*. Most of these did not attend board meetings because they were too busy with business affairs, lived outside the district or had high profile political careers at Westminster. They tended to turn up in April, following guardian elections, to ensure that their interests would be represented over the coming year. Three, however, did attend meetings regularly and were influential members of the board. Of the remaining forty-three elective seats, one remained unallocated due to a sudden death, the rest were held by three landowners, three land agents, three clergymen and thirty-two farmers (one farmer held two seats). The landowners seldom attended meetings because their land agents represented their interests. The clergy represented their patrons, usually *ex-officio* guardians. Thus, the block vote of thirty-two farmers should have controlled policy but as most were the tenant farmers of *ex-officio* guardians they acted conservatively. Under their stewardship, the numbers in receipt of outdoor relief fell from a high of 1,068 in January 1873 to a low of 658 in the following July.[2] Thereafter numbers stabilised with about fifty claimants being removed every half year. Gradually, therefore, outdoor relief registers were purged.

In about 1875 some guardians were critical of the social cost of *crusading* initiatives. Several farmer guardians tried to push through a number of outdoor relief cases but a majority out-voted their proposals, refusing to relax regulations. The *crusading* party, motivated by deep convictions and the pursuit of personal aggrandisement, decided that it was time to implement four major cost-saving strategies, which would save money and further consolidate their power on the Brixworth union board. It is not possible to reconstruct fully who voted in favour of which cutbacks because voting patterns were not recorded in the guardian minute books in this period. But records are available to retrace the government-authorised, as well as informal, strategies that the guardians implemented. At first, the *crusaders'* party decided to prosecute the adult children of elderly paupers to force them to pay towards the maintenance of their relatives both inside and outside the workhouse. At the same time they refused outdoor relief to those in receipt of charity or resident in an almshouse as technically they were not destitute. Then the number of relieving officers in the area was reduced to give guardians greater control over the local poor law decision-making process. Finally, the chairman and a number of his key supporters asked the remaining relieving officer to refer all

---

1   Brixworth union guardians' minute books, 1870–3, P/L 2/16.
2   Ibid.

outdoor relief applications from elderly deserving paupers to a private charity fund, which they set up and financed. They hoped that this would mean that they would never have to grant outdoor relief again. Unsurprisingly, the labouring classes resented these changes.

In 1875 the first cost-saving measure was debated. Privately, guardians discussed how they could further reduce outdoor relief and match LGB cost-saving targets. Despite posting a *crusading* charter throughout the district, elderly applicants had not been deterred. The chairman of the board explained that guardians must not be sentimental:

> Of course it is said why it is no fault of theirs. To this I think one might reply to say maybe then the question and effect be their fault as they say only *reap as they have sown* – but if it be purely their misfortune, it is a misfortune, <u>not of our</u> making. I've only <u>found</u> them in misfortune and it is our own duty to help them in the way <u>least</u> impervious to the community; and the rates were never meant to relieve misfortune but only to relieve destitution and I am experienced enough to think that very many of the abuses prevalent among us, are the result of so called caring attempts to be more merciful than God.[3]

A majority proposed that the Brixworth union should prosecute the adult children of elderly paupers who were failing to support their parents. Court records after 1870, as David Thomson argues, are 'filled with similar reports of prosecutions of sons, and a few daughters as well'.[4] The *crusading* party, however, needed Earl Spencer's support if the scheme was to succeed; as lord lieutenant he controlled the county bench and could persuade three *ex-officio* guardians to convict cases when they came before them at petty sessional hearings in Northampton. At first magistrates supported the policy. Seventeen out of twenty-six cases were convicted at Northampton petty sessions between April 1872 and April 1877.[5] Magistrates adjudicated that adult children should be responsible for the upkeep of parents, and ordered families to pay a maintenance allowance for their pauper parents, generally fixed at 2s. 6d. per week. This was to be paid into the court, which would then pass it on to the poor law union where the pauper resided. The relieving officer granted an equivalent outdoor relief allowance to each elderly pauper once receipt of money from the court had been confirmed. However, after 1877 magistrates refused to co-operate because they believed that the numerous complaints sent to the LGB protesting about this legal action were justified. Magistrates 'chose not to exercise their legal, social and economic powers' because they believed the strategy was 'alien and offensive'.[6] For example, a labourer from Holcot village complained that he had been ordered to pay 1s. per week for the maintenance of his mother:

3   W. Bury to Spencer, 10 Mar. 1874, MSS Althorp, K156.
4   Thomson, 'Welfare of the elderly', 217.
5   Northampton petty session records, NRO, misc. volumes, ML 44, V2911.
6   Thomson, 'Welfare of the elderly', 200.

I am not A Able boyd [able-bodied] man myself have had one rib fractured and one shoulder dislocated which fails me very much at times I have lost one eye I get my living by doing a little shoework but as I was not brought up to it I cannot get much. I have not had much to do this last few weeks nearly fifty years old my wife is over fifty years of age. I have house rent to pay and everything to find towards living out of what I get and barely make both ends meet.[7]

The pauper was temporarily awarded '2s. 6d. and 1 loaf' for four weeks but once the publicity had died down the allowance was cancelled. The LGB refused to intervene.[8]

There was considerable debate in the *Northamptonshire Guardian* about this controversial prosecution strategy.[9] As a more radical Liberal newspaper it gave widespread coverage to the labourers' cause. A number of NALU correspondents also publicised the plight of impoverished labourers in the district. They stated that NALU membership had steadily grown in the Brixworth union since 1871: it was claimed that some 2,407 members were affiliated to the politically active Market Harborough district office by 1874.[10] They explained that the prosecution strategy was swelling NALU ranks because the union promised to represent summonsed members in court. A 'poor labouring man from Moulton' was amongst the first to be defended by NALU counsel for Northamptonshire. His defence team warned magistrates that NALU members were determined to oppose the policy by fighting for 'their social and political rights ... every man had a right to a voice in the making of the laws he was called upon to obey' and this law was unjust.[11] The *crusading* party was very wary of NALU involvement but they were also determined to press ahead.[12] However, the prosecution strategy coming so soon after bitter NALU feuds about the withdrawal of charity and poor relief seemed to deepen labourers' sense of injustice. As a result there was considerable disagreement on the Brixworth board over the strategy.

Some farmers calculated that since prosecution was expensive, at an average cost of 10s. per summons, it was no longer worth pursuing so controversial a policy. *Ex-officio* guardians were divided. Pell's supporters believed that the strategy was justified. The three sitting *ex-officio* magistrates who opposed his policies did not. They did not refuse to convict cases, but instead tactically adjudicated minimum fines, of 6d. in 59 per cent of cases between

---

7   G. Faulkener, Holcot parish, to LGB, 19 Apr. 1873, MH 12/8699.
8   Internal memorandum 'on how best to reply to George Faulkener' dated 'April 1873', ibid.
9   *Northamptonshire Guardian*, 5 Aug. 1876.
10 Horn, 'Northamptonshire agricultural labourers', 372.
11 C. Stevenson to LGB, 'February 1874', MH 12/8700. There was a lengthy inter-departmental correspondence following Stevenson's complaint about NALU defence strategies in Norfolk and Northamptonshire.
12 Beasley to Spencer, 27 Mar. 1873, and Boyle to Spencer, 8 Apr. 1872, MSS Spencer, Sox 571, both document local NALU activity and the reaction of farmers.

1875 and 1877. Moreover, they refused to fine defaulters, adjudicating that those who could pay did pay and those who could not, did not. After 1877 they decided to throw all cases out of court. English courts often decided that the *crusade* was not an official legal change to the New Poor Law, but rather a set of central government recommendations and this gave them considerable discretion to interpret the law leniently.[13] This meant that a second cost-saving drive was needed that involved non-prosecuting modes of saving money.

In 1875 guardians set up a committee out of the Brixworth union board to investigate whether charity was indiscriminately awarded to poor relief claimants. The committee reported that it was customary to allow paupers to claim both outdoor relief and charity, and this practice had to stop. Numerous almshouse trusts misappropriated their funds by allowing pauper residents to claim outdoor relief. Technically, they should not have been allocated a place in an almshouse if they could not show that they had independent means.[14] Thus, after 1875, elderly applicants were not granted outdoor relief if they were living in an almshouse or in receipt of a charitable benefit. A block, though still minority, vote of farmers opposed the policy and convinced a number of guardians to change sides during key motions. Nevertheless, this initiative was implemented, to the detriment of the aged poor. This meant that each board meeting became a battle-ground over the issue of outdoor relief, for although in public staunch *crusaders* were determined to retain regulations, in private their rank and file supporters argued about the pace of change in the locality. As even Spencer explained to Pell, 'The indiscriminate bestowal of out-door relief [is an] encouragement to improvidence ... in the question of Widows houses my views do not differ from your own ... but reform <u>must</u> be slow when dealing with old people.'[15]

Those who opposed the provision of outdoor relief were ambivalent about how to support deserving elderly paupers but, like central government, they took the view that 'only by cutting assistance to all, even the welfare core, could the policy emphasising self-responsibility be successful'.[16] For example, policy became contested regarding the almshouses which the Spencer family had built in the Brixworth union in the early nineteenth century to house long-serving estate workers. *Crusaders* felt that they should be administered according to the strict letter of the poor law, with no resident receiving outdoor relief. The labouring poor, however, believed that residence was a customary right which should not be subject to a means test. Spencer decided to implement an experimental almshouse grant-in-aid scheme to test whether outdoor relief could be abolished. Residents had to prove that they could support themselves with a minimum weekly allowance of 2s. 6d. Spencer

<hr />

[13] Thomson, 'Welfare of the elderly', 198–9.

[14] Report of the Brixworth union charities committee, Northampton 1875, NRO, 49p/46.

[15] Spencer to Pell, 28 Jan. 1877, MSS Althorp, K159.

[16] Thomson, 'Welfare of the elderly', 217.

promised those who were semi-independent an equivalent dole. However, if any resident defaulted their almshouse would be repossessed by Spencer's land agent, thus preventing almshouses from becoming 'refuges for paupers'.[17] Spencer hoped to raise the means test threshold to 3s. and then to withdraw his proportion of the dole. This would ensure that only labourers of fully independent means applied for an almshouse place and thereby discourage paupers who had to accept compulsory admission into the workhouse instead.

There was considerable disagreement amongst clergy guardians about this policy. Their spokesman warned Spencer that his proposals would 'destroy the <u>special</u> paternal character [of almshouses], which was particularly valuable because it promoted a bond between landowner and dependants'. The provision of almshouses improved community relations at a time when the *crusading* initiatives were undermining traditional relationships. Moreover, the cumulative effect of these two major cost-saving measures meant that the chairman lost support: just seventeen guardians were committed *crusaders* in 1878. They were still in the majority but their opponents had won the respect of a growing number of farmers and of the labouring classes in the district, as the issue of outdoor relief crossed traditional 'class' boundaries. These divisions were exposed in public when an elderly pauper, John Howard, applied for, and was refused, outdoor relief in the early summer of 1878.

Howard, a blind widower aged seventy-nine from Harlestone parish, applied to the Brixworth union for a small outdoor relief allowance because he could no longer work. Two farmers proposed that Howard should be given a permanent allowance of 2s. 6d. per week. However, *crusaders* put a stop to the motion by instructing Howard to apply to a local Harlestone charity instead. The chairman of that charity was outraged:

> The Great Question to be decided between the Brixworth Guardians and the Parish of Harlestone is this: – Is such a man as Howard who is nearer 80 years of Age ... and now blind ... without any means of his own, after having worked all his days whilst he was able, on the Land at Harlestone to be supported by the occupiers of the Land or merely to be sympathised with and sent for help to the Trustees of a Fund the Donors of which never imagined that their gifts would be used to lessen the burden imposed on ratepayers.[18]

He explained that the charity could not afford to fund outdoor relief pensions for elderly paupers in the parish. Its income was only £125 per year. It gave £50 to fund the local school to educate the children of the poor and spent £75 on shirting, blankets, sheets and flannel. Howard's case was widely publicised because the charity's chairman wrote to the LGB, the *Local Government*

---

17 Bury to Spencer, 15 Jan., 11 Nov. 1880, MSS Althorp, K382; M. Calverley to Bury, 1, 13 Dec. 1880, 8 Mar. 1881, K144.

18 David Morton, rector of Harlestone, 9 May 1878, Brixworth union guardians' minute books, P/L 2/19; 'Brixworth: power of the chairman questioned', *Local Government Journal* xxvii (July 1878), NRO, ZA 2246.

Chronicle and both regional and national newspapers. The *Midlands Free Press*, for example, reported that Howard had been categorised as 'able-bodied so long as he could walk'. Adverse publicity alienated even committed *crusaders* like Earl Spencer. He was angry that some *crusaders* had ignored his earlier advice regarding the need for gradual change. He loathed bad publicity and wanted the case resolved as quickly as possible. Pell acted decisively and offered a weekly pension of 2*s*. 6*d* from a private source.[19] Farmer opponents asked if this donation had been granted in perpetuity but no details were given. The LGB refused to make any further enquiries on their behalf, relieved that the issue had been resolved by private means. It was evident that *crusaders* needed to take greater control over the management of poor relief to avoid further bad publicity. But how could they achieve this?

The *crusading* party decided on a third major cost-saving initiative. It was agreed that the only way to exercise greater control over the administration of outdoor relief was to appoint one relieving officer to oversee all applications. This passed on the board by '17 against 11' votes but the minority refused to accept the result. A petition was sent to the LGB which investigated the measure.[20] Poor law regulations laid down that in populous districts a minimum of two relieving officers must be employed to ensure efficient and uniform administration. The LGB wanted to know how one man could oversee such a large geographical area, travelling a distance of up to 200 miles per week to serve a population of 13,866 inhabitants. The chairman of the board reported that by appointing a 'competent' and 'energetic' officer on a large salary of '£160' all the logistical difficulties would be overcome and outdoor relief would be administered uniformly. Central government told the chairman that as his request was unique, it would have to be authorised at the most senior level of the LGB. A senior civil servant commented to the president of the LGB that it was 'Anything but sound policy to reduce the number of Relieving Officers and if the present proposal is applied to, the District of the Relieving Officer ... will contain over 60,000 acres ... this is Pell's union and I own I am surprised that the proposal should come from such a quarter.'[21] Nevertheless the LGB authorised the new experiment for twelve months. If the scheme worked, it could become permanent. It is noteworthy that the Brixworth union was the only poor law union in England and Wales permitted to take such action in the later nineteenth century. Numerous internal memos discussed the proposal at length. The LGB decided that it did not want to lose such a valuable ally as Pell in its fight against outdoor relief. Civil servants were also concerned that reductions in national pauperism rates were stagnating because many guardians refused to institutionalise vulnerable claimants in workhouses: poor law unions often

19 Alfred Jeffrey, union clerk to LGB, 'July 1878', MH 12/8701..
20 'Petition by the Revd John Drake J. P., Mr Richard Lee Bevan J. P., Mr Francis Eady and Mr Francis Chevalier Jeyes all guardians of the poor in the Brixworth union protesting against policy of having only one relieving officer', 13 Dec. 1879, ibid.
21 'Southam, Lambert and the President', memos, 3 Jan. 1879, ibid.

argued that outdoor was cheaper than indoor relief, and more humane. Thus the LGB needed the support of, and to retain, flagship poor law *crusaders*, like Brixworth. *Crusaders* knew this and exploited that situation to consolidate their poor law power.

Clearly the local context sometimes shaped the national *crusade*, rather than the reverse. In the Brixworth union *crusaders* were both creative and exploitative. Although the LGB did not want to distrust the political motives of committed ideologues, none the less civil servants were aware that central government statistics often belied poor law realities. Only primary research can uncover the real character and sentiment of the poor law in this location and its role in the bigger poor law picture. Meanwhile, it soon became apparent that a fourth major *crusading* initiative was underway in the Brixworth union.

Crusaders wanted just one relieving officer chiefly because they had devised a new scheme to deter aged paupers. The highly paid relieving officer agreed that each time a deserving claimant made an application for outdoor relief his or her case should be diverted to a leading *crusader*, like Pell, rather than being reported to the board of guardians. The pauper was then given a small private charitable donation (from a fund run initially by four guardians) for around four weeks on the strict provision that they did not reapply for outdoor relief. Any pauper who broke this rule was rejected on the grounds that he or she was technically no longer destitute because of the charitable payment. Fewer deserving cases, therefore, ever came before the board to trouble guardians who were wavering. *Crusaders* implemented this cost-saving measure unofficially in 1878 because it was too controversial to ask the full board to vote on. However, by 1883 the number of cases had grown steadily and the charity lacked funds. Leading *crusaders* organised a fund-raising drive and asked Spencer to become patron to encourage others to subscribe. As one contributor wrote, he was

> Sure the time [had] come when we could do away altogether with out-door relief in the Union ... the really deserving cases and destitute cases are very few ... a small sum ... raised as a charity fund ... administered by a select committee on certain fixed principles would work. [He had] talked to a good many intelligent people [but we] <u>must</u> have your support to set the ball rolling.[22]

Since Spencer insisted that the scheme remained a private unaffiliated venture it was dubbed the 'Secret Service Fund'.[23]

The fund was a local version of the COS. It was similar to most

[22] Bury to Spencer, 6 Mar. 1883, MSS Althorp, K382.

[23] Spencer hoped that *ex-officio* guardians would enthusiastically welcome the new scheme because the COS had recently been established in nearby Leicester. See, for example, Leicester Charity Organisation Society minute books, 1876–81, Leicester Records Office, DE/2340, and J. D. Martin, *The Leicestershire COS, 1876–1976: a contemporary review*, Leicester 1976.

nineteenth-century organised charities administered by an upper-middle-class committee, which adopted a case-study method of investigation to categorise the labouring poor. It promoted self-help, as it saw poverty as springing from moral failure. The 'Secret Service Fund' was the most despised of the inititiaves implemented in the Brixworth union during the decade 1875–85. The gift relationship it established tried to legitimise social subordination. The labouring classes in the district viewed poor relief as a customary right. Charitable pensions destroyed the natural claims of labour. Thus, the labouring poor refused to express gratitude for the loss of community funding. Many also suspected that the 'Secret Service Fund' was an ill-disguised attempt to penalise the poor for their poverty. After all, guardians were refusing to implement a tried and tested social welfare formula like outdoor relief.[24] Its subscribers knew that the fund was controversial but it was the only way they could achieve year-on-year outdoor relief gains.[25] *Crusaders* hoped that this fourth *crusading* initiative would help them win the economic argument.[26] The onset of a severe rural recession by the early 1880s, however, threatened to upset the pace of their *crusading* measures.

Rural recession: agricultural crisis in the Brixworth union

Since the 1960s there has been considerable debate amongst agricultural historians about the timing and extent of economic change in British farming over the course of the nineteenth century.[27] Although the reasons for the crisis in agriculture are complex, few welfare textbooks have examined the impact of rapid economic change on poor law practices in the later Victo-

---

[24] No detailed records of the 'Secret Service Fund' have come to light. John Morley, the 5th Earl Spencer's land agent, recorded that Spencer paid an annual subscription of £10 (about £700 today) to the fund. See, for example, Morley's financial statement of Earl Spencer's private accounts, 26 Oct. 1895, MSS Spencer, Sox 551; 'Secret Service Fund' circular to Spencer, 'January 1894', MSS Althorp, K345.

[25] Bury to Spencer, undated draft notes of a proposed speech at the inaugural meeting of the 'Secret Service Fund', 15 Mar. 1882, MSS Althorp, K382.

[26] Sidney Ward, a labourer from Brixworth parish, gave evidence to the *Royal Commission on the Aged Poor*, qq. 15653–764, that Jeyes, the guardian of Brixworth parish, was asked and declined to subscribe to the 'Secret Service Fund'.

[27] See, for example, S. Wilmot, '*The business of improvement': agriculture and scientific culture in Britain*, c. 1700–c. 1870, Bristol 1990; F. M. L. Thompson, 'The anatomy of English agriculture, 1870–1914', in B. A. Holderness and M. Turner (eds), *Land, labour and agriculture, 1700–1920*, London–Bowling Green, OH 1991, 210–40; M. E. Turner, 'Output and prices in UK agriculture, 1867–1914, and the great depression reconsidered', *AgHR* xxxx (1992), 38–51; N. F. R. Crafts and S. N. Broadberry (eds), *Britain in the international economy, 1870–1914*, Cambridge 1992; E. J. T. Collins, 'Why wheat? Choice of food grains in Europe in the nineteenth and twentieth centuries', *JEEcH* xxii (1993), 7–38; and R. Perren, *Agriculture in depression, 1870–1940*, Cambridge 1995.

rian countryside.[28] Knowledge of the policy decisions that strict 'model' rural unions, like Brixworth, took during the agricultural crisis is still limited.[29] This means that it is difficult to 'mingle with the crowd', getting beneath an increasingly rigid poor law system to understand the local dynamics of the *crusade*.[30] However, revisiting traditional analyses of the national agricultural crisis and then rethinking its local effects in both Northamptonshire and the Brixworth union, can allow welfare historians to begin to engage with the sorts of economic changes that often impacted on the poor law.

Agricultural historians often refer to the late 1860s as the 'Indian summer' of British agriculture, a time when high profits seemed to have been guaranteed because farming benefited from a lack of overseas competition and from good weather patterns.[31] Most textbooks stress the relative affluence of farmers before agriculture became a 'contracting sector of the economy in both relative and absolute terms'.[32] Essentially, at the end of the high-farming era, an agricultural crisis began to unfold in areas where farming was overcapitalised.[33] This was caused by the growth in American and Australasian exports flooding British markets that coincided with a series of 'adverse seasons', which 'drained' domestic 'farming reserves'.[34] Thus most historians now stress that 'the last quarter of the nineteenth century was a period of agricultural crisis'.[35] There is agreement that farming trends reflected a deepening rural recession in most Midlands and southern English counties where the 'collapse in cereal prices' was 'the quintessence' of the agricultural crisis.[36]

In an attempt to improve rental incomes, which fell by an average of 26 per cent nationally between 1879 and 1895, most landowners converted arable land to grass.[37] Consequently, the total acreage of wheat under cultivation in England contracted by some two million acres between the early 1870s and

---

[28] See, for example, introduction, n. 14. Few poor law textbooks discuss the impact of the later Victorian agricultural crisis.

[29] Greenall, *Northamptonshire*, gives an overview of some of them. Likewise, Thompson, 'Anatomy of English agriculture', 225–40, assesses conditions in Northamptonshire. However, there is no comprehensive study of farming in mid-Northamptonshire where the Brixworth union was situated.

[30] R. Jeffries, *Hodge and his masters*, Stroud 1992 edn, p. xv.

[31] P. J. Perry, 'Where was the "great agricultural depression?" A geography of agricultural bankruptcy in late Victorian England and Wales', AgHR xx (1972), 30–45 at p. 31.

[32] Thompson, 'Anatomy of English agriculture', 212.

[33] Ibid. 214; Perren, *Agriculture in depression*, 5. This included areas such as East Anglia, the East Midlands regions and Yorkshire in England and Lothian in Scotland: Howkins, *Reshaping rural England*, 134–52.

[34] P. J. Perry (ed.), *British agriculture, 1875–1914*, London 1973, p. xxvi.

[35] Ibid. p. xi.

[36] Ibid. p. xiv; Floud, *The people and the British economy*, 102–6, estimates that on average wheat producers experienced the largest percentage decrease in their profit margins, prices falling around 63 % in the period 1860–95.

[37] M. Overton, 'Agriculture', in Langton and Morris, *Atlas of industrialising Britain*, 34–54, estimates that 45% of farming land was under cultivation in 1866, but that figure had fallen to 32% by 1905.

the 1890s.[38] Likewise the size of the agricultural labour force nationally shrank by 21 per cent between 1871 and 1911.[39] Michael Thompson emphasises that the psychological impact of this flight from the land and 'the contraction in the opportunities for employment in farming' was profound, even though the rural exodus solved the problems of underemployment in many regions.[40] Although average weekly wages between 1860 and 1890 rose from some 12s. to 17s., these rates of pay were low compared to other occupations, even though cheap wheat prices (which cut food expenses) reduced the cost of living. Thus, a smaller labour force (often comprised of older men) was asked to increase productivity rates to replace lost farming revenue. Charles Feinstein estimates that the output of an average agricultural worker increased by around 26 per cent between 1871 and 1911, when a greater volume of crops was grown to make up for the fall in prices.[41] However, since agricultural conditions differed very considerably from region to region it is very difficult to assess with any degree of accuracy how the rural labour force as a whole was affected by the agricultural crisis. 'It could be argued', Thompson observes, 'that the relative … inferiority of agricultural labourers was the necessary pre-condition for the magnetic attraction of towns and emigration' during the agricultural crisis.[42] A series of grievances, including the effects of the *crusading* campaign, probably convinced many to leave.

In a Midlands county like Northamptonshire, where classic high-farming methods were practised, meat suppliers usually adopted either 'beef-barley or lamb-barley systems', as well as producing wheat.[43] There were a number of dairy farmers and wheat growers in the county who marketed butter, cheese and milk, as well as raising pigs, poultry or selling eggs. In mixed-farming districts it is therefore very difficult to measure profitability trends because investment returns were based on a wide range of produce and it is necessary to take into account a number of variable costs, such as the price of purchased feed.[44] In addition wool prices, very important in the Brixworth union, were affected during the 1880s by the Australian wool surplus that flooded British markets at a time when sheep farmers lost a lot of stock after a virulent outbreak of liver rot.[45] Consequently, although meat prices were generally more buoyant in the 1880s because there was an increased

---

[38] Thompson, 'Anatomy of English agriculture', 220. Perren, *Agriculture in depression*, table 1 at p. 8, calculates that home production of wheat contracted from 50.7 million cwt in 1872 to 32.2 million cwt by 1902. In the same period wheat imports increased from 48.3% to 80.8%.

[39] Thompson, 'Anatomy of English agriculture', 218.

[40] Ibid. 217.

[41] C. H. Feinstein, *Statistical tables of national income, expenditure and output of the UK, 1855–1965*, Cambridge 1965, appendix, table 54.

[42] Thompson, 'Anatomy of English agriculture', 218.

[43] Ibid.

[44] Perren, *Agriculture in depression*, tables 3, 9 at pp. 12–13, gives details of the downward trend in mutton, beef and pork prices.

[45] Floud, *The people and the British economy*, 105.

demand for better quality home produce they need to be set in the context of a range of less favourable market factors.[46] Recessionary pressures meant that in mixed-farming regions most farmers tried to diversify by moving into large-scale fruit and vegetable production, though estimates on the size and spread of these ventures vary.[47] However, it is clear that exports and poor weather started to have a major impact on agriculture in the Midlands' heartland. Spencer's land agent noted that those farmers who had over-capitalised found it very difficult to absorb losses especially during inclement seasons, although he also saw a number of discrepancies.[48] If contemporaries disagreed about the impact of the rural recession on a regional basis, it is not suprising that there has been some disagreement among historians. Perry and Thompson have debated the impact of the agricultural crisis in Northamptonshire. Perry used 'bankruptcy rates as an indicator of depression for farmers'.[49] He concluded that Northamptonshire farmers in the 1880s were able to absorb some of their losses because mixed-farming practices gave them an opportunity to spread their investment risk and most did not experience a recession until the 1890s. Thompson disputes this, suggesting that Inland Revenue returns, which measure rent movements, refute Perry's work.[50] Thompson believes that rent levels give a 'reasonable indicator of the general state of farming', provided they are balanced against county figures on gross farm output.[51] He found that Northamptonshire rents decreased by 24 per cent between 1872 and 1893; this meant that it ranked eighth out of forty English counties in a league table of the steepest rental reductions. Gross farm output in the county fell by around 15 per cent in the same period, with the agricultural labour force (excluding farmers) declining by some 39 per cent in the period between 1871 and 1911.[52] Overall Thompson ranks the county in a grouping of the ten most affected areas in England where landowners

46 Perren, *Agriculture in depression*, 11.
47 Overton, 'Agriculture', 48, estimates that the number of orchards increased by 60% between 1873 and 1904. Floud, *The people and the British economy*, 105, calculates that between 1873 and 1911 the number of market gardening ventures grew by 145% and the number of woodland management schemes by 27%.
48 Land agents' records, MSS Spencer, Sox 562, 566, 567. Perry, *British agriculture*, p. xix, points out that all sectors of the economy, not just farming, slowed down because of the scarcity of gold on the world markets and that contributed to the agricultural crisis, while Perren, *Agriculture in depression*, 6, notes that these problems were exacerbated by the declining importance of agriculture in the national economy, at a time when Britain's wealth creation was concentrated on manufacturing and service industries.
49 Perren, *Agriculture in depression*, 19; P. J. Perry, *British farming in the great depression, 1870–1914: an historical geography*, London 1974, 26–34; Thompson, 'Anatomy of English agriculture', 210–40. This debate has been revived in M. E. Turner, J. V. Beckett and B. Afton, *Agricultural rents in England, 1690–1914*, Cambridge 1997.
50 Thompson, 'Anatomy of English agriculture', 233–40.
51 Thompson defines gross output as, 'crops plus stock minus quantities consumed in the farming operation'.
52 Idem, 'Anatomy of English agriculture', tables 11.1–8 at pp. 226, 232–4, 237–8.

and farmers, but probably not labourers, experienced the worst aspects of the agricultural crisis.

In the Brixworth union it has been said that 'farmers were not so much interested in what was happening to total farm output', but rather in 'what was happening to their share of the division in the proceeds between themselves, the landowners and farm workers'.[53] The Spencer papers show that tenant farmers started to complain about poor profit margins around 1879.[54] For example, a farm bailiff informed Spencer that during 1879 his wholesale wheat prices at market fell by 11s. per quarter.[55] He later reported that wheat prices fell by a further 30s. per quarter between 1879 and 1884, which meant that his profits were 50 per cent below 1860s levels. The bailiff tried to diversify his farming practices to spread his investment risk and reduce labour costs, setting aside thirty-three acres of arable land to implement a market gardening experiment, where he grew mainly root vegetables (carrots and turnips) interspersed with beans and peas. Initially the scheme was profitable but it lost money when larger farmers followed suit and undercut his prices. He then tried to improve his cereal profits by using steam machinery to drain, plough and harvest wheat, which cut labour costs, but his prices still plummeted. In 1883 he nearly went bankrupt because his cattle had to be destroyed after a severe local outbreak of foot and mouth disease, closely followed by an attack of pleural pneumonia. At the same time most of his sheep died from liver rot. The bailiff complained to Spencer that if he were forced to leave the Althorp estate because of his accumulated debts he would not receive adequate compensation for the capital he had invested in farm improvements in the 1860s. Unless he ran the farm down before giving up his tenancy, both Spencer and the next tenant farmer would be the beneficiaries of his venture capital and hard work. The compensation issue is one of the chief complaints recorded in the Spencer archive.[56] Most tenant farmers believed that they were effectively bankrupt by 1887.[57]

Throughout the 1880s tenant farmers on the Althorp estate reported that the agricultural crisis was not ephemeral because it could not be blamed on successive seasons of poor weather conditions. They predicted that the problems of mixed farming would be of a much longer duration because of the growth in overseas competition, which allowed too much cheap produce to flood British markets. In fact, prices fell so steeply that some tenant farmers in the district refused to grow grain crops. For example, in Harlestone parish one tenant explained that he stopped growing oats because it was so unprofit-

[53] Ibid. 235.

[54] Land agents' records document numerous cases: MSS Spencer, Sox 562, 566, 567.

[55] T. Eady to Spencer, 7 Jan., 2 Sept. 1880, 10, 22 Feb. 1882, 22 Oct. 1883, 10 Feb. 1884, MSS Althorp, K349.

[56] Beasley to Spencer, 19 June 1882, discusses the plight of the farmers, ibid. K599.

[57] Sir Hereward Wake to Spencer, 4, 7 May 1881, ibid. K569, warned Spencer about the farmers' plight and the effects of controversy over compensation.

able.[58] It took 170 tons of manure to cultivate an average plot of twenty-one acres, but the yield was so poor in the 1880s that it was not cost effective to purchase and plant seed. Most farmers ploughed their oat crops back into the soil because after successive wet seasons it was of such poor quality that it could not even be used for pig fodder. Another tenant farmer explained that converting arable land to grass was no more cost-effective.[59] In 1887 he had to plough both his hay and his straw back into the soil because it had lain so long on the wet ground that it had rotted away. He usually sold surplus poorer quality straw for thatching ricks, but nobody would buy his rotten stained produce. Spencer's land agents [60] reported that on the three estates they managed tenant farmers began to break their leasing agreements to recover costs, which generally they had not done before. Tenants began to sell hay, straw and clover crops, which should have been stored, because they were their only remaining sources of revenue.

Although these examples do not fully characterise the depths of recession across the Brixworth union, they do give a flavour of the sorts of difficulties many tenant farmers faced in the 1880s. Initial research seems to indicate that Perry's work on bankruptcy rates in Northamptonshire, which show that the county was 'marginally an island of prosperity' because of its 'concentration on grazing and fattening', underestimates the degree of distress in the farming community.[61] Contemporary accounts suggest that Thompson's assessment of the sharp decrease in rental returns and decline in gross farm output reflects the reality of dire farming conditions in the 1880s.[62] At the very least, tenant farmers in the Brixworth union experienced a severe rural recession, confirming that their evidence to successive Royal Commissions on agricultural distress was not unduly alarmist or exaggerated.

In the 1880s Spencer's land agent reported that the agricultural crisis was making it very difficult to retain good tenant farmers.[63] Many whose families had been employed for generations on the Althorp estate left the district, even though the agent offered rent reductions of up to 30 per cent *per annum*. John Morley, who became land agent in 1885, found that few tenants would agree to sign lease renewals with traditional long-term fixed rental agreements, until they could predict farming's prospects. The land agent decided to renew tenancies on an annual basis rather than evict loyal tenants with whom the estate had developed good working relationships. Although farming specula-

---

58 T. Alley to J. Morley, 5 Sept. 1887, MSS Spencer, Sox 566.
59 Morley to Spencer, 12 Nov. 1887, ibid. Sox 562, discusses the plight of John Wykes, a valued tenant farmer. Wykes was in dire circumstances and had broken his lease agreements.
60 There were two land agents on the Althorp estate in the 1880s. Joseph Noble Beasley served as land agent from 1874 until 1885, leaving under a cloud after it was discovered that he neglected his duties and was an alcoholic. John Morley then served on the estate until the 5th earl's death in 1910.
61 Perry, 'Great agricultural depression', 36.
62 Thompson, 'Anatomy of English agriculture', 223–40.
63 Morley to Spencer, 26 Jan. 1888, MSS Spencer, Sox 562.

tors were more common in this period, Spencer's agent was wary of entering into long-lease agreements with this new breed of agriculturist. Experience had taught him that such agreements usually resulted in evictions. There are some well-documented cases in the Spencer archive of the land agent having a great deal of difficulty trying to enforce lease agreements when farming speculators defaulted on their rental arrangements by the early 1890s.[64] Spencer's land agent seems to have found his job increasingly difficult because he had to maximise business opportunities to try to offset falling rental incomes; this meant that he had to take unpopular decisions. He reported that Spencer's rental income fell by an unprecedented £4,000 per quarter and by 1887 he had to begin to evict a number of long-standing tenants.[65] The agent's letters reveal that this was a depressing task.[66]

Spencer adopted a much more business-like attitude after the onset of the agricultural crisis. He told his land agent that 'the principle of a berth that is supposed to be hereditary' in farming was 'bad and unsound' because it usually led to 'unpleasantness in the end'.[67] He was forced to be pragmatic, even though many of his tenants had invested their capital and labour resources for generations, because he had over extended himself in the 1870s, just before the crisis in agriculture got underway. The office of lord lieutenant of Ireland, which he held twice (1868–74 and 1882–5) cost about £20,000 per appointment, but like previous holders Spencer spent almost double that amount on lavish entertainment during each tenure. On his first return from Ireland in 1874 he took up hunting, a life-long but expensive passion. By April 1879, rather than liquidate inherited assets, he had to take out a loan of £15,000 'on account of the excess of expenditure for the Hounds 1874/8'.[68] His financial records show that he was very worried about the rate at which his farming revenues were decreasing.

Thus, in 1886, he decided to close Althorp House for the foreseeable future, releasing all but a few female servants to reduce household bills.[69] Likewise, by the 1890s, Spencer's land agent was very concerned about the future of English agriculture. He warned that

> There will be a sort of agricultural collapse to face – the poor old ship agriculture has been up against bad winds for many years – Her machinery has broken down and she has put to her sails, and the question is whether her provision (capital) will last out until she reaches the haven of better

64 Morley to Spencer, 12 Jan. 1887, ibid., discusses problems of lease agreements with speculators from the north.
65 Spencer to S. Hartington (copy), 23 Dec. 1881, MSS Althorp, unnumbered misc. box, discusses the fall in Spencer's rental income in some detail and his concerns about the future of farming.
66 Morley to Spencer 1887–9, MSS Spencer, Sox 562.
67 Morley to Spencer, 12 Nov. 1887, and Spencer to Morley, 13 Nov. 1887, ibid.
68 Spencer memorandum on his finances, 26 Apr. 1879, MSS Althorp, unnumbered misc. box; Gordon, The red earl, 1–34, gives an overview of Spencer's financial situation.
69 John Dasent to Spencer, 10 Sept. 1886, MSS Althorp, K398.

times and remunerative prices – … Oh that a smarter hand would arise to place on the old ship the Plimsoll mark of a fair rent and a fair burden of taxation.[70]

During the 1880s everyone in the Brixworth union was affected by the agricultural crisis. It is evident that if the largest landowner in the area, Spencer, was forced to cut costs dramatically then labourers unable to claim outdoor relief must have been suffering too. Some guardians decided to offer employment on a number of privately funded welfare-to-work schemes to claimants seeking outdoor relief. It was hoped thus to keep rates low and avoid substantial tax increases. What do they tell us about the character and sentiment of the poor law during a rural recession?

Welfare-to-work

Lynn Hollen-Lees, in her recent appraisal of the English poor laws, comments that 'welfare transactions offer a window into the functioning of societies at the local level, one which brings into view the destitute alongside the affluent'.[71] The poor law during a period of agricultural crisis therefore should be of prime interest to welfare historians because economic tensions would have reshaped welfare priorities. It is evident that during a period of agricultural crisis working people needed more generous outdoor relief. Rural boards of guardians, however, dominated by farmers with falling incomes, wanted to cut expenditure. Shifting local imperatives coincided with the development of new policy instruments at a national level. Thus, around 1885, central government became alarmed at growing social unrest in London and major English towns as a result of recessions in trade and agriculture.[72] As unemployment levels in urban areas rose, creating exceptional distress amongst the working classes, attitudes to pauperism slowly began to change. This process coincided with new social scientific investigations into the causes of poverty and pauperism.[73] It was evident that individual outdoor claimants could not be held responsible for the vagaries of poor weather or the prevailing trade recession in an industrial economy. A new outdoor relief directive was thus issued in March 1886.

The Chamberlain Circular authorised guardians in depressed areas to set up employment schemes, funded from the rates, to alleviate unemployment.[74] Such projects should 'not involve the stigma of pauperism'.[75] Claim-

[70] Morley to Spencer, 21 Feb. 1893, MSS Spencer, Sox 563.
[71] Hollen-Lees, *Solidarities*, 12.
[72] Englander, *Poverty and poor law reform*, 27–9, summarises the background to the Chamberlain circular (1886).
[73] See chapter 1 above.
[74] The Chamberlain circular (1886) is discussed in Harris, *Unemployment and politics*, 76–7; Hollen-Lees, *Solidarities*, 287–93; and Kidd, *State, society and the poor*, 58–63.
[75] Englander, *Poverty and poor law reform*, 109–11.

ants to outdoor relief were to be given the option of labouring on a variety of community schemes such as laying paths, cleaning streets or doing 'spade husbandry on sewage farms'. They were to be paid at a rate lower than local wage levels but paupers could apply for outdoor relief supplements to avoid the workhouse. Central government would not fund the schemes, but as an alternative to rate increases guardians had the option of borrowing money to defray costs until conditions improved. Predictably, this new set of recommendations alarmed *crusaders* in the Brixworth union who were unwilling to increase their borrowing. They complained that the scheme would increase local rates and undermine their *crusading* achievements.[76] Pell summarised their views in a speech to the North Midland poor law conference:

> Aid from a public fund ... only makes matters worse in the end unless applied to assist in the accomplishment of changes arising from economical causes, which are as irresistible as they are natural. ... The victim to this and similar schemes is the Forgotten Man – the ratepayer – the man who had watched his own investments, made his own machinery safe, attended to his own plumbing, and educated his children; who, just wants to enjoy the fruit of his own care, is told that it is his duty to go and take care of some of his negligent neighbours. ... He is passed by for the noisy, pushing, importunate and incompetent. ... Misery enough we shall always find in this world, the result of improvidence, intemperance and idleness ... but whether there be more or less of this sort of habitual misery, it should never be taken into the account of exceptional distress, or met or relieved in the same way. This sort of distress is more a matter for public police than public bounty.[77]

Yet Pell also considered the Chamberlain Circular opportune. He proposed that *crusaders* should adapt the new guidelines to suit their interests, by setting up a number of welfare-to-work schemes funded by private enterprise. These were portrayed as benevolent gestures to alleviate unemployment; in reality they were an ill-disguised attempt to force the labouring poor in the area to migrate to local towns.

In this way Brixworth union guardians exported their outdoor relief problems to their poor law union neighbours, a common *crusading* practice. Meanwhile, three welfare-to-work schemes, which had a clear cost-saving purpose, were set up on Spencer's Althorp estate. In 1884 Spencer authorised his land agent to set aside 'a hundred to two hundred acre' site to create a large-scale allotment farm on the outskirts of Harlestone parish as close to Northampton as possible.[78] The land was divided into plots of 'one, two or three acres'.

---

[76] Brixworth union guardians' minute books, P/L 2/17: the issue was debated throughout the summer of 1886.

[77] A. Pell, 'Exceptional distress', in *Annual poor law conference for the East Midland district: poor law conference reports*, London 1888, 412–14.

[78] 5th Earl Spencer and his allotment farming scheme, NRO, misc. ZA 2246: files contain details of his welfare-to-work initiatives.

In theory, the allotment farm was created to provide work for labourers in low-paid rural employment or for the non-able-bodied unemployed. Spencer's land agent gave the impression to local newspaper reporters that any resident of the Brixworth union could apply to grow produce on the allotment farm to feed their families and that this would allow them to remain outside the workhouse.[79] In reality, the allotment scheme was discriminating because although it was portrayed as a charitable initiative it was set up as a profit-making business enterprise. Spencer told the chairman of the board of guardians that he had got his land agent to draw up a contract specifying that only the able-bodied who were already employed in town and who were members of an existing allotment society could join the scheme.[80] Spencer took this decision because he was concerned about the high level of cottage arrears on his estate and his aim was to encourage men employed in regular urban work to stay in the area. He hoped that this would force the unemployable to migrate and not become a burden on the local economy.[81] Despite the scheme's welfare-to-work rhetoric it was a speculative business venture with a social engineering objective that discriminated against the most vulnerable members of the labouring community.

Janet Howarth has argued that in the Brixworth union 'there was no record of an unsatisfied demand for land before 1885' because it had been 'Spencer's policy ... to give allotments when asked'.[82] However, that assertion is mistaken because most labourers were disqualified from signing up to the allotment scheme. Spencer's agent threatened even those who were allocated a plot with eviction if rent was not paid on time. This became a problem during the frequent bouts of inclement weather in the 1880s. The allotment holders harvested poor quality produce, which was difficult to sell and many who could not pay their full rent had their plots reduced in size proportionally or withdrawn. After 1885 Spencer decided to change the allotment scheme by limiting all plot sizes. He cited financial reasons for this decision, stating that in a three-year period, 1884 to 1886, a plot of one acre lost on average £7 2s. 7d.[83] Although labour charges in the first year were high, the scheme never subsequently broke even and Spencer calculated that it was not worth investing in such an unprofitable venture. Instead, he decided to invest in a

---

[79] Both the *Northampton Mercury* and the *Northampton Herald* interviewed Spencer and his agent about the initiatives in March 1884.

[80] Land agent records reveal that Spencer got his solicitor to draw up a number of regulatory contracts in 1884–7 to cover the welfare-to-work schemes: MSS Spencer, Sox 566. The contracts have not survived but the agent expressed concern about their harshness to a number of his close confidantes.

[81] Spencer to Bury and reply, 8, 9 Jan. 1887, ibid. Sox 565, reveals Spencer's views on the need to disperse underemployed labour in the district to towns.

[82] Howarth, 'The Liberal revival', 110–11.

[83] *Royal Commission on Labour* (1894), appendix 'F', q. 87 and appendix 'C', xiv, q. 107, gives details of the financial arrangements on the allotment and co-operative farms respectively.

second welfare-to-work scheme, a co-operative farm, hoping that it would be more profitable.[84]

In October 1885 a fact-finding delegation, comprising *crusading* guardians, inspected a co-operative farm at Radbourne in Warwickshire. They were impressed by its achievements and thought a similar scheme might provide employment opportunities in the Brixworth union. This would avoid them having to reintroduce outdoor relief. In 1886 they persuaded Spencer to take the lead by establishing the Harlestone Co-operative Farm Ltd.[85] He lent the venture £3,000 at 3 per cent interest (2 per cent below average loan charges) because he was determined to ensure that the enterprise was profit-able. If the farm went into profit he would review the interest rate, with a view to increasing loan repayments. Two leading *crusaders*, Pell and Bury, also subscribed £25 each. A farm of twenty-one fields, comprising 160 acres of arable land and 140 acres of pasture, was set aside on the glebe farm at Harle-stone. Again Spencer got his solicitor to draw up a contract. It stated that eight able-bodied labourers would be elected by a committee from amongst the respectable labouring poor at Harlestone to work the farm. The stock, farm equipment and any improvements were valued at cost. Spencer decided to charge a fair and equitable rent, set at £410 16s. 8d. in 1886. It was agreed that each co-operator would be paid average wages for the district, around 13s. per week. Profits would be distributed as follows. Three-quarters would be put into a reserve account, to fund further work on the farm, and the remaining quarter would be divided equally amongst the co-operators and the manager. If the farm made a loss the profits' bonus would not be paid until any deficit had been made good.

Once again, the *crusading* party portrayed the co-operative scheme as a benevolent welfare-to-work gesture. But it too was discriminatory because its contract undermined the spirit of co-operation that it was supposed to be promoting. Even though labourers were paid 13s. per week, they were not recompensed for their extensive unpaid overtime during the first six months. The scheme would not have got off the ground if they had not worked the extra hours because the previous tenant had left the farm in such 'bad order'. It is also worth emphasising that this wage level was below that achieved by the NALU in the district in the 1870s (15s. per week). Morale amongst the labourers was soon low because the farm made a year-on-year loss. Over an eight-year period, between 1886 and 1893, it lost £1,818 7s. 4d. and it was evident that their bonus would never be paid.[86] The labourers complained that the venture was not a true co-operative.

Spencer's land agent asked a valued tenant farmer to assess whether the labourers had a legitimate complaint. The tenant farmer replied that 'it isn't

---

84 Calverley to Spencer, 5 May 1885, MSS Althorp, K324.

85 5th Earl Spencer and his allotment farming scheme, NRO, misc. ZA 2246.

86 The co-operative lost on average £259 16s. 9d. annually, a deficit of 176s. 6d. per acre which equates to an average loss of $8^3/5\%$ on the £3,000 capital that Spencer invested.

co-operation at all in the strictest sense of the term ... the benefit to be received by any co-operator under this scheme is microscopic and remote'.[87] He noted that labourers should have had the same rights as shareholders in a company. However, as the contract conferred 'absolute and autocratic power upon Lord Spencer', the labourers had no rights. Spencer could dismiss labourers at a week's notice. He could wind up the concern without notice. He could usurp any decision of the management committee or the manager. He could buy or sell stock without consulting anyone. The tenant farmer confirmed that although labourers received a weekly wage they were considerably out of pocket. Unlike their fellow day labourers in the district they were not paid piece-wages but according to a fixed wage agreement. This might seem an advantage, guaranteeing them employment, but in reality they were being exploited, working much longer hours.[88] The farmer calculated that a farm of 300 acres with capital bearing interest could not make a substantial profit. Even if it did, eight labourers and a manager had to share a 25 per cent bonus. Each would get a maximum of 2.7 per cent from negligible profits. He believed that the co-operative ethos was a sham and as so few were employed on the farm it was a hollow gesture, rather than an effective welfare-to-work initiative.

Numerous protests by angry labourers opposing the privately funded charitable and welfare-to-work schemes were reported in local newspapers.[89] In 1881, for example, the chairman of the board informed Spencer that his parishioners in Harlestone reacted angrily to the 'Secret Service Fund' by refusing to attend church, even before the welfare-to-work schemes got underway. He admitted that his sermons on charity, self-help and the evils of outdoor relief were not popular amongst the labouring poor:

> the poor people of Harlestone will naturally look upon me with suspicion and it may be some time before they understand that I am not so bad as I have been painted. I quite anticipate empty benches at Church but luckily I have long ceased to regard the size of a congregation as a measure of good work.[90]

It is impossible to determine from the records why a labourer decided not to attend church. Most likely it was a visible means of registering a protest, since the poor law boardroom was now closed to them. The Spencer papers reveal that political activity amongst labourers was extensive at this time because few accepted either the abolition of outdoor relief or the welfare-to-work substitutes. A wry poem was circulated in the district mocking the inability

---

[87] D. Rice to Morley, 27 Oct. 1887, MSS Spencer, Sox 566.

[88] Morley to Spencer, 25 June 1890, ibid. Sox 562, noted that this was an ongoing wage grievance.

[89] See, for example, the *Northampton Mercury* throughout 1884–7, when the letter page was filled with complaints.

[90] Bury to Spencer, 31 Oct. 1881, MSS Althorp, K382.

of Anglican clergy guardians in the 1880s to increase their congregations without resorting to new tactics:

> I can't get the parish to come to my church,
> They all go elsewhere and leave me in the lurch.
> So I'll tackle them now in a different way
> And at the same time I shall make them all pay.
> I've hit on a scheme to set up a club
> And incidentally compete with the pub...
> I shall be boss and take all the dough.
> I shall also decide where the money's to go.
> I shall not allow them to have a committee,
> They might not want me and that would be a pity...
> The pick of my rules is the last number ten,
> I shall get all their money and on Sunday's when
> I rise in my pulpit to give a discourse,
> You'll see that I preach to a much larger force.
> As you can't join my club if you don't go to church
> I think this will stop my being left in the lurch.[91]

Likewise, guardians reported numerous protests to Spencer's land agent. For example, Harlestone labourers held a number of meetings to oppose the conversion of their village store and public house to similar co-operative contracts. They applied to several clergy guardians to support their cause, with little success.[92] One clergyman admitted to Spencer that labourers felt very aggrieved about how in reality *crusaders* were forcing them to leave.[93] Most agricultural workers, who needed regular employment, felt excluded.

In the mid-1880s many labourers from the Brixworth union migrated to find regular work in shoe-manufacturing towns, such as Kettering, Northampton and Wellingborough. Few unemployed able-bodied agricultural workers could afford to stay in a district where there was no outdoor relief provision and most refused to enter the workhouse. As a result, the population of the Brixworth union fell by 15.2 per cent between 1871 and 1901.[94] Spencer's land agent was concerned that this meant that a large underemployed pool of older labourers would roam the district in search of work. Poorer families and the aged usually lived in tied estate cottages and could not afford to give up their homes to seek work in town. In any case there was little work available in town because manufacturing was also experiencing a trade recession.[95] The land agent noted that the non-able-bodied were experiencing

---

91 M. D. Wilford, *Clipston heritage*, Market Harborough 1991 edn, 5. Clipston village lay on the edge of the Brixworth union and local people were angry that the *crusaders* influenced nearby poor law unions, such as Market Harborough, where outdoor relief was more difficult to obtain.
92 [?] Stewart to Spencer, 3 Mar. 1885, MSS Althorp, K381.
93 Ibid.
94 Brixworth union, census returns, 1871–1900.
95 Bobby Spencer's political speeches, 'Depression in trade', 1885–6, MSS Spencer, Sox

great difficulties outside the workhouse. One clergy guardian explained in a private letter to Spencer that elderly labourers living in Chapel Brampton on the Althorp estate walked fourteen miles per day to seek work in the spring of 1888.[96] Older labourers earned just 2s. 6d. per day for twelve hours' labour in the fields. On wet days their work was cancelled and as the work was only available in March, one of the wettest months, this happened frequently. They could not earn a living wage. Most worked a three-day week earning on average about 7s. 6d. and they needed some form of outdoor relief to avoid the workhouse. Despite such evidence, *crusaders* were determined never to reintroduce outdoor relief.

Local newspapers stepped up a campaign against private welfare-to-work schemes.[97] They publicised labourers' suspicions that they had been introduced to persuade potential poor relief applicants to become burdens on the Northampton union. Spencer's land agent became very concerned that workers on the Althorp estate believed that private initiatives were draconian; he worried that traditional social relations were being irreparably damaged. He described, for example, a rent audit in Chapel Brampton in 1888 when labourers turned up drunk and were unwilling to pay even a portion of their rent. They were generally very abusive and felt that because they were being treated harshly by farmer guardians they could ignore rental demands. He observed that on the whole labouring demands were legitimate and that the *crusading* campaign would have far-reaching repercussions:

> Unfortunately there is no one resident ... who can now fuse the different interests and schools of thought and any meeting now ... reminds one of so many barrels of the different sorts of explosives now in use. Each dangerous in itself and frightfully jealous of its neighbour.[98]

The land agent was particularly concerned because Spencer instructed him in the later 1880s to establish a third welfare-to-work initiative on the Althorp estate. This caused even more hardship and further resentment. It also showed that as the recession deepened Spencer was determined to save money at whatever social cost.

The scheme, wood faggoting for elderly labourers of pensionable age,[99] was the brainchild of Bury who argued that labourers over seventy years of age still had '10 or 15 years of good work in them'. Older worn-out labourers

---

246, outline local economic problems (rural and urban) in the county; Greenall, *Northamptonshire*, 103–6, explains that the influx of agricultural labour into the shoe industry caused a number of problems in the 1880s. It lowered wages and created a 'sweat industry'. This benefited manufacturers who were experiencing a trade recession as a result of increased competition in the industry. However, once mechanisation was phased in, which remedied problems of competition, unemployment levels increased.

[96] Calverley to Morley, 7 May 1888 and replies, MSS Spencer, Sox 567.

[97] *Northampton Guardian*, 14 Mar. 1885, reported working people's complaints in an article entitled, 'Harlestone: lecture on agricultural depression'.

[98] Morley to Spencer, 6 Mar. 1888, MSS Spencer, Sox 562.

[99] Spencer to Bury, 24 Oct. 1886, and Bury to Spencer 10 Jan. 1887, ibid. Sox 565–6.

worked in woodsheds, earning on average 11s. per week. One local clergyman complained to Spencer's agent that it was upsetting to watch the daily struggle of infirm labourers to work, even in the depths of winter, trying to earn enough to keep them out of the workhouse.[100] What saddened him most was that many were respectable labourers who had worked loyally on the Althorp estate throughout their lives. Their life savings were usually spent during their first serious illness and thereafter most went into a steady and cruelly prolonged decline. They had the option of the workhouse but most feared the stigma and monotonous daily ritual. Privately, the land agent admitted to the clergy guardian that he had opposed the scheme but intervening with Spencer was pointless.[101] He elaborated that the real purpose of such schemes was to encourage labourers to work to avoid the workhouse, to migrate or accept indoor relief at the end of their working lives. He noted that instead the schemes prolonged the older labourers' hardships and that most died after entering the workhouse, which was convenient for *crusading* farmer guardians since it kept rates low. Previously, Spencer had admitted in a private letter to Bury that putting older labourers to work was an excellent way of managing pensionable estate workers. It demonstrated to elderly paupers that they had to work to avoid the workhouse or accept indoor relief quickly when they broke down on the job. He conceded that it was 'demoralising' for younger workers when their fellow labourers died on the job but he would not compromise his poor law convictions.[102] It soon became apparent throughout the Brixworth union that some guardians, with their eyes fixed on central government targets, chose to overlook the depths of local poverty which their *crusading* initiatives exacerbated.

Three further cost-saving measures were implemented on the Althorp estate in this period. First, in July 1888, all rent reductions on the Althorp estate were cancelled.[103] This caused hardship amongst both tenant farmers and labourers. Spencer calculated that he could no longer afford to supplement the incomes of his fellow farmer guardians. He knew that this policy would not interfere with the *crusading* experiment because it would make farmer guardians more determined not to reintroduce outdoor relief as it would increase their rates. Second, tenants who lived in estate cottages, and who were considerably in arrears with their rents, were given two options. Either they accepted assisted emigration, locally or overseas, or they would be evicted.[104] Spencer asked local clergymen to interview potential migrants and stress that their homes would be repossessed shortly. The clergymen reported that most 'refuse[d] point blank' to emigrate. Middle-aged labourers stated that they were 'too old' to 'make a fair start overseas'.[105] Third, Spencer told

100 Calverley to Morley, 29 Nov. 1887, and Morley to Calverley, ibid. Sox 562.
101 Ibid.
102 Spencer to Bury, 24 Oct. 1886, ibid. Sox 565.
103 Spencer to Morley, 2 July 1888, ibid. Sox 567.
104 Calverley to Morley, 7 Mar. 1888, ibid.
105 Ibid.

his land agent to review his charitable expenditure, instructing him to cancel all contributions, including Christmas gifts of bread and meat, to the poor.[106] One clergy guardian, who supported the *crusading* cause, felt that Spencer had gone too far.[107] He asked him to reconsider his decision because Christmas charity was such a 'vital and needy distribution'. In the makeshift economies of the poor these gifts were important to annual subsistence calculations. He stressed that to withdraw them 'without any previous notice!', would have deeply impoverishing repercussions. When Spencer refused to reconsider, the clergyman felt that it was his Christian duty to take over the subscriptions personally. He could not in good conscience ignore such acute pauperism. He was also very concerned when Spencer withdrew his annual subscriptions to local burial, sickness, coal and clothing clubs, even though he was patron of numerous local friendly societies. In the 1870s Spencer had set up many of these schemes personally and assured the labouring poor that if they subscribed to them they would replace outdoor relief.[108] Most labourers had been sceptical because friendly societies often went bankrupt before subscribers could claim any benefits. Spencer promised that this would not happen because he would underwrite the schemes. In the later 1880s he reneged on this promise, citing financial pressure.

Spencer's charitable expenditure was in fact minute when compared to his net income. His land agent sent him regular statements of his financial position, detailing income and expenditure. By 1895, during the second phase of recession when he was under even greater financial pressure, he still had a total cash income of just over £94,000 (equivalent to £6.85 million today) in his private bank account. Out of this he spent £387, 0.04 per cent, on sundry charitable payments.[109] One case illustrates just how small his charitable subscriptions were by the later 1880s. In 1887 Spencer reduced his charitable payments in the parishes of Chapel and Church Brampton to £3 annually, even though local piece-wages averaged just 2s. 6d. per day. Furthermore, a clergy guardian had to divide this subscription between ten impoverished families, comprising fifteen adults and nineteen children.[110] This was an average annual payment of just 1s. 8½ d. per head, and the clergyman stepped in once more, supplementing poorer residents out of his own pocket.

The social cost of the welfare-to-work schemes and of Spencer's retrenchment was profound. As one of the largest employers in the district his deci-

---

106 Spencer to Morley, memo on charity cancellations, 'Mar. 1887', ibid. Sox 566.
107 Calverley to Morley/Spencer, 30 Dec. 1888, ibid. Sox 567.
108 Northampton Library, Local Studies Collection, misc. collection of friendly society records, *Chapel Brampton Friendly Society, annual report for the year*, Northampton 1873. The society was established by the 5th Earl Spencer, who paid an annual donation of £4 (about £210 today).
109 Morley to Spencer, 26 Oct. 1895, MS Spencer, Sox 551. The Economic History Series, www.eh.hmit/compare/, estimates that between 1861 and 1901 £1 was worth nearly £70 at 2001 values.
110 Calverley to Spencer, 26 Dec. 1887, 5 Jan. 1888, MSS Althorp, K324.

sions penalised the needy. The working life-cycle of the labouring poor, always precarious, became perilous during rural recession. For instance, one clergy guardian complained to the Althorp estate land agent, that the children of the labouring poor were 'half-starved'.[111] Older labourers in the parishes of Brington and Whilton petitioned a clergyman to help them rent an allotment site of '8 to 10 acres of arable land', which was 'urgently required' to feed them because they were living a hand to mouth existence.[112] They explained in the petition that they had tried to rent land from a local farmer but he turned 'nasty' and they were afraid to beg for help again because a second request might later 'recoil on their heads'. The labourers worried that farmers would stop employing them in the district. The Spencer archive reveals that even those in regular employment experienced poor working conditions and received meagre piecework wages of around 2s. per day. The same clergy guardian complained to Spencer that 'big farmers are without exception exceedingly hard on their men ... they are bullies and village tyrants'.[113] He 'wish[ed] their farms were cut in half' because 'it would be better for the land, as well as for [local] people'. He witnessed numerous evictions, when poor people were treated harshly. Many should have been given a month's notice before being repossessed but most were 'ejected at a week's notice'.

Initial research on the records of the Northampton poor law union for this period,[114] indicates that the town had a large pool of underemployed labourers from the Brixworth union. The Northampton workhouse did not have the capacity to house these claimants and guardians had to reintroduce outdoor relief. They complained to central government that the Brixworth union was resolving its social problems by exporting them to its neighbours.[115] Senior civil servants replied that rural depopulation was natural during a recession and had not been manufactured by guardians in the Brixworth union. This belied *crusading* outcomes. The privately funded schemes were introduced to cut the rates and prevent the reintroduction of outdoor relief by convincing many in the district to migrate. Brixworth union workhouse records (*see*

---

[111] Morley to Spencer, 3 Mar. 1888, MSS Spencer, Sox 562, discussed the clergyman's complaint.

[112] Calverley to Morley, 22 Mar. 1888, ibid.

[113] Calverley to Spencer, 26 Dec. 1887, 5 Jan. 1888, MSS Althorp, K324.

[114] Northampton union guardians' minute books, 1870–1900, NRO, misc. vols (uncatalogued).

[115] The problem of the influx of working people was a key feature of life in the Northampton union. Guardians tried to resolve their outdoor relief crisis by sending large numbers of vagrant and lunatic paupers to the county asylum at Macclesfield to free up space in the workhouse, which was filled to capacity in the 1880s. In addition John Bates, guardian of the poor for St Andrews parish, acted as an emigration agent at 28 the Drapery, Northampton, and tried to persuade claimants to go overseas. The growing crisis in outdoor relief was discussed at successive meetings in the mid-1880s and was a key election issue, as posters that have survived in Northampton Library, Local Studies Collection, attest.

Table 5
Changing age profile (%) of the Brixworth union workhouse, 1861–91

Age Date		0–9	10–19	20–9	30–9	40–9	50–9	60+	Total
1861	Female	32.0	17.0	9.0	21.0	2.0	6.0	13.0	100%
	Male	20.0	4.0	4.0	20.0	12.0	16.0	24.0	100%
1871	Female	14.0	40.0	17.0	6.0	14.0	3.0	6.0	100%
	Male	18.0	15.0	5.0	13.0	3.0	8.0	38.0	100%
1881	Female	26.0	22.0	3.0	10.0	8.0	8.0	23.0	100%
	Male	20.0	8.0	5.0	5.0	12.0	10.0	40.0	100%
1891	Female	23.0	10.0	3.0	6.0	6.0	10.0	42.0	100%
	Male	11.0	4.0	2.0	0.0	4.0	9.0	70.0	100%

Sources: Brixworth union poor law records, census returns, 1841–1900.

table 5) reveal that larger numbers of elderly persons who remained in the union had to accept indoor relief in the 1880s.

Although the data in table 5 does not take account of demographic variants, such as fertility and death rates, or of seasonal work patterns, it does indicate significant changes in age differentials. If the age structure of the population increased substantially in the period between 1861 and 1891, it would explain why the numbers of elderly persons in the workhouse increased dramatically. Yet Thomson estimates that between 1861 and 1891 the number of persons aged sixty-five or over as a percentage of the total population in England and Wales only increased by around 1.6 per cent.[116] The withdrawal of outdoor relief, together with the agricultural crisis, thus increased the percentage of elderly people in the workhouse beyond their distribution in the wider population. It is evident that by 1881 increasing numbers of older labourers, both male and female, were accepting indoor relief in the Brixworth union. The proportion of male labourers aged over sixty in the workhouse rose by 30 per cent in the decade 1881–91. This was probably because they could not find menial work in the district, whereas women could take on child-care, nursing, washing and mending work to contribute to sparse family economies.

Regional studies have shown that there was more almshouse provision for women than for men in rural unions.[117] Families often refused to let women

[116] Thomson, 'Residential care of the elderly', 46, estimates that in 1861 3.75% of the population was aged over 65, compared with 5.4% in 1891. He points out that the figures for those over 60 are more difficult to correlate and although the increase of 1.6% excludes those aged between 60 and 65, the numerical increase still does not account for the significantly higher numbers of older persons in the workhouse after 1870.

[117] Rose, 'Crisis of poor relief', 50–70, argues that on the whole women were less harshly

enter the workhouse because they had greater affection for female relatives. Nevertheless, the proportion of women over sixty in the workhouse had risen by 19 per cent in the period 1881–91 in the Brixworth union. These figures explain why the lack of outdoor relief led to deep 'class' divisions by the 1890s. The stigma of admission to the workhouse was inevitable for the majority of elderly agricultural workers and this motivated working people to oppose the *crusading* party. Most chose to act now, to avoid indignity later.

Penalising the poor

Michael Rose suggests that by the 1880s most workhouses were transferring their duties to other care institutions by boarding out paupers.[118] Yet the Webbs' model of social welfare progressivism, which stresses the development of more specialised indoor care, was not in operation in the Brixworth union during the 1880s.[119] Of course, further comparative work needs to be done to ascertain whether the same trends occurred elsewhere. However, even though Brixworth was a strict union and therefore its workhouse statistics might be atypical, Thomson's Bedfordshire studies reveal similar increases in the number of elderly residents after 1880. He explains that workhouses became institutional care homes for the elderly in rural society during the agricultural crisis, with one out of every three workhouse inmates classified as elderly (over sixty-five) by 1891.[120] This suggests that even in areas where regulations concerning outdoor relief were relaxed, many guardians tried to save outdoor costs. The social cost of the *crusading* campaign seems to have been more profound than many current welfare historians appreciate.

The Spencer archive confirms that many dispossessed older labourers sold their possessions to buy food, but in the end the majority had to accept indoor relief.[121] Today it is easy to overlook the shame and stigma of admission to the workhouse, but in the later nineteenth century it was visible proof of social failure. Mary Mackinnon stresses that the psychological impact must have been considerable because before entering paupers had to surrender their belongings.[122] When the Brixworth union workhouse was refurbished as an old people's home in the early 1970s, workmen found bundles of small possessions within the perimeter wall and hedging which had been deposited by paupers in the later nineteenth century.[123] Purses containing a few pennies, letters from loved ones and precious wedding rings were stashed for

treated and benefited from the move to boarding-out paupers after 1870 as indoor care expanded.
118 Ibid.
119 Webb and Webb, *English poor law history*.
120 Thomson, 'Decline of social security', 299–336.
121 Calverley to Morley, 29 Nov. 1887, MSS Spencer, Sox 562, discusses social problems.
122 Mackinnon, 'Poor law policy', and 'English poor law policy'.
123 Anon., *Centenary of Brixworth Rural District Council, 1894–1994*, Northampton 1994.

safekeeping. They represent an inventory of pauper dignity and the social cost of an impoverishing *crusading* experiment. Presumably paupers hoped to collect their prized bundles at a later date. Historians know so very little of those who never returned. Their lost property has become an historical analogy for the untold account of their impecunious lives.

This section has explored the effect of a rural recession and the development of the *crusading* process in the Brixworth union. It has been possible to trace the demise of paternalism and the way that union combination impacted on poor law politics and relief practices. From the late-1860s falling profit margins and poorer harvests meant that outdoor relief was scrutinised and was under constant attack on a broad front. Throughout the 1870s guardians tried to create a 'world-without-welfare' outside the workhouse. They were not oblivious to the social cost, but they judged it irrelevant to their immediate economic interests. Central government knew how reductions in pauperism were being achieved, but they too ignored the social cost in favour of the bigger poor law picture.

Local sources reveal that there may have been a *crusading* 'template' in operation, which could involve several stages. In this section the first stage has been outlined: withdrawing all outdoor medical relief; the prosecution of the adult offspring of paupers for their maintenance; the completion of a charity review to encourage philanthropists to take over poor relief bills (which might also involve cutting relieving officers); and the elimination of semi-independent paupers from relieving officer lists as well as setting up private welfare-to-work schemes (including, if necessary, private charity). There must have been subtle variations in these initiatives in different regions and at different times. None the less pauperism figures cited in part I, taken from Williams, indicate that most of these measures must have been adopted in the majority of poor law unions. However, the actual official and unofficial cost-saving initiatives that helped guardians to reduce poor law expenditure and achieve their central government targets have been elusive. Primary evidence, therefore, has allowed welfare historians to engage with how *crusading* worked in practical terms. It has been possible to observe the day-to-day operation of the poor law at a time of acute retrenchment. Evidence points to the fact that the majority of guardians, even opponents of the anti-welfare campaign, had a clear understanding of what *crusading* involved. Widespread publicity of the cost-saving benefits by both central government and local enthusiasts meant that a *crusading* template was in circulation, which could be manipulated to suit local economic and political interests. The coming of democracy, therefore, must have been the harbinger of far-reaching poor law turmoil. Part III now explores how and with what political strength the excluded demanded to be included, protesting about pauperism in a more democratic era.

PART III

PROTESTING ABOUT PAUPERISM

6

Organising Resistance:
Protesting about Pauperism

The experience of being poor has a rich and complex historiography.[1] The question of what it meant to be poor in the English past has been tackled in a wide variety of ways. Issues of definition, however, still hamper social historians in this complex field. Who was poor and why remains unresolved across the nineteenth century.[2] Thus, Lynn Hollen-Lees has tried to identify welfare continuities and disjunctures in order to ascertain what they tell us about the material context of the poor's everyday lives;[3] Pat Thane has examined the degree to which poor law guardians treated men and women equally;[4] Peter King has investigated the stage at which one fell from relative to absolute poverty, and whether poor law authorities recognised that critical economic threshold.[5] By contrast, David Thomson analyses the extent to which pauperism was exacerbated by age and whether poor law officials treated the elderly with discretion and an understanding of their life-cycle predicaments.[6] Steven King has used yardsticks, such as burial, medical relief, clothing and suchlike to measure the experience of poverty across pauper populations,[7] while Thomas Sokoll's groundbreaking work on pauper narratives has given voice to the underprivileged.[8] 'Being poor' is a vibrant historiograhical field.

Few poverty historians, however, have taken up the suggestions of either Olwen Hufton[9] or Joanna Innes[10] that in order really to understand the experience of being poor it is necessary for welfare historians to integrate research on local 'makeshift economies' with the 'mixed economy of welfare'. Nor

[1] For a summary see L. Fontaine and J. Schlumbohm (eds), *Household strategies for survival, 1600–2000: fission, faction and co-operation*, Cambridge 2000.
[2] King and Tomkins, *The poor in England*, 1–38, provides a good overview of key debates on the experience of being poor.
[3] Hollen-Lees, *Solidarities*.
[4] P. Thane, *Old age in English history: past issues, current perspectives*, Oxford 2000, and P. Thane and L. Botelho (eds), *Women and ageing in British society since 1500*, Harlow 2001.
[5] Hitchcock, King and Sharpe, *Chronicling poverty*.
[6] See, for example, Thomson, '*I am not my father's keeper*', 265–86, 'The decline in social security', 451–82, and 'The welfare of the elderly', 194–22.
[7] King, *Poverty and welfare*.
[8] T. Sokoll, *Essex pauper letters, 1731–1837*, Oxford 2001.
[9] O. H. Hufton, *The poor of eighteenth-century France, 1750–1789*, Oxford 1974.
[10] J. Innes, 'The "mixed-economy of welfare" in early modern England: assessments of the options from Hale to Malthus (c. 1683–1803)', in Daunton, *Charity*, 139–80.

have many poverty studies built upon John Broad's remark about the need for 'an holistic approach to welfare', which indicates how paupers overcame and negotiated their way around poor law policy-making constraints.[11] To omit these material considerations, it is argued here, denies pauper agency and undervalues the political reaction that *crusading* could trigger.[12]

This chapter will consider further the reality of being poor. Returning to the inception of the *crusading* initiative, it will begin to trace the first stirrings of a definitive political journey by the labouring poor who opposed acute retrenchment. It shows how, and with what political strength, the impoverished and their allies locally came together to form a proactive opposition. Their reasons for doing so were straightforward. They were motivated by the fact that increasingly they had to 'makeshift' their resources very carefully to remain independent, that welfare-to-work schemes exacerbated their impoverishment and helped to create a 'world-without-welfare'. Slowly a political journey began. It started with the advent of agricultural trade unionism and developed into more direct forms of political action. Above all, local vestries were the centre of political activity. Here opposition began its poor law fight back. Indeed, it will be shown that local vestries had political vibrancy throughout the later Victorian era, as Keith Snell first noted.[13] Poor people were neither apathetic, nor disinterested, nor indeed submissive, in the face of poor law *crusading*. They could not afford to be. Thus it is possible to trace their resistance, both sporadic and organised, by examining the potential ways in which one could start to protest about pauperism in the local vestry. Moreover, as Steven King insists, 'the issue of how poor people … should secure their weekly, monthly and yearly welfare manifested itself as *the* single most important question at local and national level'.[14] If this view is salient, then retracing the political reaction that the *crusading* initiatives stimulated would give welfare historians concrete evidence that the experience of being poor could be dire in the later Victorian period.

---

[11] J. Broad, 'Parish economies of welfare, 1650–1834', *HJ* xxxxii (1999), 985–1006.

[12] Innovative research is to be found in the histories of crime, demography and medicine. On crime see, for example, R. Jutte, *Poverty and deviance in early modern Europe*, Cambridge 1994, and S. Woolf, *The poor in western Europe in the eighteenth and nineteenth centuries*, London 1986; on demography see B. Reay, *Microhistories: demography, society and culture in rural England, 1800–1900*, Cambridge 1996; on charity and sickness see Mandler, *The use of charity*.

[13] I am grateful to Keith Snell for sharing with me a draft copy of his *Parish and belonging in England and Wales, c. 1660–1904*, Cambridge 2007.

[14] King, *Poverty and welfare*, 1.

Vestry politics: a poor law fight back

In 1870 most labourers in the Brixworth union were disenfranchised, unable to influence the local poor law decision-making process.[15] However, despite being excluded in this manner, labourers were very interested in local politics. After all, the way that the poor law was administered shaped their material lives. Intriguingly, a participatory political culture had survived in the district in local vestries. In these venues labourers calculated that it was possible to exploit the chaotic nature of local government bureaucracy to challenge the poor law *status quo* once the *crusade* was underway. Specifically, this involved manipulating the procedures for electing guardians. If an individual wanted to serve as a guardian of the poor they first had to be nominated for election in their local vestry. This remnant of parish government gave the labouring poor an important source of political leverage. Although labourers were excluded from the poor law union boardroom, they were entitled to attend local vestry meetings. Even if they could not vote, they could voice their opinions and influence local politics. If they could round up enough opposition in local vestries they could seriously disrupt the re-election, generally on a triennial basis, of *crusaders* to poor law office. Their first opportunity came three years after the *crusade* started, in 1876–7.

In three renowned local vestry contests labourers tried to oust leading *crusaders* from office in this period.[16] In the first contest, in the parish of Brixworth, a number of ratepayers and sympathetic guardians formed an alliance. They wanted to ensure that two opponents of *crusading* were elected to the office of guardian of the poor to represent their interests. Two moderate farmers agreed to stand. A noisy campaign was launched successfully and in due course the vestry selected the farmers. Their names went forward for election in April. Both farmers won a guardian seat with very substantial majorities. The incumbent who lost his seat had been a keen *crusader* and ousting him from office delighted his opposition. Politically that outcome was rather embarrassing for Spencer. Although he was a leading national and county Whig, the two farmers were well-known Liberals who were outspoken critics of *crusading*. Spencer's reputation in the district had been crucial to getting the *crusading* campaign underway, but even he could not prevent local opposition developing in the vestry and wider community.

In the second contest the acting chairman of the board, William Bury, fell victim to a local plot in his parish at Haselbech. Here the labouring poor benefited from the patronage of Selina, Dowager Viscountess Milton (a prin-

---

[15] Rural labourers were disenfranchised in parliamentary elections until the Franchise Extension Acts of 1885 equalised county and borough qualifications. In poor law elections most labourers remained disenfranchised until the passing of the Local Government Act of 1894, which abolished property qualifications. See, for example, Keith-Lucas, *English local government*, 97–101.

[16] These three vestry contests are analysed from Brixworth union poor law correspondence, 'vestry contexts and guardian election procedures, 1867–7', MH 12/8701.

cipal landowner). Lady Milton despised Bury and Pell, and their *crusading* ethos, which she believed exacerbated pauperism. She therefore formed an alliance with one of her tenant farmers and disgruntled labourers who deeply resented the *crusading* initiatives. They hatched a plot to ensure that the chairman of the board missed his reselection notice. Lady Milton instructed her tenant farmer, who happened to be a churchwarden and vestry over-seer, to arrange with the Brixworth union clerk to post a guardian reselec-tion notice at midnight on the church door in Haselbech. It was nailed up surreptitiously and removed before dawn the following day to ensure that the chairman could not read it. Moreover, they hoped that he would forget to attend the appropriate vestry meeting to be reselected. To make sure the plan was fool-proof, the vestry meeting was set on an odd day and was over in a flash. As anticipated, the chairman of the guardians did not turn up to be renominated and a farmer who opposed his policies was nominated in his place. Lady Milton ensured that the farmer chosen was popular with local people. Events at Brixworth support Keith Snell's emphasis on the critical role played by overseers in parish government throughout the nineteenth century.[17] In fact a third example of gerrymandering in the vestry exempli-fies how poor law clerks and overseers of the poor who joined the opposition could be a thorn in the side of *crusading* guardians.

During the contest at Scaldwell parish another leading *crusader*, William Hamshaw, faced strong opposition when he tried to get reselected. However, he had got wind of what had happened at Brixworth and Haselbech in the weeks before the election, so he did not forget to turn up to be reselected. Moreover he brought with him a number of prominent landowners who supported his candidacy. The vestry clerk could not therefore prevent Hamshaw's renomi-nation. However, the opposition had not been defeated. Instead, the vestry clerk, the overseer of the poor for the parish and the Brixworth union clerk hatched a plot to get Hamshaw ousted from office. This time, the Brixworth union clerk agreed to falsify electoral registers in the April guardian elections in the parish. The clerk, with the co-operation of the overseer, decided to distribute voting papers during the guardian election to a number of artisans who did not pay rates. They also left voting papers at the homes of paupers who had been in receipt of outdoor relief, did not pay rates and should have been disqualified from voting. They even manipulated procedures to allow an alternative publican candidate – local and very popular – to stand in the first instance although he had not paid rates for twelve months and was also a fellow overseer of the poor for the parish. This should have disqualified him from seeking election. In the end, the publican candidate was elected with a large majority. The LGB set up an official inquiry following a complaint by Bury, the acting chairman, about these events and his having missed a rese-lection notice:

---

[17] See n. 13 above.

Our parish meeting for the election ... was held today <u>the 26th</u> – observe the date – And as the result of a plot, which I by accident discovered only within the last few days – my election for Guardian (an office I have held for some years) was opposed and another person nominated in my stead. I am anxious if possible to spare the poor and union the expense of a contest and the further expense of legal proceedings, which my friends will take upon certain informalities in case of my defeat – ... I think it is desirable to avoid a defeat, for not only am I Chairman of the Board but I have been instrumental in effecting substantial reforms for the carrying out of which my presence is very necessary.[18]

Despite a number of extensive investigations civil servants were unable to prevent the popular candidates from being elected. Procedures were chaotic and the clerk and overseer had too many discretionary powers. Only they could provide evidence of their own election mismanagement because not until after 1879 were guardian election procedures subject to public account-ability. If they chose to falsify elections there was nothing central government could do to stop gerrymandering. In a confidential letter to the Brixworth union guardians a civil servant concluded that 'The Board direct me to state that it rests with the Returning Officer [clerk and overseer] in the first instance to decide upon his own responsibility and according to his own views of the case ... we cannot properly at present express any opinion on the subject.'[19]

This angered *crusaders* who felt let down by the LGB. A leading guardian made further inquiries and reported to the LGB on 26 March 1877 that

An attempt has just been made by nominating another person to unseat Rev. William Bury, the old guard of this parish and Chairman of the Board. Voters, I am told, have been for some time past quietly canvassed outside the parish as well as in and every preparation made by his opponent. The notice of the Election of Guardian has not this year been affixed to the Church Door, the usual place for notices or otherwise published in the parish. Under these circumstances I have declined to nominate the [alternative] Guardian, believing that no legal election can take place.[20]

In fact, this statement was duplicitous, as several private letters to Spencer later revealed. Their author, Pell, was forced to admit that 'the greater Part of the Parishioners will I am sure be pleased to hear that Rev. Bury can this year be ousted'. Pell learned that the notice had been published and removed surreptitiously and so the election was legal. He asked Spencer to help Bury get re-elected. The *crusaders*' party implemented two plans to achieve this.

Technically, magistrates still had the right to veto any vestry appointment

---

18 Bury to LGB, 26 Mar. 1877, MH 12/8701.
19 Official letter of reply, 1 Aug. 1878, ibid. Civil servants ignored complaints for almost a year before replying.
20 Pell to LGB, 26 Mar. 1877, ibid.

judged detrimental to the public interest. They could rule that a guardian of the poor was not appointed if the individual refused to administer outdoor relief efficiently by supporting a *crusading* policy. Spencer did not want to override popular votes but he did decree that the names of committed *crusaders* ousted from office be added to vestry nomination lists to allow them to stand at the next guardian elections in April 1877. Every lord lieutenant had the power to do this since they controlled the magistracy. Pell thus made extensive use of Spencer's position to secure the *crusaders'* power by means of this procedural loop-hole. In a private letter he thanked Spencer and revealed that 'I believe there is a frightful mischief going on, over which one in your position could exercise irresistible control. ... I wish your hounds would run their fox occasionally into some of the homes of the people!'[21] Subsequently he wrote:

> I do not like so good and noble a man to be disturbed in his office here by this ungracious plot. I had good grounds too for believing that the majority of the parishioners were with him.
> But reviewing this affair in the calm light in which your letter places it, I entirely admit that he will do well and will be taking higher ground by retiring [from the controversy].[22]

Spencer then arranged to re-elect Bury without a contest in Althorp parish, which he controlled. Despite this counter-action Pell regretted what he called, 'this *game of the poor*' and admitted that Bury now had to ensure that he did not 'lessen the value of what you have done for us by further noticing this insult'. They ought to congratulate themselves that 'it is sufficient that he had the opportunity of washing his hands of the whole dirty proceeding'.[23] Large landowners who supported the *crusade*, therefore, ensured that incumbents were renominated to safe seats. They achieved this because they held a large number of plural votes in closed parishes. As a result, one very unpopular *crusader* was nominated in three contests to ensure that he was not ousted from office. What do these vestry contests reveal about the nature of rural politics and the social welfare aspirations of the labouring classes in the Brixworth union?

These vestry contests were a precursor of a shift in rural politics before the advent of the extension of parliamentary enfranchisement in 1885. David Eastwood argues that 'the vestry ceased to be a theatre of local government' once poor law unions were established in the 1830s.[24] He asserts that the

---

21 Pell to Spencer, 3 Feb. 1877, MSS Althorp, K159. The early date of this letter, before the missed re-selection notice, indicates that political tensions in the district were running high.
22 Pell to Spencer, 31 Mar. 1877, ibid.
23 Ibid.
24 D. Eastwood, 'Rethinking debates on the poor law in early nineteenth-century England', *Utilitas* vi (1994), 97–116, and *Government and community in the English provinces, 1700–1870*, Basingstoke 1997, 126.

New Poor Law destroyed the participatory ethos of the Old Poor Law because vestries lost the right to administer poor relief expenditure. The vestry was down-graded in rural society, its vibrant political culture was destroyed and labourers became disenchanted with parish government. It is apparent that the evidence here indicates that Eastwood has overlooked the importance of vestry politics and in particular how they influenced elections of poor law guardians in the later Victorian period.

It is easy to miss the fact that vestries remained a focal point of rural life. Often, political historians are distracted by the implications of the Third Reform Act. Within the 'poor law and the politics of place' there were complex layers of local political reality. Moreover, in vestries, pauper agency survived intact. Some of the labouring poor who turned up to the vestry on a regular basis also joined the NALU. Thus they kept up vestry attendance in order to challenge farmers face-to-face about social conditions and a more rigorous poor law. Whereas the poor law boardroom was closed to visitors, the vestry (even if strictly 'closed') was often a space for open public debate. Furthermore, the three Brixworth union vestry contests demonstrate that *crusading* initiatives triggered a political reaction. Paupers used this outlet to express their own political will. This is instructive since historians, such as Pat Thane, have tended to take a rather one-sided view of the political ambitions and social welfare aspirations of the rural labouring classes in the later nineteenth century. At best, Hodge is portrayed as a member of a down-trodden class incapable of exerting political influence; at worst, he is consigned to the role of an apathetic bystander.[25] Such historical interpretations distort the true nature of local rural politics after 1870.

In the 1970s Derek Fraser argued that 'the politicising of local government was not the creation of the caucus politics of the 1870s'; vestries had been politicised for much of the nineteenth century.[26] In the late 1870s, when the Liberal party wanted to strengthen its position, it tried to widen its appeal by aligning with those radical forces that were already present in local vestry politics. Fraser astutely observes that the significance of the vestry, at least before the Franchise Extension Acts of 1885, has been neglected. In the 1980s a number of socio-political urban historians made important contributions to this field of poor law studies. Work on Victorian industrial towns has furthered historical understanding of the significance of urban vestries as late as the 1880s. John Garrard argues that a 'high level of social and political autonomy' was created over the course of the nineteenth century.[27] There was an important degree of devolution within the poor law system, often more than contemporaries chose to admit. This was achieved in a number of ways. For instance, vestries that continued to select guardians of the poor to

---

[25] Thane, 'The working class and state "welfare"', 892, maintains that 'nowhere did working class voters flood out to support such social reforming candidates, or indeed any others' in the late-nineteenth century. She has overlooked the impact of *crusading*.

[26] Fraser, *Urban politics*, 30.

[27] See introduction, n. 29.

stand for election had a significant amount of political leverage. Local over-seers of the poor, working alongside union clerks and relieving officers, had a considerable amount of local power at a grass roots level. The creation within boards of sectional committees that controlled key decision-making processes also produced a highly discretionary system.

Unfortunately, there have been few published local studies of these aspects of rural poor law politics in the later Victorian period. Admittedly, it is often very difficult to reconstruct how local rural politics operated because good source material is hard to find. It is evident that welfare historians still do not fully understand the nature of rural politics among the labouring poor. A good starting point, however, is to seek out evidence of where a poor law reaction may have been engendered, since that will uncover evidence of any political activity. Clearly an analysis of the *crusading* campaign can reveal how resist-ance was organised, whether low key or more overt.[28] The labouring poor in the Brixworth union may have been uninterested in national party politics but that did not mean that they were not actively involved in political issues of their own. Many labourers in the Brixworth union in the 1870s ignored the national political scene because they conceived that it did not impact directly on their lives, but the *crusading* measures did. So, they organised to resist poor law changes that they resented and could ill afford.

Organising resistance

This brief analysis of the political backdrop at Brixworth reveals underlying tensions within the poor law system. One key factor furthers historical under-standing of socio-political relations. An NALU presence in the district made a significant local impact because traditional relationships were fundamen-tally altered. After 1870 labourers came forward in public to air their griev-ances because the *crusading* initiatives undermined customary expectations of social obligation. For example, as chapter 4 recounted, one NALU branch on the Althorp estate took the unprecedented step of directly petitioning Spencer for a wage increase.[29] Other branches, as Horn has shown, held meetings to instruct members in how to use their collective voice effectively in local vestries during poor law elections and school board contests. The NALU actively encouraged labourers to seek election to local authorities, an action that alarmed farmers who felt that the rural social order was under threat again. A prominent supporter of the NALU advised labourers that

> Every occupier of a rateable cottage in every village in England, no matter whether the rates are paid by himself or his landlord, has the same right ...

[28] Ryan, 'Poplarism', 56–83, examines the impact of *crusading* in East London unions.
[29] 'Petition to the 5th Earl Spencer', 27 Mar. 1873, MSS Spencer, Sox 393. Spencer reacted angrily, informing petitioners that they had been refused permission to use local schools for their union meetings.

to attend every vestry and parish meeting, and vote for or against this or that man being churchwarden, guardian of the poor, waywarden, or on the School Board.[30]

It was a sentiment that had widespread appeal in the Brixworth union. Pamela Horn explains that, by 1878, membership of the NALU in Northamptonshire had stabilised, but it is significant that labourers used the union infrastructure extensively. Whereas under the Old Poor Law the poor had the right to appeal to a local magistrate against a decision on poor relief made by the overseers in their parish which they considered unfair, after 1870 justices were asked to convict the adult children of elderly paupers. The labouring poor had to employ an intermediary to act as their defence counsel in court because they had lost their traditional right of appeal. The NALU therefore provided a much-needed service and by protecting its members it also enhanced its role in rural society. It is evident that the NALU in this area also encouraged labourers to participate in poor law politics.[31] The prosecution strategy seems to have polarised local opinion, creating a vacuum that the NALU readily filled. The labouring poor who took part in the 1876–7 vestry contests appear to have been determined to fight back, resisting further *crusading* measures. The NALU recognised that need and identified that it was important to support their fight because the *crusading* controversy had arguably become the single most important issue in this location after 1870. In a number of poor law unions some *crusading* regulations were relaxed around 1879 because of the impact of the agricultural recession; but where a *crusading* template of measures was implemented, as at Brixworth, they dominated local politics.

The NALU was a precursor of modern trade unionism. Although it alarmed a number of farmer guardians in the 1870s, by the 1880s a considerable number of them admitted in private that the *crusading* experiment was too retributive and triggered union combination.[32] Agricultural and welfare historians have access to, but seldom exploit poor law sources that reconstruct these types of political complexities and the depths of rural deprivation they exemplify. Yet it is evident that growing grievances about a world-without-welfare created a new socio-political climate in the Brixworth union district. From as early as 1876, only three years after its inception, the *crusading* experiment faced strong opposition. Predominantly this occurred in local vestries because they were accessible political forums, a source of political leverage for the impoverished. The LGB knew that a number of procedural loop-holes were being exploited by union clerks, overseers, farmers and the labouring poor. However, civil servants had to ignore malpractice at election time because they had no powers to compel poor law officials to comply with their recommendations – a factor that helped get *crusading* underway but paradoxically also gave working people the means to fight back.

---

30 Canon Girdlestone, 'The farm labourer', *Macmillan Magazine* (1872), 261.
31 See introduction, n. 36.
32 Dunbabin, '"The revolt of the field"', 69.

In 1878 a select committee examined the issue of corruption in guardian elections, concluding that chaotic procedures undermined bureaucratic efficiency. However, they recommended that election procedures should remain unchanged because they 'would have the effect of causing elections now determined by other considerations to be regarded as political'.[33] The select committee was determined to stress the apolitical nature of guardian elections, even though its members knew that the controversy over *crusading* was a dominant political issue in many locations. This evidence supports Snell's contention that the parish 'remained a strong cultural focus amongst the poor into the later nineteenth century'.[34] Before the advent of formal changes in the suffrage these vestries had proved to be 'a quite sufficient background against which class feelings could develop' during guardian election contests.[35] The labourers' desire to reintroduce the provision of outdoor relief also attests that they had social welfare aspirations and, if provoked, were prepared to fight for them. Those who ran the *crusading* experiment knew this, and reacted to halt that challenge.

Residents in the Brixworth union, having formed a coalition for change, and started to organise resistance, were ready, and, with a growing determination, committed to fighting for the reintroduction of outdoor relief. They now extended their growing political involvement in the poor law. Meanwhile, *crusaders* committed a key error. Instead of acting with moderation and greater understanding, they pushed for more extreme *crusading* measures. This was foolhardy, since the pauperised were already politicised. The *crusaders*' obdurate response inflamed the opposition's determination to make further political headway in a more democratic era. Both sides clashed, as those in control tried to consolidate their position and those in opposition tried to wrest control over the poor law from them.

---

[33] *Report of the House of Commons select committee on elections of poor law guardians in England, Scotland and Ireland*, PP 1878, iv, appendix xvii at p. 268.
[34] Snell, 'Deferential bitterness', 178.
[35] Ibid. 179.

7

Class Coalition: Poor Law Crisis and Reaction

Political historians have debated extensively the impact on rural society of the Third Reform Act (1885) and the County Council Act (1889).[1] It is estimated that about a third of the population gained the right to vote in parliamentary elections in English counties after 1885. Yet equalising borough and county suffrage qualifications was not straightforward. Complicated registration procedures often limited the effect of the new voting provisions: Neal Blewett has calculated that less than 30 per cent of the total male adult population in England and Wales successfully registered their right to vote after 1885.[2] Moreover, the extension of the franchise still alarmed the ruling elite in rural society. In a period of rapid economic change, they feared that they were losing their 'perquisite of power'.[3] Gradually there was a change in the personnel and structure of local government, even though many landowning magistrates were elected to county councils in 1889.[4] The reform of county government also raised many controversial questions about the future structure of rural politics, most notably whether poor law unions should be democratised too. The focus of this chapter, therefore, is upon the effect of the coming of democracy on the poor law.

It is first essential to analyse the bitter political debate that broke out when the chairman of the Brixworth union criticised the conduct of the landed interest over the poor law in a national journal: an important controversy since it betrayed that in private guardians were very divided over the social cost of the *crusade* and its political ramifications. By analysing the 'class' composition and voting data of guardians, it is then possible to unravel poor law allegiances. The period 1885–9 was one of coalition politics, which made it very hard for committed *crusaders* to maintain their dominance. Moreover, the advent of caucus politics and therein the political activities of working people complicated local poor law debates. New voters took an active interest in local poor law politics. The politicisation of rural society runs counter to the traditional view that hostility to the *crusade* was low key and only organised by mavericks. In fact, there was growing opposition, which though

---

[1] See, for example, J. P. D. Dunbabin, 'The politics of the establishment of the county councils', *HJ* iv (1963), 238–50; 'Expectations of the new county councils and their realisation', *HJ* xviii (1965), 354–73; and 'British local government reform: the nineteenth century and after', *EHR* lxxxxii (1977), 777–805.
[2] N. Blewett, 'The franchise in the United Kingdom, 1885–1918', *P&P* xxxii (Dec. 1965), 27–56 at p. 27.
[3] E. J. Hobsbawm, *Industry and empire*, London 1969, 203.
[4] Cannadine, *Decline and fall*, 139–81.

tentative at first, can be traced from its early inception. Its impact can be observed in the way that the *crusaders* reacted to mounting political activity amongst the labouring poor by proposing a scheme of local government that limited poor law democracy.[5] Although their plan was unsuccessful, it reveals just how alarmed *crusaders* were at the pace of economic and political change, and how that fear shaped their actions. It soon became evident that those in power were fighting to consolidate their weakening position and those in opposition were seeking to make political capital out of their discomfort, inspired by the coming of democracy to fight together in pragmatic ways for changes in the poor law.

'Squires, spires and mires':
Northamptonshire politics and the threat of democracy

Northamptonshire politics were complex in the later Victorian period. None the less, the revival of Liberalism, as Janet Howarth has argued, was one of the most striking features of political life in the county after 1880.[6] Moreover, in 1885 a boundary commission divided Northamptonshire into four parliamentary constituencies. The Brixworth union was reallocated to the newly created mid-Northamptonshire seat, which was held until 1895 by Spencer's half-brother, Bobby Spencer.[7] Thus the success of Liberalism in the county was dependent on two factors, namely the influence of the Spencer family and the appeal of Gladstonian democracy. However, as the image of Liberalism in the area was 'not simple or uniform', both factors had limited success during the 1880s (despite the general election victories of 1885, 1886 and 1892).[8] Liberalism was a success in the East Northamptonshire constituency because it was a 'Radical-advanced' Liberal stronghold, with puritan and Chartist roots. Here Liberals, usually Nonconformists, cultivated their electoral appeal *vis-à-vis* a growing industrial electorate. In mid-Northamptonshire Liberalism was less successful. Essentially, Earl Spencer and Bobby Spencer were too conservative. Neither would support extensive social welfare reform that would have

---

[5] Few welfare historians discuss the impact of county council proposals on *crusaders*. See, for example, Kidd, *State, society and the poor*, 48–52, which makes no reference to the threat to the poor law *status quo* implicit in county council reform. Keith-Lucas, *English local government*, 82–115, still gives the most comprehensive summary of the implications of local government change; Bellamy, *Administering central-local relations*, 148–9, 233–71, discusses those who lobbied central government to protect their poor law interests in the light of local government change.

[6] Howarth, 'Liberal revival', 78–118.

[7] Ibid. 83–4 n. 14, explains that these were East Northants (Wellingborough, 'advanced' Liberal, 1885, 1886, 1892, 1895), Mid-Northants (Brixworth, Whig and Gladstonian Liberalism, Spencer family seat, 1885, 1886, 1892, lost to Conservatives 1895), South Northants (Towcester, Conservative, 1852–92, Gladstonian Liberal, 1892–95, Conservative after 1895); North Northants (Oundle, safe Conservative seat after 1870).

[8] There were elections in 1885 and 1886 because of the Home Rule crisis.

appealed to villagers anxious to reintroduce outdoor relief and desirous of old age pensions. Although the Home Rule issue was debated extensively in the area in the 1880s, it was local issues, which affected voters' everyday lives, that had the most direct appeal. In a less democratic era the Spencer family's refusal to support popular poor law reforms would probably not have affected their long-term political future. But after the Third Reform Act that situation altered considerably.

The parliamentary electorate trebled across Northamptonshire in 1885; gradually, the character of local political life changed. The rural exodus of the early 1880s ensured that most of the new electorate was 'outside the reach of the landed influence' in the area.[9] One might have expected migration to have increased the influence of the rural elite over those who stayed behind in the Brixworth union. Instead, the *crusading* experiment had the opposite effect. During the first stage of the agricultural crisis discriminatory welfare-to-work schemes polarised local opinion.[10] Against this backdrop opposition formed, determined to resist further changes in the poor law. This tense political atmosphere alarmed the chairman of the Brixworth union: he feared that parliamentary democracy was raising political expectations amongst the labouring poor who were numerically strong; and that in future those new voters would want to have a greater say in poor law matters.[11] Future poor law democracy would give members of the lower classes an opportunity to be elected as guardians. Furthermore, many farmer guardians had become rather complacent about holding power. Many had neither the time nor the inclination to devote to poor law politics during a recession. Bury was concerned that the farmers were more concerned about their falling rental incomes and poor profits, than daily poor law administration. He was convinced that the recent political changes had increased the need for his party to put on a united front. Consequently, he decided to publish an article in a leading national journal outlining his concerns.

In March 1885 Bury's article, '*Squires, spires and mires*' appeared in the *Fortnightly Review*.[12] Its theme and timing were controversial. It appeared to endorse 'Radical Liberal' criticisms of landed society and coincidentally was published just prior to Joseph Chamberlain's 'Unauthorised programme'. Bury did not intend either that political slant or to create so much adverse publicity, but his article caused a furore in Liberal circles because readers realised that its author was criticising a leading party leader and close ally of Gladstone, namely Earl Spencer. Since Spencer valued his privacy and protected his political reputation carefully, he was angered at being identified so easily and by the forthright nature of the criticisms. When it then emerged that the author was a clergyman and that Spencer was the patron

---

9   Howarth, 'Liberal revival', 90–1.
10   See chapter 5 above.
11   Bury to Spencer, 6 Mar. 1883, 24 July 1885, MSS Althorp, K382, discuss his concerns.
12   Revd W. Bury, '*Squires, spires, and mires*', *Fortnightly Review* (Mar. 1885), 352–70.

of his living, critics seized the opportunity to make political capital out of a potentially embarrassing article.

In a lengthy discussion Bury outlined why the conduct of country gentlemen in rural society ought to be censured. He stated that landowners used the countryside as a 'playground', exploiting its sporting potential, but taking little interest in local affairs. Often, for example, they refused to invest in the community by implementing basic sanitary improvements. Squires also refused to build good housing and they seldom administered poor relief regulations efficiently:

> My complaint is limited to this, that he neglects the plain duties which lie at his very door, and which require nothing from him beyond a little self-denial; that on matters of local administration properly belonging to him, and which are of really vital importance to the community, and especially to the labourer, the country gentleman is conspicuous by his absence; and that when he is brought face to face with local abuses of the gravest kind he is apparently unconcerned and that in attempts at reform he lends no hand.[13]

Bury went on to state that squires were apathetic about poor law matters. Most did not appreciate that by neglecting their local duties they were undermining their power base in rural society.

The article also criticised Bury's fellow Anglican clergymen.[14] He argued that clergymen never questioned conventional definitions of poverty. Instead they categorised poor relief claimants as 'deserving'. Most did not want to offend their congregations. Many gave alms to paupers even though they knew it discouraged an ethos of self-help and industry. He argued that withholding outdoor relief and charity 'makes the poor more self reliant, not less'. Moreover, the article asserted that guardians should abandon charity and adopt instead scientific theory and political economy. Only those approaches would remedy the social evil of poverty. Clergy should recognise that charitable donations ought to be 'temporary expedients ... stepping stones' to independence, otherwise their generosity would produce 'an utterly thriftless class'. Bury observed that rural society was on the brink of a number of important political changes the implications of which Anglican clergymen did not appreciate fully. He believed that it was every cleric's duty to guide his parishioners. The re-education of the poor would make them more industrious and shape their future voting decisions.[15]

13 Ibid.

14 Bury to Spencer, 14 Apr. 1885, MSS Althorp, K382, discusses criticisms that the article raised and the political controversy it aroused. Bury told Spencer to refer all critics to him and that he would explain that in poor law matters 'everyone knows how much the reform [i.e. *crusading*] owes to the line you took ... to the invaluable support you have given to the "reformers"'.

15 Bury to Spencer, 25 Feb. 1885, ibid. informed Spencer that Bury thought it was his duty to teach the new rural voters how they ought to participate in politics by organising

To its readership in the Brixworth union, Bury's motivation for publishing this article was self-evident.[16] The article was a political cry to arms, an appeal to *crusaders* to remain united. Bury believed that the political strength of the rural elite had always been based on a principle of unity in diversity. So long as they concentrated on policy agreements and ignored minor differences, they would remain in power. However, if they allowed internal divisions, complacency, or apathy, to determine their actions their political oligarchy would be destroyed. Bury's greatest fear was that democracy would be extended to the poor law. New voters would demand that the basis of welfare service provision must change, a negative outcome for the *crusade*. He thought that by forewarning his poor law colleagues he could reunite his party. Instead he soon learned that his article stirred lengthy debates that divided, rather than united, guardians. There were two main replies to his article.

The first to respond was Lord Stanley of Alderley, a close family friend of the Spencers and ironically co-editor of the *Fortnightly Review*. He had not seen Bury's article before publication. Had he done so, Spencer would have been given an advance copy for approval. Stanley felt that it was his public duty to defend Spencer who was in Dublin at the time of publication, serving his second term as lord lieutenant of Ireland (1882–5). His reply to Bury, published in the *Fortnightly Review* in July 1885, and entitled 'Two days in the Brixworth union', informed readers that he had visited the district in May 1885 to ascertain whether Bury's claims were true and in particular whether his criticisms of Spencer were warranted.[17] Bury complained to Spencer that the visit had been a difficult one:

> He came to Harlestone & ... wandered about the neighbouring parishes to see whether or not I had overstated my case in my Article – ... He refused my hospitality for fear lest he should become too friendly with me and be disarmed ... but this didn't prevent him talking to me 'sixteen to the dozen' – quite ignoring my replies – I gather however he quite accepts facts but quarrels with conclusions.[18]

Stanley reported that he had interviewed a cross-section of guardians. He learned that many were very critical of the chairman: although they did not vote against him on the poor law board, many abstained because they disliked his self-styled administrative methods which seemed to exacerbate pauperism. Clergy guardians were very angry about Bury's criticisms of their charitable work. Stanley recorded that Bury used private charitable schemes,

a series of meetings that he would chair. He ended, 'it is high time the new voters should learn something about politics'.

16 Bury to Spencer, 6 Mar. 1883, ibid. explains that Bury had earlier set out his views on the importance of poor relief management and how it protected the interests of the landed influence in a very lengthy letter to Spencer.

17 Stanley, 'Two days in the Brixworth union', 42–55. S. Lee (ed), *Dictionary of national biography, 1901–1911*, London 1911, 383, summarises Stanley's career.

18 Bury to Spencer, 16 May 1885, MSS Althorp, K382.

such as the 'Secret Service Fund', to suit his economic interests even if this meant ignoring 'deserving' poor law applicants. Thus, Stanley alleged that the chairman's charity, couched in COS rhetoric, only served Bury's political expediency. He concluded that 'Mr Bury surveys the world from the serene altitudes of the political economist' failing to recognise that 'the new gospel … of legislative change, scientific and economic improvements' often ignored the 'considerable number of human beings silently suffering below' it. In his opinion Bury was a penny-pinching bureaucrat who ignored basic economic calculations (indoor relief was more costly than outdoor). This made him nothing more than a 'pestilent meddler, *an unmitigated evil* and an intolerable nuisance!'

A leading Liberal *ex-officio* guardian, who was a Northamptonshire squire and a close friend of Spencer, published a second reply, 'Country gentlemen and agricultural labourers', in the *Northampton Mercury*. He described the chairman's criticism as a '*stinking fish*'.[19] He denied any *ex-officio* dereliction of duty. Moreover, he revealed that if landowners had not supported the 'Secret Service Fund', the *crusading* campaign would have failed by 1880. He was angry that Bury criticised clergymen for giving charity to the poor. Wasn't Bury doing the same when he diverted genuine and 'deserving' claimants to outdoor relief to his 'Secret Service Fund'? In the squire's opinion the *crusade* did not work in practice. It accentuated, rather than resolved, the problem of endemic poverty. Moreover, rates were cut as a result of *crusaders'* ruthlessness not the *crusade's* economic logic. If everyone rejected had chosen to enter the workhouse, it would have been filled to capacity and cost rate-payers more in local taxes. Often, nearby poor law unions inherited their social problems. The squire concluded that Bury was a politically ambitious clergyman who used poor law ideology to further his career. The obstinacy of the *crusaders* radicalised working people. He warned Bury that 'labourers are as independent as their incomes allow; they bitterly resent the accusation that they would sell their freedom for a dole'. And it was unwise to ignore such popular sentiments in a more democratic era.

A number of local clergymen also wrote lengthy criticisms to local newspapers. One described the chairman as a man of 'candour and caustic vigour'. He noted that Matthew Arnold 'held that the State Church' should provide 'for each parish an educated man as a diffuser of *sweetness and light*'.[20] The same clergyman pitied Bury's parishioners: 'Imagine the Anglican Church appointing someone who used his position to impoverish the labouring poor.' The labouring classes also took a keen interest in these articles because this was a public debate. One correspondent aptly summarised their position:

By the kindness of a friend I continue to receive the *Guardian* from your office … and I want to say that I am glad that you keep pegging away …

[19] Sir Hereward Wake, 'Country gentlemen and agricultural labourers', *Northampton Mercury*, 11 Apr. 1885.
[20] *Northampton Guardian*, 30 May 1885.

two million of our fellow creatures are about to give their votes for the first time. To *whom* shall they be given? ... Let me say as a worker what kind of men we need to make laws for us. Is it quite necessary that they must be rich men and of high social position, men born, as we say, 'with a silver spoon in their mouths', men quite removed from the experience of the struggling multitude. ... I say no, a thousand times no. ... Now the kind of man I want to represent me is a plain straight upright large-hearted broad minded a 'be just and fear not' man – a man who knows by actual experience what the tussle of life is. ... If we workers are properly represented ... we shall have *better times ... we want fair play, just laws and a chance to live.*[21]

This letter, one of several written to local newspapers, revealed that there was a growing awareness amongst the labouring classes of the implications of the chairman's controversial action. His defensive attitude belied just how divided guardians were in private about the *crusading* controversy. Parliamentary democratisation and its extension into local government would give the labouring poor an opportunity to challenge the *crusade* through the ballot box, where it most mattered. Correspondents commented that Bury's article strengthened their political resolve to resist those who used the poor law 'to protect the interests of the few, at the expense of the many'.[22] At the same time, the ongoing controversy also revealed that Bury's article had backfired. Paradoxically, he had accentuated divisions among the guardians. Thus, the scene was set for working people to forge alliances with sympathetic farmer and tradesmen guardians, as they had done during the advent of agricultural trade unionism. In the future, it might be possible for them to gain a foothold on the Brixworth union board, at a time when its social profile was undergoing significant change.

The changing social profile of guardians

The social structure of the Brixworth union board of guardians changed in several fundamental ways in the period 1885 to 1889.[23] The guardians' minute books reveal that this was a time of more intense coalition politics. This created a strained atmosphere during fortnightly board meetings. Table 6

[21] Letter, 'What we workers want and should have', *Northampton Guardian*, 14 Mar. 1885.
[22] Ibid.
[23] Unfortunately, as guardians' voting patterns were not recorded in this period on a regular basis, it is very difficult to reconstruct guardian divisions definitively. However, the clerk of the Brixworth union did keep a record of votes during controversial motions. Sampling these allegiances gives an insight into party politics: *crusaders* versus an opposition. To test the accuracy of this analysis, voting patterns have been cross-checked against figures for the 1890s when it was a legal requirement to keep voting records. These provide a useful comparison with earlier data. The exercise reveals that those guardians who attended board meetings on a regular basis usually voted in a consistent manner; they therefore provide an insight into party loyalties.

Table 6
Class composition of the Brixworth union board of guardians, 1885–9

	1885	1886	1887	1888	1889
Non-elected					
Ex-officio	14	14	14	14	16
Elected					
Landowner/ householder	2	1	2	2	2
Land agent	2	4	4	4	4
Clergy	5	4	6	5	5
Farmers					
Group 1	8	7	6	5	4
Group 2	7	3	5	3	2
Group 3	13	14	18	19	19
Tradesmen	3	3	2	2	2
Artisans	0	0	0	0	0
Labourers	0	0	0	0	0
Other					
Double nominations/ vacant seats	4	8	1	4	6
Subtotal					
Elected	44	44	44	44	44
Total votes	58	58	58	58	60

Source: Brixworth union guardians' minute books, P/L 2/17–18.

outlines the basic 'class' divisions, divided into three catgories in order to take account of their occupational diversity and shifting poor law allegiances.[24] Group 1 farmers consistently supported the *crusade*. By contrast, some group 2 farmers were *crusaders* and others were not, so table 7 and fig. 7 display party allegiances. Meanwhile, group 3 farmers represent a floating block whose allegiances wavered considerably. Seldom were they loyal either to *crusaders* or the strong opposition party. Thus, for the purpose of this discussion about how coalition politics worked, group 3 farmers need to be treated with caution. What the figures show is that in 1885–9 *crusaders* gained an average

[24] Compiled from *Royal Commission on Labour* (1894), 'Brixworth union', appendix i, 895–995; P. Kirton, *Census of Brixworth: an analysis and transcription*, on behalf of Brixworth History Society, Northampton 1994 (NRO, ROP 2765).

Table 7
Class composition of the Brixworth union board of guardians with political allegiances identified where possible, 1885–9

	1885	1886	1887	1888	1889
Crusaders' party					
Non-elected					
Ex-officio	11	11	11	12	14
Elected					
Landowner/					
householder	2	1	1	1	1
Land agent	2	4	4	4	4
Clergy	4	3	5	4	4
Farmers					
Group 1	8	7	6	5	4
Group 2	4	1	4	1	0
Group 3	–	–	–	–	–
Tradesmen	0	0	0	0	0
Artisans	0	0	0	0	0
Labourers	0	0	0	0	0
Subtotal	31	27	31	27	27
Opposition party					
Non-elected					
Ex-officio	3	3	3	2	2
Elected					
Landowner/					
Householder	0	0	1	1	1
land agent	0	0	0	0	0
Clergy	1	1	1	1	1
Farmers					
Group 1	0	0	0	0	0
Group 2	3	2	1	2	2
Group 3	–	–	–	–	–
Traders	3	3	2	2	2
Artisans	0	0	0	0	0
Labourers	0	0	0	0	0
Subtotal	10	9	8	8	8
Floating voters					
Farmers					
Group 3	13	14	18	19	19
Double/vacant					
seats	4	8	1	4	6
Total votes	58	58	58	58	60

Source: Brixworth union guardians' minute books, P/L 2/17–18.

Figure 7

Party divisions on the Brixworth union board of guardians, c. 1885–9

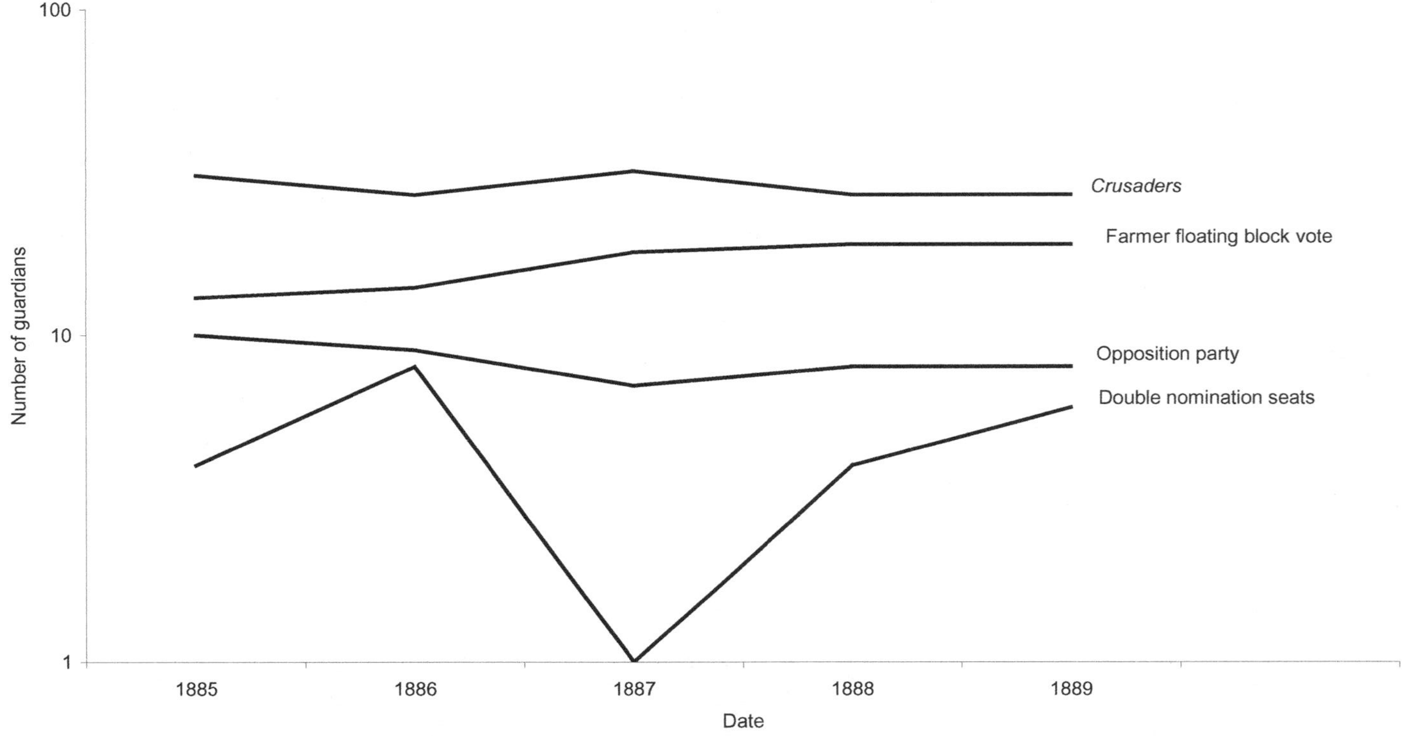

Crusaders

Farmer floating block vote

Opposition party

Double nomination seats

Number of guardians

Date

1885   1886   1887   1888   1889

100

10

1

Source: Brixworth union guardians' minute books, P/L 2/14–20

of twenty-nine out of a possible fifty-eight guardian seats. However, that crude calculation belies the reality of boardroom politics, for in fact *crusaders* gained the bulk of their support from unelected members of the board who seldom attended meetings. Elected supporters therefore held the balance of power and determined the success or failure of the *crusading* party. Recalculating that figure reveals that on average *crusaders* elected to office totalled around seventeen, against eight guardians on the opposition party. This meant that Pell and Bury had to work harder to convince elected *crusaders* to turn up to key meetings, to ensure that they retained a comfortable majority. They also had to negotiate on a more regular basis with some of the farmers in group 3. It is interesting to speculate that had this floating block entirely migrated to the opposition, *crusaders* would have lost power in years when *ex-officio* (unelected *crusader*) attendance was low. In fact, guardian minute books show that *crusaders* faced a potential voting crisis in 1888–9. Pell and Bury calculated that for personal reasons no *ex-officio* guardian could attend. This meant that the group 3 farmers, who often supported the opposition party, threatened *crusaders*. Counting the votes shows that the board might often be tied at twenty-seven votes apiece. Pell disliked coalition politics, favouring a more autocratic style of leadership. Reluctantly, he had to bargain more to retain power. Against this background Bury felt it necessary to publish his controversial article in the *Fortnightly Review*. He foresaw that some *ex-officio crusader* guardians were complacent. The figures also confirm that they did need to regroup and take a greater interest in poor law matters, otherwise their future power was threatened.

Voting figures also reveal that an opposition party was starting to gather momentum, and in the longer term threatened to become more established. Although fewer in number, members of this group were regular attendees, and included a small but significant number of influential *ex-officio* guardians. Moreover, some of the larger farmers from group 2 joined the opposition; they seem to have had the financial independence to devote time to poor law politics. It is interesting to note that dependence on a large landowner for rent reductions did not always compromise their political leanings. An example was Francis Chevalier Jeyes, elected to serve for Brixworth in 1876 during a controversial vestry contest that year, who ran one of the largest farms in the area. He employed on average seven men and several boys. However, he did not rely on farming for his sole source of income: his relatives owned a pharmaceutical company in Northampton in which he had a share.[25] Semi-

---

[25] Francis Chevalier Jeyes's family fortune was derived from Jeyes fluid, which his father manufactured in Northampton. The family fortune was established during the Crimean War when Jeyes fluid was used to combat the spread of typhoid amongst British soldiers. The family also developed the recipe for Worcester sauce, which they manufactured in Worcester. One of Jeyes's brothers, a renowned Northampton chemist named Philadelphius Jeyes from Boughton, was also a guardian of the poor in the Brixworth union. I am indebted to Miss Doreen Jeyes of Earls Barton who was kind enough to recount the Jeyes's family archive, which is still held in private hands at Moulton.

independent farmers often had diverse business interests which lay outside the control of major landowners, and in this case it had political repercussions.

In this period several influential tradesmen who owned public houses in the district became long-serving members of the board. They were all elected in parishes where no single landowner dominated. To stand as a guardian of the poor a candidate had to pay rates of between £15 and £40 *per annum* (rates varied in different locations).[26] The three publicans on the board were self-made men who rented or owned land on which they paid rates of £15 *per annum*. Although many tradesmen's profits must have been affected by the migration of the local population to nearby towns, these men seem to have accumulated enough capital to ride out the recession. Most of them also farmed smallholdings, where they grew wheat and barley for beer production.[27] They appear to have joined the opposition party on the Brixworth union board of guardians for two reasons.

First it was probably in their interests to uphold the rights of those who gravitated to the public house, making them a centre of opposition: some of the first agricultural trade union meetings were held in the back room of the pub and friendly societies often met there too, probably reinforcing the development of a labouring class critique of poor relief arrangements.[28] Publicans were thus kept abreast of public opinion amongst the labouring poor and were keenly aware of the underlying anger about retrenchment.

A second motivating factor is evidenced in the guardians' minute books: some publicans were Nonconformists. They appear to have held strong views about the impoverishment of working people.[29] It is difficult to assess to what degree this motivated their actions, because key-note speeches were not recorded in sufficient detail, but it cannot be discounted as a factor in their opposition. It is also entirely possible that they had friendship or kinship ties with those who had been refused outdoor relief and this may also have influenced their actions.

Against this background Pell had to rely upon on a limited cohort of committed *crusading* guardians. Yet, despite growing opposition he remained in power. By the time opponents (taking account of a higher turnover of farmers during the recession) had learned how to oppose controversial motions they were out of office. By contrast, those in the *crusaders'* party were long-serving members of the Brixworth union board. Poor law regulations also gave the chairman the power to cast a second discretionary vote to resolve controversy on cases of outdoor relief. Predictably, this was always

---

[26] Keith-Lucas, *English local government*, 82–115, outlines voting scales.

[27] Details derived from *Kelly's directories*, 1885–9, and Brixworth union guardians' minute books, annual electoral returns to LGB, P/L 2/17–18.

[28] Feingold, *The revolt of the tenantry*. Howkins, *Poor labouring men*, 33–4, discusses the importance of the pub as a political venue and place of entertainment in rural life.

[29] Brixworth union guardians' minute books (P/L 2/17) detail some key speeches in the period 1878–87.

cast in favour of the *crusaders*. Yet in many respects this picture of coalition politics is too rosy. Local political life was further complicated by the advent of caucus politics, which seemed to threaten radically to change the political tenor of the district.[30] At a time when county council legislation was proposed, caucus politics seemed to undermine the poor law *status quo*; fear of even more democratic change thus shaped the actions of the *crusading* party.

Caucus politics

Although there has been considerable debate amongst historians about whether democratisation under the Third Reform Act constituted a watershed in English politics, there is agreement that it did start to change the tenor of rural life.[31] After 1885 national parties perceived that it would be unwise to ignore the new rural electorate.[32] Consequently a number of political associations affiliated to the National Liberal Federation (NLF) were formed in the Brixworth union during this period, which tried to harness the political ambitions of the labouring classes. For a time it seemed as though the Liberal caucus would help cement poor law opposition. It is not surprising that most *crusaders* feared any political development that seemed to threaten their dominance in local life. However, although a number of former NALU leaders set up Liberal associations in their villages, on the whole the labouring poor were disenchanted with caucus politics.[33]

The reasons for this were first that associations were allied to larger caucus initiatives in local manufacturing towns, such as Kettering and Wellingborough. Predominately, these urban delegates promoted the interests of middle-class voters. The Spencer family election agent commented that many Liberals in town discriminated against new rural associations. He noted that agricultural labourers were not encouraged to stand in caucus elections or local government contests. The election agent warned Spencer that the political mood in the area was changing because 'the main body of electors prefer a more advanced man', to represent them.[34] A number of Spencer's correspondents reported that labourers regularly experienced some form of electoral discrimination.[35]

---

30 Howarth, 'Liberal revival', 92–6, explains that in the rural districts of Northamptonshire a leading farmer often organised local caucus branches.

31 Blewett, 'Franchise in the UK', 43; J. Davis and G. Tanner, 'The borough franchise after 1867', *Historical Research* lxix (1996), 306–27.

32 Charles Parker, MP for Perth, *Hansard* iv, 25 May 1892, speech 1814, noted the registration problems but also observed that working people's aspirations could not be ignored; Blewett 'Franchise in the UK', table 4 at p. 49, explains that as late as 1911, 11% of the electorate in the Mid-Northants division (covering the Brixworth union) were exploiting complicated registration procedures to obtain votes in multiple divisions.

33 Howarth 'Liberal revival', 92–3.

34 J. Becke to Spencer, 10 Jan. 1885, MSS Althorp, K277.

35 F. A. Channing, MP for East Northants, discussed with Spencer how the new Liberal

Second, and predictably, the fact that the Spencer family opposed the reintroduction of outdoor relief began to undermine the Liberal party's fortunes in the mid-Northamptonshire division, where Bobby Spencer was the sitting member. At a time when it was crucial for the Spencer family to take the lead in the district by supporting labourers' causes, they acted conservatively.[36] In parishes where Spencer owned substantial property he refused to let labourers, even Liberal caucus members, use schoolrooms for political meetings. Spencer told labourers that national schools could only be used for matters of a disinterested nature, which ruled out political gatherings. In private he admitted that he knew schoolrooms would be used as a platform to criticise the *crusaders'* policies. He refused to permit the development of that type of free speech on his estate.[37] The Spencer papers reveal that as a result of Spencer's actions support for a Liberal caucus in the district was patchy. In public, Spencer always maintained that support for the *crusading* cause was widespread amongst independent labouring Liberal voters. However, in reality, Liberalism failed to 'nurse support' in the Brixworth union, where the party was too closely associated with the *crusading* campaign.[38] Working people appear to have been unconvinced by Spencer's political rhetoric. Most argued that substantial social welfare provision would have improved their material lives.

The Spencer papers confirm that new rural voters were disenchanted with the local Liberal party and thus rejected caucus politics. They complained that the established rural order did not welcome a new political voice. Bury commented to Spencer that he felt very uneasy about further democratisation – 'what a deplorable condition the political world is in! Liberals and Tories trying to outbid each other for the popular vote regardless of principle' – which was something he refused to do.[39] Bury also touched upon alternative forms of political activity amongst the labouring poor in the area. He was worried that he had recently turned down a request from 'a labourer called Brambley who hailed originally from Brington and asked to be able to use the school room' for a political discussion.[40] In April 1886 another clergyman wrote to Spencer that Brambley had mounted a very successful opposition campaign by rallying supporters against the *crusade*. Brambley accused the Liberal party in the county of failing local voters in poor law matters. The clergyman noted that Brambley was a former agricultural trade union leader

associations were formed at Kettering and Wellingborough in the mid-1880s. He noted that the population of Kettering increased dramatically from 11,000 to 14,000 in 1888, and the strongly middle-class emphasis of the NLF caucus. See, for example, F. A. Channing to Spencer, 10, 11 Apr., 11 Aug. 1888, ibid. K252.

36 Gordon, *The red earl*, 1–34, describes the political outlook of Earl Spencer and Bobby Spencer in the 1880s.

37 Bury to Spencer, 25 Feb., 24 July 1885, MSS Althorp, K382.

38 Howarth, 'Liberal revival', 97.

39 Bury to Spencer, 24 July 1885, MSS Althorp, K382.

40 Bury to Spencer, 25 Feb. 1885, ibid.

and 'owing to his present position as supposed leader in a working men's question his remarks were always received with cheers', wherever he spoke.[41]

Brambley seems to have ignored his local Liberal association. Instead, he travelled about the district campaigning for the rights of the poor, which, as local newspapers reported, earned him a considerable amount of support.[42] Spencer told his land agent to refuse any request from Brambley to hold meetings in his estate villages. This seems only to have increased his popularity.[43] Instead, Brambley spoke at numerous venues – in public houses, in Nonconformist chapels and by the side of fields at the end of the working day. Local newspapers reported that he was taking up a series of grievance on behalf of the labouring poor. At a typical meeting he spoke in favour of employment with fair wages, basic food, better cottages, fair rent and outdoor relief allowances in times of illness and old age.[44] Spencer's correspondents complained that labourers became adept at holding meetings in venues where they had been refused permission to congregate. One local clergyman gave permission for a school hall to be used to discuss general agricultural questions. However, after the discussion finished a second meeting took place at the rear of the hall, where local people debated the *crusading* controversy. Despite the clergymen's intervention he failed to disperse the large crowd that had congregated.[45] These are only a few examples of the drift away from Liberalism and are not representative of every shade of labouring opinion. However, the Spencer papers do reveal that meetings were becoming more popular and that the political climate was changing. His correspondents confirmed that the third Reform Act had raised expectations amongst agricultural workers. This seems to have made them more determined to oppose the *crusade* by campaigning alongside, rather than from within, the Liberal rank and file. Moreover, the Spencers' stance over the *crusading* controversy had some bearing on this trend.

It is evident that some working people had embarked on a political journey in response to their growing opposition to the *crusade*. This started with the advent of agricultural trade unionism. Vestry politics then proved a political outlet for poor law frustrations. Later, caucus politics might have rallied opposition. But the conservatism of prominent Liberals, like the Spencers, in this part of Northamptonshire, appears to have trigged a political drift away from Liberalism. How widespread this was elsewhere is unclear. Yet, as Howarth

---

41 Stewart to Spencer, 5 Apr. 1886, ibid. K381. There is little evidence in the Spencer papers about any surviving support for agricultural trade unions by 1885.

42 *Northampton Guardian*, 14 Mar. 1885.

43 After the Liberal party election defeat in 1895, Brambley agreed to become the leader of the Harlestone Liberal Association, but only because Bobby Spencer had been ousted from office and the *crusading* experiment on the Brixworth board of guardians had been overturned. For Liberal party support amongst the working classes see pp. 215–26 below. See also the *Northampton Mercury*, 21 June 1895.

44 Bury to Spencer, 21 May 1894, MSS Althorp, K345, discusses Brambley family history.

45 Stewart to Spencer, 5 Apr. 1886, ibid. K381.

points out, the growth of class-consciousness among the rural and urban poor in Northamptonshire was underway after 1885.[46] Moreover, it is ironic that Liberalism promoted 'democratic local government reforms', which was the 'source of weakness to the Liberal party, and contributed to its collapse in 1895' in both national and local elections. Evidence suggests that voters in the Brixworth union were divided above all by the *crusading* experience and that 'it was the Liberals who lost most by it', in the decade 1885 to 1895.[47]

The testimony of the Spencer papers corroborates this viewpoint. It indicates that political historians who debate the demise of Liberalism in the later Victorian and Edwardian eras may need to take into account the political ramifications of poor law controversies when they assess the success or failure of municipal socialism.[48] For example, Brian Harrison has recently stated, 'nor is there strong evidence of working-class pressure for public welfare, which was a prominent election issue between 1885 and 1914 ... Interventionist ideas were not prevalent in working class organisations' or politics.[49] The poor law and its complex political configuration seems to refute traditional views: rather it would feed into the establishment of a local independent labour movement. Meanwhile, until further work is produced on the local political ramifications of the *crusade* elsewhere (amongst extremists and moderates) both political and welfare historians remain unclear about, and may have undervalued, working people's active interest in public welfare issues. A related issue is whether the coming of county council reform changed the terms of local debates about welfare provision and this discussion now turns to that important question.

County councils

Around 1870, when the LGB was trying to persuade poor law unions to implement a *crusading* campaign, it established a number of regional poor law conferences throughout England and Wales.[50] Guardians were encouraged to send representatives to debate poor relief issues. Senior civil servants believed that sharing experiences and best practice would encourage guardians to become more proficient administrators. Each regional conference usually nominated two guardians to attend an annual poor law conference held in London. Senior civil servants, and a number of prominent COS members, such as Charles Loch, attended and gave papers on contemporary poor law subjects. The LGB used these regional and national forums to test reac-

[46] Howarth, 'Liberal revival', 117.

[47] Ibid. 113.

[48] For Liberalism see pp. 31–9 above.

[49] B. Harrison, *The transformation of British politics, 1860–1995*, Harmondsworth 1996, 71.

[50] See MH 19/93, 21 July 1883, which records discussions amongst inspectors about the value of poor law conferences, 1870–83.

tions to forthcoming government legislation. Naturally, the chairman of the central committee of poor law conferences had a considerable amount of influence in central government circles. Pell chaired this central committee from its inception in 1868 until his retirement in 1896. His position gave him a unique opportunity to promote a COS ethos.[51] Conference proceedings are invaluable in revealing the issues that were being debated and how *crusaders* tried to influence government policy.[52]

In 1885 Pell decided to use the platform at the poor law conference to outline an alternative model of county government. It envisaged poor law unions occupying a central role in local democracy. He hoped this alternative plan would enhance the role of poor law unions, protect the political interests of the traditional leaders in county life and thereby prevent the reintroduction of outdoor relief.[53] Pell recognised that county council reform was needed. There were too many overlapping agencies in local government with no clearly demarcated lines of responsibility. However, he felt that the LGB did not fully appreciate the implications of such reform. He believed county councils would be too democratic and would eventually take over the administration of the poor law. This would undermine the *crusading* campaign and destroy the power of the guardians in rural society. Pell therefore argued that it was imperative that poor law unions be selected as the new unit of county government.[54]

Pell proposed that central government should legislate that each area must have a local government unit containing four poor law unions in each county to oversee all administration.[55] The new local authority would be so structured that a rural poor law union would have jurisdiction over all villages in a county; a borough poor law union would oversee each county town; a large urban poor law union would administer manufacturing districts in the county; and a major metropolitan poor law union would cover cities. Each county would have a council comprised of representatives from each of the four feeder poor law unions in its geographic area. Members could not serve on the county body unless they had first served on a local poor law union board and proved their expertise in a particular area of local administration. The county council would thus be 'an intermediate between the primary local authorities and the Imperial government'. Each county council would distribute

---

[51] Digby, 'The rural poor', 600, discusses the importance of the poor law conference lobby.

[52] See, for example, Editorial 'Local government and its responsibilities', COR xv (Mar. 1886), 81, and xvi (Apr. 1886), 145–50, for the types of discussion that arose from poor law conference proceedings.

[53] W. Rathbone, A. Pell and F. C. Montague, *Local administration*, London 1885.

[54] Pell rejected the alternative Liberal proposal that the parish should become the new unit of local administration. He felt that individual villages were too small to work as the basis of an effective system of county government. Sykes, *Rise and fall*, 128–76, discusses Liberal party policy between 1885 and 1890.

[55] A. Pell, 'Local government in counties: a paper delivered to the 14th annual poor law conference', in *Poor law conference report*, London 1885, 294–308.

financial awards to those poor law unions that were prudently administered. The most proficient managers of outdoor relief would be awarded the largest county grants. To resolve the problem of too many competing agencies in local government, legislation would stipulate that there would be one rateable valuation, one method of voting and one county authority to oversee the four poor law boards in each area.[56]

Pell knew that it was important to preserve the property qualification in guardian elections otherwise the labouring classes might out-vote the landed interest in the future. He therefore proposed that one third of the membership of each county authority would be appointed by Justices of the Peace, and two-thirds elected by the ratepayers. The latter group would be split in two, half elected directly by ratepayers and the rest co-opted by ratepayer guardians who sat on the four local poor law union boards. All members of the county authority and feeder poor law boards would serve a minimum three-year term of office. Ratepayers would accept the principle of direct taxation in return for greater representation on the county authority. Pell conceded that poor law union boundaries would have to be redrawn as many crossed county lines. He believed that the most effective way of overcoming this problem would be to amalgamate parishes along county boundaries into whichever poor law union was most convenient for administrative purposes. Essentially, Pell's scheme aimed to distribute local government duties amongst poor law unions, and thereby concentrate the power of the rural elite. He explained that 'these principles must surely be the guiding ones in local government where, at any rate, the conservative is the true reformer, for he desires to apply principles, which have answered since the birth of civilisation'.[57] He also hoped to compel the new county authorities to adopt profitable business practices by tendering out their services and cutting costs where possible to save ratepayers' money: this would appeal to the electorate and guarantee the success of the new scheme.

Unquestionably Pell's local government scheme was proposed in response to the growth of caucus politics and the changing political character of the Brixworth union, which alarmed his party. It was an astute measure that exemplified his real political ambitions and fears about poor law democratisation. Its main aim was to preserve the power of guardians who supported the *crusading* cause. If one examines the proposed voting arrangements they reveal how the new county infrastructure would not only have protected but enhanced his party's interests in local life.

An average poor law union in the 1880s comprised *ex-officio* members and elected guardians who held approximately 20 per cent and 80 per cent of the available seats respectively. Under Pell's proposals the *ex-officio* block vote in each feeder poor law union would be increased from 20 per cent to 33 per cent. The elected guardian block vote of 80 per cent correspondingly fell to

66 per cent. However, Pell limited the number of directly elected guardians on the county authority to just 33 per cent of that 66 per cent. Elected guardians on each of the four poor law unions in a county appointed only 8.25 per cent of their members to sit on the county authority. Consequently, the new county authority was made up of a 33 per cent *ex-officio* block, 33 per cent (8.25 per cent x 4) directly elected members, and 33 per cent (8.25 per cent x 4) co-opted members appointed from amongst the elected guardians.[58] This rather complex system meant that once *crusaders* were elected to office they could dominate the county authority by forming a formidable coalition with the *ex-officio* representatives, allowing them to have effective control over all local administration. The principle of democracy was a sham for only about one third of the county delegates would be elected members and the rural elite would always outvote them.

Pell sponsored numerous private members bills at Westminster to get these measures onto the statute books.[59] Ultimately, the scheme was rejected in 1888 when a boundary commission reported that implementing the proposal would have meant redrawing constituency boundaries, including those in Ireland.[60] The Conservative government refused to introduce any changes that would have political ramifications for Irish Home Rule. Nevertheless, Pell's proposals did carry considerable weight with MPs on both sides of the House of Commons.[61] Spencer was one of a number of prominent Liberals interested in the scheme. He even convened a private meeting at Althorp in April 1888 to discuss the proposals with leading *crusaders* from Northamptonshire to see how they could work together to persuade the government to adopt the plan. In advance of the meeting, Pell told Spencer that if his county scheme was rejected then poor relief would be administered in a 'frothy and harmful' manner because further democratisation was inevitable. He feared that the new 'mischievous' form of 'political feeling' would determine local government in the Brixworth union and that the growth of caucus activity was a harbinger of that change.[62] Spencer's response has not survived: it would have provided an interesting insight into a Whig view of local democracy. Bury admitted to a packed meeting of the Northampton Chamber of Agriculture on the eve of the new county council legislation that he was alarmed by the reconstruction of county politics that was taking place. He pointed out the dangers of widening political discussion and greater representation:

[58] Ibid.
[59] Pell sponsored private members' bills on 16 February and 21 May 1880, on 19 June 1881, 13 February 1882 and on 2 April 1883.
[60] Keith-Lucas, *British local government*, 96–8.
[61] Prominent supporters included Lord Edmond Fitzmaurice, William Rathbone, Clare Sewell Read, James Yorke, Albert Gray, A. Doyle (LGB inspector for Wales), G. F. Henley and C. T. Ritchie (president of the LGB after 1886).
[62] Pell to Spencer, 1, 2 Apr. 1888, MSS Althorp, K372.

Debates and discussions must take place. … Eloquence must be aired and, of course, reported; election pledges, however vast, must be kept and the 'penny wise and pound foolish' policy may often triumph over the true economist. The work to be done calls for men of independence and public spirit, as well as ability and business-like capabilities. Plainly the Council is no place for drones or dunces or dummies, still less for political adventurers or charlatans … the Court of Quarter Sessions was not always infallible but was always above suspicion … popular government is not always wise, nor is it always pure, [for] it also has its peculiar dangers and temptations for [there] will always be prophets to prophesy falsely if the people will have it so.[63]

Despite Pell's best efforts the County Council Act of 1888 failed to mention poor law reform and his scheme was abandoned in order to get the rest of the legislation through parliament.[64] None the less, each county council was comprised of elected members and co-opted aldermen. Outside of London 40 per cent of those elected to the new county authorities were magistrates and in most counties the chairman of quarter sessions was elected chairman of the county council.[65] Spencer became chairman of the Northamptonshire county council and Pell was one of a number of Conservative magistrates elected.[66] To the anger of the local populace, Spencer and Pell co-opted Bury onto the council's technical education committee to serve as an alderman. Not until the more democratic changes in the 1890s did working people gain the opportunity to govern themselves for the first time.

The danger of the coming of democracy

In the period 1885–9 four political developments troubled those in control of the Brixworth union. The first was the threat of further local democracy as revealed when the chairman admitted in print that he was alarmed by the implications of the Third Reform Act. Although historians have seen this publication as a straightforward attack by a clergyman who felt that the landed elite was acting irresponsibly in rural society,[67] Bury's motives were in fact more complex. Viewed in the context of the *crusading* campaign, the article was a political call to arms. It tried to motivate landed society to regroup and unite to protect their class interests. Bury believed that *crusaders*

[63] *Northampton Guardian*, 22 Dec. 1888.
[64] W. Henage to Spencer, 7 May 1886, MSS Althorp, K170. Henage, former Liberal chief whip, advised Spencer to distance himself from Pell because he believed that one of the reasons for the Liberal party losing the general election of 1886 (aside from the issue of Home Rule) was its support for 'Mr Pell's Taxation Resolution for county councils', which was 'unpopular'. There is no record of Spencer's reply.
[65] Dunbabin, 'British local government', 793.
[66] J. Bradbury, *Government and county: a history of Northamptonshire county council, 1889–1989*, Northampton 1989, 91.
[67] Howarth, 'Politics and society', 269–74.

must take a proactive, not reactive, stance in poor law matters regardless of personal financial pressures. Moreover, since the development of local democracy coincided with an era of coalition politics in the poor law theatre, he felt that his worst fears about losing power were being substantiated. Unfortunately, his article backfired. It was too controversial and exposed deep divisions within his party. Ironically this may have encouraged working people openly to criticise the *crusading* campaign even more.

The second was that the poor law entered an era of coalition politics. Guardians' minute books reveal that farmers were split into three groupings. Pell had to negotiate with a group of farmers who had no firm party allegiance which forced his party to engage in coalition politics. This type of political management did not suit Pell's autocratic style. It was unfortunate from his party's viewpoint that the rural recession coincided with a more democratic era in county politics, since once land was devalued the power inscribed in that land started to diminish too. This process was slow but it was also irreversible. The establishment of an opposition party on the board of guardians must have seemed very alarming; the harbinger of how further economic change would determine local political life. Indeed, publicans and other tradesmen were a now a permanent fixture on the board of guardians and they had a very different political outlook. John Garrard's equivalent urban studies show that tradesmen favoured local over national elections.[68] Those with successful local government careers seldom tried to get elected to parliament, not because they lacked ambition but because they could bring about more radical policy changes, gaining greater influence than in national politics. Since tradesmen and publicans tended to align themselves carefully for business reasons in their local community, their staunch support for the opposition party on the board of guardians is noteworthy. Overall, their developing allegiances further understanding of how, in political terms, different social groupings reacted negatively to *crusading*.

The third development was triggered by the advent of caucus politics. Greater political participation by the labouring poor in local political life alarmed *crusaders* and thus a fear of further democratisation shaped their actions. At the same time, the failure of a Liberal caucus in mid-Northamptonshire meant that critics of the poor law questioned in public the basis of the older rural order.[69] Caucus politics thus led to debates about the need for poor law democracy too. These fed into the issue of county council reform and its consequences for the longer-term future of the poor law. Naturally, this alarmed *crusaders*, who were even more obdurate.

The final development was that the creation of county councils seemed to threaten to erode the influence of the landed interest in Northamptonshire life. Thus, Pell tried to redraft county council legislation before it reached the statute book. Although in reality county council legislation was conserva-

---

68 See, for example, introduction, n. 29.
69 Howarth, 'Liberal revival', 97.

tive at first, fear of more democratic change shaped his party's action. It is intriguing that the type of local authority he envisaged is not that dissimilar to fund-holding administrative systems in local government today. Pell would have rejoiced in their ethos of business enterprise and local taxes combining to provide profit-making healthcare and welfare services. At the time, however, his proposals only further isolated the labouring poor, who already felt excluded from political life. Thus, former agricultural trade union leaders filled the political void created by *crusaders* and leading Liberals like the Spencers.

Initial research appears to indicate that an independent and parallel labour movement was forming alongside Liberalism in the Brixworth union. Peter Clarke observes that 'for many illiterate labourers, the meetings of 1884–5, whether held under union auspices, or convened to demonstrate feeling over the franchise, or straightforwardly organised in support of Liberal candidates, were a breakthrough' into politicisation 'of a novel kind' in local political life.[70] There is one important qualification to this viewpoint: it was poor law politics that captured the political imagination of the labouring poor.[71] (Of course, social and political historians, notably Alun Howkins, Keith Laybourn, Jon Lawrence and David Taylor, have debated the meaning in political terms of 'class labels', such as 'labouring poor' and 'working people'.[72]) In the Brixworth union opposition to harsh poor law policies involved a cohort of individuals coming together to stage a political fight back. Some were aware of, or had experienced, and indeed were very critical of, the withdrawal of outdoor relief. Others, such as independent farmers, publicans and tradesmen agreed that *crusading* initiatives damaged the delicate balance of social relations. As a result, it is possible to find tangible proof that a model of traditional social relations – exemplified in Peter King's notion of a triangular nexus of landowner/ farmer/ labouring poor – had started to shift.[73] This realignment was new, significant and unstoppable.

At the time of the Third Reform Act a flagging economy and an obdurate landed elite could not halt the tide of democratic change in many areas. In the Brixworth union these factors coincided with a political awakening. Working people aligned with, but were not absorbed by, the democratising influence of caucus politics. Instead, the promise of increased democracy in local government gave the labouring poor the means, vision and hope to move on. Resolutely they grasped that chance.

---

[70] Clarke and Langford, 'Hodge's politics', 129.

[71] Harrison, *Transformation*, 71. This refutes Harrison's view that working people were not interested in public welfare issues in the later Victorian era.

[72] See, for example, Howkins, *Reshaping rural England*; P. Taylor, *Popular politics in early industrial Britain: Bolton, 1825–1850*, Keele 1995; and Lawrence, *Speaking for the people*.

[73] Hitchcock, King and Sharpe, *Chronicling poverty*, 1–14, provides an excellent overview of how to approach studies of the experience of being poor in the context of socio-economic relations.

8

Begging for a Burial:
Fighting for Poor Law Funding

To be poor is a human condition that few would choose. Seldom will any individual who is confronted with economic hardship relish the deterioration of their material circumstances from relative to absolute poverty.[1] For these reasons, as Edward Thompson remarked, the poor will fight back in defence of their 'moral economy'. Often they will do so in complex ways, especially if they believe that key customary rights are being ignored.[2] After all, when you have nothing, fighting for something is a gain in real terms. Anthropologists have identified that death in a family can produce a financial crisis. Those left behind will react angrily if they experience absolute material hardship as a result of political economy encroaching in a detrimental way on their meagre state of affairs.[3] Typically, the poor will expect recognition of their straitened circumstances and acknowledgement of their cultural mores. Often, bereaved families will apply for, and expect to, receive some form of welfare assistance to bury loved ones 'decently'.[4] If these claims are rebuffed, a bitter sense of injustice can ignite social unrest.

Crusaders either ignored, or had little understanding of, such basic facts about human nature at times of bereavement. They also failed to appreciate that, as the *crusade* took hold, it impoverished more social groups. Once the rural recession cut deep and began to affect the incomes of tenant framers, small businessmen, artisans and unskilled labourers, more people were dragged into the vortex of poverty. The economic ties of kinship, family and neighbourhood were damaged. A ground-swell of opposition to the *crusade* was also created. Failure to appreciate that fact meant that *crusaders* were the architects of their own political downfall, though they did not see it that way. They decided to act more conservatively in the face of economic pressures, ignoring changing welfare ideas about individual responsibility for pauperism. Whereas with the coming of democracy *crusaders* needed to respond in ways that were more, not less, sympathetic to the genuine economic needs of poorer residents, in the Brixworth union at least they were obdurate. Thus, a key political debate broke out in the area, summed up in a bitter letter to

---

1   Sen, *Inequality re-examined.*
2   E. P. Thompson, *Customs in common*, London 1993 edn.
3   G. D. Jones, *Speaking for the dead: cadavers in biology and medicine*, Abingdon 2000.
4   See, for example, J.-M. Strange, '"She cried a very little": death, grief and mourning in working-class culture *c.* 1880–1914', *SH* xxvii (2002), 143–61, and 'Only a pauper who no-one owns: reassessing the pauper grave, *c.* 1880–1914', *P&P* i (2003), 148–78.

a local newspaper: 'Why did there have to be another push to save poor law costs – Hadn't the *crusade* gone far enough already?' Controversy surrounding the cancellation of traditional pauper funeral provision now kindled a slow but determined political journey amongst opponents of the *crusade* in a more democratic era.

To extend the discussion about how the politics of the vestry and the political aspirations of the working class became radicalised by the later 1880s, this chapter uncovers a new *crusading* initiative, one that offended the poor in numerous unions, not just at Brixworth. This, the policy of selling 'unclaimed' cadavers for anatomical teaching when paupers died in the work-house and their families could not afford to bury them,[5] was by far the most despised policy of the *crusading* decades. It was practised by both moderate and extreme poor law unions as a means of making ongoing savings. An aspect of the *crusading* experience overlooked in welfare literature, in the literature on the cultural history of death and also in work on the history of medicine, it was deeply offensive to the poor, contravening their cultural, religious and social mores. They responded by pooling their meagre resources in order to bury their loved ones. Rare reports in central government files, written by the poor, reveal their determination to fight for provision for pauper funerals. Women and children often had to beg in order to bury their dead. As the Anatomy Act of 1832, which authorised the sale of 'unclaimed' pauper cadavers, came into full force under the later Victorian poor law, the economic interests of poor law authorities, asylums and anatomists converged to the detriment of the poor.

Begging for a burial

Under the terms of the Anatomy Act nobody in England and Wales was guaran-teed a pauper funeral paid for from local rates in England and Wales.[6] Instead, guardians of the poor had the right to reclaim any poor relief costs associated with parish care, both indoor and outdoor relief funding, by selling pauper

---

5   See, for example, the following relevant studies: G. Rowell, *Hell and the Victorians*, Oxford 1974; R. Houlbrooke, *Death, ritual and bereavement*, London 1989; J. Litten, *The English way of death: the common funeral since 1450*, London 1991; P. Jupp and G. Howarth (eds), *The changing face of death: historical accounts of death and disposal*, Basingstoke 1997; G. Avery and K. Reynolds (eds), *Representations of childhood death*, Basingstoke 2000; J. Wolffe, *Great deaths: grieving, religion and nationhood in Victorian and Edwardian Britain*, Oxford 2000.

6   See, for example, R. Richardson, 'A dissection of the Anatomy Acts', *Studies in Labour History* i (1976), 8–11, and *Death, dissection and the destitute*, London–New York 1987; T. Laqueur, 'Bodies, death and pauper funerals', *Representations* i (1983), 109–31, and 'Cemeteries, religion and the culture of capitalism', in J. A. James and M. Thomas (eds), *Capitalism in context: essays on economic development and cultural change in honour of R. M. Hartwell*, Chicago 1994, 138–55; and P. Jalland, *Death and the Victorian family*, Oxford 1996.

body parts to teaching hospitals. Legislation stipulated that the body of any deceased person, still unclaimed for burial six weeks after death, could be used for anatomical tuition. The act outlawed the commercial use of whole corpses, but it did permit poor law guardians to use their discretion to sell pauper cadavers for dissection or dismemberment, for use in research and for the training of doctors. Ruth Richardson has described the Anatomy Act as an 'advance clause' to the New Poor Law Amendment Act of 1834. Together they 'forged a wedge, which sundered the two nations of rich and poor' in England and Wales.[7] She stresses that this was why pauper burial were so feared amongst the impoverished since guardians could use legislation as a 'class reprisal' to dispose arbitrarily of the remains of the poor.[8] In an age when the dismemberment of a cadaver was visible proof of both social and religious failure, the poor used every resource within their limited means to avoid such a fate.[9]

What little research has been done on the subject of pauper funeral rites suggests that it was not common in the earlier Victorian period for cadavers to be sold to recover the costs of poor relief.[10] Instead, many guardians agreed to pay for a series of customary local funeral arrangements using medical outdoor relief orders. However, when the LGB was established in 1871, the *crusading* template reveals that all medical provision came under a renewed attack. Even then the issue of pauper funeral rites paid on medical orders did not become a contentious issue in the Brixworth union until the passing of the Third Reform Act. In 1885 politicians agreed that sick paupers should not be prevented from voting in parliamentary elections. Provided claimants received poor relief on medical grounds they could register their right to vote. This new stipulation was codified in the Medical Relief (Disqualification Removal) Act of 1885 (MRDRA).[11] It meant that for the first time the sick poor were enfranchised.[12] Predictably, some Brixworth union guardians, believing in 'no representation without rates', resented that fact. They maintained that if a person did not pay local taxes then they should not be allowed to vote on how they were spent. As a result, *crusaders* were even more determined to eradicate medical outdoor relief. Their resentment manifested itself in a campaign to abolish traditional pauper funerals paid on medical orders. Ratepayers in the area were determined to stop the sick poor voting and paupers were even more determined to mobilise their new voting rights. Predictably, the two sides clashed. Thus, at a time when the *crusading* experiment was at its most rigorous, the issue of pauper funerals became a flash-point for opposition. Local people sent petitions, letters of protest and evidence about controversies over pauper funerals. The sources that survive

---

7   Richardson, *Death and dissection*, 266–7.
8   Ibid.
9   Laqueur, 'Bodies', 109.
10 Digby, *The poor law*, 19–26, details misuse of medical orders by boards of guardians.
11 Englander, *Poverty and poor law reform*, 25.
12 Williams, *Pauperism*, 102.

are compelling: they give a rare glimpse of working-class funeral *mores* and experiences at the hands of *crusaders*. The harshness of the *crusading* experiment appears to have brought into public view, and given voice, to a subject that was normally taboo in pauper society. A rare set of dossiers containing details of the death customs of the poor and their fears about losing pauper funeral provision have survived in central and local government records. Basic record linkage techniques facilitate an analysis of four of the best-documented cases in the Brixworth union.[13]

The first involved Sarah Ward, an elderly pauper, aged eighty-five, from Spratton village.[14] The Brixworth union letter book and central government records reveal that she had applied for medical outdoor relief in late June 1887 after she broke her leg. Her relatives sent a messenger to the union doctor asking him to attend Sarah as soon as possible. They feared that her injury was more serious than it appeared because she was in considerable pain. The DMOP refused to visit Sarah at home because his conditions of service had been altered and he was no longer authorised to make home visits without the presence of the relieving officer and the authority of a full board meeting of the Brixworth union guardians. His contract also stipulated that he was not allowed to attend paupers in cases of 'sudden accident'. He told Sarah's family that their only option was to take her to Northampton Infirmary, some seven miles away, where she would receive the necessary medical treatment. However, Sarah's family were too poor to pay her transportation costs. She was therefore left overnight, in considerable pain. The doctor attended the following day free of charge and arranged for her transportation at a reduced cost. Despite this Sarah later died after entering the infirmary, on 24 August 1887, from a thrombosis-related condition. Although there was no evidence to link her demise to medical neglect, the doctor believed that the Brixworth union guardians had undermined his professionalism.

The letter book and central government files reveal that Sarah's family was now confronted with two dilemmas.[15] They suspected at first, but could not prove, that had she received immediate medical attention she might not have died. If they requested an official inquiry into the case it was likely that it would focus on the action of the doctor and they had no desire to criticise him because he had acted in Sarah's best interests under the circumstances, providing free medical care. A second problem was that Sarah's cadaver was now in the Northampton Infirmary.[16] Unless her family pooled their meagre

---

[13] These cases are not detailed in date order but in the sequence in which they were discussed in official records at the LGB or elsewhere.

[14] This case has been analysed from 19 July 1887, MH 12/7805, and Brixworth union general letter book (1886–9), entry for 19 July 1887, NRO, LG 21/07.

[15] Ibid.

[16] The *Lancet*, 7 Sept. 1889, noted that there was a teaching hospital in anatomy and *materia medica* and a practical pharmacy next to the Northampton Infirmary. Its pupils were charged £25 *per annum* with a perpetual fee of £50. The anatomy school seems to have been set up there so that students could study cadavers from the infirmary, though in

resources to pay for a private burial, the parish authorities might step in and sell the dead body for dissection and dismemberment. Though at this stage few residents guessed where such remains would be sent, in fact their destination would have been Cambridge University's anatomy department. All the family knew was that they wanted to avoid dissection and this meant fighting for a pauper burial held publicly so they could make sure that the body was in the ground. The correspondence between the guardians and Sarah's family indicates that the bereaved relatives knew that it was pointless to apply for a medical outdoor relief order, as this would be refused. After consulting the doctor a decision was taken to report the case to the LGB. The family hoped that central government would intervene if they created a controversy and would force the board of guardians to act more leniently and fund a customary pauper funeral.

An official inquiry began but the guardians' minute books reveal that it was the doctor, not the board of guardians, who came under attack from central government.[17] Guardians were very careful to distance themselves from charges of medical culpability and they were determined not to act leniently in this case because they did not want to set an unwarranted precedent. The doctor defended his actions at a board meeting on the grounds that medical regulations in the Brixworth union were unworkable and undermined his professionalism. After a lengthy investigation the inquiry concluded that Sarah's death was the result of natural causes and was the responsibility of neither the doctor, nor of the guardians. However, this verdict did not resolve the problem of Sarah's burial and her family had to accept the ignominy of guardians taking over responsibility for the body. No details have survived concerning the fate of Sarah's cadaver. It is difficult to assess whether the doctor portrayed this case in a bad light to complain about his heavier workload and salary cut, but it is evident that a lack of medical outdoor relief provision had forced a pauper to leave her home to get essential medical care. Sarah was placed in a vulnerable position that heightened the danger of her body being dismembered or dissected if she died.[18]

The second case occurred in the autumn of 1885 when an elderly widower, Samuel Brains, died from natural causes. Central government records and Samuel Ward's evidence to the Royal Commission on the Aged Poor (1894) reveal the circumstances of this case.[19] Brains had been a resident in the Brix-

fact Cambridge University bought most available cadavers in the Midlands and north of England.

[17] Brixworth union guardians' minute books, P/L 2/17–18.

[18] The case and subsequent inquiry was reported in local newspapers throughout July 1889. See, for example, the *Northampton Mercury* and the *Northampton Herald*. There was no discernible bias in their coverage but a sense of outrage amongst the community at the turn of events was apparent.

[19] This case has been reconstructed from 19 Sept. and reply 2 Oct. 1890, Wilson (DMOP) to LGB, and 27 Sept. 1891, MH 12/8705; *Royal Commission on the Aged Poor* (1894), Ward, qq. 15696, 15698, 15702; and reports on the case kept by local poor law officers, 23 June 1887, 6 May 1888, NRO, LG 21/07.

worth union but his body was in the Northampton Infirmary at the time of death. He had recently been transferred there because the doctor was not authorised by the guardians to attend terminally ill paupers at home, unless it was to arrange to transfer them to the workhouse or a local hospital. Samuel's body lay in the Northampton Infirmary for a week after death. This delay was a deliberate tactic employed by his wife, friends and neighbours to give them more time to organise a funeral fund to bury him without recourse to a pauper burial. Central government files reveal that they knew that leaving his body in the Northampton Infirmary was a risky strategy because if they failed to collect enough funds to bury him guardians could sell his body for dissection or dismemberment.[20] Even though guardians were not authorised officially to sell the corpse for dissection until six weeks after death, in reality the cadaver might be dismembered at any time without consultation. After seven days it became apparent that his wife, friends and neighbours could not raise enough money to bury Samuel. The 'makeshift' economies of the labouring poor in the area were already over-stretched because of the impact of the agricultural crisis. Consequently Samuel's wife asked their daughter to travel to the area from a nearby county and arrange to claim her father's body for burial on behalf of his relatives. However, as she too was impoverished the daughter had to apply to the Brixworth union for a medical outdoor relief order to bury her father, as had been the custom in the area before 1870.

Samuel's daughter made a burial application to the Brixworth union relieving officer. Samuel Ward informed the Royal Commission on the Aged Poor that three times she applied and three times her request was refused.[21] The relieving officer informed her that guardians would only lend her money to bury her father, otherwise she had to accept a scaled-down pauper funeral arranged by the parish authorities. Samuel's daughter refused to take out a loan because she would have to sign a contractual agreement to repay the debt in weekly instalments, which she could not afford to do. The Brixworth union letter book suggests that paupers feared that if they defaulted on their repayments guardians would prosecute them at the petty sessions in Northampton for the recovery of the outstanding debt.[22] Ward explained that Samuel's daughter pleaded with the relieving officer to assist her to bury her father's body 'decently'. She wanted a small parish allowance to pay for a customary burial. LGB records suggest that funeral allowances were modest and would provide for a local woman to wash her father's body and to dress him in a new woollen funeral shroud, to ensure that the body could be laid out for inspection by neighbours and friends. Such arrangements, as Julie-Marie Strange has highlighted, appear to have been important signifiers of the family's respectability, indicating that the deceased had the right to be

---

[20] Ibid.

[21] *Royal Commission on the Aged Poor*, Ward, q. 15696.

[22] Brixworth union letter book, LG 21/07, reveals that although guardians did not prosecute they still regularly used the threat of doing so.

buried in consecrated ground because his death was natural, and not the result of a violent suicide.[23]

In his evidence, Ward explained that Samuel's daughter was determined to ensure that her father's body was buried in a wooden coffin with a basic Christian service. Records of local burial boards indicate that it was conventional for poorer people to be buried in a communal grave marked with a numbered cross and probably located to the north of the churchyard (wealthy residents were buried in the eastern section of churchyards).[24] It was also customary to arrange to bury loved ones in a nailed coffin otherwise there was no guarantee that the body would reach the grave before being sold. Samuel's daughter was thus determined to bury her father in a coffin, otherwise it might be exhumed and sold privately for anatomical purposes.

Ward stated that the Brixworth union relieving officer refused to make an exception in the case of Samuel Brains. He informed Samuel's daughter that if she could not afford a coffin and a funeral service she would have to do without one.[25] He instructed her to claim her father's body from the Northampton Infirmary and arrange with the hospital authorities to prepare the body for burial herself. She was told to wash her father's cadaver, wrap it in a cotton sheet and sew the body in personally.[26] She could then accompany it on a return journey back to her father's parish of birth, having paid a local carter to transport her and the cadaver. The body could then be buried in a communal grave. This would give her an opportunity to ensure that her father's body was placed securely in the ground. Samuel's daughter was outraged. It was unlikely that a carrier would agree to transport a body that had been putrefying for several weeks wrapped in a thin sheet. Ward said that he 'could hardly believe' the relieving officer's instructions, as reported by Samuel's daughter.[27] He 'wrote to the guardian of the parish' to ascertain the full facts of the case and the guardian wrote back 'confirming the statement'. Clearly, the furtive funeral arrangements that the relieving officer suggested undermined the sense of respectability of poorer families in the local community, offending both their cultural and their religious sensibilities.

After considerable local controversy about the fate of Samuel's cadaver a sympathetic guardian intervened in the case. He could not get the medical

---

23 E. Howlett, 'Burial customs', *Westminster Review* (Aug. 1893), 166–74, discusses the history of pauper funeral rites. The basic conventions were very similar to those evident from the Brixworth union. They included a woollen shroud (p. 168); laying out a body to prove death was natural (p. 171) (although this was often done for inheritance reasons in a wealthier family); tolling a bell to bid mourners to a funeral (p. 174); and a wake (p. 166). See also Strange, 'She cried', and 'Only a pauper'.

24 *Rules of the East Haddon burial board, adopted 12 Jan. 1892*, Northampton 1892, Northampton Library, Local Studies Collection. This pamphlet reiterates basic conventions that had been in use since the 1860s and sets new regulations on the cost of burial sites, and so on.

25 *Royal Commission on the Aged Poor*, Ward, q. 15696.

26 Ibid.

27 Ibid. qq. 15695, 15697–704.

outdoor relief decision overturned but he gave Samuel's daughter a charitable contribution towards the cost of a coffin. He also wrote a begging
letter for her, authorising her to collect house-to-house around the union
from wealthier ratepayers in the community until she had enough donations
to bury her father decently.[28] Begging for a burial was replacing customary
funeral payments in this area; these revised medical outdoor relief policies
were deeply resented amongst the poor.

The third case was that of a pauper, Elizabeth Simons,[29] aged seventy-eight,
from Moulton village. In May 1888 she applied for medical outdoor relief
because she was infirm and could no longer work.[30] Her husband Daniel, aged
seventy-four, was also unemployed. Her application was refused but because
her case was deserving, she was funded for one month from the 'Secret Service
Fund'. Three weeks later she died and her destitute husband applied for a
medical outdoor relief order to bury his wife. He thought that this would be
a straightforward matter. However, the poor law union records and Ward's
evidence before the Royal Commission on the Aged Poor reveals that Daniel
Simons could not get the guardians to agree to pay for his wife's funeral even
though he was impoverished. Since his wife had been in receipt of charity
prior to death and was therefore not legally destitute, guardians would not
pay for a coffin or any associated conventional funeral expenses on medical
outdoor relief orders. Instead, Elizabeth's body was left at home to putrefy,
whilst her husband appealed to local overseers and the sanitary inspector to
help him bury his wife's body privately from public funds. When that failed
he solicited the help of a sympathetic guardian who brought the case before
local magistrates on his behalf. This was a risky business because the inspector
of nuisances could remove the body on health grounds or arrange with the
relieving officer to sell it to anatomists, recovering parish costs, without
consulting the widower. This technicality in the Anatomy Act seems to have
roused deep anxiety amongst the impoverished in the Brixworth union and
to have shaped their actions.

At a petty sessions hearing in Northampton magistrates decided that they
could not interfere with due process in the Brixworth union. However, they
did indicate that in their opinion the cadaver was the responsibility of the
sanitary inspector because a putrefying corpse was a health hazard.[31] Several
magistrates who served as ex-officio guardians in the Brixworth union felt very
uneasy about this decision and there was heated debate during successive

---

28 Ibid. qq. 15696-7.
29 There is some disparity in the evidence as to the correct spelling of this name, sometimes referred to as Simons or Symons. It is taken here as the former, as this was recorded
in the guardians' minute books. Her age was also disputed as seventy-three or seventy-
eight at the time of death. As it is cited twice as seventy-eight this has been accepted
here.
30 See memos of 16 May 1888, LG 21/07, and 16 May 1888, MH 12/7805. See also *Royal
Commission on the Aged Poor*, Ward, q. 15701.
31 Brixworth union guardians' minute books, P/L 2/17-18.

board meetings about the case. Guardians agreed to refer the matter to the local sanitary inspector but he refused to take responsibility for the case. He informed guardians that a dead body displayed at home was a private, not a public, nuisance. He argued that he was a poorly paid official, on just £5 *per annum*, whose low wages did not recompense him for taking unpopular decisions. He recommended that the case should be referred back to the relieving officer who was on a salary of £160 per year. The latter adjudicated that as the widower had 'been to work, was able to work, and had the prospect of work' he should be offered a loan to cover the costs of the coffin to be repaid in weekly instalments.[32] If he remained unemployed he could ask his relatives to repay the funeral debt. Again the DMOP refuted that assessment. At a time when young men found it difficult to get employment in the district, an aged, worn out labourer was all but unemployable. His family could not support him as they were already struggling to make ends meet.

The doctor approached the magistrate who had been uneasy about the case during the original hearing in Northampton and asked him to support a move to overturn the burial policy of the board of guardians. The sympathetic guardian proposed a motion that censured the conduct of the relieving officer. Of the twenty-six guardians attending the meeting twenty voted, six abstained, and the vote was carried by eleven votes to nine.[33] The chairman was outraged and to deflect attention from the funeral controversy focused on the need to rally support for the relieving officer who had been criticised. He moved a new motion to 'approve the action' of the relieving officer, reiterating that he was the instrument, not the instigator, of the policy. At the request of the chairman an LGB inspector, Mr W. Peel, intervened in the case. The relieving officer was not censured but it was noted that a minority of guardians strongly disapproved of the unpopular burial policy. In the end Elizabeth Simons had a customary funeral but only because two sympathetic guardians paid the costs of the burial out of their own pockets.

As a result of the public outcry in the district over these burial controversies, Bury, as the chairman of the Brixworth union, decided to make a statement to local newspapers, in which he defended his actions:

> in a parish where they have learnt to help themselves and where the Guardian has the reputation of being hard-hearted ... an old woman dies. There can be no question about destitution. She was a widow, and had been an inmate of the Workhouse until quite recently and possessed literally nothing but her clothes. What happens here? The difficulties which staggered Moulton and convulsed the Board of Guardians ... with a threat of popular *emeute* [unrest] ... is very simply settled. The neighbours who had taken it in turn to sit up with her during her illness perform all the necessary offices after her death. The carpenter makes the coffin at cost price; first one gives help, then another ... and the poor woman is quietly

---

32 Entry for 16 May 1888, LG 21/07.
33 Brixworth union guardians' minute books, May–June 1888, P/L 2/18, and ibid.

and decently buried. ... I only ask lovers of poor relief ... to ... look at this picture ... and say which exhibits the better side of human nature?[34]

The letter is revealing. Firstly in that Bury was sufficiently concerned about the threat of a popular reaction to defend his action in a letter to a local news-paper. Evidently it must have been general public knowledge that residents in the Brixworth union were bitterly divided over the pauper burial issue. Secondly, the action of residents reveals that they used their friendship and kinship networks to overcome parsimonious poor relief policies.[35] Thirdly, even the chairman admitted that a burial was not 'decent' unless a pauper was buried in a coffin 'quietly', in a private manner. His stance over the pauper burials attacked working-class culture and was deeply offensive, confirming Strange's work on the importance of burial and funeral rites amongst the poor.[36] But the chairman would not stop there.

The final case was that of a labouring man from Spratton, John Wykes, aged twenty-seven, with a wife and two young children.[37] Letters from the same caring and by now over-worked doctor and a sympathetic local guardian describe the circumstances. After the harvest of 1889 Wykes contracted 'quinsy', an inflammation of the throat. He never fully recovered and by Christmas his condition had worsened after a severe dose of influenza. The doctor explained that he made no application for medical outdoor relief and 'during this time he was destitute and dependent on private Charity'.[38] In April 1890 Wykes tried to return to work at the iron pits at Brixworth but contracted pleurisy and a severe inflammation of the lungs. He now had to apply to the local medical officer for outdoor relief. LGB records indicate that the doctor certified that the patient was too ill to be moved but guardians refused his application, offering only indoor relief. Meanwhile the pauper's condition deteriorated further. The doctor explained that Wykes developed a 'pulmonary inflammation which resulted in an ulceration of the lung with a constant discharge of a most malignant and offensive character'.[39] The smell of infection was so bad that neither the doctor, nor a local clergyman, nor a farmer guardian from the parish could enter the sickroom for more than a few minutes where he lay dying. His wife and mother nursed him because the stench of his condition was so bad that no paid nurse would attend. The cler-gyman tried to get Wykes to enter the workhouse but he refused because he wanted to die at home and avoid the stigma of a pauper burial after death.

The Brixworth union doctor supported Wyke's case for special treatment to central government. He stated that any sudden movement would be fatal. His family also complained separately to the LGB that once Wykes was placed in

---

34 *Northampton Guardian*, 18 May 1888.
35 See, for example, Mandler, *The uses of charity*.
36 Strange, 'She cried', and 'Only a pauper'.
37 Revd J. L. Roberts to LGB, case of John Wykes, 9 July 1890, MH 12/8705.
38 Roberts and Harpur to LGB, 9 July 1890, ibid.
39 Ibid.

the workhouse he would be placed in a male ward where his female relatives could not enter to nurse him. There was no trained nurse in the workhouse, no officer who cared for patients during the night and he would be left in the care of 'aged male paupers who would desert him in his need'.[40] The doctor pleaded with the LGB, stating the extenuating circumstances, but they adjudicated that the pauper had to enter the workhouse. The chairman of the Brixworth union offered to relax workhouse regulations by allowing the pauper's wife to nurse him in an upper sick ward. If she did not accept this adjudication parish-funded medical treatment would stop unless the doctor offered to attend Wykes free of charge. Reluctantly his wife accepted that she had no choice but to arrange to transport her terminally ill husband, on a cart, one chilly autumn morning three miles to the Brixworth union workhouse where, unsurprisingly, he soon died. The family could not afford to pay for his funeral expenses. Their farm on the Spencer estate had failed during the agricultural recession and they had been evicted without compensation. Wykes's wife had to accept the ignominy of a pauper burial. Regrettably no details have survived concerning the fate of the cadaver. It disappeared from all official records and so his case caused a furore in the district.

There is no doubt that the facts of these four cases need to be set in the context of the doctor's grievances and the poor's resentment of the *crusading* initiatives, notably the withdrawal of outdoor medical care. However, it is evident that paupers were being refused customary funeral payments on medical orders on a regular basis. Local newspaper reports about these cases suggest that Brixworth union residents believed that guardians had withdrawn medical outdoor relief funding of customary funerals for both economic and political reasons. They were not hoodwinked and made the connection with the changes in local democracy.[41] The four cases show just how impoverishing the revised medical regulations were in practice, and confirm that this policy was a form of 'brutal dispauperisation'.[42] Although the poor had no evidence that guardians regularly authorised the dismemberment or dissection of corpses in this location, they had learned to fear that they did. This further undermined traditional social relations in the area and deepened the climate of mistrust. It must also have accentuated the stress that poorer families experienced during mourning.

Sidney Ward told the Royal Commission on the Aged Poor that too many claimants were refused a coffin in the Brixworth union. When a young mother died even 'the children had to collect round the village to bury her'.[43] He claimed that 'people would rather die of want than go into the house' because of the burial policy. Ward's statements are compelling because even though he raised the cases for political purposes, it seems unlikely that he

---

40 Case files, July 1890, ibid.
41 See, for example, letter pages of the *Northampton Guardian*, May 1888.
42 Williams, *Pauperism*, 107.
43 *Royal Commission on the Aged Poor*, Ward, q. 15702.

would have given such damning evidence in front of Pell and Spencer, who sat on the Royal Commission on the Aged Poor, if it had been untrue and hence could be challenged immediately. In fact, although both Spencer and Bury questioned Ward at length about other aspects of his evidence, they did not pursue the matter of the lack of outdoor relief burial payments, an omission that reveals how controversial the burial policy was.[44] It is evident that in the Brixworth union poorer families could not afford the luxury of private grief; instead they had to put aside their intimate feelings to wheedle for basic customary funeral rites.

There is evidence to show that 'model' metropolitan unions did authorise dismemberment and dissection practices regularly. The Whitechapel union in London, for example, sold corpses, which their workhouse officials might have buried, to major London teaching hospitals.[45] Similarly, the *Lancet* reported in November 1889 that clause 4 of the Poor Law Act (1889) had been altered. It now permitted hospitals of the Metropolitan Asylums Board to be used for medical instruction because of the availability of pauper cadavers.[46] In addition, the Paddington union passed a resolution 'permitting the friendless or unknown dying in the Paddington Workhouse Infirmary to be used for purposes of dissection'. An editorial in the *Lancet* welcomed this trend because it noted that 'the number of subjects at present in the dissecting rooms is less than the supply for many past years and we are glad to see another source of supply has become available'.[47] Williams argues that the *crusading* experiment encouraged guardians to act in a devious manner to make greater savings, an assertion supported by controversies over pauper funerals.[48] It is evident that medical funding changes had a detrimental impact on some of the most vulnerable members of later Victorian society as a result of which they often suffered the stigma and shame of pauper funeral practices. In the Brixworth union the poor renamed the board of guardians the 'Bury-al Board' in this period,[49] a pun on the chairman's name, and a wry comment on the nature of poor relief care in the area. The Brixworth union was the poor law board that would rather bury you, than care for you outside the workhouse, and then might not bury you in the conventional manner. The poor feared death less than dissection or dismemberment, a far more demeaning fate.

Tom Laqueur argues that working-class funerals were usually much simpler affairs than their middle class counterparts.[50] However, the poor had one

---

[44] The chairman was given an opportunity to defend his poor relief management in the appendix to the *Royal Commission on the Aged Poor*. Although he gave details of a number of general outdoor relief cases, no medical cases were discussed, nor did he defend his practice on the matter of provision for pauper funerals.
[45] Richardson, *Death and dissection*, 243.
[46] *Lancet*, 9 Nov. 1889, 971.
[47] Ibid. 1129.
[48] Williams, *Pauperism*, 102.
[49] W. R. O. Adkins (ed.), *Our county*, Northampton 1893, 89–92.
[50] Laqueur, 'Bodies', 125–6.

priority, namely to avoid a pauper fate at death. Consequently, many paid into burial societies to ensure a decent burial. In the Brixworth union Sidney Ward became an insurance agent for a friendly society that provided this service. He collected weekly subscriptions around the district to ensure that the poor had a customary funeral. In some areas mourners organised a funeral raffle or an evening's entertainment at the local public house to pay for funeral expenses. Ruth Richardson points out that it was often women who took responsibility for funeral funds. She found evidence of women taking round 'the basin to collect for the burial of a pauper'.[51] The pauper funeral controversies in the Brixworth union confirm this. Begging for a burial became a more common sight in the district during the agricultural crisis and it was women and children who pleaded for charitable donations. It is also evident, as in the case of Samuel Brains, that certain elements of funeral practice 'were a powerful articulation of social aspiration and attainment'.[52] A woollen shroud, displaying the body, a wooden coffin and a Christian service demonstrated 'distance from the workhouse'.[53] Unlike the upper or middle classes the poor could not afford a lead coffin secured by 'stout rows of coffin nails'. This was a status symbol beyond their means. However, they could claim a body, accompany it until it was laid out, arrange a wake and finally ensure that it was buried whole. This was the register of their respectability, the scale of their cultural expectations and conventions.[54] Working-class mores were not dissimilar to those of the middle classes, as Pat Jalland observes, and were equally important.[55] They ensured that a loved one did not become an anonymous cadaver taken from a shallow pauper grave or degraded during an anatomical teaching seminar.[56] The dignity of private burial was society's final judgement of the deceased. For this reason in the Brixworth union the relatives of deceased paupers begged to bury their dead. But were the poor's fears of dissection justified?

Pauper cadaver trafficking: an untold *crusading* story

Research on the Cambridge University anatomy school suggests that their concerns were warranted. Anatomy records indicate that many more unions adopted *crusading* elements than is currently appreciated. Paradoxically, the

---

51 Richardson, *Death and dissection*, 277.
52 Ibid. 273.
53 Ibid.
54 The general fear and distrust on the part of the labouring poor of the meagre provision for pauper burial provided by poor law officials is discussed in Kidd, *State, society and the poor*, 138, and Hollen-Lees, *Solidarities* 294–8. The importance to the poor of decent burial is emphasised in E. T. Hurren and S. A. King, '"Begging for a burial": form, function and conflict in nineteenth-century pauper burial', *SH* xxx (2005), 321–41.
55 Jalland, *Death and the Victorian family*, 3.
56 Pauper graves were usually shallow because up to twelve bodies were placed in one hole. This meant that it was easier to steal bodies for dissection: ibid 279.

Brixworth union was moderate on the matter of trafficking in pauper cadavers. Others who denied involvement in fact championed it. This confirms how little welfare historians understand the diversity of the later Victorian poor law experience. Thus the demography, geography and scale of pauper trafficking activities in England has been ignored although Michael Sappol has examined the close working relationships that developed between American anatomy departments and their suppliers.[57] In broadening this discussion of a hidden aspect of the *crusading* process, four key issues would allow English historians to complement his work.

First, how was the supply and demand for corpses organised regionally? Second, given that the poor resented the Anatomy Act of 1832, its application must have been controversial and shaped popular views of medicine. Even though initial reactions to it are documented, notably in Richardson's and Strange's studies, its longer-term impact is under-researched at a local level.[58] If, therefore, the fate of those of Brixworth's poor who were denied a pauper burial could be discovered, this might substantiate the poor's claim that dissection was happening and contravened their death practices. Third, if the *crusaders* did sell the bodies of the poor for dissection and dismemberment on a regular basis, studying the ways that complex mechanisms of contact and payment with individuals and institutions were negotiated would reveal an unwritten aspect of the *crusading* history. Furthermore, welfare historians might discover to what extent the timing and scale of pauper cadaver supply chains mirrored the *crusading* campaign. Was it, for instance, just *crusaders* who sold on the dead poor or did more moderate unions follow suit and engage in extensive pauper trafficking? Finally, it is evident that the best way to acquire cadavers was to exploit lunatics and the poor. Thus, *crusaders* could sell bodies to recover welfare costs. At the same time, anatomists needed to increase their supplies, both of whole cadavers and body parts for research, for the Medical Act (1858) stipulated that all medical students had to pass a two-year training course in anatomy and hence more cadavers were needed to train increased numbers of fee-paying students. But how much profit was made from each cadaver, how did the economic priorities of *crusaders* and anatomists converge during the *crusading* decades? Trafficking in pauper cadavers reveals an unwritten history from above (anatomists and *crusaders*) and a history underneath (the poor lacking basic funeral provision) the umbrella of the later Victorian poor law.

In 1885 the workhouse master in the Brixworth union started to record the fate of pauper cadavers. In the workhouse death register he notes three possible outcomes: 'buried by friends'; 'buried by kin'; 'buried in the parish'. These entries referred to cadavers claimed by friends and family, to ensure a basic funeral and interment. For other types of cadavers there appeared to be

[57] M. Sappol, A traffic of dead bodies: anatomy and embodied social identity in 19th-century America, Princeton 2002.
[58] Richardson, Death and dissection; Strange, 'She cried', and 'Only a pauper'.

a considerable delay between the date of death and interment, as much as two years in some cases. The records indicate that sometimes a body was returned later from somewhere and this necessitated a delayed burial. Where was each body during that period? The remaining entries provided a date of death but no record of the parish of interment. The cadavers appear to be missing. The fact that the workhouse master started to keep more accurate burial records suggests that he may have been made more accountable for the destination of cadavers. His notes reveal that the poor now demanded to know the fate of their dead relatives' bodies. This worried him as it appears that the poor had every reason to resent the withdrawal of pauper burial payments on medical outdoor relief orders. The fate of a dead child in 1885 helps to explain both more accurate workhouse record-keeping, the possible destination of 'delayed bodies' and where guardians of all political persuasions (strict, moderate and liberal) may have traded pauper cadavers on a regular basis.

On 26 July 1885 William Henry Austin, 'an infant' from Holdenby village, died in the workhouse.[59] His family could not afford to bury him. Technically his cadaver now had an 'unclaimed' status under the Anatomy Act. Guardians had the option of paying for a pauper burial but this was refused. Instead, they opted to sell his body to the Cambridge anatomy school, on the Downing College site. Following preservation, dissection and dismemberment, the body was returned by rail, by prior arrangement to avoid a scandal, to Brixworth parish churchyard. The child was buried in a pauper grave on 27 June 1887, almost two years later after he died. The boy's family did not know what had happened to the body, nor is there any indication that it was able to take an active role in the delayed interment. The records of the anatomy school indicate that the practice of selling a pauper child's body for research purposes was quite normal. Delayed interment was, however, unusual. Most of the cadavers sold to the Cambridge anatomists were buried in the city centre and never returned to source.[60]

Burial records provide the key to understanding the fate of missing pauper cadavers.[61] They reveal that a total of 2,953 cadavers was interred in Mill Road cemetery in Cambridge between 1855 and 1920 (see fig. 8 for the number purchased and subsequently buried). Data collated suggests how economic and political change affected the local supply of bodies, while anatomists actively sought to acquire specific types of cadaver, notably infants. Ruth Richardson has asserted that the number of bodies acquired by regional anatomical schools under the Anatomy Act was much smaller than antici-

---

[59] Brixworth union death registers, 1837–95, NRO, P/L 2/12. These were checked against interment records held at Brixworth parish church. I am grateful to Canon Watson for his assistance in reconstituting these burial records.

[60] See E. T. Hurren, 'The pauper dead-house: the expansion of Cambridge University anatomical teaching school under the late-Victorian poor law, 1870–1914', *Medical History* i (2004), 69–95.

[61] St Benedict's burial records, Cambridge Records Office, P25/1/21–3.

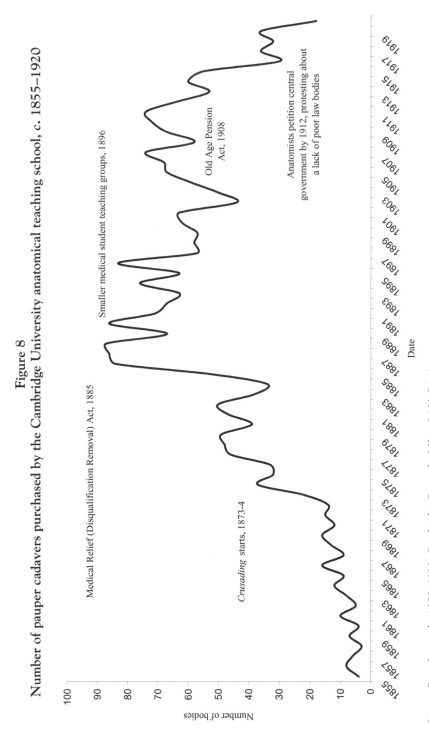

Figure 8

Number of pauper cadavers purchased by the Cambridge University anatomical teaching school, c. 1855–1920

Source: Burial records, 1855–1930, Cambridge Records Office, P25/1/21–3

pated in the mid-Victorian period.[62] She points out that the legislation was ill-thought-out, inefficient and resented. The figures for Cambridge, however, show different outcomes because they include the bodies sold under the late-Victorian poor law, which was beyond the scope of Richardson's work.

The number of bodies obtained by the Cambridge school between 1855 and 1870 was small. On average five bodies were dissected annually in the 1850s, rising to ten in the 1860s. The level of material was adequate because of small classes. However, by 1865, an average class contained sixty students and so there was an increasing demand for a wider range of material for dissection to satisfy the new training requirements.[63] This was still a problem in the early 1870s when only about seventeen dissections were performed annually. Significantly, however, cadaver numbers increased by 100 per cent to thirty-four anatomical demonstrations by 1873–4. This date marks the start of the *crusading* campaign. Thus during one of the most radical phases in the history of the nineteenth-century poor law anatomists were able to acquire more cadavers. *Crusading* therefore enabled anatomists to secure more teaching material provided they reimbursed asylum and poor law agencies for supplying human remains. Fee income was generated by passing on the costs of preparing, transporting and burying pauper cadavers to anatomists, thereby recovering some of the poor relief costs previously paid out. These covert payments were not declared on central government returns and an illicit trade in pauper cadavers developed, which underpinned medical training.

Figure 8 shows that while the number of bodies acquired rose between 1873/4 and 1884 to an average of forty-four annually, around 1885/6 the number fell to just thirty-two. By then the *crusading* campaign in more moderate areas had begun to abate because of a series of urban trade slumps and the rural recession in agriculture that followed the growth of overseas competition. Many poor law unions refused to withhold outdoor relief payments when poverty was not the fault of the individual but a national problem. Cambridge anatomists, therefore, faced an uphill task. They needed more bodies for an increased number of pupils. The professor of anatomy wrote to J. Pickering Pick, the government's anatomy inspector for the provinces, recalling that

> We have had very many difficulties in carrying on a School of Anatomy in a town with a small population in a thinly peopled centre, but we draw our supply from many and distant sources, as you will see from our certificates … I am sorry to say that the larger East Anglican towns, Norwich, Ipswich and Colchester, have a sentimental objection to send [ing] us any bodies.[64]

Surviving archives at Downing College reveal that regular drives to acquire more bodies were successful again, but only after 1885: within two years the number of bodies procured had increased by another 100 per cent on the

[62] Richardson, *Death and dissection*, 247.
[63] C. W. M. Pratt, *The history of anatomy at Cambridge*, Cambridge 1981, 13.
[64] Alex Macalister to J. Pickering Pick, memo, 9 Oct. 1896, Anatomy Inspectorate correspondence for the University of Cambridge, MH 74/11.

Table 8
Suppliers and number of cadavers sold to the Cambridge University anatomical teaching school, 1870–1920

Location of body suppliers	No. of bodies supplied	Location of body suppliers	No. of bodies supplied
Cambridge city centre	700	Hitchin union	27
Hull union	315	Leeds union	21
Addenbrooke's Hospital	305	Huntingdon union	17
Cambridge uuion	178	Whittlesey union	13
Doncaster union	146	Whitechapel union	11
Finchley union	138	Bishops Stortford union	9
Leyton union	129	Chelmsford union	9
Brighton union	104	Hardingstone union	8
Fulborn asylum	100	Kingston-upon-Hull union	8
Mildenhall union	86	Southampton union	7
Wisbech union	72	Basford union	6
Biggleswade union	70	Bury St Edmunds union	4
Anatomical school	59	Haverhill union	4
Colney Hatch asylum	58	Reading union	4
Hertford union	54	Ely union	3
Luton union	53	Nottingham union	3
Bedford union	43	Saffron Walden union	3
Three Counties asylum	42	Thetford union	3
Manchester union	36		
Yarmouth union	33		
Chesterton union	32	**Subtotal**	**2,944**
London county asylum	31	Other suppliers (2 cadavers or less)	9
		Total	**2,953**

Source: St Benedict's burial records, P25/1/21–3.

1873–4 figures. In fact, anatomists benefited from a much overlooked and underrated piece of minor poor law legislation, the MRDRA. This explains why body numbers increased between 1873 and 1883, then fell off in 1884 before rising once more in 1885/6.

Although the MRDRA was passed to remove the stigma of poor law medical treatment, in fact it did the opposite, penalising sick paupers by taking away their right to medical care and exacerbating the grieving process for bereaved families who now lacked basic funeral provision.[65] This was the background to the story of William Henry Austin.[66] Brixworth, however, was not alone in this furtive practice. Many other guardians, committed, moderate and liberal, sold similar unclaimed cadavers to regional anatomical schools (*see* table 8), which suggests that the *crusading* campaign and the expansion of anatomical training were inextricably linked.

Pauper cadavers were supplied to the Cambridge anatomical teaching school from more than forty sources between 1855 and 1920 (*see* table 8). The data reveals that, despite the anatomy department's claims in various memoranda to the Anatomy Inspectorate in London, they procured around 34 per cent of their dissection material from Cambridge city centre and Addenbrooke's hospital. A plotting of the streets in the city from which they obtained cadavers reveals that the closer the proximity of the death to the anatomy school, the Cambridge workhouse or Mill Road cemetery the higher the chance of ending up as dissection material. The poorer districts of the city provided most of the dissection specimens. So far no evidence has emerged to suggest how this was achieved on such a regular basis and scale. Again, it is only possible to conjecture about local arrangements between doctors, undertakers, bereaved families and the anatomy department.[67] All that can be said is that given the high numbers of bodies secured, a system must have been in place.

Figures from sources supplying 10 per cent or more cadavers to the anatomy school reflect late nineteenth-century regional demographic trends. Hull, for example, was one of the chief suppliers, with 315 bodies. It was one of the five English cities with the highest mortality rates during this period. Demographic historians often note the north–south divide in mortality patterns, with the exception of London.[68] Again, the cadaver figures for Cambridge broadly verify this for Hull and Doncaster unions lead the list of suppliers, closely followed by the Finchley union in London. The Leyton union (in east London), which supplied 129 bodies (4.37 per cent), was a logical supplier too.

---

65 See, for example, Englander, *Poverty and poor law reform*, 25.

66 Brixworth union death registers, 1837–95, P/L 2/12.

67 It is difficult to ascertain whether arrangements were made between doctors and undertakers, or by families direct. The high numbers suggest that various agencies may have been involved. There may have been neighbourhood intermediaries too.

68 E. Garrett, A. Reid, K. Schurer and S. Szreter, *Changing family size in England and Wales: place, class and demography, 1891–1911*, Cambridge 2001, 355, discusses broad north–south demographic trends.

Brighton union followed closely with 104 cadavers (3.52 per cent). Although Brighton seems to run counter to the trend towards a north–south divide, it was a mortality hot spot after 1870.[69] Moreover, despite public health in the city improving because of the work of the medical officer Arthur Newsholme from 1888, the local poor relief regime favoured anatomists.[70] Its poor law union was also a *crusading* leader. The aged poor, therefore, lost their customary funeral payments. Mistrust of *crusaders* and fear of being stigmatised meant that many paupers did not seek medical relief in the workhouse until it was too late. Their 'last resort' attitude resulted in increasing numbers of pauper cadavers being sold to Cambridge anatomists.

Other East Anglian and Midlands poor law unions were also regular suppliers. Indeed, the Downing anatomy archive reveals that once a board of guardians passed a motion in support of anatomical provision, the arrangement continued for many years. Following the passing of the MRDRA the Yarmouth guardians, for example, approved a motion in 1885 to sell cadavers to Cambridge. Their policy was not reconsidered until it was discovered that a body was missing from the local cemetery. Adverse publicity stopped supplies from Yarmouth after 1902. It is relevant that most poor law guardians were elected to office every three years. Few people were willing to undertake this unpaid and often tedious work, and those who were prepared to serve were often in office short-term. They had no reason to revisit controversial issues unless they had been the focus of an election campaign, like those following the democratisation of the poor law under the Local Government Act (1894). Indeed, guardians often had no knowledge of anatomical arrangements during their term of office. Workhouse personnel were not interested in drawing attention to a controversial policy that generated a regular income for them. These factors fostered a furtive administrative climate of close co-operation. The policy seems to have been say nothing, record nothing and evade all enquiries.

It is also evident that while some specifically *crusading* leaders supplied cadavers regularly, notably Brighton, Manchester, Oxford, Reading, Southampton and Whitechapel, they were not alone. A wide cross-section of asylums and poor law unions followed suit. Some unions, like Hull, claimed to have rejected the *crusading* campaign but in private complied. Widespread co-operation by unions in the supply of cadavers demonstrates the impor-

[69] Ibid. 362, though these trends were reversed by 1911.
[70] J. M. Eyler, 'Poverty, disease, responsibility: Arthur Newsholme and the public health dilemmas of British Liberalism', *Millbank Quarterly* lxvii (1989), 109–26; 'The sick poor and the state: Arthur Newsholme on poverty, disease and responsibility', in C. Rosenberg and J. Golden (eds), *Framing disease: studies in cultural history*, Rutgers 1992, 276–96; and *Sir Arthur Newsholme and state medicine, 1885–1935*, Cambridge 1997. New health policies sponsored by the LGB's medical division often ran contrary to the same department of state's desire to keep poor relief costs low, exemplified by the *crusade*. See, for example, E. T. Hurren, 'Poor law versus public health: diphtheria and the challenge of the *crusade* against outdoor relief to public health improvements in late-Victorian England, 1870–1900', *JSHM* xxviii (2005), 1–25

tance of looking beyond central government pauperism statistics to 'regional systems of welfare' and their local context.[71] It is also clear that those historians who have dismissed the *crusading* experiment as irrelevant, as a policy only pursued by mavericks, need to look again at its administrative record and the close links with anatomical teaching.

The location of supplier poor law unions and asylums within the eastern counties' railway network reveals that Cambridge anatomists targeted towns on the Great Eastern, Great Northern and Midland main and branch lines.[72] For example, Bedford, Biggleswade, Hertford, Hitchin, Huntingdon, Luton, Stevenage and Three Counties were all stations on the Great Eastern line going out of Cambridge. Similarly, Bishops Stortford, Bury St Edmunds, Ely, Haverhill, Histon, Fulbourn, Lakenheath, Mildenhall, Saffron Walden and Thetford were on branch or main lines out of Cambridge. Railway expansion at Cambridge got underway in the Victorian period because of a desire to link London to northern coal and industry via an eastern-counties stop-over: the anatomists benefited from networks linking the city to areas with high mortality rates. From September 1882 they could use a thrice-daily freight service between Liverpool Street and Doncaster via Cambridge. Similar coal and cattle services were operating between Cambridge and Leeds (via the Leeds and Selby branch line) by 1892. Other important direct links to Hull, Huntingdon and Nottingham had created opportunities to develop anatomical links further afield by the later 1890s. Railway connections explain why smaller unions, like Mildenhall, Wisbech and Biggleswade, with populations of only around 5,000 in the 1890s, supplied proportionately more cadavers. Quite simply, they were ideally located. Commentators often note that the railway was one of the chief symbols of modernity in Victorian England. It is seen as an engine of progress that expanded entertainment and employment opportunities for poorer working people. Paradoxically, it also regularly carried a cadaver freight that ignored cultural, religious and social sensibilities. This was more widespread than many social historians have appreciated.

Anatomy and the later Victorian poor law

There was a very wide network connecting poor law unions, asylums and anatomists within which anatomists, asylum superintendents, guardians of the poor, medical officers and workhouse personnel had close working relationships.[73] These took time to develop fully, coming to fruition only after

---

71 King, *Poverty and welfare*, makes this point forcibly in the conclusion.
72 D. I. Gordon, *A regional history of the railways of Great Britain*, V: *The eastern counties*, Newton Abbott 1968, chs vi–vii, outlines Cambridge's main and branch line links.
73 E. T. Hurren, 'Why did we fail to learn the medical lessons of the past?', in A. Gestrich, S. A. King and L. Raphael (eds), *Being poor in modern Europe*, Oxford 2004, 352–87, discusses cadaver trafficking by the Oxford anatomy school.

1870 during the most radical phase of poor law administration and the peak of expansion in anatomical teaching. Four significant features are evident.

First, the timing of the *crusading* campaign mirrors patterns of cadaver purchase by anatomists. In Cambridge, the start of the *crusading* initiatives increased pauper specimens 100 per cent in 1873–4. After the passing of the MRDRA cadaver numbers increased by a further 100 per cent in 1885–6. The economic interests of asylums and guardians of the poor converged with the research and training agendas of anatomists. Many poor law unions that denied their involvement in the *crusading* process were supplying pauper cadavers to recover the costs of relief. Further empirical work needs to be completed on the value of cadaver sales to ratepayers. Nevertheless, one should not understate that *crusaders* judged it worth the time and effort to become involved in this complex and covert trade.

Second, the Anatomy Act gave regional anatomical schools a high degree of autonomy. To what extent a general lack of public accountability shaped anatomical training is as yet unclear. Perhaps it dictated the research agendas of anatomists and shaped major scientific breakthroughs, such as the first x-ray in Britain (in Cambridge, using a pauper child), early tissue culture laboratory work and suchlike. Whatever the scientific outcome, welfare historians still need to engage with the regional complexities of this legal but duplicitous trade pioneered by *crusaders* and their moderate counterparts.

Third, the demographic profile of the bodies that passed through Cambridge is instructive. The data explains why so many of the aged poor dreaded admission to the workhouse in the later Victorian era. Living within close proximity to the anatomy school, cemetery or workhouse enhanced the chances of ending up as research material, as did being treated in a workhouse infirmary or at Addenbrooke's. In Oxford, similarly, the dead poor were purchased from the workhouse on Cowley Road, or came via the Radcliffe infirmary. In this way Oxford medical students too relied on a pauper cadaver trade. Moreover, some so-called 'liberal' poor law unions, like Leicester, that denied involvement and refused Cambridge's offers to purchase cadavers, were lying about their involvement in the body trade: they sold on cadavers for a higher price. Secretly, Oxford outbid Cambridge in its determination to secure plenty of bodies so that it could increase its numbers of fee-paying medical students. A large medical and poor law historiography emphasises the benefits of the expansion of workhouse infirmaries under the later Victorian poor law,[74] but it tends to omit any discussion of the anatomy trade and its high social cost. It is unlikely that the majority of aged paupers viewed their anatomical fate as progressive in an era when the dissection or dismemberment of human remains signalled social failure for bereaved families.

Fourthly the anatomy trade explains why the Brixworth poor were so fearful when customary funeral payments were withdrawn. When the records of cadaver sales to Cambridge University are examined it is clear that for

---

[74] See, for example, introduction, n. 13.

many reasons their fears were justified. Significant numbers of bodies were not sold from the Brixworth union, but not because guardians did not want to upset the local poor. Rather, the dossier of pauper burial controversies reveals that when crucial funeral rites were halted the poor in the Brixworth union somehow managed to claim their cadavers. Often this meant using delaying tactics, relying on neighbours as well as kinship networks and, if necessary, even begging. Anything and everything was done to ensure a 'decent' burial. They suspected something sinister was happening and that perception shaped their strong reaction. Elsewhere, those who did not know about cadaver trafficking had no reason to react. They assumed, incorrectly, that reassurances about poor law moderation meant that their loved ones were buried 'decently'. In fact, many were sold onwards, but quietly. This suggests that it is inappropriate to use the generic term a 'crusade against outdoor relief' to describe the entire later Victorian poor law experience, since welfare historians still know so little about its fine details. What was actually happening was a series of *crusades* at a local level.

It is clear why the poor in the Brixworth union were very sceptical about further changes in the poor law and motivated to resist any further retrenchment. *Crusaders* had taken away their economic options. They had compounded their impoverishment by undermining what little dignity the grieving poor had left at times of bereavement. Some were even reduced to begging to bury their loved ones. Others were either unaware or tried to prevent the remains of their friends and close relatives being anatomised. Thus the development of local democracy and the guardians' failure to respond to fundamental human needs, ensured that by the 1890s the *crusaders* were the architects of their own downfall. The end was in sight.

9

Campaigning for Change:
Democracy and Poor Law Politics, 1890–1900

The end of the *crusading* experiment 'is conventionally fixed in 1893'. This was the year that qualifications to vote in guardian elections changed, reduced from a rateable value of £25 to £5 *per annum*.[1] Then, in 1894, the Local Government Act (LGA) introduced one-man-one-vote suffrage in both guardian and new parish council elections.[2] The plural voting system was abolished and for the first time non-property owners could stand as guardians of the poor.[3] At the same time, the office of *ex-officio* guardian was discontinued and poor law unions were redesignated as urban or rural district councils. Although there has been considerable debate amongst political historians about the impact of the extension of the parliamentary franchise, the democratisation of the poor law is still understudied.[4] The standard view is that the nature of local government in the English provinces did not change significantly after the passing of the LGA because there was more continuity than discontinuity in the personnel involved in the new district and parish councils.[5] However, whilst that may have been the case in other poor law unions, democratisation had a major impact in the Brixworth union. For the first time working people had the opportunity to take control of the poor law system that had excluded and impoverished so many, and they acted decisively.

This chapter explores the political reaction amongst working people when the property qualification in guardian elections was lowered. By 1894 the political tide at both the national and local levels had turned against committed *crusaders*. This gave tradesmen, the labouring poor and paupers the means to win the majority of seats on the board of guardians by 1896, thus ending the protracted battle over the *crusading* campaign in the Brixworth

---

[1] Williams, *Pauperism*, 103.

[2] See, for example, a basic outline of the provisions of the Local Government Act (1894) in Pugh, *Modern British politics*, 69–112, and Pearce and Stewart, *British political history*, 185–231.

[3] Women, for example, could be elected guardians from 1872 provided that they owned property and paid rates of £15 *per annum* in the provinces or £200 in London. In 1893 this was reduced to the £5 threshold everywhere and then abolished in the 1894/5 election. Hollis, *Ladies elect*, 195, 267–302, estimates that around 800 women were elected for the first time in 1894. I am grateful to S. A. King, for allowing me to read an advance copy of his *Women, welfare and local politics, c. 1880–1920: 'We might be trusted'*, Brighton 2005.

[4] See, for example, introduction, n. 30.

[5] Sykes, *Rise and fall*, is a recent monograph on political history that adopts this view; Kidd, *State, society and the poor*, is a welfare textbook that takes a similar stance.

union. It was time for a ground swell of opposition to launch a successful counter-offensive.

Democratic action

In December 1892, at Gladstone's request, Spencer convened a meeting at Althorp to discuss with senior members of the Liberal government proposals to establish parish councils. This had been a key manifesto commitment of the Newcastle Programme of 1891 and had helped the Liberals to win the 1892 general election.[6] Many Liberals feared that the party could not introduce a new local government act to create parish councils without also democratising the poor law. The Chancellor of the Exchequer, Sir William Harcourt, told Spencer that the problem with the parish council scheme was that 'we have moved too fast and too far towards the extreme left on every subject at once, and quite sensible folk don't like it'.[7] Spencer agreed that the future was 'very dark' for the party but he conceded that the democratisation of the poor law was inevitable because of the manifesto commitment to create parish councils. Before the meeting a number of correspondents wrote to Spencer to ask him to oppose the parish council scheme because of the effect it would have on the administration of the poor law, which was the last stronghold of the rural elite in local government. For example, a clergyman asked Spencer whether ratepayers would be given more votes on village councils than non-ratepayers: he could not believe that the Liberal party was going to repeal the principle of 'no representation without rates'. Spencer told his land agent that the clergyman's enquiry 'was a difficult one' because the Liberal party was 'supposed to be the champion of householders'.[8] Predictably, the *crusaders'* party in the Brixworth union felt threatened. Bury wrote to Spencer:

> I am quite in accord with the provisions of the Bill, but I would argue that it must have a serious effect, at any rate for a time, on administration and that it will excite speculative hopes in the minds of potential recipients, which, whether realised or not must have a mischievous tendency. All considerations of expense or modification sink into insignificance compared to the enormous power which poor law administration has to improve or demoralise every class of the community ... – will you let the importance of this subject be my apology, for earnestly praying you to use your great influence in the direction of enquiry <u>before</u> legislation.[9]

After the meeting at Althorp the Liberal government introduced local government legislation, which created parish councils in villages with populations

---

6 Sykes, *Rise and fall*, 145, discusses the background to the 1892 election victory.
7 W. Harcourt to Spencer, 17 July 1892 and Spencer to Harcourt, 18 July 1893, Bodleian Library, Oxford, MSS Harcourt, 711, fos 10, 16.
8 R. Abbay to Spencer, and Spencer to Abbay, 14 Dec. 1891, MSS Althorp, K329.
9 Bury to Spencer, annotated by Spencer, 10 Nov. 1891, ibid.

of more than 300 people. Under the terms of the LGA poor law unions in rural areas were to be democratised too and as an interim step the Liberal government reduced the property qualification for voting in guardian elections to a rateable value of £5 *per annum* in 1893. In reply to an angry letter from Bury, Spencer wrote:

> I cannot agree with your view that those who prepared the bill were unconscious of the effect it would have on the Poor Law. We considered it and discussed it. We knew that by doing away with the plural vote we were giving more direct control of P.[oor] Law to the poorer classes of the Electors who might desire to give more out-relief than is given in some Unions like Brixworth. We cd.[could] not however defend the present voting or ex-officio JP guardians. The battle wh. [which] you have fought at Brixworth will no doubt have to be fought if ... the Bill is carried but I believe that in the end the principle of relief wh.[which] you have been champion will be carried. Pray remember that this method, this sound method is really exceptionally practised. I thought that maybe a majority of the Bd. [Board] as at present carry not a lax policy of relief?[10]

Spencer seemed to have done a *volte-face*, because, unlike ardent *crusaders*, he was a pragmatist and a political realist. He was not in favour of the democratisation of the poor law, but he sensed that the political scene was changing and he appears to have judged that it was better for the Liberal party to adapt than stagnate and lose office. His election agent also warned Spencer after the election victory in 1892 that, 'unless something is done for the agricultural labourer *pari passu* with Home Rule or even before it we cannot keep our hold on the Counties or this part of the County'.[11] He recommended the reintroduction of outdoor relief for elderly paupers, which 'would do more for us in villages than Parish Councils, one man one vote or a Good Allotment Act all found together'. The chairman of the Brackley union, a leading Liberal in south Northamptonshire, told Spencer that their party should 'pronounce in favour of old age pensions of 5/- [shillings] per week to every man or woman arriving at the age of 65 [so that] the workhouse with its preceding nightmare would be abolished'.[12]

Although these local proposals anticipated the Liberal welfare reforms of 1906, in the Brixworth union working people wanted first to reform the poor law. Spencer was ambivalent about social welfare reform and so when asked about the *crusading* campaign he responded in a typically Whig fashion, citing his apolitical stance. He sat, for example, on the Royal Commission

---

[10] Spencer to Bury, 'Nov. 1891', ibid. K344. There is some confusion over the dating of this letter as the 7th Earl Spencer, who catalogued his family papers in the 1950s, wrote that it was written in 1893. This was a cataloguing error as it was written in response to Bury's letter of 10 Jan. 1891.

[11] Ryland Adkins to Spencer, 17 July 1892, ibid. K333. *Pari passu* is a term in English land law meaning 'alongside', where charges on a property are not ranked in order of debt but have equal weighting in the event of bankruptcy.

[12] Thomas Judge to Spencer, 6 Dec. 1891, ibid. K330.

for the Aged Poor (1894), but would not support state pensions. He spoke in favour of local government changes, but would not endorse the reintroduction of outdoor relief. Leading *crusaders*, notably Pell, thought Spencer's appraisal of further local government proposals, in particular the democratisation of the poor law, was naïve. Pell wrote to *The Times* protesting that 'under the Bill ... however, this control reduced ... passes into the hands of a class which comprises the recipient numerically strong and whose influence becomes dominant. Should this Bill pass in its present form the prospect is a sad one for the country'.[13]

Local government debates convinced working people, ratepayers and guardians who opposed the *crusading* initiatives in the Brixworth district that the time was right to launch an opposition campaign.

In late January 1893 an advertisement appeared in the *Northampton Mercury*:

> To the Electors of the Brixworth Board of Guardians
> A meeting of Delegates will be held in the Brixworth School Room
> on February 2nd 1893,
> in respect of the recent reduction of qualification for guardians.
> Chair to be taken at seven p.m.
> All villages in the district are requested to send delegates.[14]

Approximately 200 people met at the Red Lion public house in Brixworth village, where they formed the Brixworth District Out Door Relief Association (BDODRA). This political pressure group was the brainchild of Sidney Ward, a labouring spokesman encountered throughout this poor law journey.[15] There were similar associations elsewhere that may have influenced Ward. For example, in 1888 working people in Oxford formed an association to fight against the *crusading* experiment of the Oxford union board of guardians.[16] The Oxford union was dominated by leading COS members such as the Revd L. R. Phelps and working people tried to get their own candidates elected but failed. It is not clear whether the Oxford association provided the blueprint for BDODRA, but its activities were renowned in poor law circles and Ward admired their stance.

Sidney Ward was born in Brixworth parish in 1864, an illegitimate only child, whose mother had been harshly treated by the union guardians.[17] During her confinement guardians refused to pay the cost of a home midwife

---

13 *Times*, 25 Nov. 1893.
14 *Northampton Mercury*, 27 Jan. 1893.
15 See pp. 104–5 above.
16 Misc. vols, 1888, MSS Phelps, Oriel College, Oxford; *Jackson's Oxford Journal*, 24 Mar. 1888; L. R. Phelps, 'Oxford poor relief', in VCH, *Oxfordshire*, London 1952, 349; *Oxford Chronicle*, 24 Mar. 1888; *Berkshire and Buckinghamshire Gazette*, 24 Mar. 1888.
17 Ward's illegitimacy was recorded on the 1881 census return for Brixworth parish. Recent family members seem to have been unaware of it. See, for example, J. Gould, 'In search of Sidney Ward', *NP&P* viii (1993/4), 393–406.

and she had to enter the workhouse to give birth. However, she refused to hand her child over to the parish authorities, raising him at home with the help of her family and friends. Little is known of Ward's early life, except that he acquired a rudimentary education at the Church of England school in Brixworth parish and had a Nonconformist background, attending Sunday school at the local Methodist church. In 1893, when BDODRA was founded, he was a single man aged twenty-nine, standing over six feet tall and sporting a large beard. He had three part-time jobs during the second phase of the agricultural crisis: as a jobbing gardener, a lamplighter and an insurance representative for the Royal Liverpool & Victoria Friendly Society. As an insurance collector, Ward travelled weekly throughout the district collecting sickness and burial club subscriptions from local people who needed some form of insurance to replace outdoor relief. He often visited subscribers during family crises when he called to assess their insurance claims. Contemporary accounts suggest that Ward was a popular member of the community, both admired and respected by his peers. In adulthood he was an active member of the Salvation Army in Brixworth parish, often preaching at services. Since the Salvation Army had no meeting place in the village they usually hired either the school hall or the village hall or held open-air services, frequently accompanied by a band. Ward's Salvation Army work taught him how to make an effective public speech and organise rallies. Although he had learned to read and write at school his bible studies appear to have given him a thirst for wider political knowledge. Like many Nonconformists he favoured radical texts, such as Tom Paine's *The rights of man*. He often quoted the speeches of Keir Hardie, which he read in the *Daily News*, an 'advanced' Liberal newspaper widely circulated in the Brixworth union that seems to have influenced many of the labouring community.[18] In the years 1890 to 1891 the *Daily News* published a series of rural reports about the effects of the agricultural crisis and the *crusading* experiment on the lives of the labouring poor in rural England. A typical editorial concluded that 'in the abstract principle the [poor] law is right; the practical application of it ... is often a cruel wrong'.[19] Ward's illegitimacy and Nonconformist upbringing gave him the motivation, contacts and skills to organise the local community into a political pressure group to exploit the democratisation of the poor law. He argued that the time was ripe to overthrow the *crusaders*.

In 1891 and 1892 Ward recruited leading opponents of the *crusading* policies whom he met at Nonconformist meetings or on his travels throughout the district. For example, in Walgrave he enlisted the help of Stephen Norton Walker, a Baptist lay-preacher and former agricultural labourer. Walker was a self-made man who manufactured army boots in a small factory in his

---

[18] *Royal Commission on the Aged Poor* (1894), Ward, 27 Feb. 1894, q. 15955.

[19] *Daily News*, 3 Aug. 1891, quoted in E. Bellamy, E. Razzell and J. Ward (eds), *Life in the Victorian village: the Daily News survey of 1891*, i, London 1999, 112.

village, employing a large number of local people.[20] At Pitsford he recruited Josiah Turner, also a member of the Baptist Church, a carpenter and builder with strong 'advanced' Liberal views.[21] George Page (baker, grocer and beer retailer) joined these men from Holcot parish. Ward also enlisted a number of outspoken agricultural labourers, originally NALU members. Sam Brambley, for example, had led one of the first union meetings in the spring of 1872 and petitioned Spencer in March 1873 for higher wages. He had also campaigned alongside the Liberal caucus in 1884–5 against the *crusading* activities of the Brixworth union. A series of grievances in this rural community, but most notably the issue of outdoor relief, contributed to this nascent independent labour movement in 1893, which was led by a combination of moderate farmers, traders, artisans and common agricultural labourers.

At the inaugural meeting of BDODRA members voted in a president (a sympathetic farmer guardian) and eight executive committee members (a farmer guardian, four artisans and two labourers) to oversee their political activities.[22] Most were Nonconformists and all nine members of the committee were 'advanced' Liberal party supporters. Two of them (Ward and Walker) were illegitimate, but in fact all seem to have had friends or relatives who had been harshly treated by the guardians. BDODRA's executive committee invited 'any competent working man' who paid rates of £5 *per annum* in 1892/3 to apply to be selected to stand as a guardian of the poor on their behalf. As the guardian election was set for April 1893 BDODRA ran a very short campaign. Meetings were convened in most of the larger parishes in the district, where no major landowner predominated.[23] A local BDODRA member usually hired a school or church hall in his or her parish and canvassed ratepayers to attend. In the course of each meeting a committee of five men was elected to oversee BDODRA's campaign in that village. Each BDODRA member subscribed 6*d. per annum* to a union fund, so that any newly-elected working guardians could claim an allowance of 2*s.* 6*d.* per day in compensation for lost earnings every time they attended a fortnightly poor law union board meeting.

To publicise BDODRA Ward wrote to incumbent guardians asking them to answer a series of questions about the *crusading* controversy, which he planned to publish in local newspapers: 'whether, if you are returned at the next election as a guardian of the poor, if you would vote for out-door relief to be given to the deserving poor, such cases that are recommended by the

[20] Walker to LGB, 'March 1893', MH 12/8706, LGB ref. 31225/93. I am indebted to Miss Doreen Norton, niece of Stephen Norton Walker for sharing with me her private family archive at Walgrave and her memories of her uncle.
[21] I am indebted to the present Turner family of Pitsford village for sharing with Peter King and me family memories and a photograph of Josiah Turner.
[22] *Northampton Mercury*, 3 Mar. 1893.
[23] The *Northampton Mercury* and the *Northampton Herald* gave weekly accounts of BDODRA's activities and funding arrangements in March 1893.

committee and guardians of their own parish'.[24] His letter to Spencer stated that 'in some parishes the men are *afraid* to vote *against* the Guardians who are opposed to out-relief because by doing so they would come under your Lordship's displeasure'. Spencer replied that this was nonsense but he later admitted that the 1893 guardian election had been partisan.[25] Ward then invited local newspaper reporters to attend a meeting in the chairman's parish, Harlestone, on 21 March 1893, six days before polling. It was one of the last chances BDODRA had to campaign and Ward hoped to belittle the chairman in public. He also invited a number of Northampton town council-lors, who were members of the Northampton Liberal Radical Association, to attend the meeting. He hoped that they would persuade ratepayers who were wavering to vote for BDODRA.

The Harlestone meeting was reported in all the local newspapers. The *Northampton Mercury* stated 'that Harlestone ... was the scene of a meeting the like of which has rarely taken place'.[26] BDODRA's president chaired the meeting. Ward spoke first, attacking, the 'Secret Service Fund', which was being used to fund deserving paupers, instead of the poor being given outdoor relief. He stated that 'if there were cases in the Brixworth district that were deserving enough to get a charity fund relief, they were deserving enough to get relief from the parish'. The town councillors from Northampton seconded this motion. Their spokesman, Frederick Covington JP, confirmed that 'if a man was entitled to private benevolence, he was certainly entitled to the public benevolence'. Proceedings were so rowdy that henchmen, hired by the chairman of the board of guardians in anticipation of political feeling running high, had to intervene when scuffles broke out. Order was restored but broke down again as soon as Bury rose to speak. He challenged BDODRA to produce 'ten really hard cases' that had suffered because of the *crusading* experiment. Bury offered to refer them to the Royal Commission on the Aged Poor, which had just convened in London. He promised that for every poor relief decision that was judged too harsh he would pay £5 to the Harlestone Benefit Society. The editor of the *Northampton Mercury* commented 'that from communications which have reached me at different times, I should say it would not be difficult to accept that challenge!'[27]

Before polling day the *crusaders* defended their chairman in a series of letters to local newspapers. One correspondent, styled 'Fairplay', stated that 'the rector of Harlestone has been badly treated, and if the Out-Door Relief Association thinks to make or retain friends they are on the wrong track'.[28] Unfortunately a number of long-serving members of the *crusaders'* party ignored popular opinion, acting in a very offensive manner during the elec-tion campaign. For example, at East Haddon, the local vestry de-selected

[24] Ward to Spencer, 17 Mar. 1893, MSS Althorp, K344.
[25] Spencer to Ward, 18 March 1893, ibid.
[26] *Northampton Mercury*, 24 Mar. 1893.
[27] Ibid.
[28] Ibid. 31 Mar. 1893.

the incumbent guardian, the vice-chairman of the Brixworth union, who had offended the local community by telling working people that, 'he was too busy' to answer their criticisms and that 'in his experience ... men of the lower class ... had a tendency to bully'.[29] An editorial in the *Northampton Mercury* explained that the *crusaders'* party had lost support in the community:

> The Board is responsible to the law, as well as to the ratepayers, and to the poor; it cannot justly deliver over its duty to any private arrangements [*Secret Service Fund*]. There is never smoke without fire; and it is inconceivable that there can have been the strong and bitter feeling over this question ... if there were not the pressure of a hardship, difficult perhaps to reduce to a particular shape but yet very present in the minds of the aged poor, living ever on the brink of starvation but still clinging to life outside the Bastille. ... The hardship is often difficult to prove, but it is hard to define the terror which seizes with undefineable grip the multitudes of the poor and because you cannot measure in a pint pot the pangs of hunger and misery of the cold which freezes aged blood. I feel that the balance of humanity and justice, as well as of policy, is in favour of discriminating 'out-relief' and should, therefore, advise the casting of the vote in support of those candidates who carry it out.[30]

Local newspapers in Northamptonshire had always reported poor law matters objectively, so this change of editorial policy, and by a Liberal newspaper, reveals that the political climate in the area had indeed been radicalised. Years of poverty had engendered a reaction unfavourable to the *crusaders*. Two particular factors, the 'Secret Service Fund' and the treatment of elderly paupers, had solidified opposition amongst a cross-section of the community. For BDODRA to have won such a resounding endorsement from a local newspaper it must have conducted a very successful election campaign. The next issue of the paper reported that BDODRA had won nine out of the ten seats they had contested in the April 1893 elections, confirming changing poor law allegiances.

In the 1890s poor law procedures were altered in two significant ways: the clerk to the Brixworth union board of guardians had for legal reasons to keep a record in the guardians' minute books of the votes cast during fortnightly meetings, and reporters were admitted to meetings for the first time and permitted to report all proceedings in full. Accurate guardian voting patterns can therefore be compiled, matching regular attendance to definitive party allegiance. In 1890 there were fifty-five guardians sitting on the Brixworth union board. Thirty-nine were elected (five smaller seats had been amalgamated in the late-1880s, for example Moulton Park merged with Moulton parish), and sixteen were *ex-officio* appointments. On average forty-two guardians attended meetings regularly between 1890 and 1896, and voting patterns reveal that the opposition party held seven seats or 16 per cent of the avail-

29 Ibid. 24 Mar. 1893.
30 Ibid. 31 Mar. 1893.

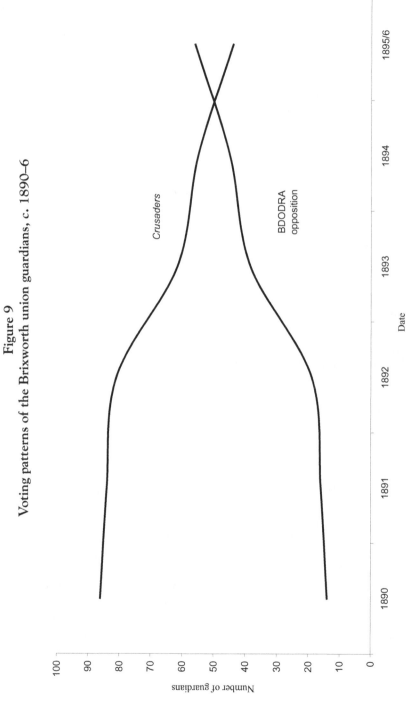

Figure 9
Voting patterns of the Brixworth union guardians, c. 1890–6

Source: Brixworth union guardians' minute books, P/L 2/14–20

Table 9
Levels of support for *crusaders*, 1890–6

	1890	1891	1892	1893	1895	1896
Number of seats						
A						
Pell's party	37	36	30	27	23	20
B						
Opposition party	6	7	7	17	19	25
C						
Opponents who were						
Members of BDODRA	(2)	(2)	(1)	(9)	(10)	(11)
D						
Guardians who						
abstained regularly	0	1	0	0	0	0
Totals						
A+B+D	43	44	37	44	42	45
(attending guardians)						

Source: Brixworth union guardians' minute books, P/L 2 /19–20.

able votes on the board between 1890 and 1892 (*see* table 9 and fig. 9).[31] This compared favourably with its average share of the votes in 1885–9. However, that situation changed following the April 1893 election.

For the first time there were more marked class divisions on the board over the *crusading* issue. In 1893, 59 per cent of farmers supported the *crusaders'* party. Although this was a significant proportion of the board, it represents a reduction of 22 per cent in the 1890–2 figures, which showed that 8 per cent of farmers were ardent *crusaders* (*see* tables 10–12). Those farmers with no fixed allegiance who had supported the *crusaders* in 1885–90 period were starting to migrate to the opposition. The figures also reveal that around three times as many artisans and traders were elected to office in 1893 and constituted 16 per cent of the available votes. One candidate described himself as 'an agricultural labourer' and was the 'first of his class' to be elected to office. The *crusaders'* party held a 61.5 per cent block vote on the board in 1893 and their opponents 38.5 per cent. Overall the *crusaders* had lost a 19.5 per cent share of the votes on the board. It was clear that the loss of the farmers' support was significant because they held the largest block of votes: any change in their allegiance alarmed committed *crusaders* like Pell and Bury. It also indicated that the coming of democracy had given residents who paid rates of £5 *per annum* the opportunity for the first time to make their feelings felt at the poor

[31] Since each seat gave every guardian one vote, the share of the votes and the number of seats were equal. Percentage share of votes held will therefore be referred to throughout.

Table 10
Occupational structure (%) of the Brixworth union board of guardians, 1890–6

Occupation	1890	1891	1892	1893	1895	1896
Ex-officio	9	7	8	4.5	0	0
Elected						
Landowners/householders	7	12	13.5	9	16.5	11
Clergy	12	9	11	9	9.5	9
Land agents	14	19	19	20.5	14	11
Farmers	53.5	46	43	39	29	29
Artisans/traders	4.5	7	5.5	16	21.5	29
Labourers	0	0	0	2	7.5	9
Female guardians	0	0	0	0	2	2
Totals:	100	100	100	100	100	100

Source: Brixworth union guardians' minute books, P/L 2 /19–20.

Table 11
Crusaders' party (%) on the Brixworth union board of guardians, 1890–6

Occupation	1890	1891	1892	1893	1895	1896
Ex-officio	9	7	8	4.5	0	0
Elected						
Landowner/householder	7	12	8	4.5	12	8
Clergy	12	9	11	9	7	7
Land agents	14	19	19	20.5	14	11
Farmers	44	37	35	23	20	16
Artisans/traders	0	0	0	0	0	0
Labourers	0	0	0	0	0	0
Female guardians	0	0	0	0	2	2
A Subtotal	**86**	**84**	**81**	**61.5**	**55**	**44**

Source: Brixworth union guardians' minute books, P/L 2/19–20.

Table 12
Opposition party (%) on the Brixworth union board
of guardians, 1890–6

	1890	1891	1892	1893	1895	1896
Occupation						
Ex-officio	0	0	0	0	0	0
Elected						
Landowner/householder	0	0	5.5	4.5	4.5	3
Clergy	0	0	0	0	2.5	2
Land agents	0	0	0	0	0	0
Farmers	9.5	9	8	16	9	13
Artisans/traders	4.5	7	5.5	16	21.5	29
Labourers	0	0	0	2	7.5	9
Female guardians	0	0	0	0	0	0
B Subtotal	14	16	19	38.5	45	56
A+B Total	100	100	100	100	100	100

Source: Brixworth union guardians' minute books, P/L 2/19–20.

law ballot box where it mattered most. All the artisan, labourers and trader guardians were BDODRA candidates who joined the opposition party on the poor law board. The *crusaders'* party still held the largest block of votes, but it was dependent on higher attendance levels.

The first meeting of the newly elected guardians took place at the Brixworth union workhouse on 23 April 1893.[32] Bury took the chair and welcomed the new members stating 'that as they were new to the work he might state one or two elementary principles to them'. He announced that as 'they were a public body, with a public duty and public funds to administer' they must observe central government guidelines. Pell also hoped that 'new members would divest themselves of the view that they were there to sit as opposing bodies'; guardians should try to work efficiently together to administer the board's policies.[33] However, BDODRA guardians refused to co-operate, since they had been elected to create as much agitation as possible until outdoor relief was reintroduced. By August 1893 tensions between the two sides had reached such a peak of bitterness that most meetings were being headlined in local newspapers as 'disorderly'.[34]

BDODRA guardians wanted to challenge all cases where outdoor relief was refused but discovered that applications seldom came before a full board

32 Brixworth union guardians' minute book, P/L 2/19–20.
33 *Northampton Herald*, 22 Apr. 1893.
34 Ibid. 12 Aug. 1893.

meeting. They were either redirected to the 'Secret Service Fund', or were refused by an assessment committee, which predictably was dominated by *crusaders*. Consequently, BDODRA guardians decided to concentrate their energies upon attacking the 'Secret Service Fund' which was so despised by the labouring poor. During proceedings of the Royal Commission on the Aged Poor, while Bury tried to minimise the role of the charity fund, Samuel Ward gave damning evidence against it.[35] He explained that the chairman used the charity to redirect deserving outdoor relief cases which should have been funded from the rates and that he was able to do this because he was in cahoots with the relieving officer. Together they ensured that no deserving outdoor relief cases came before the full board. If one slipped through the chairman made sure the applicant was relieved by the use of charity before the case was heard so that the application could be thrown out on the basis that the pauper was no longer destitute. Ward's integrity impressed the prince of Wales, later Edward VII, who sat in on the commission's proceedings. However, since both Spencer and Pell were members of the commission, Bury was permitted to add an appendix to the commission's final report, defending his policy decisions. Ward complained to the LGB that Spencer and Pell were biased. He emphasised that under poor law regulations it was illegal to act in this way since relieving officers were not allowed to disclose for publication any information on applications for outdoor relief .

> Sir could you let me know how it was Rev. W. Bury was allowed to reply to my evidence on the aged poor commission and why I was not allowed to see his reply before it was printed as his reply is very misleading and False Statements about the aged poor and other who have suffer [sic] enough already and who are able to give Evidence in the district also Guardian of the villages and people who have known them for years are willing to tell Truth about the poor people I refer to.[36]

Internal memoranda between senior civil servants reveal that they did not know how to reply to Ward as he was correct: Bury's reply and the relieving officer's disclosures were illegal. They decided to ignore his letter and it was simply filed. Such action by both central government and the *crusaders'* party angered BDODRA members. They became even more determined to fight for the reintroduction of outdoor relief although it was difficult to oppose a party led by prominent individuals with so many influential allies. However, in January 1894, a newcomer arrived in the district to support BDODRA's cause, the Revd Dr John Charles Cox.

---

[35] *Royal Commission on the Aged Poor* (1894), appendix, Revd W. Bury's report on outdoor relief cases in the Brixworth union; evidence of A. Pell, 27 Feb. 1894, q. 15818; and Ward, 27 Feb. 1894, qq. 15581–6019.
[36] Ward to LGB, 20 Apr. 1895, MH 12/8706, LGB ref. 53860/95.

Radical John Charles Cox

John Charles Cox was born in Parwich in Derbyshire in 1844, the second son of the Revd Edward Cox, rector of Lincombe in Somerset. Little is known of his early childhood except that he was educated at Repton and Somerset College in Bath, before being matriculated at the Queen's College, Oxford, aged eighteen.[37] He decided not to take his final degree examinations leaving at the end of his third year to become a partner in the Wingerworth Colliery Company in Derbyshire. The business did well, and having married in 1868, Cox bought a house at Belper in Derbyshire, where in the 1870s he became a justice of the peace, a guardian of the poor and chairman of the Belper school board. He was a committed 'advanced' Liberal and a strong supporter of working men's rights. In 1872 the *Ripley Advertiser* described Cox as a 'remarkable man', noting 'how rare it is to find a man without class prejudice'.[38] The success of his colliery business gave Cox the financial freedom to support numerous radical Liberal causes, such as trade union reform, a shorter working day and extension of the suffrage. He was the leader of a number of radical pressure groups in the late-Victorian era, notably the Land Tenure Reform Association. His closest political ally was Sir Charles Dilke, a life-long friend. When Dilke's national political career got underway he often delegated his radical plans to Cox. Thus, Cox took over from Dilke as a member of the executive committee of Joseph Arch's NALU in 1874. At Joseph Chamberlain's behest he stood for parliament twice as an 'advanced' Liberal candidate, in Bath and in Dewsbury, although on both occasions defeated by a small margin. He became dispirited and decided to follow in his father's footsteps and become a clergyman.[39] Cox was ordained at Lichfield Theological College in 1880 and held a number of clerical posts in northern parishes (Enville, Staffordshire, from 1883 to 1886, and Barton-le-Street, Yorkshire, from 1886 to 1894). However, as Dilke explained in his diary, 'being a man of active mind' Cox 'found the care of small parishes of ritualistic tendencies insufficient to occupy his whole time'.[40] He took up anti-

---

[37] There is no biography of Cox, despite his scholarly reputation and radical Liberal career. Brief overviews of aspects of his working life are detailed, for example, in R. F. Wearmouth, *Some working class movements of the nineteenth century*, Leicester 1948, 293–6, and the *Midland Free Press*, 26 Apr. 1873.

[38] *Ripley Advertiser*, 31 Aug. 1872.

[39] Cox's role in the education controversy has been reconstructed from the *Bath Journal*, 21 June 1873; the *Bristol Daily Times and Mirror*, 23 June 1873; Chamberlain to Morley,19 July, 10 Aug. 1873 (copies), Birmingham University library, MSS Chamberlain, JC, 5/54.3, 5/54/7; A. F. Taylor, 'Birmingham and the movement for national education', unpubl. PhD diss. Leicester 1960, 214–16; R. Jay, *Joseph Chamberlain: a political study*, Oxford 1981, 18; P. C. Griffiths, 'Pressure groups and parties in late-Victorian England: the National Education League', *Midland History* iii (1975), 19–26; and P. Auspos, 'Radicalism, pressure groups and party politics: from the National Education League to the National Liberal Federation', *JBS* xx (1980), 181–204.

[40] Sir Charles W. Dilke diaries, 1873, BL, MSS Dilke, lix, entry no. 43932.

quarian research, became a renowned local historian and gained the degree of doctor of divinity.[41] Gladstone admired Cox's historical work and when the crown living of Holdenby in Northamptonshire became available in 1893 he asked Cox to accept it.[42]

Holdenby, with its historical connections to Cromwell, the battle of Naseby and the imprisonment of Charles I, was an ideal choice for a radical historian. It was also a small parish with a generous stipend of £500 *per annum*, which was welcome given that Cox had ten children to support.[43] The small ministry would also give him the time to pursue his historical research and local politics. At first Cox was unsure whether to accept the appointment because it involved a major move for his family, but he changed his mind when the bishop of Peterborough, Mandell Creighton, intervened. It was rumoured that this had been done at Gladstone's behest because he deplored the actions of the *crusaders* on the Brixworth union board of guardians. The *Northampton Independent* recalled in Cox's obituary in 1919 that 'it was currently understood that the offer was made' by Gladstone 'in order to introduce vigorous contention within the Brixworth district, where Liberals thought the agricultural labourers could not secure justice'.[44] There is no primary evidence to substantiate this, although the Webbs repeated the story in their history of the English poor law.[45] It may be significant that Cox moved very quickly into the district, ensuring he could register in time to stand for election to the Brixworth union board of guardians in December 1894.[46]

Cox became a leading spokesman for BDODRA as soon as he took up his clerical appointment, declaring that he intended to stand for election to the board of guardians as soon as possible. His previous radical credentials ensured both national and local publicity for the BDODRA cause. He had always held complementary political ideals:

> I do not hold what are generally understood as Socialist views ... but I do believe very strongly that the present distribution of wealth, as it is in England, is gross and iniquitous ... all of history teaches us that a dispro-

[41] Anon., *The third council for Northamptonshire 1895: no. 862. a record of the elections reprinted from the Northampton Mercury; a summary of the career of Rev. Dr. J. C. Cox*, Northampton 1895, Northampton Library, Local Studies Collection.

[42] J. Cox to Gladstone 25 Apr. 1892, MSS Gladstone, cccxxix, 44514, fo. 204; Cox to Gladstone 28 Dec. 1889, ccxxiii, 44508, fo. 262 (discusses mutual historical interest and Gladstone's scholarly patronage of Cox's work). H. C. G. Matthew (ed.), *The Gladstone diaries*, ix, Oxford 1986 (entry for 7 Jan. 1876); xii, Oxford 1995 (entry for 20 Sept. 1889), make reference to visits by Cox to Hawarden Castle to discuss antiquarian research.

[43] Lord Chancellors' office, presentation papers for crown livings: Holdenby, PRO, C.247/3, ref.147; J. C. Cox, 'Presentation papers for the crown living at Holdenby', 24 Jan. 1894, NRO, ref. 172/9.

[44] *Northampton Independent*, 1 Mar. 1919.

[45] Webb and Webb, *English poor law*, 466 at n. 2.

[46] Guardian elections in April 1894 were postponed until December because of the changes brought in by the Local Government Act (1894). Guardians then served from January 1895 to April 1896; thereafter elections were held in April.

portion so enormous, accompanied, as it is of necessity is, with so much crime, of pauperism, of absolute misery, cannot go on forever, and will one day right itself; – and remember, the jolt will be severe if it comes on us all at once.[47]

The *crusaders'* party was very concerned about the extensive adverse publicity that Cox began to generate against them. Bury therefore decided to take strong action and bow to public pressure by revealing how the 'Secret Service Fund', was administered.[48] He set up a four-man committee of *crusaders* to oversee the charity's finances in an official capacity and published a leaflet outlining the new procedures, which he distributed to every ratepayer in the district. For the first time he sent each subscriber an annual report detailing the charity's income and expenditure. Spencer's copy shows that the chairman spent 'about £25 per annum per parish' (£1,750 per year at current values).[49] If that figure is multiplied by thirty-six (the number of parishes in the area), the fund's average annual income seems to have been around £900 in total (£63,000 at today's values). Spencer thought that the chairman was sending out the information in order to elicit larger subscriptions as the fund was overdrawn by £26 12s. Bury replied that he had paid the deficit because he wanted to maintain the scheme. He admitted it had 'been instrumental as much or more than anything else in enabling us to break the need of Outdoor relief'.[50] He also revealed that BDODRA had tried 'to break the bank' by inundating the charity committee with applications for funding in 1893–4. This had been Cox's doing as a means to bankrupt, and hence abolish, the fund. Although Cox could not hope to overturn the *crusading* initiatives in the area until he was elected a guardian of the poor, he could use his contacts at Westminster to make political capital out of the *crusading* controversy. Suddenly the Brixworth union was the focus of national debate and intense speculation about poor law democracy and the social cost of the *crusading* experiment. This was to BDODRA's electoral advantage.

The Brixworth union: national publicity

By 1894 the Brixworth union had a formidable reputation in poor law circles because of its *crusading* stance. Thus, on the eve of the LGA, when central government was debating the implications of the democratisation of the poor law, the policies of the Brixworth union became the focus of national

[47] J. C. Cox, *The advantages of trade unions! A lecture delivered at Ripley by J.C. Cox JP FRHS of Hazelwood Belper on Thursday evening August 29 1872 published at the request of the Derbyshire and Nottinghamshire Miners' Association*, Derby 1872, 1–27, BLPES, pamphlet collection, P 25129.
[48] Bury to Spencer, 11 Jan. 1892, MSS Althorp, K334; charity fund circular, dated 'January 1894', ibid. K345.
[49] Bury to Spencer, 11 Jan. 1892, ibid. K334.
[50] Ibid.

attention in periodicals and newspapers. Considerable editorial attention was given to considering what would happen in the Brixworth union once working people got the vote in poor law elections, and to debating whether the social cost of the *crusading* experiment was too high. The conservative *Quarterly Review*, for example, noted that in strict 'model' poor law unions, like Brixworth,

> The problem of the Poor Law is being dragged into the vortex of practical politics. It is all too evident that the rate devoted to the relief of the poor can be made an admirable electioneering fund. The *debacle* has already begun ... By a barefaced disregard of every principle of constitutional government, the public purse has been put at the disposal of a local electorate, the majority of which is in many cases financially irresponsible ... The *debacle* is proceeding at an accelerated pace. The temptation to make political capital by advocacy of an outdoor policy is growing irresistible.[51]

A Fabian Society tract, *The humanizing of the poor law* (1894) took the opposite view. It welcomed the electoral changes, declaring that in unions like Brixworth the labouring poor now had a crucial voice in the administration of welfare. The pamphlet claimed that 'the average guardian is prejudiced against the poor', but now the working classes had an opportunity to 'control elections' and administer outdoor relief humanely.[52] It asserted that 'the expense of relieving the poor is part of the ransom that Property has to pay to Labor [*sic*]; and it is a ransom which is not begged as a charity but demanded as an instalment of justice'. C. S. Loch, secretary of the COS, defended the policies of poor law unions like Brixworth in an article entitled 'Manufacturing a new pauperism' in the conservative *Nineteenth Century*. He worried that 'the trend of opinion in some quarters favours the abandonment of the principle which we would defend ... even the bar of the disenfranchisement of the voter on receipt of poor relief is to be removed'. Reformers were manipulating statistics on pauperism to create more support for electoral reform of local government and few understood that the funding of outdoor relief might become 'a strong electioneering weapon,' which could be exploited by unscrupulous local politicians.[53] Thomas MacKay, historian of the COS, supported Loch in his 'Politics and the poor law', published in the Liberal *Fortnightly Review*. He monitored the changing political climate on poor law matters and focused on events in the Brixworth union, describing elections in the district as 'an auction wherein election is sold to those who offer the largest donation' of outdoor relief. He deplored BDODRA, claiming that it was 'supported mainly by agitators and ... malcontents ... who will bless the policy they have been sent to curse'.[54]

[51] *Quarterly Review* clxxviv (July–Oct. 1894), 467.
[52] J. F. Oakeshott, *The humanizing of the poor law* (Fabian Society, tract liv, 1894), 1–23.
[53] C. S. Loch, 'Manufacturing a new pauperism', *Nineteenth Century* (Apr. 1895), 697–708.
[54] T. MacKay, 'Politics and the poor law,' *Fortnightly Review* (July 1895), 408–22.

The Brixworth union was also the subject of a number of articles in Anglican journals. *The Church of Today*, for example, published an article condemning the *crusaders'* policies. It noted wryly that 'Mr Loch and other reformers of his severe type are never weary of holding up this tract of Dark England as an example *to be seen and read of all men* – especially those of democratic, humanitarian or socialistic tendencies.'[55] It rejoiced that 'there has been a long-smouldering opposition, which at last has burst into fierce flames' with the formation of BDODRA. The editorial concluded that it was 'evident that the autocratic ... Abolitionist' was losing the poor law fight in the Brixworth union because 'ever-growing democracy' was stronger and 'will quickly take from him his *armour* of policy *wherein he trusted*'. As Bury was a clergyman this article, in an Anglican periodical, must have been both personally and politically embarrassing. The journal labelled the Brixworth union the rural equivalent of what William Booth had investigated in his *In darkest England* (1890). However, of all the articles written about the Brixworth union, an anonymous pamphlet, published in 1894, brought the *crusaders'* party the most unwelcome publicity.

Plain words on out-relief first appeared in 1894. It was rumoured to have been written by two senior LGB civil servants with responsibility for Scottish poor relief.[56] The pamphlet reviewed the statistical claims of the *crusaders* by testing 'whether total abstinence or moderation' in outdoor relief management was more economical. It asked why, if the retrenchment policy worked, were 'the ears' of so many guardians 'closed to the voices of Mr. Albert Pell?' It examined two places where outdoor relief had been refused for more than twenty years – the Whitechapel union in London and the Brixworth union. It gave a brief account of the history of the Brixworth union, explaining how guardians had reduced the number of paupers in receipt of outdoor relief from 1,118 in 1871 to just 55 by 1892, cutting expenditure on outdoor relief from £5,635 in 1871 to only £231 by 1892. The article stated that these results were impressive because the ratio of outdoor to indoor paupers in the area had fallen from 1:12 in 1870 to 1:127 by 1890. This meant that the Brixworth union was one of the top ten performing unions in England and Wales. However, the authors pointed out that these crude indicators did not reflect either the true financial position or the high social cost of *crusading* at Brixworth. The civil servants decided to rank poor law unions in a new league table based on the '**cost** of poor relief' per head of population in each district. They found that the Brixworth union then slipped to 149th place out of a total of 648 unions in central government league tables because it still spent 4s. 7d. per head of population on poor relief, considerably more than those poor law unions that had reintroduced outdoor relief in the 1880s. Expenditure in Brixworth was so high because its poor law officials, specifically

55 J. Frome Wilkinson, 'Poor law administration and the Brixworth union', *The Church of Today*, 15 Feb. 1895, 76.
56 Anon. *Plain words on outrelief*, London 1894, 1–65.

the relieving officer, were the most highly paid in the country and indoor relief was more expensive than outdoor. Despite the *crusader's* best efforts to deter pauperism workhouse numbers had risen because of the agricultural crisis, which forced elderly paupers to accept indoor provision. The article concluded that 'although Mr Pell and his energetic fellow athletes' on the Brixworth union board had been 'straining every nerve ... in the arduous and well-nigh impossible task of... stamping out out-relief, a very large number of Poor Law administrators, working on different lines' had left them 'hopelessly behind'.[57]

The issue of expenditure, highlighted in *Plain words*, was used as a key electioneering tool by BDODRA during their guardian election campaign in December 1894. Cheyney Halford from Naseby parish (a tailor and prospective BDODRA guardian) wrote to Spencer (a letter which Halford copied to local newspapers) protesting that ratepayers believed that the *crusaders'* policies were too expensive and that residents were 'paying ... [poor law] officers greatly in excess of what their duties call for'.[58] Likewise Ward informed the committee of the Royal Commission of the Aged Poor in 1894 that ratepayers felt that it was inhumane to refuse outdoor relief to elderly poor law claimants. He elaborated on the awkward position of ratepayers:

> Thomas and Elizabeth Campion of Holcot ... they were over 70 both of them ... They struggled for a long time [to avoid the workhouse] ... People gave to them for a time, but for people who have to pay rates ... it is very hard for them to keep people as well: They say 'We pay rates for the purpose and you ought to make an application'. Very well they did make an application. They walked over to Brixworth, and when they got there they had the offer of the house, and they pleaded very hard to have a little out [relief] ... they were refused and I believe they went back home. ... The woman went to the guardians again, she said: 'I will rather die in the street than go back to the union' ... [a] farmer ... coaxed her to go back, drove her over in his trap on a Sunday morning, and I think it was hardly so long as a fortnight before they took her back as a corpse to her own village.[59]

Cases like these that were rallying cross-community support for BDODRA.

Crusaders went on the offensive in defence of their philosophy and policies in the national press and journals. An editorial leader in the *Quarterly Review*, for example, stated that *Plain words* was an underhand attack on both the Brixworth union and central government policy. The editorial stated that if the tract's authors believed their cause was just, then they ought to identify themselves. The journal refuted the interpretation of LGB returns provided in *Plain words* and commissioned C. S. Loch to review its claims.[60] Loch said that poor law experts took three factors into account when making decisions

---

57 Ibid.
58 J. Halford to Spencer, 19 July 1894, MSS Spencer, Sox 372.
59 *Royal Commission on the Aged Poor*, Ward, q. 15680 at p. 845.
60 Editorial, 'The abuse of statistics', *Quarterly Review* clxxviv (July–Oct. 1894), 467–85.

on poor relief: 'expenditure, ... administrative experience ... and a careful analysis of human motive'. The editorial concluded that in poor relief matters 'we cannot devise any substitute for experience, common sense and detailed analysis', which were being practised at Brixworth. The COS also replied to *Plain words* in a paper entitled *Why is it wrong to supplement outdoor relief?* It stated that 'the Poor Law is a legal institution based on a compulsory rate which must be kept as low as possible in order to prevent the poorest class of ratepayers from themselves becoming applicants for relief'.[61] These national debates appear to have given considerable publicity to BDODRA and to have strengthened their election campaign in December 1894.

Protesting about pauperism at the polls

By 1894 the political climate in the Brixworth union was so rancorous that a leading Liberal squire, a life-long friend of Spencer, decided to publish an election pamphlet. Entitled *A parting of the ways?*, it stated that most moderates hoped that working people would not be suspicious or distrustful of the motives of the landed influence in the Brixworth union. He regretted that political ill-will over the issue of outdoor relief might result in a 'parting of the ways' now that the poor law was democratised and he hoped that new voters would choose a third way, a broader road of co-operation.[62] Bobby Spencer was seeking re-election to parliament for the Brixworth division in the years 1894–5. He kept Spencer informed of the public mood in the Brixworth union. He warned that many *crusaders* would not be re-elected as guardians since most were 'very low at the lapse of our old supporters' and found that 'some tenants appear to be extremely active against us'.[63] A clergy guardian summarised what happened during the election:

> It is all about the 'Out-relief' question that the fighting arises – There is very strong feeling about it throughout the Union ... One of the worst features of the business is that the latest clerical imposition Dr Cox of Holdenby is throwing himself headlong into the fray, as a resident's partisan of the 'Outs' and is spreading broad cash statements, which are misleading and grossly inaccurate – he is full of talk, but not of well digested facts and aspires to be a leader on the subject, which he has not taken pains to make himself master of. I am afraid he is well in running for the Chairmanship, which would be a most deplorable appointment as he is evidently without either knowledge or tact ... you have no doubt seen

---

61 Anon., *Why is it wrong to supplement outdoor relief?* (COS occasional paper xxi, 1893–4), 1–3 (BLPES, pamphlet collection, P. 205392).
62 Sir Hereward Wake, *The parting of the ways; or, what local government can and cannot do for labouring men by a squire: for lawyers by lawyers*, Northampton 1894 (NRO, CAM/901).
63 R. (Bobby) Spencer to Spencer, 2 Sept. 1894, MSS Althorp, K347.

one of the 'Out-Relief Association' circulars – ...the men say they vote 'not for the man, but for the principle!'[64]

Once again BDODRA increased its representation on the poor law board by winning a 45 per cent share of the total number of votes. The *crusaders'* party had a slim majority, of only 10 per cent, and the class divisions amongst guardians were growing (*see* tables 10–12). Universal suffrage meant that no *ex-officio* guardians held seats. A female guardian, Mary Calverley, was elected to office for the first time, but as she was a COS member and outspoken critic of generous outdoor relief, she became one of the *crusaders'* staunchest supporters.[65] Farmers still held the largest share of the vote, at around a third (29 per cent), but just over two-thirds of them (20 per cent) voted for the *crusade* party and just under one third (9 per cent) for BDODRA. Although *crusader* support appeared to be stabilising it was only a temporary respite. Even though the number of farmers who voted for BDODRA had decreased since the last election, the number of artisans and traders had risen correspondingly to a 21.5 per cent share. After the farmers they held the largest block of the votes, but, unlike the farmers, their holding was not split since they were all committed BDODRA supporters. Cox was the only BDODRA clergy guardian, but this did not prevent him challenging Bury for the chairmanship, which he only lost by one vote. Bury was delighted to win the contest because he automatically became a justice of the peace for his term of office under the terms of the LGA.

At the first meeting of the new board of guardians, on 21 February 1895, Cox declared that 'destitute deserving people had an absolute right to relief and the Brixworth Union had become an absolute hunting ground for selfish ratepayers and wrong intended economists of Mr. Bury's [the chairman] school ... the poor of the district thoroughly detested it'.[66] Cox put four motions before the board. First, that the union's relieving officer should stop forewarning the chairman of pending applications for outdoor relief, which would then be referred to the 'Secret Service Fund'. Second, he asked that guardians set up a committee to survey unemployment in the district to ascertain whether *crusading* methods were impoverishing the labouring poor.[67] Third, he wanted to lobby central government to reassign guardian seats more fairly on the basis of population distribution in the area. Fourth, he asked guardians to develop a close relationship with the newly created parish councils in the district. Although the *crusaders'* party defeated all four motions, the voting was close and the chairman had to cast his second discretionary vote on each occasion to prevent the proposals being passed when the board was deadlocked.

[64] Calverley to Spencer, 19 Dec. 1894, ibid. K345.
[65] M. Calverley, *'Looking back': records of the Brixworth union: Lady-day 1895: Lady-day 1896*, Northampton 1901, 1–16.
[66] *Northampton Herald*, 23 Feb. 1895.
[67] Cox to LGB, 12 Jan. 1895, MH 12/8706, no. 5448/95; Brixworth union guardians' minute books, P/L 2/19–20.

Cox ignored the ruling and decided to survey unemployment levels in the district anyway and to send his findings to the LGB. The *Northampton Mercury* reported that it was a 'scandal to our social and industrial life that hundreds of able-bodied men in our county parishes should have to face every winter two months or more unemployment'. It felt that the *crusaders'* 'attitude of "we can't do this" and "we can't do that" [was] not credit to our common humanity'.[68] Cox found that there were 315 unemployed men in the Brixworth union sixty-three of whom were skilled artisans (masons, bricklayers, builders' labourers and painters) and the rest 'respectable' agricultural labourers. He noted that the population in the area had fallen by '1600 between 1875 and 1885' and that a further '1000–1200 left or migrated between 1885 and 1895'.[69] Cox claimed that without outdoor relief the labouring poor had to migrate to the detriment of local business. Usually skilled labourers left the district first, never to return, which meant that key skills were lost forever. Even if younger men wanted to stay in the Brixworth union there was no one left to teach them a trade. Cox also complained that these less populous districts, which working people had been encouraged to leave in the 1880s, still elected more guardians of the poor than larger parishes. For instance, although BDODRA won a majority of 350 votes at the polls in 1895 it won fewer seats than the *crusaders'* party on the board of guardians. This was because small closed parishes, such as Hanging Houghton (twenty inhabitants), were allocated the same number of seats as a large open parish, like Moulton (more than 1,500 residents). A key BDODRA objective was to have seats redistributed equitably. It also tried to get working men elected to parish councils, so that it could take over all local administration. Regrettably, not all of the parish council returns have survived, but an editorial in the *Eastern Weekly Leader* gives a flavour of the new political mood in the area:

For weeks past there have been crowded meetings in the village school, and heated discussions at the bar of the inn; knots of men have lingered on the threshold of the chapel, unwilling to let go of the subject they will resume the minute the service is over; strange nods and winks, with whispered hints and cautions have passed the labourers at their work and an unwonted eagerness has been shown in their examination of the weekly paper. At the markets farmers have forgotten their standing complaints about low prices to vent their wrath at the appearance of the new enemy. In the rectory, there has been keen questioning of the servants and anxious counting up of reliable dependants, while up at the Hall Bluebooks and Handbooks have taken the place of The Times and silenced the mirth of Punch. The finger of the labourer has stopped an inch short of his cap when the parson has passed.[70]

68 *Northampton Mercury*, 11 Nov. 1895.
69 Ibid. 22 Feb. 1895.
70 *Eastern Weekly Leader*, 1894, quoted in Hollis, *Ladies elect*, 46.

Available parish council returns for the entire district show that BDODRA members won around 60 per cent of the seats.[71] Spencer told Sir William Harcourt that he was in the proud position of being chairman of the Althorp parish meeting, but that he had to make an impassioned speech for fifty-five minutes to win the contest and even then many of his tenants voted for him out of self-interest – quite an admission.[72]

During 1895–6 local newspaper postbags swelled with letters about outdoor relief. One question predominated – would the 'autocrats or the democrats win the day?'[73] Bury believed that the press coverage was biased against *crusaders* and complained to the editor of the *Northampton Mercury* that 'if the chair' of a poor law union 'of a popularly elected body [was] not a pulpit, neither [was] the chair of the Editor of a popularly conducted journal'.[74] The editor explained that his paper was reflecting popular sentiment and that he was not responsible for ill-feeling in Northampton and the surrounding district. He pointed out that the chairman had created animosity by refusing outdoor relief in the first instance and then exporting the Brixworth union's social problems to local towns, like Northampton, leaving urban ratepayers to pick up a larger pauperism bill.

This controversy came to a head when three new applications for outdoor relief came before the Brixworth union board in May 1895. Although two cases were 'deserving', the third – from the distant relative of a clergy guardian who supported the *crusaders* – was borderline. The clergyman asked BDODRA to support the borderline application. They agreed to do so, provided the clergyman defect to the opposition. He also had to agree to support a motion to prevent the union's relieving officer forewarning the chairman of outdoor relief cases. BDODRA guardians wanted to compel the relieving officer to liase with individual guardians when applications for outdoor relief came in. The chairman was furious at this turn of events and resigned in a fit of pique. He accused Cox of using underhand tactics, which made his position untenable. He asked Spencer to intervene and take the chair.[75]

Spencer was concerned and stressed to Bury that it was a chairman's duty to 'hold the balance between the two sides' on a board of guardians.[76] He told him that the *crusaders*' party should appoint an 'impartial' elected guardian to the chair until the controversy had died down. Bury felt that Spencer had let him down and he threatened to wind up the 'Secret Service Fund', stating that it might be better to 'let each Guardian who is <u>sound</u> do the best he

[71] Parish and vestry council records, NRO: Brington, 49/p/150/d; Brixworth, 50/p/109; Harlestone, 153/p/111; misc. vols, Naseby, Scaldwell parish bundles 1894.
[72] Spencer to Harcourt, and Harcourt to Spencer, 6, 7 Dec. 1894, MSS Harcourt, 47, fo. 86; 711, fo. 20.
[73] *Northampton Mercury*, 1 Feb. 1895.
[74] Ibid.
[75] *Northampton Herald*, 4 May 1895.
[76] Bury to Spencer, and Spencer to Bury, 6, 7 May 1895, MSS Althorp, K348.

can with his own parish'.[77] Spencer expressed his regret that having worked so hard 'to prevent old administration in the parishes where I have most influence' the *crusading* experiment would be abandoned without a fight. He thought that Bury should take part in the chairmanship contest in August and hope to take the chair again in the autumn of 1895. In the interval the *crusaders'* party should regroup and consider converting the 'Secret Service Fund' into a branch of the COS, with 'different sorts of men … dissenters as well as Churchmen' appointed to oversee a finance committee.[78] They should not fear this change, because the committee would have to work 'in harmony with the B.[oard] of guardians' and would still promote COS principles. Spencer told Bury that they must ensure that Cox did not use each outdoor relief case as a 'stalking horse' because that was 'dangerous and may lead to harm in the union'.[79] Spencer also spoke to Cox, whom he met by chance on the London train and told him that he should not become chairman until he had moderated both his speeches and the behaviour of his followers. Cox replied that he had consulted his friend Sir Charles Dilke who advised him that it was his duty to accept the chair. He told Spencer that 'if I have to take up the Brixworth reins, I shall do so … desirous to do right and check extremes'.[80] Cox campaigned for the chairmanship during August 1895. He attacked the 'Secret Service Fund' and promised outdoor relief to deserving applicants, but again Bury won by one vote.

Although Spencer's immediate concerns were resolved he feared that the bad publicity over the chairmanship contest was damaging Bobby Spencer's prospects in the campaign for the mid-Northamptonshire division in 1895.[81] However, Bobby Spencer's re-election campaign was already floundering because his Conservative opponent, James Pender, made political capital out of the *crusading* campaign. At a meeting in March 1895 Pender declared that

> He was personally requested to assist and support the private fund … he refused to join it, considering then, as now, that out-door relief, ought to be provided out of the rates for the support of the poor. … He hoped to see some old age pension scheme introduced and some reform in the working of the poor houses.[82]

In 1895 the *crusading* controversy was the key issue in the mid-Northamptonshire parliamentary election. Pender beat Bobby Spencer resoundingly because he favoured the reintroduction of outdoor relief. Turnout at the election were very high at 84.4 per cent, reflecting local interest in welfare

---

77 Ibid.
78 Ibid.
79 Ibid.
80 Cox to Spencer and Spencer to Cox, 30 Apr., 1 May 1895, ibid.
81 *Northampton Mercury*, 1 Mar. 1895.
82 Ibid. 22 Mar. 1895.

issues.[83] Spencer admitted to one of his old political allies, Harcourt, that he was 'dismayed at the elections' as his family had 'suffered in a very tender part in my brother's defeat ... I was anxious but never lost faith in his winning'.[84] He subsequently learned from his election agent that 'the cry of opponents to outdoor relief was used by Pender against' them. Spencer went abroad on a long winter holiday, but he still took a keen interest in poor law matters.[85] He received reports that BDODRA was making headway in the district and that the Conservative government planned to redistribute guardian seats in agricultural districts more equitably. He suspected that this would mean the end of *crusading*.

In the April 1896 guardian election the *crusaders'* party won only a 44 per cent share of the seats on the Brixworth union board. BDODRA members formed an opposition coalition with sympathetic ratepayers and farmers to secure a 56 per cent share of the seats, which gave them a majority for the first time (*see* tables 11–12 and figure 9). This meant that the situation had been reversed since the start of 1895. The opposition coalition elected Cox chairman of the board and the 'Secret Service Fund' was abolished. Cox reviewed the contracts of employment of poor law officials, increased the doctor's salary and reduced that of the relieving officer. He set up a committee to review indoor care, and the new BDODRA guardians concluded that work-house provision was substandard and should be upgraded. A new building project was implemented to equip medical wards properly and to provide shared bedrooms for married couples. Guardians also voted in favour of the reintroduction of medical outdoor relief, including funeral payments. Cox asked the LGB to sanction the proper sanitation of villages. Pell and Bury tried to stop him but the LGB intervened, authorising the appointment of a new public medical officer of health on a salary of £50 *per annum* to oversee comprehensive sanitary works.[86] Spencer's land agent reported that the villagers on the Althorp estate had elected Sidney Ward as their guardian:

> So we are saddled with the great Sidney Ward ('That splendid man' as Dr Cox calls him) for 3 years – I must say I do not like being represented by an outsider and I expect Sidney Ward may be trouble – I suppose he will bring up all the out-relief cases he can – I suppose it is the natural remedy of [the] cast-iron policy.[87]

Although outdoor relief was reintroduced, a number of controversies over public health, specifically over tax increases to pay for adequate drinking

---

[83] Howarth, 'Liberal revival', 84.

[84] Spencer to Morley, 20 July 1895, MSS Harcourt, dep. 37, fo. 87.

[85] Spencer to Harcourt, 1 Nov. 1895, ibid. ref. 711, fo. 349.

[86] 1 June 1897, MH 12/8709. Brixworth RDC minute books (LG 21/106–16) give details of ongoing sanitary controversies. See also Hurren, 'Poor law versus public health', 399–414.

[87] Morley to Spencer, 31 Mar. 1896, MSS Spencer, Sox 563.

water supplies, persisted for some time. An LGB sanitary inspector noted in 1897 that the 'Pell-Bury' school was acting 'out of spite' and that everything in the district was still 'unhappily political'.[88] From time to time Pell's supporters published articles in the COR justifying their experiment but their views were out-dated. When Cox retired from office in 1899, Ward became chairman of the Brixworth union board of guardians. It was the final realisation of BDODRA's aims – to let working men 'speak for themselves and govern themselves'. As F. A. Channing, 'advanced' Liberal MP for the East Northamptonshire division recalled, 'In 1895 dreams and ideals were crystallising into positive proposals and thought-out schemes. ... Local self-government ... would merge individualism into collective action. Guardians were not now nominees of large ratepayers but men with generous sympathies who knew the wants and miseries of the poor.'[89] BDODRA's 'new ideas, new hopes and new aims' had come to fruition. Democracy had triumphed.

Poor law victory

In the Brixworth union the unravelling of *crusading* began around 1893 because of the democratisation of the poor law.[90] Working people who had suffered under the harsh *crusading* regime, ratepayers who no longer believed in the classical economy of the *crusaders'* poor law school and moderates who had fought against *crusading* initiatives from their inception, formed a coalition to launch a successful counter-offensive. The withdrawal of funeral rites, and the threat to sell pauper cadavers for anatomical teaching, aroused deep-seated animosity and was the final catalyst in the political journey of working people. By 1890 Pell was ignoring central government in all local authority matters, adopting whatever guidelines or legislation suited his political purposes. It is evident that the Longley Strategy (1874) gave his party too much autonomy on the Brixworth union board of guardians. They paid the political price for a lack of consultation, sensitivity and understanding of the human reality of endemic poverty throughout the community, especially once the poor law was democratised.

The establishment of BDODRA, which local newspapers reported had more than 7,500 members in twenty parishes by 1896 (around one third of the adult population), was a remarkable achievement that marked the beginning of the end of *crusading*. It was a political pressure group led by a cross-section of the community, but initiated by a working man who felt that the social costs of the denial of outdoor relief were too high. Building upon a reservoir of political discontent in the Brixworth union, which had been gathering force

---

88 LGB inspector for the Brixworth union to central government, 1 Aug. 1897, MH 12/8709: private memo on ongoing sanitary controversies.
89 F. A. Channing MP, *Memories of midland politics, 1885–1910*, Northampton 1918.
90 Williams, *Pauperism*, 103.

throughout each stage of the battle over outdoor relief, Ward and Cox were facilitators who helped working people to target their grievances in a positive manner by exploiting poor law democratisation. BDODRA organised a formidable campaign and its members paid union fees at a time of higher unemployment, just as the second phase of the agricultural crisis was starting around 1891. This suggests that their commitment probably mirrored the depths of impoverishment in the area and confirms that the *crusading* experiment had a profound social cost.[91] Thus the labouring community pooled its resources, both financial and organisational, to fight *crusading* activities. Local newspapers gave their cause widespread coverage because 'advanced' Liberals who sat on the Northampton union board of guardians supported BDODRA. They objected to *crusaders'* policies swelling the numbers on outdoor relief in the 1880s, when working people left the Brixworth union in search of work and basic welfare. Whatever the numbers involved, exporting poor law problems created political tensions between rural and urban poor law unions because of the context of the *crusading* campaign.

The national debates on outdoor relief, in which the Brixworth union featured so prominently in the years 1894–5, reveal that a growing body of opinion at Westminster and amongst LGB civil servants no longer believed that the *crusaders'* claims to cut costs were financially sound. In particular *Plain words* aroused considerable controversy. Such debates indicated, though not to committed *crusaders*, that the political tide was changing because definitions of the causes of poverty were being revised. That should have signalled to *crusaders* that their poor law ideals were losing impetus. Both Spencer and Bury knew this, but the former was more pragmatic than the latter because he had to consider his political career. Spencer accepted, albeit reluctantly, that the Liberal party would have to introduce more generous social welfare provision, otherwise candidates like Bobby Spencer, who had been defeated in the 1895 parliamentary election, would not regain their seats. He therefore stressed the apolitical nature of his involvement in poor law matters, although in private he disliked the changes on the board of guardians. Bury was slow to change, unable to face the inevitable.

The national debates that focused on the Brixworth union in the years 1894 to 1895 were very significant. They added further weight to BDODRA's campaign and persuaded ratepayers who were wavering that the *crusading* experiment was too expensive. Moreover, they encouraged Spencer to distance himself from the controversy for political reasons. At the same time Pell discovered that the LGB was not a strong ally because it had few powers to support his cause when he needed help most. By 1895 Pell had fewer friends in central government because of his outspoken stance and maverick actions over many years. He personified 'COS inflexibility', the 'unbending socially marooned' who were 'obdurately indifferent to the changing tides of public

---

[91] Mackinnon, 'Poor law policy', 226–336, and 'English poor law', 603–25.

opinion'.[92] Pell's philosophical outlook was 'built on a paradox ... its primary purpose was to nurture self-sufficiency', but his 'methods demanded abject deference' from applicants for outdoor relief. Once the democratisation of the poor law got under way, Pell's administrative methods were an electoral liability.

It is clear that from 1890 there was a great deal of interest in poor law elections in the Brixworth union, with high turnouts during successive contests. There was a similar level of interest in the 1895 parliamentary election in the mid-Northamptonshire division.[93] In contradiction to the standard interpretations of welfare historians,[94] this case study reveals that working people were seldom apathetic about the poor law, local or national politics. Although events in the Brixworth union may have been an aberration, there is considerable evidence of political engagement there by ordinary people over welfare issues. BDODRA's election manifesto, with its commitment to lobby central government for poor law pensions, anticipated early twentieth-century welfare reforms. Such aspirations were a reaction against the deeply impoverishing *crusading* initiatives. They were not an expression of satisfaction with social welfare progressivism. Nor, in the 1890s did working people in the Brixworth union look 'past the poor laws to another conception of welfare'.[95] Instead they organised to reclaim lost outdoor relief benefits. Most wanted welfare reform within the poor law because only by taking control, having been excluded, could they ensure that their everyday material lives were improved. None the less, this leaves two unanswered questions: did the *crusading* experiment produce a rigorous reaction elsewhere, and what had been learned by both sides about the management of the poor law?

92 Humphreys, *Sin*, 173–4.
93 Howarth, 'Liberal revival', 84.
94 Thane, 'The working class and state "welfare"', 877–900; Harrison, *Transformation*, 71.
95 Hollen-Lees, *Solidarities*, 296.

10

Denouement: Continuity or Change?

In 1870 *crusaders* tried to create a world-without-welfare outside the workhouse. All paupers were to be deterred, whether needy, vulnerable or workshy. The majority were judged undeserving of welfare support from local taxes. By 1900 a new poor law language was in vogue. Pauper categories had been redefined to take account of innumerable experiences within a life-cycle of poverty. Thus Lloyd George declared that 'working class pride revolts against accepting so degrading and doubtful a boon' as the poor law. Essentially, poor relief discourse was restyled 'public assistance', which in turn was re-designated 'national assistance', and then became known as 'supplementary benefit'.[1] This linguistic sea change was not coincidental.[2] The probity of *crusading* was questioned by ordinary people who suffered under its excesses. In a more democratic era, strong opposition created a consensus in central government that the early Welfare State had to be seen to stand against unpopular poor law experiments. Poor law political economy was offensive. In electoral terms, no politician could afford to ignore the lesson of the collapse of the *crusade*. Quite simply, there was a growing awareness that impoverishment was not the fault of an individual but rather of a society of individuals, who had a responsibility to ameliorate the situation on behalf of all citizens, both above and below a poverty threshold.

The *crusading* decades therefore exemplify the paradox at the heart of Victorian self-help rhetoric. On the one hand reformers praised individualism and independent work effort. On the other hand that sentiment belied the fact that most individuals were powerless when confronted with the vagaries of industrial or agricultural recessions. If the complexities of social mobility, rapid urbanisation, housing crises, sanitation needs and the exodus of labourers from the countryside is factored in, then it is not difficult to see that the poor law was being forced to respond to a changing material world. Whether *crusading* rhetoric, based on such a fixed ideology, had the flexibility to adjust to such a level of change on a national basis is debatable. What is clear is that the early Welfare State could not be built on the crumbling ideological edifice of *crusading*.

That said, it is too easy, as David Thomson warns, to dismiss *crusading* initiatives as irrelevant, as 'the fading remnant of a passing, cruder, less generous society than our own'.[3] To do so would be to adopt a blinkered view

1 Fraser, *Evolution*, 132–7.
2 Thomson, 'Welfare', 255–378.
3 Ibid.

that fails to take account of the nuances of welfare continuities and changes. So what was the aftermath of the *crusading* decades? Did they bequeath a rosy nostalgia about notions of self-help, industry and *laissez-faire* economics? Or did they help to fashion a collective consensus, determined to redress endemic poverty? What about the thorny question of larger tax bills to pay for extensive welfare provision? Did late Victorians simply tinker around the edges of a tax crisis that Edwardians could not resolve and which modern governments inherited?

At the close of the *crusade* there was a general recognition that the worst aspects of poverty were seldom self-inflicted. Some basic economic facts illustrate this point well. Increase in industrial production slowed from a peak of 4 per cent *per annum* in the 1820s to just 1.5 per cent annually between 1875 and 1894. In 1870 Britain controlled about 32 per cent of the world's manufacturing capacity. By 1910 this had more than halved to just 15 per cent. In the same period, her share of world trade fell from 25 per cent to 14 per cent.[4] Her dominance was fading fast on the world markets. Faster steam ships, the growth of the railway and the advent of the telegraph meant that communications, and therefore inter-continental trading networks, improved substantially. Whilst Britain was not eclipsed in economic terms, none the less overseas competition had created fundamental fiscal problems. Admittedly, as the price of home-grown wheat tumbled to match cheaper imports, living standards improved. But, at the same time, employment was volatile. Greater investment might have obviated these trends, and the cycles of boom and bust, but there was an increasing tendency for investors to spread their risk abroad. Estimates vary, but on average around $20 million had been invested overseas by 1914. The crucial point about this level of overseas investment is that Britain's main competitors often benefited. Paradoxically this contributed to domestic economic problems. For example, of the $20 million invested abroad, around $4.5 million was sent to the USA in the late-Victorian period.[5] The fact that any new wealth generated was seldom re-imported or evenly distributed only exacerbated pauperism. Meanwhile, *crusaders* maintained that the haves should not foot the poor law bill for the have-nots.

Britain, therefore, was a nation of economic contrasts and extremes by the close of the Victorian period. Nevertheless, three lessons had been learnt over the course of the *crusading* decades. The first was that poor law reformers were forced to recognise that terms like 'welfare', 'social welfare' and so on, were complex and slippery. *Crusading* was predicated upon the notion that poor relief rules should dictate policy, but these could not resolve economic realities and were found wanting by the poor. The second lesson was that the notion of self-reliance and a belief in the ability of market forces to create opportunities to resolve social problems was naïve. It assumed that economic

---

4   Pearce and Stewart, *British political history*, 139.
5   Ibid.

change was within the control of those experiencing endemic poverty, but few paupers could reverse their dire economic fortunes without some form of public assistance. The third lesson was that minimal state interference in welfare terms was unsatisfactory as was proved by the publication of numerous ground-breaking social investigations from the 1880s onwards.[6] The *Illustrated London News* exemplified the new mood: 'Recent *revelations* as to the misery of the abject poor have profoundly touched the heart of the nation.'[7] Likewise, numerous government investigations, notably the Royal Commission on Outdoor Relief (1888) and the Royal Commission on the Aged Poor, confirmed the findings of social investigators. *Crusading* experiments, therefore, stood in opposition to a confluence of new trends in social policy. *Crusaders* could not defend themselves against either the Liberal welfare reform programme of 1906 or the Royal Commission on the Poor Laws (1909). Both started to dismantle the poor law 'from the outside, by removing from it needy groups by means of legislation on issues such as old age pensions and national health insurance'.[8] This went hand-in-hand with unstoppable political changes.

The coming of democracy sounded the death-knell of the *crusade*. Whilst legislators and social investigators took apart the poor law system from without, new voters set about dismantling the *crusading* experiments from within. In 1891 a leading socialist, Charlie Glyde, summed up the desire of ordinary people to take control of their own welfare: 'We have had two parties in the past, the can'ts and the won'ts and it is time that we had a party that will.'[9] A raft of suffrage legislation started to dismantle central and local political privilege.[10] By the time the MRDRA became law, a minor, but pivotal, democratic change had occurred, the first nail in the coffin of the previously punitive rules applied in poor law elections. It was an acknowledgement that the spirit of the poor law was too harsh in respect of genuinely sick paupers. Consequently, by the time the Liberals were swept back into power in 1892, local government democracy was inevitable. They could not renege on one of their most popular manifesto commitments, outlined in the Newcastle Programme. Democratic voices challenged the *crusaders'* obdurate views. It is apparent that, according to *crusading* rhetoric, paupers must be taught that they had no right to outdoor poor relief.[11] Rules and regulations posted on church doors, in workhouse waiting rooms and in local pubs aimed to deter them. But in a more democratic era the poor did not see why they had to be

---

6 Fraser, *Evolution*, 124–45, provides a very good summary of social investigators and their influence. See also bibliography for studies by Henry George, Andrew Mearns, George Sims, William Booth and Seebohm Rowntree.
7 This is quoted in Wohl, introduction to Mearns, *Bitter cry*, 9.
8 Thane, *Foundations*, 83.
9 Pearce and Stewart, *British political history*, 246.
10 Notably the Reform Act (1867), the Secret Ballot Act (1872), the Reform and Franchise Extension Acts (1885) and the County Councils Act (1888).
11 Williams, *Pauperism*.

degraded to get a reasonable level of public assistance outside the workhouse. Moreover, advances in the social sciences 'encouraged the tendency to look at the manifold problems of impoverishment formerly covered by the concept of "poverty" as discrete entities, each properly addressed by specialist services'.[12] Unquestionably, voting pressure from below contributed to such new welfare initiatives.

It must be conceded, however, that the extent to which new voters exerted a collective demand for welfare change is debatable. Indeed this cannot be assessed accurately until the entire *crusading* experience has been researched in much greater detail on a local basis. What mattered to contemporaries, however, is that those in power perceived that there was a pressure from below and that they needed to react accordingly. The political activities of the early labour movement indicate that this was not a simple or foregone conclusion, for 'a deeply ingrained, morally charged individualism, characteristic of the Victorian era, was by no means insignificant in Edwardian Britain'.[13] It might be easy to suppose that the Social Democratic Federation, the Trades Unions Congress, the Fabian Society and the Independent Labour Party, unified under the banner of the Labour Representation Committee (LRC) in 1900, could have made greater headway, given how much *crusading* initiatives were resented. The fact that the LRC had to fight so hard to extend the provision of state-funded welfare, despite the lessons of the *crusading* decades, indicates both continuities and change in welfare matters. *Crusading* initiatives may have ended formally but its values survived in the tone of many early twentieth-century debates on social policy. The controversy surrounding the Royal Commission on the Poor Laws illustrates this point particularly well.

Historians agree that Lloyd George was determined to deal a fatal blow to the poor law in the early twentieth century.[14] However, he inherited from the Conservative party a Royal Commission set up to study the causes of poverty and to make policy recommendations. By the time it reported in 1909 its members were divided into two camps, hence the production of majority and minority reports. Both sides agreed that a separate poor law system should end. Too much regional variation, unsystematic administration and the failure of *crusading* rhetoric rendered it out of date. In particular, participants agreed that 'involuntary poverty' was seldom redressed. The way forward was two-fold: extend the principle that all pauper categories should be reclassified and then match specialist services to specific welfare needs. If the poor law were to be replaced an alternative network of labour exchanges and some form of temporary unemployment assistance was needed. Both camps also 'assumed the existence of a ne'er-do-well class at the base of society, for whom punitive labour colonies or similar institutions would be required'.[15] Thereafter they

[12] Brundage, *English poor laws*, 133.
[13] Ibid. 133–4.
[14] Thane, *Foundations*, 81–3, provides an excellent summary of the recommendations of the 1909 commission.
[15] Ibid. 83

diverged because fundamental continuities shaped the majority's vision on social welfare.

The majority report insisted that the able-bodied unemployed lacked moral fibre. Drinkers, gamblers and spendthrifts often resorted to public welfare assistance. Thus, they emphasised the 'moral causes of poverty'. The majority agreed that guardians should be replaced, but the public assistance authorities they proposed looked very similar, except in name, to poor law unions. Anyone who was elected to the local authority or co-opted from a specialist charity in the area could serve on the public assistance committee. This would have exacerbated, not resolved, the problem of too many over-lapping personnel in local government, since the same people tended to get elected, be they county councillor, public assistance committee member, active trustee of an endowed charity or parish councillor. In this way, the recommendations of the majority report were a mixture of precedent and reform.

By contrast, the proposals of the minority report included a desire to recog-nise that unemployment might result from underlying economic constraints rather than a failure of individual morals. Likewise its authors, notably the Webbs, felt that government should set a national minimum standard of living. Those who fell below that threshold would receive some form of automatic public assistance. Furthermore, they demanded that the poor law be broken up permanently. Paupers should be reclassified and then separate specialist public assistance committees at a local level would tackle aspects of poverty like provision for the old, child welfare and so on. They advocated that medical care should come under the ambit of public health authorities. Since unemployment, they insisted, was often linked to national economic trends, it should be managed by central government.

In their entirety the reports of the Royal Commission looked back to *crusading* experiments and forward to more extensive social welfare provi-sion. The majority report was arguably the more politically expedient, and crucially was more feasible financially.[16] That said, elements of the minority report constituted a pragmatic response to new social science investigations in an era of extended democracy. What is fascinating, however, is that both contributions indicate that a *crusading* tone lingered long after its official demise. It was both reshaping and at the same time restricting the brave new world of the early Welfare State.

Here perhaps lies the true *crusading* legacy on the eve of the First World War. It left contemporaries with concrete evidence and the political will to initiate welfare change, which was needed and could no longer be ignored. However, almost forty years of debate on welfare econometrics meant that reformers did not receive a political mandate to simply spend their way towards an early Welfare State. Undeniably *crusading* initiatives did not make economic sense in practice. It cost more to feed and house a family inside, as

16 Ibid.

opposed to outside, the workhouse. But to judge *crusading* activities against that benchmark alone is to miss their underlying fiscal vision. Their real legacy was the principle of minimal taxation, a financial maxim that many succeeding governments have judged sacrosanct.

Certainly in the Brixworth union debates about rising bills for outdoor relief rumbled on. Around 1900, at successive poor law conferences, leading *crusaders* lectured moderates with tales of boom and bust if they did not check welfare spending. The tenor of their economic message survived in central government circles long after Pell, Cox and Spencer were all dead (by 1919). Only Bury settled into a long retirement and witnessed the formal demise of the poor law in 1929.[17] In the longer term the Liberal welfare reform programme after 1906 changed the *crusading* world. None the less, a century later politicians still struggle with the social policy yardsticks that the *crusaders* bequeathed in changed but equivalent contexts: how much welfare is needed? What level of taxation is appropriate? Welfare discourse may have changed, but structural economic dilemmas endure.

---

[17] Pell died in 1907 and was buried beside his wife, Elizabeth. Their graves can be found in Haselbech churchyard, by the church door. The poor said of him, 'Here lies Albert Pell, relief at last!' Spencer was laid to rest in 1905. He too was a widower and lies with his Spencer ancestors in Althorp parish church. A young Winston Churchill said of Spencer at the end: 'Poor Lord Spencer, it was rather like a ship sinking in sight of land.' Cox retired to Syndenham in 1900 and devoted the rest of his life to the study of English local history, for which he is famed. He died in 1919 and was buried in the local Roman Catholic churchyard. Bury lived into old age retiring to Uttoxeter to a generous living that Pell's brother owned. He died in 1933. He joked that he lived through three monarchs, Victoria, Edward VII and George V. He played cricket, for which he had been famed at Cambridge University, until well on in years.

Conclusion

At the close of the nineteenth century the *crusading* experiment in the Brix-worth union was overturned. The right to receive public welfare assistance outside the workhouse had been restored and the dominance of the proper-tied elite in poor law politics had waned. The Brixworth union may have been unrepresentative, for those who espoused poor law political economy there championed an extreme form of retrenchment. None the less, their radical policies throw into sharp relief a range of *crusading* measures that could be initiated. These provide an analytical framework within which to test future research in this relatively neglected area of poor law studies. It is therefore important to return to 'the Brixworth union in context' and engage with its wider historical lessons.

Being poor under the *crusading* experiment

Without doubt *crusading* initiatives had a detrimental impact on the poor. Whatever the combination of *crusading* measures, they involved a policy of 'brutal dispauperisation by every, and any means'.[1] In the Brixworth union outdoor relief was almost eradicated through a process that had never been tried before and at profound social cost. Viewing *crusading* measures from the local, rather than a national, perspective reveals what those retrenchment strategies entailed. *Crusading* was a complex jigsaw puzzle. Sometimes it was systematic, more often it was arbitrary depending on local economic circum-stances. Pauperism statistics therefore are seldom an accurate indication of the underlying sentiments of individual boards of guardians.[2] Cumulatively, *crusading* measures cut to the heart of poor relief spending. From the perspec-tive of paupers *crusading* reshaped their lived experiences of the poor law, hence their vociferous opposition to even minor poor relief cutbacks in the Brixworth union. Such experiences help welfare historians to really under-stand how reductions in outdoor relief were achieved, for what reasons, with what consistency and at what social cost.

Pauper testimony is of crucial importance, an essential historical prism. On the one hand it has been used to retrieve *crusading* measures from poor law records and contemporary accounts. On the other hand, it has stimulated debate about the need to revisit the nature of the later Victorian poor law in

---

1 Williams, *Pauperism*, 102.
2 S. A. King, 'A question of geography and taste: integrating the poor in 18th- and 19th-century rural England', *Journal of Historical Geography*, forthcoming 2007.

its entirety. Evidently, the umbrella term, 'a crusade against outdoor relief', is not an appropriate term to describe the complexities of the poor law. It is time to dispense with this outdated notion.

There were in fact different types of *crusaders*, in different places, at different times and with different economic motivations. Numerous participants – the opportunistic, moderates and extremists – deployed *crusading* techniques. Everyone did not of course necessarily pursue cost-saving initiatives at once nor with the same degree of enthusiasm. None the less it is apparent that a high degree of autonomy produced poor law opportunists determined to cut poor relief bills. A single analytical framework isolates eight common *crusading* activities that seem to constitute the major retrenchment strategies, which guardians tried and the poor resented. These key measures, ranked in order of the savings they achieved, were:

Shifting costs to your poor law union neighbours
Selling pauper cadavers to anatomists
Withdrawing outdoor medical relief
Claiming lunatic grant-in-aid funding and then shifting paupers on to
    county asylums[3]
Prosecuting the adult offspring of paupers for their maintenance
Removing semi-independent paupers from relieving officer's lists
Completing a charity review to encourage philanthropists to take over poor
    relief bills
Cutting staff costs both inside and outside the workhouse

These measures could be viewed as a *crusading* template, indicating general trends in policy. Their implementation in the Brixworth union redrew the boundaries of the provision of poor relief outside the workhouse, which exacerbated the pauperism of some of the most vulnerable members of the late-Victorian community. *Crusading* was therefore a multi-faceted financial process. Essentially, the Longley Strategy exploited classical political economy, encouraging guardians of the poor to act in a 'crudely repressive' manner.[4] At times the diversity and harshness of the various *crusading* activities was startling. No item of poor law expenditure was sacrosanct. *Crusading* often meant destroying any hope that a pauper might have of climbing back out of destitution.[5]

Unquestionably, the Longley Strategy was designed to attack the core of welfare commitment, but it was individual boards of guardians, like the Brixworth union, that made this policy work. It is apparent that this phase of poor law administration is distinctive and deserves greater prominence in the broad chronology of nineteenth-century welfare history. Welfare historians

---

3 See E. T. Hurren, 'Crusading against outdoor relief and profiting from pauperism? Revisiting the late-Victorian poor law, 1870–1900', unpubl. paper, Oxford Brookes.
4 Williams, *Pauperism*, 102.
5 Thomson, *World without welfare*.

have an opportunity to engage with demographers and medical historians to produce a revised poor law history, from above, below and around various local *crusading* experiments.

For too long studies of the late-Victorian poor law have had 'jack-in-the-box' characteristics. Whig historians sat firmly upon the lid of the *crusading* experiment, determined not to open it up to public scrutiny. They neglected evidence that it was a deeply impoverishing experience to fit their paradigm promoting the rise of the early Welfare State. As a result, early historiography misrepresented the reality of the poor law, a trend that was never fully reversed. In recent years a number of textbooks have provided general appraisal, and established a broad chronology, of the poor law.[6] It is still common to read just three or four pages, a chapter or a short overview on the *crusading* decades. This is still a 'jack-in-the-box' experience; the reader gets to peek below the lid but the reality of the poor law remains hidden. Along the way the experience of being poor is seldom given voice and hence the depths of impoverishment are still understudied, despite the important work of Mary Mackinnon and David Thomson in the 1980s. Essentially, the *crusading* 'jack-in-the-box' needs to be prised fully open to expose its contents. This means that standard historiography can no longer be taken as read. Researchers must challenge the misconception that studying the minutiae of pauperism records means losing the bigger poor law picture.

Crusading and the New Poor Law statute

For more than thirty years there has been some dispute amongst poor law historians about the rationale of the New Poor Law. Michael Rose first alerted researchers to the fact that 1834 was a watershed in social policy but that its statutory provisions may not have come to fruition until the *crusading* decades. In more extreme places, like the Brixworth union, however, *crusading* was not simply a backward-looking initiative that 'strengthened and remodelled' the existing administrative poor law system along earlier principles.[7] Rather, *crusading* guardians broke faith with the past by removing the entitlement of every pauper to claim public funds in the shape of outdoor relief. Even Thomas MacKay conceded that *crusaders* often went 'rather beyond' the New Poor Law ethos.[8] Pauperism statistics show that at least until the 1880s most poor law unions acted in this manner; otherwise the large reduction in expenditure on outdoor relief expenditure recorded at the LGB could not have been achieved on a broad front. That trend was at variance with earlier Victorian attitudes to the New Poor Law. In the 1870s many boards of guardians isolated the poor. They issued charters, the severity of which

---

6   See, for example, introduction, n. 11.
7   Rose, 'Crisis of poor relief', 65.
8   Pell, *Reminiscences*, p. xiv.

deterred even genuine claimants. Certainly in the Brixworth union there was a contrast between the sentiment of New Poor Law legislation and the hardship that the local *crusading* initiatives created. In English poor law unions, wherever a vigorous *crusading* campaign was instigated, that policy represented a fundamental disjuncture in nineteenth-century poor law history.[9]

Indeed, what was happening in the administration of the poor law might provide a crucial missing historical link connecting debates about social reform in the 1880s with intense campaigning over welfare rights in the Edwardian period. The fact that national expenditure on outdoor relief for the elderly, for instance, was halved during the *crusading* experiment should not be overlooked.[10] The Brixworth union contributed to that trend and therefore bears some responsibility for early twentieth-century welfare measures that were a reaction against a deeply impoverishing set of cost-saving policies.[11]

The severity of retrenchment might also explain why some contemporaries regarded social reform as the partisan political issue of its day by 1900. Perhaps local political controversy about the poor law anticipated the intensity of later national debates about welfare provision? Maybe overturning *crusading* measures in poor law elections raised new voters' expectations that equivalent political pressure could be applied at general election time to bring about more wide-ranging social reform? If so, the coming of democracy must have played a crucial role in both overthrowing the *crusade* and changing the tenor of British politics.

Democracy and the *crusaders*

Democratisation clearly played a key role in the demise of the *crusading* experiment. At first *crusading* zealots attacked all provision of outdoor relief; there followed a counter-attack on the part of those determined to reverse *crusading* experiments. Against this backdrop, the coming of democracy held out the promise of a transfer of power from traditional guardians of the poor to the working classes, giving them for the first time an opportunity to influence welfare decisions. Yet democracy was the tail-end of a process with deep historical roots in Brixworth and elsewhere: working people in the Brixworth union organised to fight the *crusading* experiment from its inception. It was part of their complex political journey. This began with the involvement of working people when the NALU formed and in vestry politics; it then centred on the activities of independent working-class spokesmen during the caucus phase; and, finally, it led to the establishment of BDODRA. Although linear historical models are problematic analytical tools, it is evident that some of

---

9   Kidd, *State, society and the poor*, for example, overlooks the significance of the *crusading* controversy.
10 Thomson, 'Welfare and the historians', 374.
11 Idem, *World without welfare*, 161.

the men who joined the NALU eventually led BDODRA. At each stage the working classes responded to retrenchment, rather than allowing apathy to result in further impoverishment. Working people fought to regain a series of those lost rights that had comprised their 'makeshift' economies. Throughout the *crusading* decades turnouts in both parliamentary and guardian elections were high and political activity was intense over the outdoor relief issue. In this sense, local politics were more accessible and flexible than portrayed by modern scholarship.[12]

Democratisation in the Brixworth union gave working people the chance to exercise power for their benefit and they seized that opportunity. They were not the 'helpless, hapless and hopeless sorts ... the victims rather than the makers of history' because they could exercise their right to vote.[13] It would seem that working people wanted civil and political rights for a reason, to obtain a form of basic social security. Their aspirations, therefore, anticipated the modern concept of welfare citizenship, namely that political rights without social welfare benefits are an 'empty constitutional promise'.[14] While it must be conceded that extremism on the part of guardians may have given rise to a stronger political reaction in the Brixworth union than elsewhere, there is a clear need for more regional studies. Such studies may reveal that the issue of poor relief was intimately connected to the complex nature of working-class political activism and the social welfare aspirations of the labouring classes. They may also highlight the fact that welfare historians may have overlooked a moment of triumph by working people.

By the mid-1890s ordinary voters had an opportunity to use the political vehicle of local government to bring about welfare change. They got what they wanted, and quickly, because they had a new democratic leverage. Thus the fight soon fizzled out in parish and poor law politics for a very good reason: democracy had triumphed. And, moreover, just because that process was quick does not mean that it was insignificant in the lives of the labouring poor. Perhaps the poor law was a political vehicle for a much more significant convergence of democratic forces and aspirations (involving welfare needs, economic demands and political will) than historians have hitherto appreciated? This might explain why much of the historiography has tended to focus on what was happening in places where there was a continuous and determined fight about the poor law, one that was vocal and involved prominent characters. But what if the rolling out of democracy was subtler than this elsewhere?

---

12 Thane, 'The working class and state "welfare"', 877–900, sets out the standard view. Hollis, *Ladies elect*, 290, acknowledges the influence of working-class candidates, but tends to cite examples as the exception rather than the rule. It is difficult to maintain this view with absolute certainty until more research is complete. Harrison, *Transformation of British politics*, 71, makes a similar claim.

13 Englander, *Poverty and poor law reform*, 90.

14 Finlayson, *Citizen, state and social welfare*, 12–13, explains the importance of the relationship between the right to vote and social welfare, which was a reaction against the 'mixed-economy of welfare' in the late-Victorian era.

Perhaps it triggered different types of political realignment in local government according to the severity of *crusading* measures? Where guardians had been uncompromising, poor law elections were intensely debated. Elsewhere, moderate guardians responded to working people's economic predicaments with empathy and understanding. These guardians were political realists and this satisfied new voters that their material lives were improving because local democracy worked. Thus, there was no need to shout about the need for social reform. The poor law was delivering welfare changes organically.

Although, therefore, it is important to question the degree to which working people lacked long-term enthusiasm for parish council, poor law and county council elections (a familiar historiographical theme), it seems likely that ordinary voters were not apathetic or uninterested, but quite the reverse. Democracy effectively undermined the *crusaders* and in so doing handed immediate political power to those who had been excluded from the decision-making process for so long. Rather than looking at this process of local democracy as a non-event, in fact, it is possible to observe through the prism of the poor law a widening in the scope of public welfare assistance, and at a pivotal moment in the political journey of ordinary people before full universal suffrage. For instance, Sidney Ward in 1899 petitioned central government on behalf of the board of guardians to repeal the ruling that all workhouse inmates should be disenfranchised.[15] His supporters believed that elderly people in the workhouse should have the right to vote in favour of state-funded old age pensions.[16] These sentiments, if widely held, must have meant that overthrowing the *crusading* experiment (whether by proactive or reactive means) was not the climax of working people's political journey but the start of a new phase of political inclusion. And, crucially, the catalyst for this process was the democratisation of the poor law and of parish politics.

Central–local relations after 1870

Central–local relations were complex and dynamic: the local influenced the national in hitherto unseen ways. The Longley Strategy was predicated on the basis that boards of guardians would follow *crusading* guidelines, rather than an official edict, thereby improving compliance. At the same time central government tried to foster a competitive welfare climate, by creating league tables and poor law conferences. The main problem with this strategy was that its goals were contradictory. Rarely is uniform compliance achieved when policy initiatives are issued in the form of guidelines. Too much autonomy often results in individuals interpreting recommendations and exploiting their new authority for personal gain. Central government learned this lesson to its cost: a series of problems was implicit in what happened at Brixworth

---

[15] Brixworth RDC correspondence, 1899–1900, MH 12/8710.
[16] Hollen-Lees, *Solidarities*, 298, takes the opposite view: that the desire for pension provision indicates that workers 'looked past the poor laws'.

and elsewhere because *crusading* turned into a spectacular, if unintended, own goal. Given that the New Poor Law was designed for the rural south-east, had the *crusading* experiment worked there, then it would have been an LGB triumph. Instead, it was an unmitigated failure, with central government losing control of their *crusading* campaign.

Initially, the relationship between central government and the Brixworth union worked well because it was in the interests of both sides to form a welfare partnership. Central government used the Brixworth union to raise its profile in the Midlands where it lacked real authority. This enabled civil servants to publicise the cost-saving benefits of adopting the Longley guidelines. In return, power-hungry *crusaders* exploited the Longley Strategy to pursue cost-saving goals, making radical cuts in poor law expenditure. This meant that individuals who, like Pell, dominated boards of guardians, started to exploit the close relationship they developed with central government. For instance, Pell asked central government to authorise unorthodox *crusading* schemes, such as the 'Secret Service Fund'. This placed central government in an awkward position, as did the request to reduce the number of relieving officers to just one, which contravened codes of practice. Central government did have misgivings about that request. Privately, top rank civil servants admitted in internal memoranda that they had made a fatal mistake: praise for the Brixworth union in successive annual LGB reports had been excessive and would later rebound on the LGB poor law division, which was placed in the unenviable position of having to support a maverick poor law union despite mounting public criticism.

The welfare partnership between central and local government, therefore, created a number of distinct problems. At first, leading *crusading* guardians like Pell could afford to ignore central government, acting instead in a devious manner. They were also forced into this corner because the *crusading* experiment did not make economic sense. Many soon realised that they had to be underhand in order to sustain year-on-year cuts in outdoor relief. Committed *crusaders*, who had achieved their targets against all odds, were also encouraged to think that they were welfare 'experts'. At that juncture many opted to take more complete control of their own *crusading* initiatives. Pell, for instance, became convinced that he was a welfare expert who needed no guidance, nor would he tolerate interference. It proved difficult to check his outspoken criticisms and maverick actions. A related difficulty was that *crusading* guidelines sent out mixed messages. On the one hand they promoted more humane care within workhouses; on the other this often meant forcing the impoverished indoors, with political repercussions locally. This contradiction arose because LGB policy was a 'complex mixture of the voluntary and the statutory'. As a result it lost touch with diverse 'mixed-economy of welfare' arrangements region-by-region.

In theory the new retrenchment guidelines stated that poor relief and charitable provision should operate in tandem. In reality *crusading* guardians used charitable agencies to subjugate the poor. Again, the 'Secret Service

Fund' exemplifies this outcome. The discriminating way that the charity was run motivated the labouring classes to fight collectively to overturn all *crusading* strategies Thus *crusading* contained the seeds of its destruction. A further complication was that the LGB's role was to co-ordinate the poor law policies of the government of the day. Consequently it had to take into account welfare developments that were the result of election promises. Its poor law ideology was not fixed, whereas the *crusaders* were often obdurate. By the 1890s more extensive political participation also changed the dynamic of central–local relations. Senior civil servants had to negotiate with a new class of guardian in an era when popular attitudes about the causes of poverty altered significantly. This forced government policy-makers to begin to make greater welfare concessions. Thus, at the end of the *crusading* decades a different type of local pressure was being brought to bear upon central government.

It is apparent that central–local relations went through three broad phases. In the early 1870s there was a working-down of *crusading* ideals, followed in the 1880s by a working-up of *crusaders'* demands; then in the 1890s the nature of the political pressure from local poor law unions changed again with the rolling out of democracy. Characteristically, throughout the later Victorian period, the LGB adopted the line of least resistance because it had no effective enforcement mechanism. This meant that it supported *crusaders* until the early 1890s. Thereafter, civil servants changed allegiance in line with more moderate thinking on the poor law.

Crusading and rural paternalism

The demise of local paternalism accompanied, reinforced and sprang out of the *crusading* experiment. Although paternalism is a complex historical term there is no doubt that in the late 1860s there was a 'mixed-economy of welfare' in operation in the Brixworth union. It comprised a combination of small outdoor relief doles and a range of charitable provision. These customary arrangements structured traditional social relations. Admittedly social duties and responsibilities were constantly under negotiation, usually changing according to economic conditions, with some key conventions like customary funeral payments enduring because they were deeply embedded in working-class culture. However, when *crusading* got underway at Brixworth, *laissez-faire* ideology was taken to its extreme, exploited by the landowning elite and farmers to enhance their poor law power, to the detriment of the poor. Guardians used *crusading* as an instrument of class reprisal, penalising the poor for union combination: ironically agricultural workers were combining into unions to fight for better wages to compensate for the withdrawal of poor law supplements by guardians. This seems to suggest that there was a strong link between the disintegration of paternalism and the initial success of *crusaders*. *Crusading* also seems to have been a political life-raft for the landed interest in a period of rapid economic change that threatened to undermine their dominance in rural society. Those figures, like Spencer, who needed to make major savings, particularly after the onset of the agricultural crisis, abandoned paternalism in favour of *crusading*. The social upheaval this triggered, especially with the withdrawal of customary pensions by landowners, thus abandoning the last vestiges of paternalism, had far-reaching political repercussions.

Tracing the demise of paternalism gives fresh insight into how *crusading* impacted on labourers, even though the evidence at certain junctures is fragmentary. It would be very difficult to come away from this study without gaining some sense of how deeply impoverishing the disintegration of paternalism was at a time when *crusading* initiatives hit the poor hardest. The aim throughout this book has been to let the poor speak for themselves in order to reveal the impact the demise of paternalism had on the community; and their evidence is compelling. The sudden withdrawal of paternalistic gestures, which were pivotal to pauper economies, meant that few could maintain their independence outside the workhouse. At the same time, *crusaders* were taking away outdoor relief allowances just when they were most needed. And out of all the pauper classes it was the elderly who often suffered the most. They felt keenly a lack of pension provision, fewer almshouse places and uncertainty about whether they would be buried in a dignified manner (all customary rights in the past) when their meagre outdoor relief was withdrawn. For a time some tried to fall back on their kinship and friendship networks, pooling their scanty resources, to resolve economic crises. Often after death their relatives had to beg to bury them. A lack of paternalism, therefore, resulted in deeper impoverishment. It was obvious that customary 'rights' were being eroded and at the same time *crusading* at its most extreme had a profound social cost. But working people did not accept this *fait accompli*: quite the reverse. After all, those who have nothing might as well fight for something. Committed *crusaders* believed that their actions would motivate the poor to adopt the Victorian values of industry, self-help and thrift, when in fact the poor learned fight back. Most were not deferential and acted in an expedient manner until the coming of democracy gave them the means to retaliate by playing a key role in the overthrow of *crusaders* from poor law office. The demise of paternalism, therefore, may have facilitated the *crusading* process but it also was a catalyst for democratic change.

The *crusaders*

Three men, although variously motivated, were keen *crusaders* in the Brixworth union. The activities of Pell, who dominated poor law administration for over twenty years, reveal the willingness of *crusading* fanatics to sacrifice the health and welfare of the poor in their ruthless pursuit of their ideological and cost-saving objectives. Pell never deviated in his commitment to *crusading*, even after he lost control of the poor law.[17] He was a typical COS zealot who was left 'socially marooned, obdurately indifferent to the changing tides of public opinion' because he was so 'unbending'.[18] Yet, although Pell's policies were an anachronism, the degree of political power he held and his determination to stay in office should not be underestimated. His party's conduct exemplifies the Longley Strategy's culture of performance indicators, target-setting and welfare charters. Pell sensed that *crusading* gave him the opportunity to further his political career. He could have chosen to languish on the Tory back-benches at Westminster but why do that when local government brought prominence and notoriety? *Crusading* seems to have given lack-lustre politicians opportunities to be large political players in a small poor law pond. Thus, men like Pell carved out unique roles for themselves and forged formidable reputations. Pell's contribution to *crusading* raises the question of the importance of the individual in history. Had he not dominated poor law proceedings, perhaps *crusading* would not have endured for so long. A dominant personality on a board of guardians may indeed have been a necessary precondition for the successful implementation of the Longley Strategy. Paradoxically, the radical nature of the leading individual, and the *crusading* ideology he espoused, seemed to have contained the political seeds of the *crusading* party's own destruction.

Earl Spencer's motives for becoming a *crusader* were complex and more difficult to pinpoint because he was such a private man. He usually only revealed his convictions to his peers, like Sir William Harcourt, in confidential correspondence. Yet, he did leave a record of his poor law actions, notably in the letters to his land agents. Spencer exercised control over the poor law by virtue of his birth and the extensive land and property holdings that he had inherited, which placed him at the apex of rural society. Initially he was a committed *crusader* for a mixture of ideological, economic and political reasons. But after the onset of the agricultural crisis he was more determined to cut his tax bill, withholding outdoor relief until the poor migrated. At the same time, he introduced a range of economic penalties on the Althorp estate mediated through his land agent. These included the repossession of cottages in arrears and the cancelling of all charitable subscriptions. Spencer may have been a Whig, but during the agricultural crisis he abandoned the paternalism of his forefathers. He was determined to export the social problems of the Brixworth union and for this reason he promoted welfare-to-work schemes rather than reintroduce outdoor relief. The schemes were too small-scale to alleviate unemployment and were run as business ventures. If they were not profitable, like the allotment farming scheme or the co-operative experiment, he withdrew his investment. Although Spencer was motivated primarily by economic, rather than ideological considerations by the time of the agricultural crisis, he matched Pell in ruthlessness. His charitable subscrip-

17 Pell, *Reminiscences*, p. xiv.
18 Humphreys, *Sin*, 173-4.

tions were a meagre proportion of his personal expenditure, but the impact of those cutbacks was profound. However, in one crucial way Spencer did differ from Pell; he was a pragmatist. Thus, Spencer was reconciled to the fact that the coming of democracy would change the basis of welfare provision as well as the nature of local government administration. If Spencer had not become involved in initial *crusading* activities, the campaign would still have got underway, but his support was invaluable and his reputation gave fellow *crusaders* a powerful ally. He died in 1910 on the eve of the introduction of the Parliament Bill to reform the powers of the House of Lords. His poor law career opens a window on the demise of patrician authority in national and county politics, revealing how the dispersal of territorial wealth went hand-in-hand with the transition from landed dominance to the democratisation of local government.

William Bury served as chairman of the Brixworth union board for more than twenty years, playing a pivotal role in the *crusading* controversy. Before 1870 he was a mild-mannered cleric who seldom attended poor law union board meetings. In his opinion it was in the farming community's interests to retain outdoor relief because it was part of the social fabric and therefore ensured stability. Bury believed that it was his clerical duty to mediate outdoor relief and charity to the poor on behalf of his patron. Thus he organised the construction of a local school and better quality housing in his local parish. However, once Pell moved into the neighbourhood in the 1860s, Bury underwent a radical conversion. Pell recognised that Bury would be a useful man to recruit to the *crusading* cause because he was a formidable bureaucrat. He persuaded him to take a proactive role and thus Bury became a zealous *crusader*. His unrivalled technical judgement of poor law procedures was one of the chief reasons why the *crusaders* held on to power for so long. Bury delayed controversial motions, exploiting procedural technicalities, until he could round up enough supporters to outvote any challenger. He acted as party whip and chairman, particularly during the agricultural crisis. Pell recognised in Bury the qualities of loyalty and resolute determination to follow fixed principles. They remained life-long friends and close allies. Together they demonstrate that a major factor for the successful implementation of the Longley Strategy seems to have been that whoever dominated a board of guardians needed a resolute lieutenant to recruit supporters. Bury took on that role and never wavered in his convictions after his conversion. It is difficult to gauge whether the *crusading* campaign would have failed without Bury because Pell would probably have co-opted another COS ally. However, there is no doubt that Bury played a key role throughout.

Looking forward

In her summary of the *crusading* decades, Lynn Hollen-Lees comments that Henry Longley (in the Longley Strategy) did not seek to ban outdoor relief altogether; instead 'he proposed to construct a series of high hurdles that an applicant would have to leap over before obtaining it'.[19] Yet what Longley intended did not actually happen because at first the poor reacted by trying to get under those hurdles, exploiting the system whenever, however and in whatever ways they could. The system was rife with procedural anomalies and when the *crusading* initiatives were set in motion the labouring poor had every reason to expect that they could negotiate their way around them, as they had so often done in the past. They could also mobilise their 'makeshift' economies to compensate them through poor relief peaks and troughs. Likewise, the revived customs of the high-farming era (charity, coal, clothing, almshouses, pensions and so on) held out hope of alternative income supplements. In fact, it soon became apparent that something very distinctive was evolving. The truth was that the hurdles had been removed altogether and the poor law race was cancelled. There is substantive proof that the labouring community in the Brixworth union recognised that new fact of poor law life, even adopting its analogy. During the poor law contest in 1895 BDODRA designed an election poster that was put up around the district. It described the contest as a poor law race, 'The Brixworth Stakes' (*see* plate 1). Candidates for the office of chairman of the board of guardians were given nicknames and their racing form was described in satirical terms. Spencer was 'Rufus': the fox-hunting Red Earl, a non-elected imposition and certainly not a popular runner given his track record. Pell was 'Sidesman': he manipulated the poor law from the wings: form suggested he was 'not quite up to weight'. Likewise Bury was the 'Prevaricator': he kept resigning from office when challenged, and was 'more fit for a *selling* race', reneging on the poor. At the bottom of the poster there was a wry comment: 'N.B. – No horsemen allowed on the course'. This was the labouring poor's small space to tell of their impoverishment and about how the coming of democracy would give them the political weight to enter the poor law race. This type of electioneering strategy and bitter discourse emphasises that Karel Williams's views need further refinement. He suggests that during the *crusading* decades there were oppressive outdoor initiatives alongside progressive indoor measures, and that paupers appreciated the difference. In the Brixworth union, however, whether paupers were outside or inside the workhouse, they lived not in a world, but worlds-without-welfare. Just because they were within four poor law walls did not mean that they received either adequate or satisfactory care. The number of workhouse personnel shrank, sick wards lacked professional staff, doctors were not paid enough to attend patients, pauper cadavers were turned into a

---

[19] Hollen-Lees, *Solidarities*, 262.

The Brixworth Stakes.

———

This event will be run on the Poor Law Course, Brixworth, on the 29th inst., and we understand the following are entered :

THE BRIXWORTH COLT.—This is a well bred little horse, who has always gone straight and in good form. They say he is likely to be a stayer, and although he met with a serious accident, we understand he is heavily backed to win.

SIDESMAN.—This is rather a weedy animal by " Clericus," evidently not quite up to weight. He will probably go to the post, but is more suitable to *carry a lady quietly*, than get across country.

PREVARICATOR.—Although descended from a good old sire, he runs cunning, and has lately been thrown out of training. He is, however, again entered, but his party have no confidence in him ; he's more fit for a *selling* race.

POST MORTEM.—This is a well bred horse by " Medicus," but is aged and obliged to run in blinkers. Although a good stud horse, he has not-pace enough for the present race.

RUFUS.—This horse's pedigree is not to be found in the Racing Calendar. He is stable companion to Prevaricator, and his trainer must have entered him to fill the race. He's in too good company to win.

———

N.B.—No horsemen allowed on the course.

Plate 1. 'The Brixworth Stakes': Brixworth District
Out Door Relief Association election poster, 1894–5.

medical research commodity. Little wonder that a sense of insecurity haunted the poor of the Brixworth union.

Admittedly BDODRA's election manifesto was also Janus-like. Some members looked back to older customary rights, determined to get back what was lost. They spoke about medical outdoor relief benefits, provision for pauper burial and almshouses. Others looked forward, pushing the boundaries of entitlement to poor relief: the right to have a state-funded pension, basic unemployment insurance and maternity care. Often these issues structured BDODRA political speeches. The activities of BDODRA therefore seem to indicate that in Midlands politics a new political threshold had been crossed. More research is needed to quantify levels of support for it, longer-term voter commitment and broader welfare ideals. Nevertheless, the fact that Bobby Spencer, ousted from parliamentary office in 1895, recognised the need to adopt most of BDODRA's welfare policies seems significant. His political *volte-face* ensured that he was re-elected in 1905. That reaction exemplifies how local political life was rife with contradictions. Rhetoric and statistics often belie a complex poor law landscape, peopled by politicians motivated by self-interest, as well as the poor looking both backwards and forwards and yet crossing a political boundary into a twentieth-century world of welfare.

Predicting future trends in this neglected area of poor law studies is hazardous; none the less a study of this complexity does raise a number of historical questions. It would, for instance, be instructive to examine the experiences of a much wider cohort of poor law unions that adopted the Longley Strategy to establish whether Brixworth was representative or unrepresentative, and also to determine whether it was emblematic of the *crusading* experiment. At present it is only possible to speculate on the diversity and radical nature of poor law practices elsewhere. Likewise, moving from the local to the regional and inter-regional will modify and extend historical understanding of this neglected *crusading* topic.[20] Early research indicates that there may have been regional *crusading* hot spots in the industrialised northern cities and in the less arable rural south-west of England. Other *crusader* histories await welfare historians. This should stimulate a fruitful comparison of the 'regional states of welfare' during the later Victorian poor law phase, extending the work of Steven King. Such research would facilitate more extensive studies of poor law continuity and change embedded in the type of macro-study needed to complete the *crusading* jigsaw puzzle.

In the early 1980s David Thomson recommended that *crusading* be studied in greater detail. Since few poor law historians have followed his lead, it remains the case that little is known about the diversity of politics in rural

---

[20] Hurren, '*Crusading* against outdoor relief', argues that the same 'regional states of welfare' that Steven King identified prior to 1850 appear to extend into the late-Victorian decades.

society and about the history of labour relations. And without the poor law the historical picture remains incomplete. Aspects of the *crusading* experience, especially political debates about social reform and the meaning of local government democracy, have wider significance. This book therefore aligns with newer rural studies modifying our understanding of the complexity of local political life, especially agricultural trade unionism and its links to wider changes in society. Further work also needs to be undertaken on the issue of Nonconformity and the influence of radical Liberal politics in Midlands towns like Northampton. Similarly the complex issue of the demise of Liberalism in the agricultural heartland needs to be addressed. A key question is whether these poor law events were antecedents of 'labour' politics that Liberalism tried and failed to contain before 1914. More research would facilitate this type of analysis and support studies that political historians have done on localities where the drift away from Liberalism towards municipal socialism was evident in the later Victorian period.

It is hoped that this contribution represents the start of a process of investigation. Certainly research elsewhere will help to interrogate, refine and rethink the later Victorian poor law experience. This account of events at Brixworth has only scratched the surface of the experience of being poor; none the less it has been possible to glimpse the depths of impoverishment that the *crusading* campaign must have created. The political battle over *crusading* in the Brixworth was about human dignity. A pauper, like Margaret Price,[21] exemplifies that long-forgotten rich seam of pauper evidence that has survived in many central government and county record office files. Through such material it is possible to get closer to those who lived through an embittering *crusading* experience. Thus, perhaps, the lost property of impoverished lives may finally be reclaimed.

It is appropriate to allow ordinary working people of the Brixworth union to have the last word since this is their history. At the inaugural meeting of BDODRA in 1893 Sidney Ward declared to a packed public house that it was time to pursue 'new ideas, new hopes and new aims'.[22] Giving evidence to the Royal Commission on the Aged Poor in 1894 he told the then prince of Wales why BDODRA was set up:

Suppose say now, Sir, I have the privileges of liberty, a man who has lived in a cottage for years he has got a little home; it is a little castle to him, and they say when he has lived there over fifty years he and his wife have to break up their home and go into the house. He has to sell his furniture bit by bit before they go in, because if they have anything they will not give him a paper. He has to part with all, and then when he goes in he has to part with his clothing. ... He was a man who had his liberty, and used to go about the fields all his lifetime ... being confined there after having his

---

[21] See pp. 56–8, above.
[22] *Northampton Mercury*, 3 Mar. 1893.

liberty is very hard ... I believe there is a good many would have been living to-day if it had not been for the policy of the Board.[23]

Ward explained that BDODRA was determined to oust guardians whose 'chief object had been to keep cutting rates ... for they gloried in keeping figures right ... it did not matter about the people left impoverished and suffering'. A fellow spokesman, Josiah Turner of Pitsford, reiterated the feelings of working people:

A man who had worked and paid rates all his life, for perhaps fifty or sixty years, was only asking for his own when he applied for outdoor relief. It was not charity that the working classes were asking for, but justice. Working men had never had the opportunity, which they had at present of sending men who could speak and vote. ... No law giving the working class such power as they had at present under the reduced qualifications had ever been brought forward. United they could send to the Board ... men who would do justice to their fellow workers ... they were the old people of the future ... now they had an opportunity, which they should not allow to pass, of putting men there who knew their future needs.[24]

Ordinary working men who founded BDODRA, like Ward and Turner, fought not just for political rights but for the series of welfare benefits denied to them that later became the pillars of the Welfare State. It seems David Thomson was correct when he said that

while history never repeats itself neatly, and circumstances are never the same again, there is much to be learned by considering carefully the last time 'new' welfare ideas ... were dominant ... the options facing us now are very similar to those considered, tried and discarded by previous generations.[25]

In the end, the poor were prepared to protest about pauperism and in doing so revealed much about poverty, politics and poor relief in later Victorian England.

---

23 *Royal Commission on the Aged Poor* (1894), Ward, 27 Feb. 1894, qq. 15761–4, 15676.
24 *Northampton Mercury*, 3 Mar. 1893.
25 Thomson, 'Welfare and the historians', 357, and *World without welfare*, 165.

Bibliography

Unpublished primary sources

Birmingham, University Library Manuscript Collection
MSS *Chamberlain*
J. Chamberlain, J/C, 54.3, J/C, 5/54/7, 1873

Cambridge Records Office
St Benedict's burial records, P25/1/21–3

Cambridge University Library
Pamphlet collection
P. 94/7/277 Anon., *Plain words on outrelief*, London 1894
Poor law conference reports, London 1876–1911

Leicester, Leicestershire Records Office
DE/2340, no.1 Leicester Charity Organisation Society minute books, 1876–81

London, British Library
MSS *Althorp*
Family papers
K503–5 Charlotte Spencer, 1889–96
Misc. vol. 1879, financial records
Misc. vol. 1881, political correspondence

General letter boxes
Boxes K1–K599

Official papers
K477 Home affairs, draft bills, 1893–5
K480 Local government, county council bills

Political papers
K8 W. G. Gladstone, 1884–5, 1888–95
K12 Sir Charles Dilke, 1870–1900
K19 Sir William Harcourt, 1886–1904

Unofficial papers
K24 J. Morley, land agent, 1887–96
K426 Althorp estates management
K427 Notes for speeches

K428 Undated correspondence and papers
K430 Extracts from speeches
K431 Misc. memoranda
Misc. correspondence of the 5th Earl Spencer, 1860–1910

MSS *Dilke*

Vol. lix, entry no. 43932 Diaries of Sir Charles Dilke (1873)
43874–967, Misc. correspondence and papers
43891, fos 115–86b Correspondence with the 5th Earl Spencer

MSS *Gladstone*

Add. correspondence of W. G. Gladstone (J. C. Cox letters)
cc, 44485, fos 75, 203 (14 Jan., 17 Feb. 1884)
ccxxiii, 44508, fo. 262 (28 Dec. 1889)
cccxxix, 44514, fo. 204 (25 Apr. 1892)

London, British Library of Political and Economic Science, London School of Economics

Pamphlet collection

P. 205392 Anon., *Why is it wrong to supplement outdoor relief?* (COS occasional paper xxxi, 1893–4)
P25129 J. C. Cox, *The advantages of trade unions! A lecture delivered at Ripley by J.C. Cox JP FRHS of Hazelwood Belper on Thursday evening 29 Aug. 1872 at the request of the Derbyshire and Nottinghamshire Miners' Association'*, Derby 1872
HV/578 J. C. Cox, *Outdoor relief the heritage of the poor: a paper read at the North Midlands Poor Law Conference at Grimsby on 13 Sept., 1899, with notes from a lecture delivered at Oxford on 2 Jan. 1900*, London 1900

London, House of Lords Library

MSS *Gosse*
L32 Gosse diary, 1904

London, National Westminster Bank archive, Cornhill

Northampton Union Bank Ltd collection

London, The National Archives

Public Records Office

C.247/3, ref 147 Lord Chancellors' office, presentation papers for crown livings: Holdenby
F58/ 775 Scaldwell Co-operative Industrial Society Ltd
FS/12/213 Brixworth Provident Co-operative Society Ltd, 1866–1931
FS/ 58/1359 Harlestone Progressionists Industrial Society Ltd
FS/58/2864 Hazelbech Provident Society Ltd
MH 12/8699–709 Brixworth union correspondence book, 1865–98
MH 12/8710 Brixworth RDC correspondence book, 1899–1900

MH 12/32/8 Internal memos between senior civil servants and LGB poor law division, 1877–9

MH 12/32/104 Misc. correspondence between assistant poor law commissioners and LGB poor law division, 1877

MH 19/85 LGB misc. correspondence between civil servants and poor law officials

MH 19/93 Misc. correspondence between civil servants and LGB poor law division, 1883

MH 25/24–5 LGB misc. correspondence between civil servants and poor law officials

MH 25/224 Misc. correspondence between civil servants and Margaret Price, 1874

MH 74/11 Anatomy Inspectorate correspondence for the University of Cambridge: J. Pickering Pick, inspector of anatomy to Professor Alexander Macalister, head of anatomy, 1896 files

Northampton, Northampton Library, Local Studies Collection

Friendly Society records

Chapel Brampton Friendly Society annual report for the year, Northampton 1873

Pamphlet collection

Rules of the East Haddon Burial Board, adopted 12 Jan. 1892, Northampton 1892

Anon., *The third council for Northamptonshire 1895: no. 862. a record of the elections reprinted from the Northampton Mercury; a summary of the career of Rev. Dr. J. C. Cox*, Northampton 1895

'The Brixworth Stakes': Brixworth District Out Door Relief Association election poster, 1894–5

Northampton, Northamptonshire Record Office

CAM/901 Sir Hereward Wake, *The parting of the ways; or, what local government can and cannot do for labouring men by a squire: for lawyers by lawyers*, Northampton 1894

Kelly's directory, 1885–9, 1894

Lamport rate book, 1875

172/9 Presentation papers for the crown living of Holdenby, J. C. C. Cox, 24 Jan. 1894

V2911 Northampton petty sessions records, Northampton division

ZA2246 Newspaper cutting, 'Brixworth: power of the chairman questioned', and autobiographical paraphernalia *re* the Revd W. Bury and the 5th Earl Spencer

Brixworth union poor law records

Census returns, 1841–1901

LG 21/07 Brixworth union general letter book, 1888–95

LG 21/07–9 Brixworth union sanitary authority records, 1888–95

LG 21/106–16 Brixworth union RDC minute books

Misc. ledger 267 Brixworth Rural Sanitary Authority, letter book, 1886–98

P/L 2/12 Brixworth union death registers, 1837–95

P/L 2/14–20 Brixworth union guardians' minute books, 1866–1900
49p/46 *Report of the Brixworth union charities committee*, Northampton 1875

MSS *Fischer and Saunders*

F/S/24/77, 78 Lady Milton's Haselbech land agent records and correspondence, 1870–6, 1880

MSS *Langham*

L(C) 1163 Petition of tenants, Cottesbrooke to Sir James Langham, 6 Dec. 1830

MSS *Spencer*

[all Spencer boxed material is archived as Sox i.e. S[pencer B]ox
Estate records and local affairs
Sox 246 Hon. C. R. (Bobby) Spencer's political speeches, 1885–6
Sox 393 'Brington, Harlestone and Whilton Agricultural Labourers' Union petition to the 5th Earl Spencer', 27 Mar. 1873
Sox 393 'Brixworth union parochial lists for the half-year ending Lady-day, 1879, statistics of pauperism by order of the board of guardians', Northampton 1879 (Spencer's copy)
Sox 393, 551, 562–3, 565–8, 571 Land agent records
Misc. vol. parish and parish meetings, 'parish councillors, rules as to nomination and election general order no. 31, 846', 13 Sept.1894
7b3, misc. vol. Althorp Park daily journal of labourers' work, 1859–76
7cl, misc. vol. Althorp farm labour books, 1842–57
7c2, misc. vol. Brampton farm books, 1844–53
7f 5, misc. vol. J. Beasley, 'The number of the poor and working class people in Brington parish taken in December, 1871'

Northampton union poor law records

Misc. vols (uncatalogued)
Northampton union guardians' minute books, 1870–1900
Northampton town census returns for Northamptonshire, 1841–1901

Parish and vestry council records

49/p/150/d Brington parish council records, unsorted, fragmentary papers, 1800–1930
49/p/202/e Brington parish meeting annual minute book, 1894–1951
49/p/214/e Brington parish council minute book, 1894–1919
50/ p/109 Brixworth parish council minute book, 1894–1903
150/p Brixworth All Saints vestry minute book, 1893–1938
150/p/33 Brixworth All Saints church account books, parish alms, 1876–8
153/p/22 Harlestone parish: bundle of charity correspondence and accounts, 1870–82
153/p/111 Harlestone parish council minute books, 1894–1939
153/p/112 Harlestone parish meeting books, 1894–1952
153/p/128 Harlestone parish council records, 1895–8

Misc. vol. Naseby parish: bundle of records, 1894
Misc. vol. Scaldwell parish: bundle of records, 1894
287p/50 Scadwell vestry minute book, 1876–7

Oxford, Bodleian Library

MSS *Harcourt*
Sir William Harcourt, 47, fo. 86; 37, fo. 87; 711, fos 10, 16, 20, 349

Oxford, Oriel College

MSS *Phelps*
Misc. vols 1888, 1889, 1895
Box A–B, 1908

Oxford, Oxfordshire County Record Office

OXFO, 362.5 Revd L. R. Phelps, *Poor law and charity: a paper read in the common room of Keble College, Oxford, 9 March 1887*, Oxford 1887
OXFO, 362.5 Revd L. R. Phelps, *The administration of the poor law in Oxford: a letter to the principal of Brasenose*, Oxford 1900
OXFO, 362.5 Revd L. R. Phelps, *Charity v. beggars* (Oxford COS, 1892)

Published primary sources

Official documents and publications (in chronological order)

Royal commission reports

Report of his majesty's commissioners for inquiring into the administration and practical operation of the poor laws, PP 1834, xxvii–xxxix (c44, 251, 313), including appendices
Third report from the commissioners for the inquiring into the condition of the poorer classes in Ireland, PP 1836, xxxxiii
Royal Commission on the Employment of Children, Young Persons and Women in Agriculture, 1st and 2nd reports, PP 1867, 1878, xvii
Report of the House of Commons select committee on elections of poor law guardians in England, Scotland and Ireland, PP 1878, iv, xvii (iv)
Royal Commission on Depressed Condition of Agricultural Interests: reports of assistant commissioners, and final report, PP 1882, xv, xvi
Report from the select committee of the House of Lords on poor relief, PP 1888, xv (c363)
Royal Commissions on Labour, 1st and 5th reports, PP 1895, xiv, appendixes 'C', 'F', I, xiv, xxv
Royal Commission on Poor Relief in the Case of Destitution by Incapacity for Work from Old Age: final report, PP 1895, xiv–xv (c7684)
Report of the Royal Commission on the Poor Laws, PP 1909, xxxvii (c4499), including appendices

Local Government Board reports

Annual reports of the Local Government Board, PP, 1 Apr. 1871/2–24 Apr. 1894–5
   (*Subject catalogue of the House of Commons parliamentary papers, 1801–1900*,
   iii. 581–2)
Census of Great Britain: population tables
Census of England and Wales, 1871, 1881, 1891

Hansard
Parliamentary debates (Commons and Lords), mdcccxiv, London 1892

Newspapers and periodicals
Bath Journal
Berkshire and Buckinghamshire Gazette
Bristol Daily Times and Mirror
British Medical Journal
Charity Organisation Society Review
Contemporary Review
Daily News
Eastern Weekly Leader
Economic Journal
Examiner
Fortnightly Review
Jackson's Oxford Journal
Labourers' Union Chronicle
Lancet
Local Government Journal
Macmillan Magazine
Midland Free Press
Nineteenth Century
Northampton Daily Chronicle
Northampton Guardian
Northampton Herald
Northampton Independent
Northampton Mercury
Northampton Radical
Oxford Chronicle
Punch
Quarterly Review
Ripley Advertiser
Royal Leamington Spa Chronicle
The Times
Westminster Review

Contemporary books and articles
Adkins, W. R. O. (ed.), *Our county*, Northampton 1893
Anon. *The return of the owners of land in England and Wales*, London 1873
Anon., *Why are the many poor?* (Fabian Society, tract i, 1884)

Anon., *Why is it wrong to supplement outdoor relief?* (COS occasional paper xxxi 1893–4)

Anon, *Plain words on outrelief*, London 1894

Baker, G. T., *The history and antiquities of the county of Northamptonshire*, Northampton 1823–30, 1836–41

Beasley, J., *A lecture delivered to the members of the Faringdon Agricultural Club on the duties and privileges of the landowners, occupiers and cultivators of the soil*, London 1860

Booth, C., *Pauperism and the endowment of old age*, London 1892

———— *The aged poor in England and Wales: condition*, London 1894

Bridges, J., *The history and antiquities of Northamptonshire*, London 1791

Bury, W., 'Report on outdoor pauperism in the Brixworth union', *Third annual report of the Local Government Board*, London 1873, appendix b, 119–25

———— 'Charity and the poor law,' *Poor law conference report*, London 1876, 44

———— 'Squires, spires, and mires', *Fortnightly Review* (Mar. 1885), 352–70

———— 'Poor law progress and reform', *Poor law conference report*, London 1889, 319

———— 'Out-door relief and a more excellent way', *Charity Organisation Review* (Apr. 1895), 134–38.

Calverley, Mary, 'Thrift and old age pensions', COR (Jan. 1893), 1–7

———— 'Some problems of outdoor relief', COR (Dec. 1895), 482–5

———— *Outdoor relief: a study in pauperisation: the down grade* (COS occasional papers, 1900)

———— 'Looking back': records of the Brixworth union: Lady-day 1895: Lady-day 1896, Northampton 1901

Chalmers, T., *On political economy, in the connexion with the moral state and moral prospects of society*, Glasgow n.d.

Chance, W. G., *The better administration of the poor law*, London 1895

———— 'State administration of relief', COR (Apr. 1896), 138–45

Channing, F. A., MP, *Memories of Midland politics, 1885–1910*, Northampton 1918

Cox, J. C., 'Church disestablishment and the rural districts', *Examiner*, 28 Sept. 1872

———— 'The county franchise', *Examiner*, 12 Oct. 1872

———— *The Duke of Edinburgh: the cost of the royal household*, London 1873

———— 'The right of public meeting', *Examiner*, 1 Mar. 1873

———— 'The Faringdon labourers' meeting', *Examiner*, 19 Apr. 1873

———— 'The Church and the labourers', *Examiner*, 11 Oct. 1873

———— 'The great unpaid [sic]', *Examiner*, 26 Oct. 1873

———— 'The common good and the enclosure of the commons', *Examiner*, 31 Dec. 1873

———— *Church property national property*, London 1874

———— *The rise of the farm labourer: a series of articles reprinted from the 'Examiner' 1872–3 illustrative of certain political aspects of the agricultural labour movement*, London 1874

———— *The pedigree of Cox of Derbyshire*, Derby 1889

———— *Cromwell and the great civil war*, Northampton 1899

———— 'Outdoor relief with special reference to Brixworth, Atcham and Whitechapel', *Poor law conferences*, London 1899–1900, 193–215

Editorial, 'Annual poor law conference for the north midland district held at the board room Leicester in Pockington's Walk, on Mon. 13 Dec., 1886', *Poor law conference reports*, London 1886, 407–26

Editorial, 'Local government and its responsibilities', COR xv (Mar. 1886), 81

Editorial, 'Local government and its responsibilities', COR xvi (Apr. 1886), 145–50

Editorial, 'Annual meeting report', COR (Mar. 1887), 107–20

Editorial, 'Poor relief: out-relief ii', COR (Sept. 1889), 359

Editorial, 'The abuse of statistics', *Quarterly Review* clxxviv (July–Oct. 1894), 467–85

Frome Wilkinson, J., 'Poor law administration and the Brixworth union,' *The Church of Today*, 15 Feb. 1895, 76

Girdlestone, Canon, 'The farm labourer', *Macmillan Magazine* (1872), 261

Green, T. H., *Works*, ed. R. L. Nettleship, London, 1885–8

Harcourt, Sir William, 'Speech to the National Liberal Federation, 16th annual meeting in the drill hall Portsmouth, 14 Feb. 1894', in *Liberal party pamphlets and leaflets of 1894*, London 1895, 72

Howlett, E., 'Burial customs', *Westminster Review* (Aug. 1893), 166–74

Loch, C. S., 'Manufacturing a new pauperism', *Nineteenth Century* (Apr. 1895), 697–708

Lubbock, G. (ed), *Some poor relief questions: for and against*, London 1895

MacKay, T., 'Politics and the poor law', *Fortnightly Review* (July 1895), 408–22

Marshall, A., 'How far do remediable causes influence prejudicially a) continuity of employment, b) the rate of wages?', *Industrial Conference*, London 1885, 173–4

Matthew, H. C. G. (ed.), *The Gladstone diaries*, ix, xii, Oxford 1986, 1995

Morton, J., *Natural history of Northamptonshire*, London 1712

Nicholls, Sir George, *A history of the Irish poor law*, London 1856

Oakeshott, J. F., *The humanizing of the poor law* (Fabian Society, tract liv, 1894)

Pell, A., 'Arthur Young: agriculturalist, author and statesman', *Journal of the Farmers' Club* iv (1882), 62

——— 'Local government in counties: a paper delivered to the 14th annual poor law conference', *Poor law conference report*, London 1885, 294–308.

——— 'Exceptional distress', *Annual poor law conference for the East Midland district: poor law conference report*, London 1888, 412–14

——— 'Poor law relief: out-relief', COR (Sept. 1889), 359–63

——— 'Out-relief: a paper read at a poor law conference as chairman of the central committee held at the Crewe Arms Hotel on 14 Oct. 1890', in *Tracts, 1843–93*, London 1900, 1–16

——— *The reminiscences of Albert Pell sometime MP for south-Leicestershire*, ed. T. MacKay, London 1908

——— and L. Twining, 'Local government and its responsibilities', COR (Apr. 1886), 145–50

——— and A. Wedgwood, 'The Tower Hamlets Pension Committee', COR (Nov. 1886), 401

Rathbone, W., A. Pell and F. C. Montague, *Local administration*, London 1885

Ritchie, D. G., 'Mr. Spencer's individualism and his conception of society', *Contemporary Review* (Nov. 1886), 50

Stanley of Alderley, Lord, 'Two days in the Brixworth union', *Fortnightly Review* (July 1885), 42–55

Turnell, J., *Pamphlet suggestions for the amendment of the administration of the poor law by which double relief could be given to the aged and infirm, materially increase that given to the widow and orphan, and a great reduction of the rates to the ratepayer*, Sheffield 1873

Vaughan, D. J. (ed.), *Report of the church congress held at Leicester September 28–Oct. 1, 1880*, London 1881

Wake, Sir Hereward, *The parting of the ways; or, what local government can and cannot do for labouring men by a squire: for lawyers by lawyers*, Northampton 1894

Secondary sources

Adleman, P., *Gladstone, Disraeli and later Victorian politics*, London 1970

Anon., *Centenary of Brixworth Rural District Council, 1894–1994*, Northampton 1994

Archer, J., *'By a flash and a scare': arson, animal maiming and poaching in East Anglia, 1815–1870*, Oxford 1990

Arnold, R., 'The "revolt" in the field in Kent, 1872–1879', *P&P* lxiv (1974), 71–95

Ashforth, D., 'The urban poor law', in Fraser, *The New Poor Law*, 128–48

Ashrott, P. F., *The English poor law system*, London 1902

Auspos, P., 'Radicalism, pressure groups and party politics: from the National Education League to the National Liberal Federation', *JBS* xx (1980), 181–204

Avery, G. and K. Reynolds (eds), *Representations of childhood death*, Basingstoke 2000

Beckett, J. V., *The aristocracy in England, 1660–1914*, Cambridge 1986

Behlmer, G. K., *Friends of the family: the English home and its guardians, 1850–1940*, Stanford 1998

———— and F. M. Leventhal (eds), *Singular continuities: tradition, nostalgia and society in modern Britain*, Stanford 2000

Bellamy, C., *Administering central–local relations: the Local Government Board in its fiscal and cultural context*, Manchester 1988

Bellamy, E., E. Razzell and J. Ward (eds), *Life in the Victorian village: the Daily News survey of 1891*, i, ii, London 1999

Benson, J. (ed.), *The working class in England, 1875–1914*, Harlow 1984

———— *The working class in Britain, 1850–1939*, Harlow 1989

Bentley, M., *Politics without democracy, Great Britain, 1815–1914*, London 1984

———— *The climax of Liberal politics: British Liberalism in theory and practice, 1868–1914*, London 1987

———— and J. Stevenson (eds), *High and low politics in modern Britain*, Oxford 1983

Bernstein, G. L., *Liberalism and Liberal politics in Edwardian England*, London 1986

Best, G., *Mid-Victorian Britain, 1851–75*, London 1990 edn

Biagini, E. F. (ed.), *Liberty, retrenchment and reform: popular Liberalism in the age of Gladstone, 1860–1900*, Cambridge 1992

———— *Citizenship and community: Liberals, radicals and collective identities in the British Isles, 1865–1931*, Cambridge 1996

Blake, R., *The Conservative party: Peel to Churchill*, London 1985 edn

Blaug, M., 'The myth of the old poor law and the making of the new', *JEcH* xxiii (1963), 151–84

Blewett, N., 'The franchise in the United Kingdom, 1885–1918', *P&P* xxxii (Dec. 1965), 27–56

Bock G. and P. Thane (eds), *Maternity and gender politics: women and the rise of the European welfare states, 1880s–1950s*, London–New York 1991

Botelho, L. and P. Thane (eds), *Women and ageing in British society since 1500*, Harlow 2001

Boyer, G. R., *An economic history of the English poor law, 1750–1850*, Cambridge 1990

Bradbury, J., *Government and county: a history of Northamptonshire county council, 1889–1989*, Northampton 1989

Broad, J., 'Parish economies of welfare, 1650–1834', *HJ* xxxxii (1999), 985–1006

Brown, A. F. G., *Meagre harvest: the Essex farm workers' struggle against poverty, 1750–1914*, Chelmsford 1990

Brown, K. D., *The English labour movement, 1700–1951*, London 1982

Brown, S. J., *Thomas Chalmers and the godly commonweal in Scotland*, Oxford 1982

Brundage, A., 'The landed interest and the New Poor Law: a reappraisal of the revolution in government', *EHR* lxxxvii (1972), 27–48

———— 'The making of the New Poor Law debate: redivivius', *P&P* cxxvii (1990), 183–6

———— *The English poor laws, 1700–1930*, Basingstoke 2002

Cage, R. A., *The Scottish poor law system, 1745–1845*, Edinburgh 1981

Cannadine, D., *The decline and fall of the British aristocracy*, London 1992

Checkland, O., *Philanthropy in Victorian Scotland: social welfare and the voluntary principle*, Edinburgh 1980

———— 'Chalmers and William Pulteney Alison: a conflict of views on Scottish social policy', in Cheyne, *The practical and the pious*, 130–41

Cherry, S., *Medical services and the hospitals in Britain, 1860–1939*, Cambridge 1986

Cheyne, A. S. (ed.), *The practical and the pious: essays on Thomas Chalmers*, Edinburgh 1985

Clarke, P. F., *Lancashire and new Liberalism*, Cambridge 1971

———— *Liberals and social democrats*, Cambridge 1978

———— and K. Langford, 'Hodge's politics: the agricultural labourers and the Third Reform Act in Suffolk', in N. Harte and R. Quinault (eds), *Land and society in Britain, 1700–1914: essays in honour of F. M. L. Thompson*, Cambridge 1996, 119–37

Clarke, S. and J. S. Donnelly (eds), *Irish peasants and political unrest, 1780–1914*, Manchester 1983

Coleman, B., *Conservatism and the Conservative party in nineteenth-century Britain*, London 1988

Collini, S., *Liberalism and sociology: L.T. Hobhouse and political argument in England, c. 1880–1914*, Cambridge 1979

——— *Public moralists: political thought and intellectual life in Britain, 1850–1930*, Oxford 1991

Collins, E. J. T., 'Why wheat? Choice of food grains in Europe in the nineteenth and twentieth centuries', *JEEcH* xxii (1993), 7–38

Cooke, A. B. and J. R. Vincent, 'Lord Spencer on the Phoenix Park murders', *Irish Historical Studies* xviii (1973), 585

Cowling, M., *Religion and public doctrine in England*, Cambridge 1981

Crafts, N. F. R. and S. N. Broadberry (eds), *Britain in the international economy, 1870–1914*, Cambridge 1992

Crocker, R. H., 'The Victorian poor law in crisis and change: Southampton, 1870–1895', *Albion* xviv (1987), 19–44

Crompton, F., *Workhouse children*, Stroud 1997

Crossman, V., 'Welfare and nationality: the poor laws in nineteenth-century Ireland', in King and Stewart, *Welfare peripheries*, 26–52

——— 'With the experience of 1846 and 1847 before them: the politics of emergency relief, 1879–84', in P. Gray (ed.), *Victoria's Ireland? Irishness and Britishness, 1837–1901*, Dublin 2004, 167–81

Crowther, M. A., *The workhouse system, 1834–1929*, London 1981

Cunningham H. and J. Innes, *Charity, philanthropy and reform from the 1690s to 1850*, Basingstoke 1998

Daly, M. E., *The famine in Ireland*, Dublin 1986

Daunton, M. (ed.), *Charity, self-interest and welfare in the English past*, London 1996

Davis, J. and G. Tanner, 'The borough franchise after 1867', *Historical Research* lxixiv (1996), 306–27

Dennis, B. and S. Skilton, *Reform and intellectual debate in Victorian England*, London 1987

Dickson, D., 'In search of the old Irish poor law', in R. Mitchinson and P. Roebuck (eds), *Economy and society in Scotland and Ireland, 1500–1939*, Edinburgh 1988, 149–59

Digby, A., 'The labour market and the continuity of social policy after 1834: the case of the eastern counties', *EcHR* 2nd ser. xxviii (1975), 69–83

——— 'The rural poor', in G. E. Mingay, *The Victorian countryside*, London 1981, 591–601

——— *The poor law in nineteenth-century England and Wales*, London 1982

——— *British social policy: from workhouse to workfare*, London 1989

——— *Making a medical living: doctors and patients in the English market place for medicine, 1720–1911*, Cambridge 1994

Driver, F., *Power and pauperism; the workhouse system, 1834–1844*, Cambridge 1993

Dunbabin, J. P. D., 'The politics of the establishment of the county councils', *HJ* iv (1963), 238–50

——— '"The revolt of the field": the Agricultural Labourers' Movement in the 1870s', *P&P* xxvi (1963), 68–97

——— 'Expectations of the new county councils and their realisation', *HJ* xviii (1965), 354–73

——— *Rural discontent in nineteenth-century Britain*, London 1974

———— 'British local government reform: the nineteenth century and after', *EHR* lxxxxii (1977), 777–805

———— 'The incidence and organisation of agricultural trades unionism in the 1870s', *AgHR* xvi (1986), 114–41

Dunkley, P., 'Whigs and paupers: the reform of the English poor laws, 1830–34', *JBS* xx (1980), 124–49

Dunlop, J., *The farm labourer*, London 1913

Eastwood, D., *Governing rural England: tradition and transformation in local government, 1780–1840*, Basingstoke–London 1994.

———— 'Rethinking the debates on the poor law in early nineteenth-century England', *Utilitas* vi (1994), 97–116

———— *Government and community in the English provinces, 1700–1870*, Basingstoke 1997

Emy, H. V., *Liberals, radicals and social politics, 1892–1914*, Cambridge 1973

Englander, D., *Poverty and poor law reform in 19th-century Britain, 1834–1914: from Chadwick to Booth*, New York 1998

———— and R. O'Day (eds), *Retrieved riches: social investigation in Britain, 1840–1914*, London 1995

Eyler, J. M., 'Poverty, disease, responsibility: Arthur Newsholme and the public health dilemmas of British Liberalism', *Millbank Quarterly* lxvii (1989), 109–26

———— 'The sick poor and the state: Arthur Newsholme on poverty, disease and responsibility', in C. Rosenberg and J. Golden (eds), *Framing disease: studies in cultural history*, Rutgers 1992, 276–96

———— *Sir Arthur Newsholme and state medicine, 1885–1935*, Cambridge 1997

Feingold, W. L., *The revolt of the tenantry: the transformation of local government in Ireland, 1872–1886*, Boston 1984

Feinstein, C. H., *Statistical tables of national income, expenditure and output of the UK, 1855–1965*, Cambridge 1965

Fido, J., 'The Charity Organisation Society and social casework in London, 1869–1900', in A. P. Donajgrodski (ed.), *Social control in nineteenth-century Britain*, London 1977, 207–30

Finlayson, G., *Citizen, state and social welfare in Britain, 1830–1990*, Oxford 1994

Flinn, M. W., 'Medical services under the new poor law', in Fraser, *The New Poor Law*, 45–66

Floud, R., *The people and the British economy, 1830–1914*, Oxford 1997

Fontaine, L. and J. Schlumbohm (eds), *Household strategies for survival, 1600–2000: fission, faction and co-operation*, Cambridge 2000

Fox, A., *A history of the National Boot and Shoe Operatives, 1874–1957*, London 1958

Fraser, D., *The new poor: urban politics in Victorian England: the structure of power in Victorian cities*, Leicester 1978 edn

———— *The evolution of the British Welfare State*, London 1984 edn

———— (ed.), *The New Poor Law in the nineteenth century*, London 1976

Freeden, M., *The new Liberalism: an ideology of social reform*, Oxford 1978

———— 'The new Liberalism and its aftermath', in R. Bellamy (ed.), *Victorian Liberalism: nineteenth-century political thought and practice*, Oxford 1990, 175–93

Garrard, J. A., *Leaders and politics in nineteenth-century Salford: an historical analysis of urban political power*, Salford 1977

———— 'The middle classes and nineteenth-century national and local politics', in J. A. Garrard, D. Jary, M. Goldsmith and A. Oldfield (eds), *The middle class in politics*, Farnborough 1977, 35–67

———— 'Parties, members and voters after 1867: a local study', *HJ* xx (1977), 145–63

———— *Leadership and power in Victorian industrial towns, 1830–80*, Manchester 1983

———— 'Social history, political history and political science: the study of power', *Journal of Social History* iii (1983), 105–23

Garrett, E., A. Reid, K. Schurer and S. Szreter, *Changing family size in England and Wales: place, class and demography, 1891–1911*, Cambridge 2001

Garvin, G. L. and J. Amery, *The life of Joseph Chamberlain*, London 1932–69

Gestrich, A., S. A. King and L. Raphael (eds), *Being poor in modern Europe*, Oxford 2004

Ghosh, P. R., 'Style and substance in Disraelian social reform c. 1860–80', in P. Waller (ed.), *Politics and social change in modern Britain*, Brighton 1987, 59–90

Goddard, N., *Harvests of change: the Royal Agricultural Society of England, 1938–1988*, Warwick 1988

Gordon, D. I., *A regional history of the railways of Great Britain, V: The eastern counties*, Newton Abbott 1968

Gordon, J. P. D. (ed.), *The red earl: the papers of the 5th Earl Spencer, 1835–1910*, i, Northampton 1981

Gosden, P. L. J. H., *Self-help*, London 1973

Gould, J., 'In search of Sidney Ward', *NP&P* viii (1993/4), 393–406

Gray, R., *The aristocracy of labour in 19th-century Britain, 1850–1914*, London 1981

Greenall, R. L., *A history of Northamptonshire and the soke of Peterborough*, Chichester–London 1979

———— 'Three nineteenth-century agriculturists', *NP&P* vii (1988/9), 457–9

Gretton, G. H., *A modern history of the English people, I: 1880–1898*, London 1913

Griffiths, P. C., 'Pressure groups and parties in late-Victorian England: the National Education League', *Midland History* iii (1975), 19–26.

Hamer, D. A. (ed.), *The radical programme: Joseph Chamberlain and others*, Brighton 1971

———— *Liberal politics in the age of Gladstone and Rosebery: a study in leadership and policy*, Oxford 1972

Hamilton, B., 'Gladstone's theological politics', in Bentley and Stevenson, *High and low politics*, 28–57

Hardy, A., *The epidemic streets: infectious disease and the rise of preventative medicine, 1856–1900*, Oxford 1993

———— *Health and medicine in Britain since 1860*, London 2001

Harris, B., *The origins of the British Welfare State: social welfare in England and Wales, 1800–1945*, Basingstoke 2004

Harris, J., *Unemployment and politics: a study of English social policy, 1886–1914*, Oxford 1972

——— *Private lives, public spheres: a social history of Britain, 1870–1914*, Oxford 1995

Harrison, B, *The transformation of British politics, 1860–1995*, Harmondsworth 1996

Hendrick, H., *Child welfare: England, 1872–1989*, London 1994

Hennock, E. P., 'Poverty and social theory in England: the experience of the eighteen-eighties', *SH* i (1976), 68–91

——— *British social reform and German precedents: the case of social insurance, 1880–1914*, Oxford 1987

Henriques, U. R. Q., *Before the Welfare State: social administration in early industrial Britain*, London 1979

Himmelfarb, G., *The idea of poverty: England in the early industrial age*, London 1984

——— *The demoralisation of society: from Victorian virtues to modern values*, London 1995

Hitchcock, T., P. King and P. Sharpe (eds), *Chronicling poverty: the voices and strategies of the English poor, 1640–1840*, Basingstoke 1997

Hobsbawm E. J. and G. E. Rudé, *Captain swing*, London 1969

——— *Industry and empire*, London 1969

——— *The age of empire, 1875–1914*, London 1987

Holderness, B. A., and M. Turner (eds), *Land, labour and agriculture, 1700–1920*, London–Bowling Green, OH 1991

Hollen-Lees, L., *Poverty and pauperism in nineteenth-century London*, London 1988

——— *The solidarities of strangers: the English poor laws and the people, 1700–1948*, Cambridge 1998

Hollis, P., *Ladies elect: women in English local government, 1865–1914*, Oxford 1987

Hoppen, K. T., 'The franchise and electoral politics in England and Ireland, 1832–1885', *History* lxx (1985), 202–17

Horn, P. L. R., 'Nineteenth-century Naseby farm workers', *NP&P* iii (1968/70), 167–73

——— *Labouring life in the Victorian countryside*, London 1976.

——— *The rural world and social change in the English countryside, 1780–1850*, London 1980

Horrell, S. and J. Humphries, 'Old questions, new data, and alternative perspectives: families' living standards in the industrial revolution', *JEcH* lii (1992), 849–80

Houlbrooke, R., *Death, ritual and bereavement*, London 1989

Howarth, J., 'The liberal revival in Northamptonshire: a case-study in late nineteenth-century elections', *HJ* xii (1969), 78–118

Howkins, A., *Poor labouring men: rural radicalism in Norfolk, 1870–1923*, London 1985

——— *Reshaping rural England: a social history, 1850–1925*, London 1991

——— 'Peasants, servants and labourers: the marginal workforce in British agriculture, 1870–1914', *AgHR* xlii (1994), 49–62

Hufton, O. H., *The poor of eighteenth-century France, 1750–1789*, Oxford 1974.

Humphreys, R., *Sin, organized charity and the poor law in Victorian England*, Basingstoke 1995.

Humphries, J., 'Enclosures, common rights and women: the proletarianisation of families in the late eighteenth and early nineteenth centuries', *JEcH* i (1990), 117–42.

Hunt, E. H., *British labour history, 1815–1914*, London 1981

Hurren, E. T., ' "Labourers are revolting": penalising the poor and a political reaction in the Brixworth union, Northamptonshire, 1875–1885', *Rural History* xi (2000), 37–55

——— 'The pauper dead-house: the expansion of Cambridge University anatomical teaching school under the late-Victorian poor law, 1870–1914', *Medical History* i (2004), 69–95

——— 'Why did we fail to learn the medical lessons of the past?', in Gestrich, King and Raphael, *Being poor*, 352–87

——— 'Poor law versus public health: diphtheria and the challenge of the *crusade* against outdoor relief to public health improvements in late-Victorian England, 1870–1900', *JSHM* xxviii (Nov. 2005), 399–414

——— and S. A. King, ' "Begging for a burial": form, function and conflict in nineteenth-century pauper burial', *SH* xxx (2005), 321–41

Hutchinson, I. G. C., *A political history of Scotland, 1832–1914: parties, elections and issues*, Edinburgh 1986

Innes, J., 'The "mixed economy of welfare" in early modern England; assessments of the options from Hale to Malthus (*c.* 1683–1803)', in Daunton, *Charity*, 139–80

Jalland, P., *Death and the Victorian family*, Oxford 1996

Jay, R., *Joseph Chamberlain: a political study*, Oxford 1981

Jeffries, R., *Hodge and his masters*, Stroud 1992 edn

Johnson, P., *Saving and spending: the working class economy in Britain, 1870–1939*, Oxford 1985

Jones, G., *Social Darwinism and English thought: the interaction between biological and social theory*, Brighton 1980

Jones, G. D., *Speaking for the dead: cadavers in biology and medicine*, Abingdon 2000

Jones, G. Stedman, *Outcast London: a study of the relationship between classes in Victorian society*, Oxford 1971

Joyce, P., *Visions of the people: industrial England and the question of class, 1848–1914*, Cambridge 1991

——— *Work, society and politics: the culture of the factory in later Victorian England*, Aldershot 1991 edn

Jupp, P. and G. Howarth (eds), *The changing face of death: historical accounts of death and disposal*, Basingstoke 1997

Jutte, R., *Poverty and deviance in early modern Europe*, Cambridge 1994

Katz, M. and C. Sachsse (eds), *The mixed economy of social welfare*, London 1996

Keith-Lucas, B., *The English local government franchise: a short history*, London 1952

——— *English local government in the nineteenth and twentieth centuries*, London 1977

Kidd, A. J., 'Charity organisation and the unemployed in Manchester, *c.* 1870–1914', *SH* ix (1984), 45–66

——— *State, society and the poor in nineteenth-century England*, Oxford 1999

Kinealy, C., 'The poor law during the great famine: an administration in crisis', in E. M. Crawford (ed.), *Famine: the Irish experience, 900–1900*, Edinburgh 1989, 160–85

King, S. A., *Poverty and welfare in England, 1700–1850: a regional perspective*, Manchester 2000

—— *Women, welfare and local politics* c. *1880–1920: 'We might be trusted'*, Brighton 2005

—— 'A question of geography and taste: integrating the poor in 18th and 19th century rural England', *Journal of Historical Geography*, forthcoming 2007

—— and J. G. Timmins, *Making sense of the industrial revolution*, Manchester 2001

—— and J. W. Stewart (eds), *Welfare peripheries*, Oxford 2005

—— and A. Tomkins (eds), *The poor in England 1700–1850: an economy of makeshifts*, Manchester 2003

Kirton, P., *Census of Brixworth: an analysis and transcription, on behalf of Brixworth History Society*, Northampton 1994

Langton, J. and R. J. Morris (eds), *Atlas of industrialising Britain, 1780–1914*, London–New York 1986

Laqueur, T., 'Bodies, death and pauper funerals', *Representations* i (1983), 109–31

—— 'Cemeteries, religion and the culture of capitalism', in J. A. James and M. Thomas (eds), *Capitalism in context: essays on economic development and cultural change in honour of R. M. Hartwell*, Chicago 1994, 138–55

Lawrence, J., 'Class and gender in the making of urban Toryism, 1880–1914' *EHR* 3rd ser. cxvii (1993), 629–52

—— *Speaking for the people: party, language and popular politics in England, 1867–1914*, Cambridge 1998

Laybourn, K., *The rise of Labour: the British Labour party, 1890–1979*, London 1988

—— and J. Reynolds, *Liberalism and the rise of Labour, 1890–1918*, London 1984

—— and D. James (eds), *'The rising sun of Liberalism': the Independent Labour Party in the textile district of the West Riding of Yorkshire between 1890–1914*, Bradford 1991

Lee, S. (ed.), *Dictionary of national biography, 1901–1911*, London 1911

Lee, S. J., *British political history, 1815–1914*, London 1996 edn.

Levitt, I., 'Poor law and pauperism', in Langton and Morris, *Atlas of industrialising Britain*, 160–3

—— *Poverty and welfare in Scotland, 1890–1948*, Edinburgh 1988

Lindert, P., 'Unequal living standards', in R. Floud and D. McCloskey (eds), *The economic history of Britain since 1700*, I: *1700–1800*, Cambridge 1994 edn, 357–86

Lipman, V. D., *Local government areas, 1834–1945*, London 1949

Litten, J., *The English way of death: the common funeral since 1450*, London 1991

Luddy, M., *Women and philanthropy in nineteenth-century Ireland*, Cambridge 1995

Lynch, P., *The Liberal party in rural England, 1885–1910: radicalism and community*, Oxford 2003

MacKay, T., *History of the English poor law*, III: *1834–1898*, London 1904

McKenzie, R. and A. Silver, *Angels in marble: working-class Conservatives in urban England*, London 1968

McKibbin, R., *The ideologies of class: social relations in Britain, 1880–1950*, Oxford 1991

Mackinnon, M., 'Poor law policy, unemployment and pauperism', *Explorations in Economic History* xxiii (1986), 229–336

—— 'English poor law policy and the crusade against outdoor relief', *JEcH* xlvii (1987), 603–25

McLeod, H., *Religion and the working class in nineteenth-century Britain*, Basingstoke 1984

Mandler, P (ed.), *The uses of charity: the poor on relief in the nineteenth-century metropolis*, Philadelphia 1990

Marsh, P., *The discipline of popular government: Lord Salisbury's domestic statecraft, 1881–1902*, Brighton 1978

Martin, J. D., *The Leicestershire COS, 1876–1976: a contemporary review*, Leicester 1976

Mearns, A., *Bitter cry of the outcast of London* (foreword A. Wohl), London 1970

Mitchinson, R., *The old poor law in Scotland: the experience of poverty, 1574–1845*, Edinburgh 2000

Morgan, D. H., *Harvesters and harvesting, 1840–1900: a study of the rural proletariat*, London 1982

Morgan, K. O., *Rebirth of a nation state: Wales, 1880–1980*, Oxford 1981

Mowat, C. L., *The Charity Organisation Society, 1869–1913: its ideas and work*, London 1963

Neeson, J., *Commoners, common right, enclosure and social change, 1700–1820*, Cambridge 1993

Nicholls, D., *The lost prime minister: a life of Sir Charles Dilke*, Oxford 1985

Overton, M., 'Agriculture', in Langton and Morris, *Atlas of industrialising Britain*, 34–54

Parry, J. P., *Democracy and religion: Gladstone and the Liberal party, 1867–1875*, Cambridge 1986

—— 'High and low politics in modern Britain: review article', *HJ* xxix (1986), 753–70

Peacock, A. J., *Bread or blood: a study of the agrarian riots in East Anglia in 1816*, London 1965

Pearce, M. and G. Stewart, *British political history, 1867–1995: democracy and decline*, London 1996

Pedersen, S. and P. Mandler (eds), *After the Victorians: private conscience and public duty in modern Britain: essays in memory of John Clive*, London 1994

Pelling, H., *British trade unionism*, Oxford 1965

—— *Popular politics and society in late-Victorian Britain*, London 1979

Perren, R., *Agriculture in depression, 1870–1940*, Cambridge 1995

Perry, P. J., 'Where was the "great agricultural depression"? A geography of agricultural bankruptcy in late-Victorian England and Wales', *AgHR* xx (1972), 30–45.

—— *British farming in the great depression, 1870–1914: an historical geography*, London 1974

—— (ed.), *British agriculture, 1875–1914*, London 1973

Phelps, L. R., 'Oxford poor relief', in VCH, *Oxfordshire*, London 1952, 349

Pickstone, J., *Medicine and industrial society: a history of hospital provision in Manchester and its regions, 1752–1946*, Manchester 1985.

Powell, D., 'The Liberal ministries and Labour, 1892–1895', *History* lxiii (1993), 408–26

Pratt, C. W. M., *The history of anatomy at Cambridge*, Cambridge 1981

Price, R., *Labour in British society: an interpretative essay*, London 1986

Prochaska, F. K., *Women and philanthropy in nineteenth-century England*, Oxford 1980

Pugh, M., *The Tories and the people*, Oxford 1985

——— *The making of modern British politics, 1867–1945*, Oxford 2002 edn

Reay, B., *Microhistories: demography, society and culture in rural England, 1800–1900*, Cambridge 1996

Redlich, J. and F. W. Hirst, *The history of local government in England*, 2nd edn, London 1970

Reed, N., 'Gnawing it out: a new look at economic relations in nineteenth-century rural England', *Rural History* i (1990), 83–94

Richardson, R., 'A dissection of the anatomy acts', *Studies in Labour History* i (1976), 8–11

——— *Death, dissection and the destitute*, London–New York 1987

Roberts, D., *Modern Scottish Catholicism*, Glasgow 1979

——— *Paternalism in early Victorian England*, London 1979

——— *Making English morals: voluntary association and moral reform in England, 1787–1886*, Cambridge 2004

Roberts, E., *A woman's place: an oral history of working-class women, 1890–1940*, Oxford 1984

——— *Women's work, 1840–1940*, London–New York 1988

Rose, M. E., 'The allowance system under the New Poor Law,' *EHR* 2nd ser. xxix (1966), 607–20

——— 'Settlement, removal and the New Poor Law', in Fraser, *The New Poor Law*, 25–44

——— 'The crisis of poor relief in England, 1860–1900', in W. Mommsen and W. Mock (eds), *The emergence of the welfare state in Britain, 1850–1950*, London 1981, 50–70

——— *The poor and the city: the English poor law in its urban context, 1834–1914*, Leicester 1985

——— *The relief of poverty, 1834–1914*, London–New York 1986 edn

Rowell, G., *Hell and the Victorians*, Oxford 1974

Rubenstein, W. D. (ed.), *Wealth and the wealthy in the modern world*, London 1980

——— *Men of property: the very wealthy in Britain since the industrial revolution*, London 1981

——— *Elites and the wealthy in modern British history: essays in social and economic history*, London 1987

Ryan, P., '"Poplarism", 1834–1930', in P. Thane (ed.), *The origins of British social policy*, London 1978, 56–83

——— 'Politics and poor relief: East End unions in the late nineteenth and early twentieth centuries', in M. E. Rose (ed.), *The poor and the city: the English poor law in its urban context, 1834–1914*, Leicester 1985, 130–72

Sappol, M., *A traffic of dead bodies: anatomy and embodied social identity in 19th-century America*, Princeton 2002

Scotland, N., 'The National Agricultural Labourers' Union and the demand for the stake in the soil, 1872–1896', in Biagini, *Citizenship and community*, 151–67

Scull A. (ed.), *Madhouses, mad-doctors and madmen*, London 1981

Searle, G. R., *The Liberal party: triumph and disintegration, 1886–1929*, Basingstoke 1992

Sen, A., *Inequality re-examined*, Oxford 1992

Shannon, R., *The age of Disraeli, 1868–1881: the rise of Tory democracy*, London 1992

Shaw-Taylor, L., 'Labourers, cows, common rights and parliamentary enclosure: the evidence of contemporary comment c. 1760–1810', *P&P* v (2001), 95–127.

———— 'Parliamentary enclosure and the emergence of an English proletariat', *JEcH* iii (2001), 640–62

Smellie, K. B., *A history of local government*, 4th edn, London 1968

Smith, J., *Northamptonshire: a Shell guide*, London 1968

Smith, P., *Disraelian Conservatism and social reform*, London–Toronto 1967

Smith, R. M., 'The structured dependence of the elderly as a recent historical development: some sceptical thoughts', *Ageing and Society* iv (1984), 409–28

Smyth, J. J., *Labour in Glasgow, 1896–1936: socialism, suffrage, sectarianism*, East Linton 2000

———— ' "Seems decent": respectability and poor relief in Glasgow, c. 1861–1911', in Gestrich, King and Raphael, *Being poor*, 1–27

Snell, K. D. M., *Annals of the labouring poor: social change in agrarian England, 1660–1900*, Cambridge 1985

———— 'Deferential bitterness and the social outlook of the rural proletariat in eighteenth- and nineteenth-century England and Wales', in M. L. Bush (ed.), *Social order and social classes since 1500: studies in social stratification*, London–New York 1992, 158–79

———— *Parish and belonging in England and Wales, c. 1660–1904*, Cambridge 2007

Sokoll, T., *Essex pauper letters, 1731–1837*, Oxford 2001

Song, B. K., 'Continuity and change in English rural society: the formation of poor law unions in Oxfordshire', *EHR* lxiv (1999), 314–38

Southall, H., 'Poor law statistics and the geography of economic distress', in J. Foreman-Peck (ed.), *New perspectives on the late-Victorian economy: essays in quantitative economic history, 1860–1914*, Cambridge 1991, 180–217

Spencer, C., *The Spencer family*, London 1999

Steane, J. M., *The Northamptonshire landscape*, London 1974

Steel, D., *Lord Salisbury: a political biography*, London 2000

Stewart, J. W. and S. A. King, 'Death in Llantrisant: Henry Williams and the New Poor Law in Wales', *Rural History* i (2004), 69–87

Stone, L. and J. C. Fawtier Stone, *An open elite? England, 1540–1880*, London 1984

Strange, J.-M., ' "She cried a very little": death, grief and mourning in working-class culture c. 1880–1914', *SH* xxvii (2002), 143–61

———— 'Only a pauper who no-one owns: reassessing the pauper grave, c. 1880–1914', *P&P* i (2003), 148–78

Sykes, A., *The rise and fall of British Liberalism, 1776–1988*, Harlow 1997

Tanner, D., *Political change and the Labour party, 1900–1990*, Cambridge 1990

Taylor, H., 'Rationing crime: the political economy of criminal statistics since the 1850s', *EHR* 3rd ser. xi (1998), 569–90

Taylor, P., *Popular politics in early industrial Britain: Bolton, 1825–1850*, Keele 1995

Thane P., 'The working class and state "welfare" in Britain, 1880–1914', *HJ* xxvii (1984), 877–900, repr. in D. Gladstone (ed.), *Before Beveridge: welfare before the Welfare State*, London 1999, 86–113

———— 'Old people and their families in the English past', in Daunton, *Charity*, 113–38

———— *Old age in English history: past issues, current perspectives*, Oxford 2000

———— (ed.), *The foundations of the Welfare State*, London–New York 1996 edn

Thompson, E. P., *Customs in common*, London 1993

Thompson, F. M. L., 'The anatomy of English agriculture, 1870–1914', in Holderness and Turner, *Land, labour and agriculture*, 210–40

Thompson, R. N., 'The working of the poor law amendment act in Cumbria, 1836–1871', *Northern History* xv (1979), 117–37

Thomson, D., 'Workhouse to nursing home: residential care of elderly people in England since 1840', *Ageing and Society* iii (1983), 43–69

———— 'The decline of social security: falling state support for the elderly since early Victorian times', *Ageing and Society* iv (1984), 451–82.

———— '*I am not my father's keeper*: families and the elderly in nineteenth-century England', *Law and History Review* ii (1984), 265–86

———— 'Welfare and the historians', in L. Bonfield, R. M. Smith and K. Wrightson (eds), *The world we have gained: histories of population and social structure*, Cambridge 1986, 225–378

———— 'The welfare of the elderly in the past, a family or community responsibility?', in M. Pelling and R. M. Smith (eds), *Life, death and the elderly: historical perspectives*, Oxford 1991, 194–222

———— *World without welfare: New Zealand's colonial experiment*, Auckland 1998

Tucker, T. G., 'Memories of Pitsford one hundred years ago', *NP&P* i (1978), 51

Turner, M. E., 'Output and prices in UK agriculture, 1867–1914, and the great depression reconsidered', *AgHR* xxxx (1992), 38–51

———— J. V. Beckett and B. Afton, *Agricultural rents in England, 1690–1914*, Cambridge 1997

Vincent, A. W., 'The poor law reports of 1909 and the Charity Organisation Society', *Victorian Studies* xxvii (1983–4), 343–65

Vincent, J., *The formation of the Liberal party, 1857–1868*, Cambridge 1966

———— *How Victorians voted*, Cambridge 1967

———— *The governing passion: cabinet government and party politics, 1885–6*, Brighton 1974

Wearmouth, R. F., *Some working class movements of the nineteenth century*, Leicester 1948

Webb, S. and B. Webb, *English poor law policy*, London 1910

———— *English poor law history*, London 1927–9

Weiler, P., *The new Liberalism: Liberal theory in Great Britain, 1889–1914*, London–New York 1982

Wells, R., 'The development of the English rural proletariat and social protest, 1700–1850', *Journal of Peasant Studies* vi (1979), 115–39

Wilford, M. D., *Clipston heritage*, Market Harborough 1991 edn

Williams, K., *From pauperism to poverty*, Manchester 1981

Wilmot, S., *'The business of improvement': agriculture and scientific culture in Britain, c. 1700–c. 1870*, Bristol 1990

Winter, J. (ed.), *The working class in modern British history: essays in honour of Henry Pelling*, Cambridge 1983

Wohl, A., *The eternal slum: housing and social policy in Victorian London*, Belfast 1977

Wolffe, J., *Great deaths: grieving, religion and nationhood in Victorian and Edwardian Britain*, Oxford 2000

Woolf, S., *The poor in western Europe in the eighteenth and nineteenth centuries*, London 1986

Wrigley, C. J. (ed.), *A history of British industrial relations, 1875–1914*, i, London–New York 1982

Unpublished dissertations and papers

Banks, S., 'Open and closed parishes in nineteenth-century England', PhD diss. Reading 1982

Collins, E. J. T., 'Harvest technology and labour supply in Britain, 1780–1870', PhD diss. Nottingham 1979

Driver, F. F. S., 'The English Bastille: dimensions of the workhouse system, 1834–1884', PhD diss. Cambridge 1988

Feehan, L. J.,'The relief of poverty in Liverpool, 1850–1914', PhD diss. Liverpool 1988

Horn, P. L. R., 'Agricultural labourers in four midlands counties, 1860–1900', PhD diss Leicester 1968

Hurren, E. T., 'Crusading against outdoor relief and profiting from pauperism? Revisiting the late-Victorian poor law, 1870–1900', unpubl. paper, Oxford Brookes

Lewis, Bridget, 'Charitable provision in Northamptonshire, 1785–1870', PhD diss. Leicester 2002

Markland, F. T., 'Boot and shoe industry buildings: an examination of the large 19th-century factory buildings in Northamptonshire', MSc. diss. Oxford Brookes 1998

Taylor, A. F., 'Birmingham and the movement for national education', PhD. diss. Leicester 1960

Thomson, D., 'Provision for the elderly in England, 1834–1908', PhD diss. Cambridge 1981

van der Velde, N.,'The Brixworth union workhouse: its regime, officers and inmates', unpubl. BA diss. University College, Northampton, 1999

Index

Lightning Source UK Ltd.
Milton Keynes UK
UKOW06f1024070116

265961UK00005B/59/P